LITERATURE, LEARNING, AND SOCIAL HIERARCHY
IN EARLY MODERN EUROPE

PROCEEDINGS OF THE BRITISH ACADEMY · 246

LITERATURE, LEARNING, AND SOCIAL HIERARCHY IN EARLY MODERN EUROPE

Edited by
NEIL KENNY

Published for THE BRITISH ACADEMY
by OXFORD UNIVERSITY PRESS

Oxford University Press, Great Clarendon Street, Oxford OX2 6DP

First edition published in 2022

British Library Cataloguing in Publication Data
Data available

Library of Congress Cataloging in Publication Data
Data available

Typeset by Newgen Publishing UK
Printed in Great Britain by TJ Books Ltd, Padstow, Cornwall

ISBN 978-0-19-726733-2
ISSN 0068-1202

Contents

List of Figures

Notes on Contributors

Warren Boutcher is Professor of Renaissance Studies in the School of English and Drama, Queen Mary University of London. He is the Principal Investigator for TextDiveGlobal ('Textuality and Diversity: A Literary History of Europe and its Global Connections, 1545–1659'), which is funded by the ERC Advanced Grant scheme to run from 2021 to 2026. He will be general editor of the main output: *Europe in the World: A Literary History, 1545–1659* (contracted to Oxford University Press). His publications include *The School of Montaigne in Early Modern Europe*, 2 vols (Oxford University Press, 2017).

Colin Burrow is Senior Research Fellow at All Souls College, Oxford, Professor of English and Comparative Literature, and a Fellow of the British Academy. His publications include *Epic Romance: Homer to Milton* (1993), *Shakespeare and Classical Antiquity* (2013), *Imitating Authors: Plato to Futurity* (2020) – all with Oxford University Press – as well as editions of the *Complete Sonnets and Poems* for the Oxford Shakespeare and of the poems of Ben Jonson for the *Cambridge Edition of the Works of Ben Jonson*.

Neil Kenny is Senior Research Fellow at All Souls College, Professor of French at the University of Oxford, and a Fellow of the British Academy, where he is Lead Fellow for Languages. His publications include *The Uses of Curiosity in Early Modern France and Germany* (2004), *Death and Tenses: Posthumous Presence in Early Modern France* (2015), and *Born to Write: Literary Families and Social Hierarchy in Early Modern France* (2021), all with Oxford University Press.

Ian Maclean is a Fellow of the British Academy, an Emeritus Fellow of All Souls College, Oxford, an Emeritus Professor of Renaissance Studies in the University of Oxford, and Honorary Professor of History in the University of St.Andrews. His most recent publications are *Episodes in the Life of the Early Modern Book* (Brill, 2020) and (edited, with Dmitri Levitin) *The Worlds of Knowledge and the Classical Tradition in the Early Modern Age* (Brill, 2021).

Richard McCabe is a Fellow of Merton College Oxford, Professor of English Language and Literature at Oxford University, and Fellow of the British Academy. His publications include *Incest, Drama, and Nature's Law* (Cambridge University Press, 1993), *Spenser's Monstrous Regiment: Elizabethan Ireland and the Poetics of Difference, 1580–1650* (Oxford University Press, 2002), and *'Ungainefull Arte': Poetry, Patronage, and Print in the Early Modern Era* (Oxford University Press, 2016). He has also edited *Edmund Spenser: The Shorter Poems* (Penguin

Books, 1999) and *The Oxford Handbook of Edmund Spenser* (Oxford University Press, 2010).

Richard J. Oosterhoff is Lecturer in Early Modern History at the University of Edinburgh. His books include *Making Mathematical Culture: University and Print in the Circle of Lefèvre d'Étaples*, Oxford-Warburg Studies (Oxford University Press, 2018), the co-authored monograph *Logodaedalus: Word Histories of Ingenuity in Early Modern Europe* (University of Pittsburgh Press, 2018), and *Ingenuity in the Making: Materials and Technique in Early Modern Art and Science*, edited with José Ramón Marcaida and Alexander Marr (University of Pittsburgh Press, 2021).

Simon Park is Associate Professor of Medieval and Renaissance Portuguese at the University of Oxford and Tutorial Fellow at St Anne's College. He is the author of *Poets, Patronage, and Print in Sixteenth-Century Portugal: From Paper to Gold* (Oxford University Press, 2021).

Jonathan Patterson is Lecturer at St Edmund Hall and in the Sub-Faculty of French at the University of Oxford. His research explores how literature interacts with broader cultural forces of early modern French society. His publications include *Villainy in France (1463–1610): A Transcultural Study of Law and Literature* (Oxford University Press, 2021), and *Representing Avarice in Late Renaissance France* (Oxford University Press, 2015).

Sarah Gwyneth Ross is Professor of History at Boston College. Her publications include *The Birth of Feminism: Woman as Intellect in Renaissance Italy and England* (2009) and *Everyday Renaissances: The Quest for Cultural Legitimacy in Venice* (2016), both with Harvard University Press. Ross has now embarked on a multi-generational study of the Andreini family – the actors, poets, soldiers, friars, alchemists, and painters.

Helena Sanson is Professor of Italian, History of Linguistics, and Women's Studies at the University of Cambridge, and Fellow of Clare College. Among her publications are *Donne, precettistica e lingua nell'Italia del Cinquecento* (Accademia della Crusca, 2007), *Women, Language and Grammar in Italy, 1500–1900* (British Academy/Oxford University Press, 2011), and the co-edited volumes *Conduct Literature for and about Women in Italy, 1470–1900: Describing and Prescribing Life* (Classiques Garnier, 2016), and *Women in the History of Linguistics* (Oxford University Press, 2020). She is the editor-in-chief of the book series *Women and Gender in Italy, 1500–1900* and the journal *Women Language Literature in Italy*.

Christine Stevenson is Professor of Early Modern Art and Architecture at the Courtauld Institute of Art, University of London. Her publications include *Medicine and Magnificence: British Hospital and Asylum Architecture, 1660–1815* (2000) and *The City and the King: Architecture and Politics in Restoration London* (2013), both with Yale University Press/The Paul Mellon Centre for Studies in British Art.

Jane Stevenson is Senior Research Fellow at Campion Hall, Oxford, and a member of the University of Oxford English Faculty. Most of her publications relate to Latin and the classical tradition, women's history, and exiles, particularly recusants. They include *Women Latin Poets: Language, Gender and Authority from Antiquity to the Eighteenth Century* (Oxford University Press, 2005). Her most recent books are *Baroque Between the Wars* (Oxford University Press, 2018), and a study of Federico da Montefeltro, *The Light of Italy* (Head of Zeus, 2021).

Susan Wiseman is the author of *Writing Metamorphosis in Renaissance England, 1550–1700* (Cambridge University Press, 2014), *Conspiracy and Virtue: Women, Writing, and Politics in Seventeenth Century England* (Oxford University Press, 2006), and *Politics and Drama in the English Civil War* (Cambridge University Press, 1998).

Acknowledgements

I am grateful to All Souls College, Oxford for supporting the research underlying this volume in many ways, including by funding and facilitating for almost a decade a research seminar that shares its name with the volume's sub-title. Collective thinking on this question has been advanced by the scores of researchers who have addressed that seminar (including all contributors to this volume), as well as by many others who have contributed to the seminar discussions. Warm thanks are due to the several anonymous readers who commented with rigour, generosity, and expertise on early drafts of the chapters. The same qualities were shown by Peter Burke when commenting on a draft of the Introduction. Helpful suggestions were received from the British Academy's Publications and Conferences Committee and its assessors. Geetha Nair and Portia Taylor (the British Academy's Publications Manager and Production Editor respectively) and Helen Flitton (Project Manager, Newgen Publishing) provided valuable guidance and support. Gail Welsh copy-edited the volume with great skill and tact. Permission to use the images reproduced in the volume was kindly granted by all the rightsholders. Finally, my gratitude goes to the 12 authors of chapters. Some encountered considerable pandemic-related and other difficulty; others showed much patience in waiting for everyone to have finished; all operated as a team.

NK

1

Introduction

NEIL KENNY

WHAT WAS THE relationship, from the fifteenth century to the seventeenth, between two major facets of early modern European life – social hierarchy, and on the other hand literature and learning (understood together as literate cultural activity and production)?[1]

These two facets were not just contiguous. They also overlapped. In other words, literature and learning were, to an extent, part *of* social hierarchy; they constituted one element, among many others (including other cultural ones), in the processes that produced social hierarchy and that distributed differential degrees of dignity and status to groups and individuals.[2] At a time when literacy was confined

---

[1] Literature is here understood in the broad early modern sense of letters (so overlapping partly with learning).

[2] Scholarship on early modern European social hierarchy is voluminous. Overviews include the following. For Europe: Armand Arriaza, 'Mousnier and Barber: The Theoretical Underpinning of the "Society of Orders" in Early Modern Europe', *Past & Present*, 89 (1980), 39–57; M. L. Bush (ed.), *Social Orders and Social Classes in Europe since 1500: Studies in Social Stratification* (London and New York: Longman, 1992); Jeffery Denton (ed.), *Orders and Hierarchies in Medieval and Renaissance Europe* (Basingstoke: Macmillan, 1999); Jonathan Dewald, *The European Nobility, 1400–1800* (Cambridge: Cambridge University Press, 1996); Andreas Gestrich, 'The Social Order', in Hamish Scott (ed.), *The Oxford Handbook of Early Modern European History, 1350–1750: Volume I: Peoples and Place* (Oxford: Oxford University Press, 2015), pp. 295–312; Wolfgang Reinhard, 'Introduction: Power Elites, State Servants, Ruling Classes, and the Growth of State Power', in Wolfgang Reinhard (ed.), *Power Elites and State Building* (Oxford: Clarendon Press, 1996), pp. 1–18; Hamish M. Scott (ed.), *The European Nobilities in the Seventeenth and Eighteenth Centuries*, 2 vols (1995; 2nd edn Basingstoke: Houndmills, 2007). For England: David Cressy, 'Describing the Social Order of Elizabethan and Stuart England', *Literature and History*, 3 (1976), 29–44; Alexandra Shepard, *Accounting for Oneself: Worth, Status, and the Social Order in Early Modern England* (Oxford: Oxford University Press, 2015); Lawrence Stone and Jeanne C. Fawtier Stone, *An Open Elite? England 1540–1880* (Oxford: Clarendon Press, 1984); Keith Wrightston, *English Society 1580–1680* (London: Hutchinson, 1982); Keith Wrightston, 'The Social Order of Early Modern England: Three Approaches', in Lloyd Bonfield, Richard Smith, and Keith Wrightson (eds), *The World We Have Gained: Histories of Population and Social Structure* (Oxford: Basil Blackwell, 1986), pp. 177–202; Keith Wrightston, '"Sorts of People" in Tudor and Stuart England', in Jonathan Barry and Christopher Brooks (eds), *The Middling Sort of People: Culture, Society and Politics in England, 1550–1800* (Basingstoke: Macmillan, 1994), pp. 28–51. For France: William Beik, *A Social and Cultural History of Early Modern France* (Cambridge: Cambridge University Press, 2009); Fanny Cosandey (ed.),

Proceedings of the British Academy, **246**, 1–13, © The British Academy 2022.

to a minority of the European population,[3] this role of literature and learning as one of many contributors to social status was also largely confined *to* that minority. Which is not to say that culture itself was: the rich oral cultures of early modern Europe[4] are largely beyond the scope of the present investigation, though they will make indirect appearances (for example in relation to peasants in a French village, illiterate women and men in the Italian peninsula, 'gypsies' in England, or scribe-hirers in Portugal).[5]

Conversely, social hierarchy was, to an extent, part of literature and learning. It was one element, among many others, within the various worlds (whether purportedly real or overtly fictive) that were conjured up and described by works of literature and learning. Those works represented human relations as being embedded in social hierarchies. That representing was sometimes passive, but sometimes active, in the sense that it was designed to intervene in social hierarchy, to effect an elevation of the status of some groups (such as poets and relatively uneducated lay people) or else a lowering or even an erasing of the status of others ('gypsies' again).[6]

So the relationship of social hierarchy to literature and learning was two-way. Sometimes it was so two-way that, within the area of their overlap, it is difficult to tease them apart as two discrete elements.

The nature of that relationship is arguably still understood rather little relative to its importance. That goes for the early modern period and for others, including

---

Dire et vivre l'ordre social en France sous l'Ancien Régime (Paris: Éditions de l'EHESS, 2005); Fanny Cosandey, *Le Rang. Préséances et hiérarchies dans la France d'Ancien Régime* (Paris: Gallimard, 2016); Robert Descimon, 'La Société française avant les Lumières: une société hiérarchique?', in Gilles Chabaud (ed.), *Classement, déclassement, reclassement* (Limoges: PULIM, 2011), pp. 51–69; Arlette Jouanna, *Ordre social: mythes et hiérarchies dans la France du XVIe siècle* (Paris: Hachette, 1977); Roland Mousnier, *Les Hiérarchies sociales de 1450 à nos jours* (Paris: Presses universitaires de France, 1969); Ellery Schalk, *From Valor to Pedigree: Ideas of Nobility in France the Sixteenth and Seventeenth Centuries* (Princeton: Princeton University Press, 1986). For the Germanic territories: Tom Scott, *Society and Economy in Germany, 1300–1600* (Basingstoke: Houndmills, 2002). For the Italian peninsula: Christopher F. Black, *Early Modern Italy: A Social History* (London: Routledge, 2000). For Spain: James Casey, *Early Modern Spain: A Social History* (London: Routledge, 1999).

[3] See for example David Cressy, *Literacy and the Social Order* (Cambridge: Cambridge University Press, 1980); François Furet and Jacques Ozouf, *Lire et écrire: l'alphabétisation des Français de Calvin à Jules Ferry* (Paris: Éditions de Minuit, 1977); Richard Gawthrop and Gerald Strauss, 'Protestantism and Literacy in Early Modern Germany', *Past and Present*, 104 (1984), 31–55; Harvey J. Graff, *Legacies of Literacy: Continuities and Contradictions in Western Culture and Society* (Bloomington: Indiana University Press, 1987); Paul F. Grendler, *Schooling in Renaissance Italy: Literacy and Learning, 1300–1600* (Baltimore and London: The Johns Hopkins University Press, 1989); Robert A. Houston, *Literacy in Early Modern Europe: Culture and Education, 1500–1800* (London: Longman, 2001); István G. Tóth, *Literacy and Written Culture in Early Modern Central Europe* (Budapest: Central European University Press, 2000).

[4] See for example Adam Fox, *Oral and Literate Culture in England, 1500–1700* (Oxford: Oxford University Press, 2000).

[5] Respectively in the chapters by Warren Boutcher, Helena Sanson, Susan Wiseman, and Simon Park.

[6] Chapter 13 (poets), Chapter 8 (relatively uneducated people, though with a distinction between moral and social status), and Chapter 9 ('gypsies').

the modern period, when, especially from the eighteenth century onwards, the language of social hierarchy (and of dignity, honour, estate, rank, order, and degree) was increasingly displaced by the language of class (subtended by more overt economic criteria and by relations to the means of production).[7] The relationship of literate culture to hierarchy did receive attention in the heyday of twentieth-century Marxist and post-Marxist approaches to culture, especially from the 1930s to the 1970s (from György Lukács to Lucien Goldmann and Raymond Williams). Along with other traditions, Marxism also partly informed the class-based dimensions of the study of the literary field in one country and period (nineteenth-century France) that was provided by Pierre Bourdieu.[8] The New Historicism of the 1980s and 1990s explored the relation of literature (especially early modern) to power structures, but without focusing in a sustained way on the relationship highlighted by the present volume. Other work using a variety of approaches has explored aspects of the relationship of literature and learning to social hierarchy, especially for individual countries.[9] Yet, not surprisingly given the relationship's complexity, we still lack an overarching understanding of it, even for individual countries, and few have ventured to examine the relationship on a European scale, though some

---

[7] On this shift, see for example David Cannadine, *Class in Britain* (1998; London: Penguin Books, 2000), pp. 24–34; Peter Calvert, *The Concept of Class: An Historical Introduction* (London: Hutchinson, 1982), pp. 12–25; David Parker, *State and Class in Ancien Régime France: The Road to Modernity?* (London: Routledge, 1996); P. J. Corfield (ed.), *Language, History, and Class* (Oxford: Basil Blackwell, 1991).

[8] Pierre Bourdieu, *Les Règles de l'art: genèse et structure du champ littéraire* (Paris: Seuil, 1992).

[9] In addition to studies listed in n. 3, see for example, on England: Peter Holbrook, *Literature and Degree in Renaissance England: Nashe, Bourgeois Tragedy, Shakespeare* (Newark: University of Delaware Press; London and Toronto: Associated University Presses, 1994); Mark Netzloff, *England's Internal Colonies: Class, Capital, and the Literature of Early Modern English Colonialism* (Basingstoke: Palgrave Macmillan, 2003); Laura C. Stevenson, *Praise and Paradox: Merchants and Craftsmen in Elizabethan Popular Literature* (Cambridge: Cambridge University Press, 2002); Ceri Sullivan, *The Rhetoric of Credit: Merchants in Early Modern Writing* (Madison and London: Associated University Presses, 2002); Christopher Warley, *Sonnet Sequences and Social Distinction in Renaissance England* (Cambridge: Cambridge University Press, 2005). On France: George Huppert, *The Bourgeois Gentilshommes: An Essay on the Definition of Elites in Renaissance France* (Chicago and London: University of Chicago Press, 1977); Neil Kenny, *Born to Write: Literary Families and Social Hierarchy in Early Modern France* (Oxford: Oxford University Press, 2020); Michael Moriarty, *Taste and Ideology in Seventeenth-Century France* (Cambridge: Cambridge University Press, 1988); Jonathan Patterson, *Villainy in France (1463–1610): A Transcultural Study of Law and Literature* (Oxford: Oxford University Press, 2021); Alain Viala, *La France galante: essai historique sur une catégorie culturelle, de ses origines jusqu'à la Révolution* (Paris: Presses Universitaires de France, 2008). On Italy: Robert Black, *Humanism and Education in Medieval and Renaissance Italy: Tradition and Innovation in Latin Schools from the Twelfth to the Fifteenth Century* (Cambridge: Cambridge University Press, 2001); Robert Black, *Education and Society in Florentine Tuscany: Teachers, Pupils and Schools, c. 1250–1500* (Leiden: Brill, 2007); Brian Richardson 'The Social Connotations of Singing Verse in Cinquecento Italy', *The Italianist*, 34.3 (2014), 362–78. On Spain: Clive Griffin, *Journeymen Printers: Heresy and the Inquisition in Sixteenth-century Spain* (Oxford: Oxford University Press, 2005).

studies have shown that a way of doing so is to adopt a distinct focus, whether on one social group[10] or on one writer.[11]

Moving a little along the disciplinary spectrum into the discipline of history, while many historians have studied early modern social hierarchy,[12] those who have perhaps verged most on examining its relationship to literature and learning are certain social historians who have examined the *language* of social hierarchy (whether for one country[13] or for Europe more widely[14]). That is because they, like some literary historians, examine the role played by linguistic representations in the constituting of social hierarchy. The representations that these social historians have examined are typically short (titles, honorific epithets, forms of address, phrases from ordinary language), whereas those studied by literary scholars or intellectual historians are typically long (works of various kinds). But there is a surprising affinity between their aims, since both groups investigate the role played by linguistic representations in the constituting of social hierarchy.

So, building on existing examinations of the early modern relation of literature and learning to social hierarchy, focused as they are on specific regions, nations, themes, or genres, this volume extends the investigation to a broader, Western European perspective and to a greater spread of genres, discourses, and social groups. The aim is not to be comprehensive or systematic but to open up the study of this key relationship to a wider geographical, social, and literary range, helping to open a door through which future researchers can pass. The volume is also designed to show that various methods can be used to unlock different facets of the relation of literature and learning to social hierarchy, rather than imposing any one-size-fits-all method. Some tools from earlier work, such as Bourdieu's notions of 'habitus', 'field', and 'capital', are here tested by, and applied to, new contexts.[15] But they and other tools are used heuristically, rather than in the service of any theory of the relation of culture to society. None of the ensuing chapters are constrained by an overarching hypothesis about (or by definitions of) base, superstructure, and ideology. At the same time, they are alert to tensions between socio-cultural

---

[10] James Amelang, *Flight of Icarus: Popular Autobiography in Early Modern Europe* (Stanford: Stanford University Press, 1998); David M. Posner, *The Performance of Nobility in Early Modern European Literature* (Cambridge: Cambridge University Press, 2004).

[11] Warren Boutcher, *The School of Montaigne in Early Modern Europe*, 2 vols, i: *The Patron-Author*; ii: *The Reader–Writer* (Oxford: Oxford University Press, 2017).

[12] See n. 2.

[13] Robert Descimon, 'Un langage de la dignité. La qualification des personnes dans la société parisienne à l'époque moderne', in Fanny Cosandey (ed.), *Dire et vivre l'ordre social en France sous l'Ancien Régime* (Paris: École Pratique des Hautes Études en Sciences Sociales, 2005); Keith Wrightson, 'Estates, Degrees, and Sorts: Changing Perceptions of Society in Tudor and Stuart England', in Penelope Corfield (ed.), *Language, History and Class* (Oxford: Blackwell, 1991), pp. 30–52.

[14] Peter Burke, 'The Language of Orders in Early Modern Europe', in M. L. Bush (ed.), *Social Orders and Social Classes in Europe Since 1500: Studies in Social Stratification* (London: Routledge, 1992), pp. 1–12.

[15] Especially Chapter 5.

representations and their socio-economic conditions,[16] in other words to bumpiness and opacity in the relation of literature and learning to social hierarchy.

Although the volume is intended to help open up a field rather than to survey it definitively, its selective analyses do combine to uncover certain cross-European tendencies, albeit with much local variation and divergence. Let me mention three fundamental tendencies.

First, literature and learning tended to be supportive of and constitutive of social hierarchy, rather than corrosive of it. As soon as one formulates such a tendency, exceptions to it, resistances to it, and period critiques of it all come to mind; indeed it is often they that provide the most engaging takes on social hierarchy, as the volume will show. Nonetheless, a default tendency towards mutual reinforcement between letters and social hierarchy becomes visible as a historical phenomenon (albeit a longlasting one) if one steps back to adopt a long view. Warren Boutcher does just that and deploys – again heuristically rather than dogmatically – Sheldon Pollock's thesis of a 'vernacular millennium' in Europe as well as South Asia.[17] Nuancing the European dimension of Pollock's thesis, Boutcher proposes a millennium stretching especially from the twelfth and thirteenth centuries (though with roots in the ninth) up to the early nineteenth century. In that long period, elite languages – both cosmopolitan vernaculars and Latin – became vehicles for political, bureaucratic, and prestigious literary communication, due to a convergence of numerous factors. The shorter, two/three-century window covered by the present volume includes new variants within that longer-term trend, such as Renaissance humanism, confessionalisation, and colonialism, argues Boutcher. Nonetheless, the trend was far from straightforward: it was counterbalanced, shows Boutcher, by considerable fear that new knowledge and new language skills could disrupt the peaceful reproduction of natural and traditional hierarchies and orders, with disastrous results.

Why consider that this centuries-long trend faded eventually in the early nineteenth century? Boutcher's case for this periodisation is bolstered by Ian Maclean, who reminds us below of the arrival in the early nineteenth century of mass printed literature on the one hand and of a new relationship of literature and learning to social hierarchy on the other: 'the field of cultural production was then inversely related to economic and class interests', since 'the most successful artists or writers in [high art] might be those who earned the least'.[18] So *longue durée* history suggests that the largely mutually reinforcing relationship between letters and social hierarchy that this volume identifies and examines was a historical one, with perceptible temporal contours, even if their precise detail can always be debated. That historical character of the phenomenon studied here does not prevent it from having numerous consequences in

---

[16] Especially Chapters 4 and 5.
[17] Chapter 2.
[18] Chapter 5, pp. 99–100.

our own present, whether through the continuing cultural lives of early modern works (such as those by Shakespeare and Montaigne) or through a continued tendency of cultural capital to bolster social standing.

That first fundamental tendency identified by this volume has a second as its corollary: whereas literature and learning provided representations of the gamut of social hierarchy (from gentry to 'gypsies'), on the other hand it was elites that benefited the most from the mutual reinforcement between social hierarchy and literature/learning. What is meant by 'elite'? Its precise definition varies by context, as the studies below will show. But one starting-point is to define it roughly by literacy: because literacy was restricted to a minority of the population in this period that preceded mass education, it was that literate minority that benefited the most from the mutual reinforcement between social hierarchy and literature/learning, and that acquired or maintained social status from literature and learning. When defined as the literate minority, the 'elite' was not just composed of nobles. It also encompassed the many commoners who figure in this volume and who were for example writers, publishers, or building contractors. Numerically speaking, the position of the 'middling sort' lay not in the mid-quartile range of the population, but towards the top. Certainly, some of the studies below will show how literature and learning, by facilitating social mobility, contributed to a wider porosity between some estates, ranks, or orders.[19] But that mobility was largely in and out of 'elite' groups (as defined by literacy). And the more extreme examples of mobility (such as that of the artisan-class woman Latin poet Marta Marchina, studied by Jane Stevenson[20]) are striking because they were so unusual; also, even the example of Marchina shows that the effects of mobility should not be overstated; while mobility changed her life and legacy, even it changed her physical circumstances but little.

Finally, the third tendency identified by this volume is for literature and learning, despite being broadly supportive of the upper reaches of social hierarchy, to convey (intentionally or not) a sense that often social status is actually rather contradictory or blurry at the edges, rather than clear and entirely determinate. Literature and learning tend to convey more tensions and indeterminacy in social status than do other criteria for assessing status or media for communicating it (such as birth, occupation, dress, heraldry, notarial documents), because literature and learning produce particularly rich, complex, and multilayered representations, in which a degree of interpretative freedom and indeterminacy may be fostered and in which social hierarchy has to find its footing in relation to many other concerns.

Those other concerns, which border on, overlap with, and partly merge with social hierarchy, without however being entirely coextensive with it, appear repeatedly in this volume. What is the relation of social hierarchy to morality,[21] to

---

[19] E.g. Chapters 2, 5, 6, 7, 11, 12, and 13.

[20] Chapter 7.

[21] Especially in chapters (6, 10, and 11) devoted to different genres of theatre, respectively by Sarah Gwyneth Ross, Jonathan Patterson, and Richard McCabe.

the theological equality of humans before God,[22] to knowledge,[23] to wealth,[24] to gender,[25] to ethnicity,[26] to fame,[27] to excellence *in* literature and learning,[28] to hierarchies of literary genres,[29] and to 'fictive' elaborations upon a person's status?[30] Are these other value-systems and areas of experience part of what constitutes social hierarchy? Or are they distinct from it? Moreover, far from necessarily supporting social hierarchy, can they sometimes conflict with it, for example because the wealth that was usually a *sine qua non* of high social status was often gained by mercantile means, which conflicted with the values associated *with* that status?[31] The studies in this volume indicate how deeply such questions preoccupied early moderns, how hard they were to answer, and how persistently they were explored in works of literature and learning. People had trouble determining exactly where social hierarchy ended and where these other value-systems or areas of experience began. One contributor calls this negotiating, in the period, between social hierarchy and these other elements a 'dappled language of moral, epistemic, and social hierarchy'.[32] Another contributor, in a similar vein, calls it the 'interplay of social, moral, and literary assets in the complex calculus of "status"'.[33] Works of literature and learning produced a range of dappled languages in which social hierarchy sat alongside other elements, whether easily or uneasily, and whether largely distinct from those other elements or merged indistinguishably with them.

The wider question that arises is whether this tendency of literature and learning to foster relatively nuanced takes on social status tells us only something about literature and learning, or else also something about early modern social hierarchy more generally. Different chapters may suggest different answers to that question. On the one hand, literature and learning of a less instrumental kind (for example in the theatre), designed to entertain and to provoke reflection rather than to achieve

---

[22] E.g. Chapter 8.

[23] E.g. Chapter 3.

[24] E.g. Chapters 4 and 11.

[25] Most continuously in Helena Sanson's overview (Chapter 3), Sarah Gwyneth Ross's study of the Andreini couple (Chapter 6), and Jane Stevenson's study of Marchina (Chapter 7), but also in Chapters 2, 8, and 12.

[26] Chapter 9. Susan Wiseman's chapter on representations of 'gypsies' is the one that raises most the question of how outsiders or semi-outsiders of all kinds (from 'foreigners' in general to racialised groups in particular) are dealt with in literary and other representations of social hierarchy.

[27] E.g. Chapters 7 and 13.

[28] Referred to as 'literary status' in Chapter 13. See also Chapter 6.

[29] E.g. Chapters 6, 10, 11, and 13.

[30] E.g. Chapters 6 and 13.

[31] This tension is flagged up by Christine Stevenson, Ian Maclean, and Richard McCabe in their studies of builders, printers and publishers, and the middling sort (Chapters 4, 5, and 11). See also for example Jonathan Patterson, *Representing Avarice in Late Renaissance France* (Oxford: Oxford University Press, 2015), esp. pp. 53–64, 160–200.

[32] Chapter 8, p. 172.

[33] Chapter 6, p. 122.

very determinate outcomes (for example of a social, legal, or political nature), can often allow itself to communicate more open-ended takes on status than can say, a notary, who has to focus on achieving outcomes within a legal framework. But on the other hand, it seems likely that some of the tensions surrounding social hierarchy that are writ large in literary or learned works are *also* present in other contexts, outside the domains of literature and learning. For example, as Robert Descimon has shown, although some widespread criteria for determining social status were factual, many were not: they were based on elements of fictionality, of symbolism, or of neighbourly appraisal; moreover, a person's exact status (and even their selection of titles and honours) could vary according to the requirements of a given context. Or again: the uneasy faultline in notions of 'dignity' between a dominant hierarchical understanding (which limited dignity to elites) and a more equalising theological one (which distributed it to everyone) was not confined just to literature and learning but was more widespread.[34] So, while poets and dramatists stretched the elasticity of status in new ways,[35] they thereby highlighted an elasticity that also existed beyond the domain of literature and learning. To put the point more strongly: literature and learning, as well as being distinctive, provide evidence of a unique kind about early modern social hierarchy more generally.

As already indicated, the volume is designed to foster Europe-wide, socially and generically varied consideration of the relation highlighted by its title, rather than to provide a systematic survey organised by territory, genre, discourse, or period. So the volume's structure emphasises underlying, Europe-wide issues, with individual chapters providing an initial sense of the numerous variations on them (helping pave the way for future research that will reveal wider variations still). For example, Pollock's conception (underpinning his 'vernacular millennium' thesis) of vernacular polities as ones that promoted one cosmopolitan vernacular alongside Latin is shown to work less well for the highly multilingual Holy Roman Empire than it does for, say, France;[36] the opportunities offered by print for social status were sometimes available to women in different parts of Europe, but nowhere more than in the Italian peninsula;[37] or to take a more specific phenomenon, the option for people (of high or low status) to hire public scribes was available not just in Lisbon but elsewhere in Europe too, though probably only patchily, judging from the available evidence.[38]

The territories featured are Western European – England, France, Germany and the Low Countries, Italy, and Portugal – though with Hungary making a brief appearance.[39] The selected genres, discourses, and practices to be featured

[34] Descimon, 'Un langage de la dignité', especially pp. 75–6, 94–8.
[35] Especially Chapter 13.
[36] Chapter 2, p. 21.
[37] Chapter 3, p. 60; Chapter 7, p. 139.
[38] Chapter 12, p. 243.
[39] Chapter 2.

include poetry, theatre, masque, architecture, philosophy, law, printing, publishing, translating, and scribe-hiring. Future research could extend the investigation to other genres, discourses, and practices.

The volume leads roughly from panoramic overviews[40] to more specific examples. It also leads through four successive angles of approach. Yet, although chapters are grouped according to the angle that they adopt most, each chapter actually adopts more than one of these angles, and demonstrates the interconnectedness between them.

The first two angles highlight ways in which literature and learning were part of social hierarchy. The very first angle (Part I) examines the role played by languages – especially elite written ones such as Latin, cosmopolitan vernaculars, or technical vocabulary – in enabling some groups to acquire what Warren Boutcher calls a social literacy and what other contributors call a practice or a Bourdieusian habitus. Examples of such social literacies include the ability to deploy humanistic dialectic or architectural knowledge or the ability to participate in high-literary culture by reading the Tuscan literary vernacular. Each chapter focuses not just on the process of acquisition but on the exclusions, the resistances, the doubts, the ambivalence, and the contradictions that constantly beset the process.

Warren Boutcher's overview begins by critically assessing and adapting Pollock's 'vernacular millennium' thesis. Boutcher's focus then shifts to those exclusions and resistances as he examines selected late sixteenth- and early seventeenth-century vernacular texts in order to see how they represent the irruption of new forms of social literacy into societies shaped by traditional customs, beliefs, and hierarchies. His main examples are Montaigne and Shakespeare but he ranges over Italy and Spain too, with respectively Boccaccio and Cervantes (among others). Next, another overview is provided, this time of one geographical area (the Italian peninsula) and primarily of one sex (women): Helena Sanson examines the extent to which women acquired the different linguistic varieties that existed and in turn the extent to which that acquisition enabled them to participate in the production and reception of literature and learning. Sanson's discussion of the lionisation of one variety – the literary vernacular based on fourteenth-century Tuscan – so that it became the language of literature and of the printing presses provides a model instance of the processes identified by Pollock and Boutcher, though, like Boutcher, Sanson is highly attentive to the way in which that lionisation excluded more people than it included. Her analysis of women's participation in, and exclusion from, cultural exchange embraces other linguistic varieties too, such as local vernaculars, the eclectic *koinai* of the Italian courts, classical Greek and Latin, and foreign languages.

Part I then ends by shifting from these overviews to a more specific instance of the linguistically grounded acquiring of knowledge, in this case architectural. Focusing on one country (England) and period (the later seventeenth century), Christine Stevenson explores both the extent to which the Latinate vocabulary

---

[40] Chapters 2, 3, and 5.

of classical ornament could be a source of social and professional distinction for builders, and also the limits of the extent to which mastery of that idiom provided such distinction. The acquisition of language is examined by Stevenson as just one means (and not the most important one) among others by which building contractors (such as her main protagonist, Thomas Fitch) could acquire social and professional recognition. At the same time, Stevenson's analysis shows how the social status of building contractors and of 'architects' (an elusive term) had a degree of indeterminacy and elasticity that provides an example of the status ambivalences mentioned earlier in this Introduction.

The second angle (Part II) continues to examine the acquiring of social literacies and of consequent benefits, but now with less focus on the role played by language-acquisition itself, although language-learning does still feature to an extent. The beneficiaries are not just writers but other agents in cultural production (printers and publishers, now joining the builders and contractors of Part I as ones in an industry that had an artisanal as well as mercantile grounding while encompassing a wide status range). Throughout Part II, as also elsewhere in the volume, the printed book itself is shown to be a key artefact affording a multinodal generation of status-inflected social relations.[41]

First comes another overview, this time a Europe-wide one of a whole sector, that of publishers of learned texts. Ian Maclean focuses on a similar period to that from which Boutcher's examples were drawn (in this case 1560–1630). Publishers have previously been excluded from wider considerations of the relation of literature and learning to social hierarchy. Maclean rectifies that omission by examining their social status and the extent to which it was inflected by their activity. He shows that publishers of learned texts came from a range of social backgrounds and that the knowledge of letters that they themselves acquired varied greatly, ranging from a modest grasp of their own vernacular to considerable humanistic philological expertise. Perhaps because of their belonging to a relatively new industry, these publishers of learned texts had, like Stevenson's building contractors, a social status characterised at times by a certain indeterminacy and uncomfortableness, caught as it was between artisanal, mercantile, and scholarly spheres of activity.

Part II then shifts gear from this overview and provides two case studies of the role played by cultural production in social status, each Italian, each seventeenth-century, the first focusing on the theatre of the commedia dell'arte (as well as on poetry and letters), and the second focusing on poetry. First, a singular attempt to derive spectacular social status from the unpromising springboard of commedia dell'arte performance is examined by Sarah Gwyneth Ross. Despite the social and moral disrepute that was widely associated in Catholic Italy with acting in general

---

[41] E.g. Elizabeth and Jacobean collections of plays or poems (studied by Colin Burrow), Richard Blome's *The Gentlemans Recreation* of 1686 (studied by Christine Stevenson, who makes this particularly explicit, Chapter 4, pp. 83–4), the early seventeenth-century books published by Francesco Andreini after his wife Isabella's death (studied by Sarah Gwyneth Ross), or Marchina's *Musa posthuma* of 1662 (studied by Jane Stevenson).

and with the commedia in particular, the actor and writer Francesco Andreini used the medium of print to try to provide his deceased actor-writer wife, the celebrated Isabella Andreini, and thereby himself, with a remarkably elevated social status, by associating the commedia with vernacular humanism and Christian morals. Judged by at least some measures (such as the granting of honorary citizenship to Francesco by the ducal secretary of the Mantuan court), the attempt was successful. At least as remarkable, and in some respects perhaps swimming even more against the socio-cultural tide, was the social mobility and fame gained by Marta Marchina through her Latin poetry, as shown by Jane Stevenson. The conditions that made it possible for Marchina's talent to develop and to be known were created by the confluence of different circumstances, including her mother's death, the educating of her brothers (of whom she was now in charge) by an Oratorian, and the fact that another Oratorian was from the upwardly mobile Spada family. The extent of the singularity or typicality of Marchina's case in the light of the obstacles that often hampered women's access to humanistic expertise and learning can be gauged by setting this case against the broader backdrop sketched by Jane Stevenson elsewhere and by Helena Sanson in Part I.

Next, the third angle (Part III) for analysing the relation of literature and learning to social hierarchy reverses the direction of travel between them. It shows how social hierarchy was part of literature and learning. It focuses less on cultural producers and more on what they produced – representations of social hierarchy and of the place within it of particular groups, though that 'place' is often shown to be shifting, nuanced, or indeterminate. As mentioned, while this is the dominant angle in Part III it is not the only one: the status of the cultural producers themselves is still linked to the representations they offer (for example in the case of Cusanus[42]). The same was true, the other way round, of Parts I and II, which, while taking as their starting-point cultural producers, included study of actual representations.

The first representations to be examined in this way are from the earliest part of the period on which this volume focuses, the mid-fifteenth century, and by one major figure in the history of thought – Nicolas of Cusa, or Cusanus, steeped in the devotional literature of Upper Germany as well as in learned theology. Certain dialogues by Cusanus are shown by Richard Oosterhoff to undermine the assumption – challenged by those devotional currents but widespread in the early modern period – that social hierarchy corresponds to a hierarchy of morality and wisdom, with more of both being found near the summit. These representations by Cusanus *of* social hierarchy, and in particular of the hierarchy that places clerics above lay people, are intended (argues Oosterhoff) not to overthrow social hierarchy but to change people's understanding of it, to bring them to recognise that exemplary knowledge belongs to the humble, whether they happen to be rich or poor, cleric or lay, male or female. The focus then remains on representations of low-status people with Susan Wiseman's analysis of how some people were

---

[42] Chapter 8.

constructed in the period as being 'gypsies'. Here the focus is on England, from the early sixteenth century to the early seventeenth. Constructed is the key word here, for Wiseman does not purport to describe the life of early modern Roma people, but rather how different kinds of representations – ranging from positive laws to a masque by Ben Jonson – combined to create a 'gypsy' type that continually evolved but had a relatively stable set of features and connotations, and that sat partly at the bottom of social hierarchy, partly outside it altogether. Legal and literary representations here play distinctive roles within an exclusionary doubleact, but with a degree of vagueness characterising law at least as much as literature (since the legislative programme was to an extent notional and ambiguous).

The examination of textual representations of social hierarchy then continues by putting theatre centre stage in the two remaining chapters of Part III. England remains the main focus, though Jonathan Patterson's analysis of Antony and Cleopatra tragedies includes two French ones (by Jodelle and Garnier) alongside English ones (by Shakespeare, Mary Sidney Herbert, and Samuel Daniel). Patterson shows how these dramatic representations use variations on the story of Antony and Cleopatra to question the conflation of social with moral hierarchy. Does social grandeur correspond to moral greatness? Although the language, the period, the genre, and the nationalities are far removed from the world of Cusanus in the previous century, the faultline in dominant conceptions of social hierarchy that is being questioned here is broadly the same as the one analysed by Richard Oosterhoff for the Rhinelander. Finally, with the focus now remaining on a similar period to that of Patterson's examples and now being squarely on England, the representations of social hierarchy found in a different dramatic genre are studied by Richard McCabe. 'Greatness' is a preoccupation here too, but now in the context of the new-style 'domestic' tragedies that showed that the protagonists of tragedy did not have to be Antonys and Cleopatras but could be the middling (and upper-middling) sort, such as wealthy landowners, merchants, or aldermen. Yet inserting these groups into the representational system of tragedy has the effect, once again, of asking troubling questions about the moral foundations of social hierarchy, since the credit-based system underlying the social status of this new kind of protagonist is in tension with Christian morality.

Finally, the fourth angle (Part IV) for analysing the relation of literature and learning to social hierarchy is a composite of the others, since here literature/ learning is both part of social hierarchy and vice versa, with the relation between them being even more two-way. In the first case that is because consideration of the social status of public scribes gives way to consideration of a literary representation *of* them.[43] In the second case, it is because consideration of how poets (and dramatists) used books to shape their status moves from book history to literary criticism, from paratext to text.[44] For the first case, we move to Portugal, in particular to sixteenth-century Lisbon, and to the distinctive commercial practice of

---

[43] Chapter 12.
[44] Chapter 13.

scribe-hiring that lent the power of literature to those who, for a range of social and literary reasons, commissioned a bespoke literary product for their purposes instead of producing one themselves. In Simon Park's study of these scribes for hire, a certain degree of status-indeterminacy is evident both from the historical information that can be gleaned about them and also from the literary representation *of* them that is provided by an anonymous farce, printed in 1625 but probably written a century earlier. Earning more money than one might anticipate, these scribes occupy, like some of Ian Maclean's publishers and some of Christine Stevenson's builders, a slightly hazy social position at the interstices of craft and learning, and in their case because they moved outside the clearer-cut hierarchies of Lisbon's institutions of power (such as court and church). Finally, the volume closes by returning to England, and again to the late sixteenth and early seventeenth century, with Colin Burrow's examination of both the social status of poets (and dramatists) and also the representations *of* that status that were furnished by the printed books in which their work appeared. Burrow shows that those two halves of the equation are inseparable: although the social status of these authors was not coextensive with the status-claims communicated by those printed books, the books did serve partly to shape the authors' social status (for example through various bibliographical markers of status). On the other hand, literary representations did not serve only to *claim* social status: Burrow shows how they could also complicate, mimic, and ironise it, not least in the sonnets by the writer who, with his restless representations of hierarchy, has re-appeared more than any other throughout this volume: Shakespeare.

What emerges overall from the volume is that, although the relation between cultural production and social status often had intense implications for individuals, the implications were also profoundly collective. Writers and other kinds of practitioners produced manuscripts, books, and buildings that concerned, and at times affected, not only their own social status but that of their multiple users, whether the latter were precisely envisaged or entirely unknown. Marta Marchina's poems served to enhance not only *her* status, but also that of the relatively parvenu Spada family. Prestige books helped socially not just their printers and publishers but also the latters' patrons. One composition by a public scribe of Lisbon could make more of a social difference to its commissioner than to its composer. So this volume shows that the relationship of social hierarchy to literature and learning was not just a two-way one but also a circuit of relations between three elements – producer(s), product, and user(s).

Part I

Language, Social Literacy, and Social Status

2

'Noble ambition': New Social Literacies and Traditional Hierarchies in Early Modern European Literature and History

WARREN BOUTCHER

THIS CHAPTER CONCERNS a particular period in the long history of the relations between, on the one hand, letters and learning across Latin and the major Western European vernaculars and, on the other, social relations and distinctions within the European society of orders. The *longue durée* begins in the twelfth century, when a literate world and a social elite emerge together in the European archive. During that century, we see the pan-European revival of Latin learning in the universities and the church, and the first pan-European creation of related vernacular literatures and lay readerships. The latter centre on the Anglo-Norman moment, the chivalric turn, and the emergence of French and Occitan as transregional vernaculars. Where in later centuries they became essential ingredients of gentility, Latin and Tuscan vernacular humanisms develop between 1250 and 1350 in the northern Italian peninsula, as urban, lower-class rivals to aristocratic, chivalric literary cultures. These trends combine with the accelerated growth of a state and lay documentary culture and the consolidation of a pan-European noble elite (including the clergy as part of a newly authoritative pan-European papal hierarchy) who distinguish themselves from commoners and, in some contexts, their superstitions.[1]

---

[1] These developments – bureaucratic literacy, Latin learning, literate vernacularisation and chivalry, the formation of a noble class – all of course had antecedents in the earlier medieval period in various regions of Europe. The claim is that they accelerated and converged on a pan-European scale during the twelfth century and that they continued to interact in changeable and various ways – not, of course, in linear fashion towards ever greater European cultural integration – through to the nineteenth century. See George Holmes, 'Editor's Postscript', in George Holmes (ed.), *The Oxford History of Medieval Europe* (Oxford: Oxford University Press, 1992), pp. 324–29; Jane Gilbert, Simon Gaunt, and William E. Burgwinkle, *Medieval French Literary Culture Abroad* (Oxford: Oxford University Press, 2020); Ronald G. Witt, *In the Footsteps of the Ancients: The Origins of Humanism from Lovato to Bruni* (Leiden: Brill, 2000); Anne Duggan, *Nobles and Nobility in Medieval Europe: Concepts, Origins, Transformations* (Woodbridge: Boydell Press, 2000); David Crouch, *The Chivalric Turn: Conduct and Hegemony in Europe before 1300* (Oxford: Oxford University Press, 2019); Martin Aurell, *Le chevalier lettré: savoir*

Proceedings of the British Academy, **246**, 17–45, © The British Academy 2022.

Across the centuries that followed, there were two persistent elements in the construction of nobility as a matter of social distinction, of honour and dignity: one was birth, blood, lineage; the other was lifestyle, mores, intellect. The latter included social literacies valued by the elite, and for which they were imagined to have innate predispositions. These social literacies varied across time and space, in their importance relative to more material signifiers of social status, and in the extent to which they were open to women and minorities, or offered social mobility to commoners and outsiders. They ranged from scholastic learning and chivalry in the twelfth century, to humanistic dialectic and civil conversation in the sixteenth.

Language replete with superior knowledge and/or style was, however, fundamental to most forms of elite social literacy, whether the language deployed was Latin or a cosmopolitan or illustrious vernacular fashioned to rival or imitate Latin. Dante, writing in Latin in the early 1300s (*De vulgari eloquentia*), bucked the trends of his day by placing the illustrious Tuscan vernacular amongst other customary practices and qualities that call for elite users, rather than for rustic mountain-folk. This elite is defined not by birth but by personal worth or dignity gained in the practice of commerce, chivalry, or government. Just as the quality of magnificence demands people of great means, and grand purple attire asks for the nobility, so the illustrated vernacular looks for those who excel in intellect and *scientia*. Just as the best horses are appropriate only to the best knights, so the best speech or discourse (*loquela*) is suited to the best thinking.[2]

The *longue durée* to which I referred at the beginning ends in the first half of the nineteenth century, with the social transformations brought by industrialisation and the greatly accelerated nationalisation of Western European culture after the French Revolution. Sheldon Pollock has influentially described this as the vernacular millennium in Europe and South Asia.[3] Pollock's central argument – for which Dante's intervention is evidence – is that vernacularisation is not straightforwardly to be identified with democratisation and increasing egalitarianism. Across several centuries, social elites based in courts fashioned cosmopolitan vernaculars in relation to a superordinate classical language (Latin, Sanskrit), while challenged by counter-cosmopolitan vernacular voices and revolutions. Vernacularisation, as conceptualised by Pollock, comprises processes which irrupt into pre-literate, oral

---

et conduite de l'aristocratie aux XIIe et XIIIe siècles (Paris: Fayard, 2011); Andreas Gestrich, 'The Social Order', in Hamish Scott (ed.), *The Oxford Handbook of Early Modern European History, 1350–1750: Volume I: Peoples and Place* (Oxford: Oxford University Press, 2015), pp. 295–312. When I use 'literacy' within the phrase 'social literacy' it designates a learned and applied competence or *habitus* – written, oral, behavioural – in any form of knowledge, rather than the narrower sense of the ability to read and write. For the concept of 'social literacies' see Brian V. Street, *Literacy in Theory and Practice* (Cambridge: Cambridge University Press, 1984); Brian V. Street, *Social Literacies: Critical Approaches to Literacy in Development, Ethnography, and Education* (London: Longman, 1995).

[2] Marianne Shapiro, *De vulgari eloquentia: Dante's Book of Exile* (Lincoln: University of Nebraska Press, 1990), II.i, pp. 69–70.

[3] Sheldon Pollock, *The Language of the Gods in the World of Men: Sanskrit, Culture, and Power in Premodern India* (Berkeley: University of California Press, 2006).

worlds: literisation, a society's transition to the use of writing for bureaucracy and documentation; literarisation, a society's invention in writing of literary-learned and poetic modes of expression – which can follow centuries after literisation; and the superposition of a dominant language and literary formation in response to which the literary vernacular emerges.[4]

Pollock's focus is on nexuses of political centralisation and written culture in South Asia and Western Europe; there is no room for the Ottoman Empire, which in our period may make a more natural comparison.[5] He sees the irruption both of writing per se and of the writing of literary vernacular works as sudden and decisive ruptures in a society's history. He pays no detailed attention to social hierarchy, to gender, to the interplay between oral, behavioural, and written practices. He risks reconfirming certain ideological foundations of social inequalities by denying that oral cultures have 'literature' or forms of literacy.[6] But for studies of early modern vernacular literature the wider perspective he brings is salutary: universalising, superordinate languages and literatures, cosmopolitan vernaculars, and demotic or religiously insurgent vernaculars, should be considered together, across regions and larger periods, and as a matter of choices made by agents in history.

The portion of the vernacular millennium of interest in the present chapter runs from the 1530s to the 1660s. Pollock's framework, with some adaptation, works well for this period. It is one in which pre-literate oral worlds, superposed Latinate literary formations, cosmopolitan or illustrated vernacular cultures, and demotic and religiously insurgent vernacular cultures all co-existed, interacted, clashed.[7] In what follows, I combine attention to broad historical trends in the relations between high social literacies and social hierarchy with analysis of representations of those trends in particular vernacular texts. I focus on 1580 to 1620 in England and France (especially Montaigne), and to a lesser extent Italy and Spain.

From Pollock's perspective, the long sixteenth century sees the continuation of a trend that began in ninth-century England and accelerated across Western Europe in the twelfth and thirteenth centuries: the emergence of the 'vernacular polity' understood as a regionalised form of literary production and political communica-tion and as a forerunner of the modern nation-state. Pollock concentrates on par-ticular writings that defend the vernacular, and jumps from Lorenzo de' Medici and Nebrija at the turn of the fifteenth and sixteenth centuries to Du Bellay's treatise of 1549, which he associates with the Pléiade and the influence of the court of

---

[4] Pollock, *The Language of the Gods*, pp. 4–5, 23, 298. Pollock does not, then, use 'vernacular' in the commonly accepted sense.

[5] Cornell H. Fleischer, *Bureaucrat and Intellectual in the Ottoman Empire: The Historian Mustafa Âli (1541–1600)* (Princeton: Princeton University Press, 1986).

[6] Karin Barber, *The Anthropology of Texts, Persons and Publics: Oral and Written Culture in Africa and Beyond* (Cambridge: Cambridge University Press, 2007).

[7] For a case study in the socio-cultural tensions and clashes at the heart of vernacularisation in England in this period see Jenny C. Mann, *Outlaw Rhetoric: Figuring Vernacular Eloquence in Shakespeare's England* (Ithaca: Cornell University Press, 2012).

François I.[8] If one is seeking to supplement Pollock by establishing a more precise, Europe-wide turning-point in cultural politics, the combination in the 1530s and 1540s of transformations in the arts curriculum in many educational institutions and the cultural policies of Henry VIII, François I, Charles V, and the first Dukes of Florence, Alessandro and Cosimo de' Medici makes sense.[9] Whether or not his 'vernacular polity' thesis stands up for all of Western and Central Europe, it seems clear that by these decades oral and written language-literature is becoming a more widespread means of social self-identification across Europe and its new colonies and outposts.

A number of new variants of the longer-term trends already mentioned converge in the 1530s and 1540s: the dissemination, shaped by humanist pedagogy, of multilingual, Latinate and cosmopolitan vernacular literacies to European social elites; the dissemination of newly reformed religious literacies (Reformed and Catholic) to communities both in Europe and, in a completely new development, in the colonial Americas, where both Latin and cosmopolitan vernaculars such as Castilian were imposed on indigenous vernacular cultures; the intensification and acceleration of centralised state bureaucracies – rule by paper and ink across regions and continents.

Where do these trends lead? To Pollock's 'vernacular polity'? At the other end of our larger period (the 1530s to the 1660s) we find the clearest example – not mentioned by Pollock – in sixteenth- and seventeenth-century European history of a hegemonic, court-based, cosmopolitan vernacular culture and accompanying state bureaucracy, and of the integration of literature and court and state politics: on the one hand, the court of Louis XIV's maturity in the 1660s, and its relationship to the literature of Racine, Boileau, and others – a new relationship between literature and power that had been emerging since the 1620s and 1630s; on the other hand, the state-based system of intelligence and scholarship created by Colbert. This is traditionally seen as the beginning of the ascendancy of France in ancien régime Europe, of French over Latin and the other vernaculars as the cosmopolitan language of Europe's social and intellectual elite, and, more generally, of the stabilisation of secular 'letters' as the classicised and academic foundation of elite cultures that define themselves against popular cultures.[10]

---

[8] Pollock, *The Language of the Gods*, pp. 466–9, 481, 573.

[9] Konrad Eisenbichler (ed.), *The Cultural Politics of Duke Cosimo I de' Medici* (Aldershot: Ashgate, 2001); Judith Bryce, 'The Oral World of the Early Accademia Fiorentina', *Renaissance Studies*, 9 (1995), 77–103; Greg Walker, *Writing under Tyranny: English Literature and the Henrician Reformation* (Oxford: Oxford University Press, 2005); Claude Albert Mayer, Pauline M. Smith, and I. D. McFarlane (eds), *Literature and the Arts in the Reign of Francis I: Essays presented to C.A. Mayer* (Lexington: French Forum, 1985).

[10] Oded Rabinovitch, *The Perraults: A Family of Letters in Early Modern France* (Ithaca: Cornell University Press, 2018); Larry F. Norman, 'The Baroque as Anti-Classicism: The French Case', in John D. Lyons (ed.), *The Oxford Handbook of the Baroque* (Oxford: Oxford University Press, 2018), pp. 623–41; Jacob Soll, *The Information Master: Jean-Baptiste Colbert's Secret State Intelligence System* (Ann Arbor: University of Michigan Press, 2009); Adrian Marino, *The Biography of 'The Idea of Literature' from Antiquity to the Baroque* (Albany: State University of New York Press, 1995),

But, as I have already implied, there are respects in which Pollock's narrative and approach need to be revised and nuanced if they are to provide the basis of a viable literary history of this period. Walter Cohen has done some important work to this end, adding the distinction between vernaculars that were cognate and non-cognate with Latin, and the importance of horizontal interaction between the vernaculars.[11] This is related to the question – not raised by Pollock in relation to Europe – of multilingual cosmopolitanism across Latin and different vernaculars. Some courts *were* promoters of particular regional vernaculars that were responding to superposed models, while others were centres of multilingual learning.[12]

On the one hand, not only the French, but the Italian case fits Pollock's paradigm well. The papal monarch Alexander VII absorbed the literary heritages of other Italian states whose learned families gained prestige from ducal courts, and vice versa. In 1658, he was present in person to receive the famous manuscript library of the Duchy of Urbino, which he noted was a repository of the Latin-and-Italian learning of illustrious lineages of learned and noble *urbinati* from the 1520s to the early 1600s. He picks out the vernacular Tasso manuscripts, but also works of neo-Latin scholarship and important manuscripts of classical authors.[13]

On the other hand, the paradigm does not work so well for the Hispano-Burgundian court of Charles V and his successors in the Holy Roman Empire. For there are problems with Pollock's notion of the 'vernacular polity' as the dominant politico-cultural entity throughout this period, including the fact that it relies heavily on the case of France. Charles V, as head of a multilingual and composite dynastic empire, cannot be singly identified with the promotion of a cosmopolitan vernacular (Castilian) on the model of *trecento* Tuscan and in relation to Latin. Courts such as Heidelberg and Vienna were multilingual; Latin was dominant but not alongside one regional, cosmopolitan vernacular (there were still different varieties of 'German' and none were yet 'illustrated'). In the Spanish-conquered Americas, the project of Castilianisation and Latinisation – which provided a route for indigenous people to higher social status in the colonial administration – ran alongside a project of evangelising in indigenous languages, creating complex multilingual texts and interactions. In post-conquest Peru, from 1550, Spanish priests and missionaries codified and imposed a single written standard, based on a variety of Quechua spoken in the former Inca capital of Cuzco – an important variant of the process

pp. 151–200; Caroline Castiglione, 'Cultures of Peoples', in Scott (ed.), *The Oxford Handbook of Early Modern European History, 1350–1750: Volume I*, pp. 694–719; Vladislav Rjéoutski, Gesine Argent, and Derek Offord (eds), *European Francophonie: The Social, Political and Cultural History of an International Prestige Language* (Oxford and New York: Peter Lang, 2014).

[11] Walter Cohen, *A History of European Literature: The West and the World from Antiquity to the Present* (Oxford: Oxford University Press, 2017).

[12] Jean Balsamo and Anna Kathrin Bleuler (eds), *Les cours comme lieux de rencontre et d'élaboration des langues vernaculaires à la Renaissance (1480–1620) = Höfe als Laboratorien der Volkssprachigkeit zur Zeit der Renaissance (1480–1620)* (Geneva: Droz, 2016).

[13] Warren Boutcher, 'Collecting Manuscripts and Printed Books in the Late Renaissance: Naudé and the Last Duke of Urbino's Library', *Italian Studies*, 66.2 (2011), 206–20 at 216–18.

of vernacularisation not considered by Pollock.[14] And it is arguable that not only the Spanish Habsburg empire but many of the major politico-cultural entities that emerged in this period more often looked like multiregional, multilingual, dynastic agglomerates than like forerunners of monolingual, modern nation-states.[15]

Moreover, works in regional cosmopolitan vernaculars composed and published towards the end of our period could take very different forms and have very different types of relationships with court culture and social hierarchy. Take, for example, two vernacular epics from different ends of Europe. On the one hand, Miklós Zrínyi was of the high military nobility, a Croatian-Hungarian aristocrat of Habsburg-ruled Royal Hungary, and an active military leader against the Ottomans. He had vexed and distant relations with the Habsburg court at Vienna. In the writing of the first great epic in the Hungarian language, immediately translated into Croatian, he deployed a multilingual linguistic culture including engagement with Latin and Italian classics.[16] On the other hand, Milton, a Latin secretary, moved from the 1645 *Poemata*, embedded in aristocratic connections and patronage, to the elite Republican version of vernacular *Latinitas* – distant from the ethos of the Restoration court – found in the greatest English epic, *Paradise Lost*. His multilingual range, though different, included a Latin-and-Italian heritage in common with Zrínyi.[17] But he gives cosmopolitan and epic vernacular form to biblical history, rather than – as Pollock's model assumes, and as Zrínyi does – to regional history and space.

We need, then, to adapt Pollock's framework to incorporate the different variants and spaces of multilingualism that were were fundamental to the literary history of this portion of the vernacular millennium. We need to add consideration of the other institutions and forms of literature that were significant beyond princely courts and poetry or expressive writing. But, broadly, his framework remains useful. Latin, as a language taught to be spoken and written as well as read, was on the rise across Europe – its pan-European empire, from one perspective, was just beginning – at the

---

[14] Jan-Dirk Müller, 'Mehrsprachigkeit am Kaiserhof. Multilinguisme à la cour impériale', in Balsamo and Bleuler (eds), *Les cours comme lieux de rencontre et d'élaboration des langues vernaculaires à la Renaissance*, pp. 51–69; Miguel Martínez, 'Language, Nation, and Empire in Early Modern Iberia', in José Del Valle (ed.), *A Political History of Spanish. The Making of a Language* (Cambridge: Cambridge University Press, 2013), pp. 44–61; Paul Firbas, 'Language, Religion and Unification in Early Colonial Peru', in Del Valle (ed.), *A Political History of Spanish*, pp. 135–51; Alan Durston, *Pastoral Quechua: The History of Christian Translation in Colonial Peru, 1550–1650* (Notre Dame: University of Notre Dame Press, 2007).

[15] J. S. Morrill, 'Dynasties, Realms, Peoples and State Formation', in Robert Von Friedeburg and J. S. Morrill (eds), *Monarchy Transformed: Princes and their Elites in Early Modern Western Europe* (Cambridge: Cambridge University Press, 2017), pp. 17–43.

[16] Miklós Zrínyi, *The Siege of Sziget*, ed. George Gömöri, trans. László Kőrössy (Washington, DC: Catholic University of America Press, 2011).

[17] Peter Lindenbaum, 'John Milton and the Republican Mode of Literary Production', *The Yearbook of English Studies*, 21 (1991), 121–36; Thomas N. Corns, 'Milton's Quest for Respectability', *The Modern Language Review*, 77 (1982), 769–79; John K. Hale, *Milton's Languages: The Impact of Multilingualism on Style* (Cambridge: Cambridge University Press, 1997).

same time as the cosmopolitan vernaculars.[18] It was standard for Latin and regional vernaculars to be taught or used together in humanistic education – through double translation. This was a different process, culturally, for Latin-near Romance and Latin-distant Germanic languages and for alphabetised indigenous vernaculars, and in general for students in Europe and in the colonial Americas.

The 'illustration' of regional vernaculars in relation to particular states and courts, or religious institutions, and the construction not just of a learned Latin cosmopolis but of a multilingual, cosmopolitan European space of elite social and intellectual honour, were overlapping and complementary processes.[19] So the Tuscan variant of Italian was both promoted on the European stage as the language and heritage of Medici Florence and taught internationally as one of a run of literary languages (Italian, French, Spanish, but also Latin as a 'modern', spoken language) available to European social elites as cultural capital. When considering this twinned fostering of both Latin and vernaculars, courts need to be considered alongside other institutions such as academies, universities, schools, churches, law courts, parliaments, and families; 'literature' needs more explicitly to include professional and humanistic Latinate learning, which had a role to play in all these institutions.

How are these broad developments registered in vernacular literature of the period? There are many approaches to answering this question. I focus on one that does not feature in Pollock. I ask how texts represent the irruption, both in writing and in oral and social practice, of new forms of social literacy into societies shaped by traditional customs, beliefs, and hierarchies. This is not quite the same as Pollock's exclusive focus on moments of inauguration of writing per se and of literary expressivity in particular vernaculars. I begin with the extended example of Montaigne, a Latin-educated nobleman both caught up in and critical of processes of literisation, literarisation, and superposition.

Montaigne chooses the French vernacular to speak literarily from a regional home. He is very much concerned with histories of the irruptions mentioned in the last paragraph, including the irruption of Latin learning into his own family history. His position in relation to these processes, is, though, ambivalent. His own social identity as a nobleman is from one perspective vernacular-cosmopolitan; though destined by his father for a career in Latin letters he chooses regional culture and speech as the home from which he participates in a wider world by means of letters and travel. But his text is also counter-cosmopolitan; it contains stories about the deleterious effects of the arrival of that same wider world and of letters and bureaucracy – bureaucracy in which he participated as a magistrate – on the

---

[18] Françoise Waquet, *Le latin, ou, l'empire d'un signe: XVIe-XXe siècle* (Paris: Albin Michel, 1998).

[19] Jean Balsamo, '"Voici venir d'Europe tout l'honneur": identité aristocratique et conscience européene au XVIe siècle', in David Cowling (ed.), *Conceptions of Europe in Renaissance France: Essays in Honour of Keith Cameron* (Amsterdam: Rodopi, 2006), pp. 21–34.

social order and health of traditional, self-contained, oral-based communities.[20] Ambivalence concerning the irruption of new social literacies in traditional social hierarchies proves to be typical of many of the representations we shall go on to consider in the final part of the chapter.

In *Essais* II 37, 'De la resemblance des enfans aux peres' ('Of the resemblance of children to fathers'), Montaigne tells the story of Lahontan, a village in the Atlantic Pyrenees, on the confines of Béarn and Guyenne, about 120 miles or two days' travel south of St. Michel-de-Montaigne in Périgord. Montaigne says that it is with the inhabitants of this region as it is said to be with those of the valley of 'Angrougne', where, for a long time, the villagers had lived happily apart from the world beyond, living by their own particular customs. Then someone was sent away from Lahontan to learn how to write so that he could be a *notaire*, and corruption set in. When a medical doctor arrived things got even worse.[21]

What might now be considered an instance of social and cultural mobility, facilitated by the advent of professional literacy in an isolated community, is here narrated by Montaigne as a secular Fall. Before the Fall, there had been knowledge of local customs, transmitted orally by the fathers and received with reverence by the sons. But then one of the fathers conceives a 'noble ambition', which Montaigne probably intended to sound like a paradox. He wants to become a village notable, to render his name honourable, by sending one of his sons away to acquire 'letters' and the title of 'maistre'. Hierarchy is introduced into Lahontan *with* letters, in the form of professional knowledge. It is the hierarchy that goes from a *maître* near the bottom to a royal judge near the top. In the 1580–8 text the son becomes 'monsieur', in the 1595 text 'grand'.[22] Part of the process of becoming 'monsieur' is to show intellectual excellence by disdaining local customs and showing knowledge of glorious regions in distant France.

But the villagers, and their rules and customs, are now subjected to the legal and political hierarchy of that distant France, in the form of royal judges called in for the first time. Lahontan was administered according to the *coustumes* of the *prévôté* of nearby Dax, which in turn fell in Montaigne's time under the jurisdiction of the Parlement of Bordeaux.[23] The publisher of the first edition of the *Essais*, Simon Millanges, had in 1576 published the 'coustumes … particulieres' of this *prévôté* as approved and authorised by the court of the Parlement at Bordeaux. It included

---

[20] My thanks go to George Hoffmann for the suggestion I consider Montaigne in relation to Pollock's work.

[21] Michel de Montaigne, *Les Essais*, ed. Jean Balsamo, Michel Magnien, and Catherine Magnien-Simonin (Paris: Gallimard, 2007), pp. 817–19, henceforward abbreviated as 'NP'; Michel de Montaigne, *Complete Essays*, trans. Donald M. Frame (Stanford: Stanford University Press, 1958), pp. 591–92. I have also consulted Michel de Montaigne, *The Complete Essays*, trans. M. A. Screech (London: Penguin, 2003).

[22] NP 1709.

[23] Louis Batcave, 'Commentaire historique d'un passage de Montaigne', *Revue des études historiques*, 67 (1901), 127–40.

some specific mentions of 'Lafontan', with respect to the territory's customary exceptions to the feudal right of *seigneurs* to be presented with the goods their tenants wish to sell, and to the prohibition against putting one's animals to pasture on others' enclosed land.[24] The context is the relationship between *consuetudo* (customary law) and *lex* (written law) and the question of the superiority of local 'custom' or of the 'reason' of a judge in interpreting the law as it applies in a given case. The first half of the sixteenth century in France sees a process of literisation as written and printed *coustumiers* register and codify the operation of various local, municipal, regional and national customs and laws under a centralised, royal administration.[25]

Meanwhile, in Montaigne's account, the daughters of Lahontan are beginning to attract socially worthy suitors from elsewhere, suitors who bring in other kinds of professional learning and distinction such as medicine. A new doctor who marries into the area likewise disdains the local customs, including the way the local people have learned to use garlic to tackle most illnesses. He teaches them a new *science*, also brought from afar, consisting of technical terms from pathology and anatomy. He begins to accumulate wealth from his trafficking of this knowledge, which makes them ill and even kills them. He teaches them that the *serein* – the night air – and over-heated drinking are bad for them.

The arrival of this new medical literacy in Lahontan, by oral means, is associated allusively in Montaigne's text with the vernacular literarisation of medical knowledge in sixteenth-century France. Montaigne is throughout this part of II 37 alluding to learned vernacular texts by a commoner, Laurent Joubert.[26] Joubert partly made his reputation by debunking popular errors in matters of health in print. He had risen to become Chancellor of the Montpellier Faculty of Medicine and royal physician. In one paratext, he attributed his own and his family's success to his mother's arrangement of good marriages for her daughters and education of her four surviving sons in theology, law, medicine, trade and commerce – all the types of professional learning that Lahontan had so healthily avoided. The Jouberts are an example of what Neil Kenny describes as a state–family compact which takes commoners like Joubert from their mother's homes to honourable service

---

[24] *Les coustumes generalles et particulieres de la ville et prevosté d'Acs, lesquelles ont esté approuuees, & par Edit perpetuel decretees, & auctorisees par la Cour de Parlement a Bordeaux* (Bordeaux: Simon Millanges, 1576), pp. 24, 31, 32. A text with the same title had already appeared in Bordeaux in 1553, with another publisher (USTC 41013).

[25] Ian Maclean, *Interpretation and Meaning in the Renaissance: The Case of Law* (Cambridge: Cambridge University Press, 1992); Library of Congress, European Law Division, *The Coutumes of France in the Library of Congress* (Washington, DC: Library of Congress, 1977); Ullrich Langer, 'Montaigne's Customs', *Montaigne Studies*, 4 (1992), 81–96. My thanks go to Ian Maclean for his assistance on this point.

[26] NP 1709–10; Laurent Joubert, *Erreurs populaires au fait de la medecine et regime de santé* (Bordeaux: S. Millanges, 1578); Laurent Joubert, *Segonde partie des erreurs populaires et propos vulgaires touchant la medecine & le regime de santé* (Paris: Abel L'Angelier, 1579).

in universities and royal courts.[27] In the case of Lahontan, the new *science* brings unaccustomed maladies to the people and a general decline in their former vigour.

Montaigne is here anticipating modern sociological approaches. He treats new literacies not as neutral, beneficial technical skills and knowledge transmitted via formal education but as social practices whose introduction has an ideological context. That context might typically be the imposition of new kinds of social order or disorder. The passage relates to several others in the *Essais* that narrate the consequences – in terms of social health and hierarchy – for families, communities, and nations, of the transfer of new literacies and the new elites that come with them. This transfer can be between European regions or between Europe and other regions.

One example is the peoples indigenous to the new world, which Montaigne describes in the 1580s as still in its infancy, learning its ABC, having known no letters until 50 years previously, in the 1530s. Like the arrival of the *medecin*'s knowledge in Lahontan, the arrival of 'nos opinions et nos arts' ('our opinions and our arts') in the new world proves to be a kind of contagion – analogous to the diseases the Europeans brought with them – that hastens its decline. Montaigne alludes to the fact that a document (the *requerimiento*, which he describes as 'leurs remonstrances accoutumées') that is read aloud to the native people requires their submission to the royal Catholic hierarchy of Spain and educates them in the monotheistic theology they are now instructed to accept. Written records of these occasions were kept and signed documents sent back to Spain.[28]

Montaigne records a defiant response to the Spaniards' 'remonstrances' (NP 955–6). And we might ask how, in historical practice, the attempted imposition of European Latinate, religious, and bureaucratic literacies in the Americas was received, and how those literacies were assimilated or turned against the colonisers by indigenous peoples whose own literacies were devalued. How did it relate to the transition from pre-Conquest to post-Conquest social hierarchies? There is much new research on this question. On the one hand, in 1656, a Timucua cacique in Florida used European literary communications to coordinate a Timucua and Apalachee uprising against the Spanish. On the other hand, by the 1660s, new creole elites, defined by exclusive social literacies and new bodies of knowledge, had emerged as part of a new social order in colonial Mexico.[29]

Irruptions of learning also occurred closer to home. Men of *science* arrived at the estate at St. Michel-de-Montaigne during the same decade of the 1530s. Montaigne

---

[27] Neil Kenny, *Born to Write: Literary Families and Social Hierarchy in Early Modern France* (Oxford: Oxford University Press, 2020), pp. 70–3.

[28] NP 953, 955, 1768; Colin M. MacLachlan, *Spain's Empire in the New World: The Role of Ideas in Institutional and Social Change* (Berkeley: University of California Press, 1988) pp. 30–1.

[29] Alejandra Dubcovsky and George Aaron Broadwell, 'Writing Timucua: Recovering and Interrogating Indigenous Authorship', *Early American Studies*, 15 (2017), 409–41; Anna Herron More, *Baroque Sovereignty: Carlos de Sigüenza y Góngora and the Creole Archive of Colonial Mexico* (Philadelphia: University of Pennsylvania Press, 2013).

narrates this at the beginning of II 12, which starts with his evaluation of *science* considered as a quality of a person. It is a great and universal quality; those who despise it reveal their animal stupidity (*bestise*). Some philosophers make it the sovereign good, able to make a person wise and content. But if it is true, as others have said, that knowledge is the mother of all virtue, while all vice is produced by ignorance, then the statement requires a long commentary – in the form, we might surmise, of the famous chapter that follows (NP 458). Underlying this commentary are some simple notions. Knowledge, in the form of wisdom, is a gift from God, not equally bestowed on all. Some claim it as a kind of social privilege, giving them authority over others and over God, for worldly reasons. Likewise, faith is a gift from God, not equally bestowed on all, and to be received unconditionally from the divine giver. But it, likewise, is claimed by some beyond the divinely sanctioned church as a privilege, a form of knowledge they can profit from and disseminate, and that makes them 'elect'.

Montaigne is talking at the beginning of II 12 about a moment in his father's time when the social elite took their lead from the king in acting on a belief that knowledge was the mother of all virtue. They embraced letters, as François I did, with new ardour, and raised their social esteem in the eyes of all those who looked to the royal court. They founded new institutions, such as the Collège Royal in 1529–30. This royal raising of the social esteem of men with the quality of *science*, and of *lettres* per se, also had effects in the provinces. The humanistic Collège de Guyenne was founded in Bordeaux in early 1533, around the time Michel was born. Pierre Eyquem invested time and money in gaining the acquaintance of *gens de sçavoir*, receiving them in his house – as Montaigne put it at the beginning of II 12 – like holy persons inspired with divine wisdom, partly because neither he nor any of his forebears were learned men. He was determined that would change.

One of these *gens de sçavoir*, Pierre Bunel, gifts Pierre a book (Sebond's *Theologia naturalis*) as a rational defence of the articles of the Christian religion. This was probably between 1542 and 1546, when, as Montaigne says, the 'Lutheran' novelties or new ideas of the Reform movements were spreading in France. From Montaigne's perspective, what happened to Lahontan when it raised the esteem of men of letters, men of knowledge of law and medicine, was beginning to happen across France in the 1540s. Bunel, by *discours de raison*, saw that the credit being given to the new ideas, and to the new doctors of theology who propounded them, amounted to a sickness shaking France's ancient religion. The sickness, as in Lahontan, spread amongst the *vulgaire*, the mass of common people who speak the *patois*. They now treated their long-held beliefs about salvation as 'opinions' to be doubted and tested, subject to personal approval (NP 458–9). Montaigne later makes it clear, when addressing his learned female dedicatee (probably Marguerite de Valois), that these new doctors were also spreading the contagion through her courts, and that his Pyrrhonist arguments are designed as a medicinal preservative she can use *in extremis* (NP 591–2).

But what about religion in Lahontan? And how does that *conte* relate to the story its narrator tells us in the same and other chapters about his own and his family's relationship to learning and the social hierarchy? Montaigne is putting in writing a local, orally transmitted narrative about something that happened within the memory of the villagers' fathers. It is popular wisdom about the dangers of listening to doctors or lawyers, wisdom he is overwriting in a more learned vernacular vein. The tradition is attested only by an old saying in Béarnais: 'Noutarii de Lahontaa – Medici de Lahontaa', meaning suspect professionals.[30] And Montaigne literarises it. He inserts it within the literary framework of his humanistic culture by aligning it with a classical Latin epigram by a Bordelais rhetorician and Roman official, Ausonius. Ausonius joked in verse about the classical surgeon Alcon having the power to kill, with a mere touch, a marble statue of Jove, so that it is carried from the ancient shrine to a grave (NP 817). This resonates with the story of Lahontan, in which men of knowledge also kill the old gods of a community. As Montaigne narrates that story it also recalls literary myths of the golden age and humanist Utopias, and of their corruption and decline. It is redolent of pastoral satire, and was incorporated into a pastoral drama in Renaissance England.[31] It alludes to other texts and histories, including Joubert's.

For those in the know, one such allusion colours the whole narrative of Lahontan as he delivers it. Montaigne says that it was with the inhabitants of this region as it was said to be with those of the valley of 'Angrougne' – Angrogna, as it now is, in Italian Piedmont. Contemporary readers who had read or heard about one of the many contemporary accounts of what happened to the inhabitants of the valley of Angrogna in the mid-sixteenth century would have received the story of Lahontan differently. By invoking that valley, on the other side of France, in the territories disputed with the Duchy of Savoy, Montaigne is adding the third plank of the professional triumvirate, theology. He is alluding, more particularly, to the irruption of reformed theology and learned pastors into an isolated community's time-honoured and orally transmitted religious tradition, and the consequent imposition both of forms of church hierarchy from Geneva and politico-juridical hierarchy from France and Savoy. For just as the inhabitants of the valley of Lahontan called a *maître-notaire* and a doctor into their communities to teach them new *science*, so the Waldensian inhabitants of the valley of Angrogna received doctors of the new theology, educated in the academies of the newly Reformed cities of the alpine regions. This in turn led to their being assimilated by the Reform and subjected both to the French state and church hierarchy at Turin and to the authority of the Duke of Savoy.[32]

---

[30] Vastin Lespy, *Dictons du pays de Béarn* (Pau: L. Ribaut, 1875), pp. 175–6.

[31] Warren Boutcher, *The School of Montaigne in Early Modern Europe Volume Two: The Reader-Writer* (Oxford: Oxford University Press, 2017), pp. 261–2.

[32] The best modern historical account of these events and their wider context is to be found in Euan Cameron, *The Reformation of the Heretics: The Waldenses of the Alps, 1480–1580* (Oxford: Clarendon Press, 1984). Cameron emphasises that many of the contemporary sources, produced by Reformed intellectuals, underplay the obstacles in assimilating the Waldensians to the Reformed church.

The history was recounted by many mid-sixteenth-century chroniclers including Lentolo (1561), Noël (1562), Crespin (1564), and La Place (1565). Both Scipione Lentolo and Étienne Noël were appointed pastors at Angrogna.[33] La Popelinière's account in the 1581 text of his *Histoire de France*, based on Noël, is the most useful here because it is contemporary with the publication of the *Essais*.[34] La Popelinière does not describe the valley as completely cut off from the world. But he does refer to the sixteenth-century inhabitants as Vaudois peasants and labourers who lived peacefully and apart. They recognised their *seigneurs*. They differed in their religion from papal orthodoxy, but they maintained their way of life and *doctrine* without trouble. Suddenly, however, in 1555 they begin preaching more boldly in public, in new temples such as that built at Angrogna, boosted by books and ministers called in from Geneva ('livres et ministres sortis de Geneve').[35] This is confirmed by the most authoritative modern history: with Calvin's organisation in Geneva firmly established, ministers were sent into the Waldensian valleys in the spring of 1555. They were well received by many, and more ministers followed, including the martyr Varaglia, sent to Angrogna in 1557, only to be burnt at Turin in 1558.[36]

Would Montaigne have put this irruption of Reformed theology and learned preaching into Angrogna's isolated community down to 'noble ambition' breaking out amongst the valley-dwellers? It certainly involved defying one Church hierarchy, and the noble Catholic *seigneurs* integrated with it, and gaining recognition within another, centred on Geneva, partly by learning from books. In this case the 'thoughts of the glorious world beyond' brought by the educated outsiders, the Genevan-trained pastors, would be of the New Jerusalem they were building within the royal Catholic regimes to which they were meant to be subject. In Montaigne's mind, perhaps, the booksellers began to do business out of their very salvation. The new drug of Calvinist theology alerted them to problems they did not even know they had, then killed many of them.

Modern historians describe how the *barbes* or 'uncles', the Vaudois elders who had preached their religion, were in this moment displaced by learned Calvinist ministers trained in Geneva and elsewhere. The *barbes* had not, as Reformed historiography insisted, reached agreement with Calvinist ministers as early as 1532

---

[33] Lancelot-Voisin sieur de La Popelinière, *L'Histoire de France: Tome III (1561–1562)*, ed. Denise Turrel, Paul-Alexis Mellet, and Odette Turrias (Geneva: Librairie Droz, 2019), p. 120n. 417; Jean-François Gilmont, 'Aux origines de l'historiographie vaudoise du xvie siècle: Jean Crespin, Scipione Lentolo et Etienne Noël', *I Valdesi e l'Europa* (Torre Pellice: Società di Studi Valdesi, 1982), pp. 165–202.

[34] The whole section devoted to the history of the Vaudois in the eastern Alpine valleys from 1555 can be found in La Popelinière, *L'Histoire de France: Tome III (1561–1562)*, pp. 119–69, corresponding to Henri Lancelot-Voisin de La Popelinière, *L'Histoire de France, enrichie des plus notables occurrances survenues ez provinces de l'Europe et pays voisins ... depuis l'an 1550 jusques à ces temps* (La Rochelle: Abraham Haultin, 1581), fols 244v–254v.

[35] La Popelinière, *L'Histoire de France: Tome III (1561–1562)*, pp. 121–2.

[36] Cameron, *The Reformation of the Heretics*, pp. 157–9, 161–2, 171.

at the Synod of Chanforan near Angrogna – this had been more like the opening of an inconclusive disputation (of which a written record survives) about the relationship of Reformed and Waldensian religion. But for a generation after 1555 what Peyrot called '"a new Waldensian ruling class" was raised up' in the valleys 'by the structures of Genevan church-government'. These were men of learning; many were probably of high birth. Scipione Lentolo, pastor at Angrogna, had studied at Venice and was a doctor of theology; he later formed the canons of Italian grammar in a well-known Latin treatise.[37]

After this irruption in 1555 the trouble starts, and it involves books and writing. The Parlement of Turin – in place since France had taken the city from Savoy in 1536 – and its royal judges get involved and a commission of justices is sent to investigate them for heresy. Their credo is carried back from the valleys by the justices in writing, including the statement that they will obey their civil superiors, princes and magistrates, as long as they do not command them to do anything against the honour of God, the sovereign prince of all. There is then a relatively peaceful hiatus as the whole *procès* takes a year to reach the king, a hiatus during which those of Angrogna banish the mass from their valley.[38] Individuals are, however, martyred. Crespin, in the *Livre des martyrs*, described the bookbinder Barthélemi Hector taken distributing Genevan devotional texts and bibles in the valley in 1556, for which he was executed at Turin.[39] After 1559, when he regained the city of Turin and Piedmont, the Duke of Savoy sends the troops in to extirpate heresy from the valleys, especially Angrogna – followed later by Spanish troops. Despite some heroic resistance, there is carnage, as 'ceux d'Angrongne' continue to protest that they and their ancestors had observed their religion, the pure word of God as announced by the prophets and the apostles, for centuries and that they would rather die all together than renounce it for the Roman religion. Only in mid-1561 did the skirmishes cease and the Waldensians gain some toleration of their religion.[40]

But Montaigne points to this whole history only with a single, prefatory phrase. His discourse is too prudent to enter directly into the controversies surrounding contemporary religious troubles and massacres. And the subtext is perhaps that neither he nor his fathers have been guilty of the 'noble ambition' that ended Lahontan's

---

[37] Cameron, *The Reformation of the Heretics*, pp. 132–3, 138–44, 171–5 (172), 177–8; Gabriel Audisio, *Preachers by Night: The Waldensian Barbes, 15th–16th Centuries*, trans. Claire Davison (Leiden: Brill, 2007), pp. 237–9.

[38] La Popelinière, *L'Histoire de France: Tome III (1561–1562)*, pp. 122–4; Cameron, *The Reformation of the Heretics*, p. 160.

[39] Jean Crespin, *Actes des martyrs deduits en sept livres, depuis le temps de Wiclef et de Hus, jusques à present* ([Geneva]: Jean Crespin, 1564) livre VI, pp. 839–43; Cameron, *The Reformation of the Heretics*, p. 161.

[40] La Popelinière, *L'Histoire de France: Tome III (1561–1562)*, pp. 125–42 (133, 136–7), 148–69; Cameron, *The Reformation of the Heretics*, pp. 162–3. See also William Monter, *Judging the French Reformation: Heresy Trials by Sixteenth-century Parlements* (Cambridge, MA: Harvard University Press, 1999).

tranquillity. In his apology for his conduct in the office of mayor of Bordeaux, in III 10, Montaigne celebrates the fact that he was born of a family that from way back has 'coulé sans esclat, et sans tumulte ... ambitieuse de preud'hommie' ('flowed along without glamour and without tumult, a family ambitious for probity') – *preudhommie* being the quality that had defined the conduct of the courtly elite even before the twelfth century (NP 1068).

We can now turn, however, from Montaigne's representation of Lahontan's history to his representation of the irruption of humanistic learning into his own lineage and family household. Could his father Pierre's motive for bringing men of the new learning into his household not be described as a matter of 'noble ambition'? Pierre famously brought, to his estate in the Dordogne river valley, radical new plans from Italy for his sons' education. Latin was to be superposed on the household's vernacular culture. He hired a German humanist who later became a famous doctor in France, and had him speak to Montaigne from the earliest age only in Latin. The house at Montaigne and the surrounding villages were Latinised. Latin names for artisans and tools took root in the neighbourhood (NP 179–80). Montaigne's contemporary Tabourot des Accords described this plan as a 'recepte de grands Seigneurs' ('a prescription for great Lords') and doubted whether the native vernacular of relatives, servants, and children could be displaced in this way. It would take ten or twelve fathers of the same village to get together and bring in four or five German Latinists.[41] Nevertheless, through the dissemination of Montaigne's text and the paratextual summary of his life (included with most editions) the plan was well-known and much discussed through into the eighteenth century.[42] This was despite the fact that the text makes it clear that Pierre, when his son was six, panicked about the outcome of the ambitious new method he had brought in; he sent his son to the prestigious new Collège de Guyenne (NP 182).

Montaigne states that this learned, Latinate bequest from his father did not work in the way intended (NP 181). He did not go on to become a brilliant royal judge and neo-Latin poet, a citizen of the Latin cosmopolis. And his own scheme for the education of a young nobleman minimises the disruption of the household hierarchy by putting a gentleman, not a learned doctor, in charge, and by removing the primacy of Latin (NP 154–64). He proposed mingling learning with nobility in a different way, a more vernacular and knightly way. I am referring here to the English essayist Cornwallis's comment around 1600: Montaigne, he says, 'hath made Morrall Philosophy speake couragiously, and in steed of her gowne, given her an Armour; he hath put Pedanticall Schollerisme out of countenance, and made manifest, that learning mingled with Nobilitie, shines most clearly'.[43] This is the

---

[41] Étienne Tabourot, *Les bigarrures* (Lyon: Jean Anard et héritiers Benoît Rigaud, 1599), fol. 14. My thanks go to John O'Brien for this reference.

[42] Neil Kenny, 'Que devient le statut social de Montaigne au XVIIIe siècle?', in Myrtille Méricam-Bourdet and Catherine Volpilhac-Auger (eds), *La Fabrique du XVIe siècle au temps des Lumières* (Paris: Classiques Garnier, 2020), pp. 225–45, 239–40.

[43] William Cornwallis, *Essayes* (London: Edmund Mattes, 1600–1), sig. H4v.

time-honoured transaction between nobility and letters/learning, whether Latin
or illustrated vernacular or both. Several centuries earlier, Dante had emphasised
the way the illustrated vernacular calls for elite users, but in social practice it is a
two-way transaction. Learning and the learned are illustrated, given more shine,
rendered visibly more worthy or honourable by mingling with nobility; the noble
are in turn illustrated by letters and learning in the same way they are by possession
of the best horses, the best clothes, the best armour.

Is the very narration of the history of Lahontan redolent of vernacular moral
philosophy dressed in armour? How do we understand its author to be mingling
learning with nobility in that passage, in that chapter? And what about the fact that
Montaigne is speaking for the rustic mountain-folk on this occasion, putting their
own story in writing? Montaigne is careful to mention the nature of his connection
with Lahontan. He shares the right of patronage of an ecclesiastical benefice there
with the Baron de Caupène (NP 817–18). This means that Montaigne's family
somehow – probably in the sixteenth century – acquired a feudal privilege, one of
the *abbacomites* or noble lay abbotships given to knights by medieval French kings.
They consisted of the tithes and rights attached to particular monasteries, including
the right to appoint the *curé*, the village priest. Montaigne's uncle Pierre was *curé*
of Lahontan.[44] So rather like Gonzalo in *The Tempest*, Montaigne describes himself
as lord of a domain that he would keep free of subjection and hierarchy.[45]

This is not the only mention in the chapter of his 'race' and its qualities,
possessions, and noble connections in the southwest regions of France. Montaigne
is sceptical about 'race' considered as any kind of guaranteed transmission of noble
predispositions within a family. But he does lay claim to a hereditary antipathy to
the art of medicine, going back three generations to the birth of his great grandfather in 1402 (NP 802). This also happens to be the stretch of time and generations
during which the Eyquem, merchants and bourgeois of Bordeaux, were gradually
accepted as the noble *seigneurs* of Montaigne.

But Michel's specific claim is that he has taken an inherited disposition – one
which cannot be considered distinctive or noble in itself – and given it by philosophical study a more reasoned form, turned it into a virtue. He has, in other words, for
good philosophical reasons resisted the jurisdiction of the art of medicine. He knows
its whole history; he has studied it, tested it in his own case. Unlike Lahontan, and
unlike one of his uncles who was a *conseiller*, he has not subjected himself to the
empire of doctors' rules and regimes (NP 803). Again, he has done so not just out
of the kind of instinctive antipathy for doctors that any *muletier* might have, but

---

[44] Batcave, 'Commentaire historique d'un passage de Montaigne', 130–1, 134. See also the entry for
'Abbacomites' under 'Abbas' in du Cange *et al.*, *Glossarium mediae et infimae latinitatis* (Niort: L.
Favre, 1883–7), t. 1, col. 011a, accessible online at http://ducange.enc.sorbonne.fr/ABBAS.
[45] William Shakespeare, *The Tempest*, ed. Stephen Orgel (Oxford: Oxford University Press, 1987),
II.i.141–54: 'GONZALO: Had I plantation of this isle, my lord ... And were the king on't, what would
I do? ... I'the'commonwealth I would by contraries/Execute all things ... no name of magistrate; ... No
sovereignty—/SEBASTIAN Yet he would be king on't.'

through his philosophical 'discours', his conversation (NP 826). This is part of what makes him, personally, noble. This is not to say that he dissociates himself from the non-gentle people of his neighbourhood. The next story he tells sees him leading what should have taken place in Lahontan – an investigation into the efficacy of a new remedy (billy-goat's blood) that was all the rage with men of understanding like Joubert, but that he did not want to see distributed blind by the women on his estate who distributed such cures to the local people for all ailments (NP 819–20).

If there is 'noble ambition' in the chapter, then, this is where we find it, offered up at the end of the chapter as a vernacular philosophical discourse that claims judgemental autonomy over mores and *consuetudines* but – or so Montaigne would presumably maintain – in a different spirit to that of the *notaire* and the doctor of Lahontan.[46] It is worthy of his dedicatee Madame de Grammont, a representative of the higher Catholic nobility of his region (NP 823–5). It also identifies, as the root malaise of his troubled age, the way in which opinions harden into vocabularies and institutions of prestigious learning or knowledge by means of their appeal to people of 'noble ambition'. This process creates new social elites, arranged in new hierarchies of power and knowledge, from village level in the regions to the level of the court in Paris or the consistory in Geneva. The best example of this is the one that he does not really mention openly: the prestige of the doctors of new evangelical theologies in the eyes of the village notables of the valley of Angrogna and of the ladies at the courts of Navarre. These doctors' conviction that society needs to be rationally re-ordered in a godly manner, by a self-selecting spiritual and intellectual elite who see through popular superstitions and customs, greatly antagonises the aristocratic traditionalist in Montaigne. He does not see the value in the valley-dwellers of Lahontan and Angrogna, the *menu peuple* of France, or the peoples of the Americas being given the tools to question – or simply being deprived of – those forms of traditional religion, and other knowledges and customs, that had kept their societies in good, if not rational, order.

Let us now leave this extended discussion of the ways in which the irruption of new social literacies into traditional society is represented and alluded to in Montaigne's *Essais* in order to return to the broader historical trends with which we began – trends to which the *Essais* are clearly a response. What was distinct about the history of the relations between letters and learning and social hierarchy in the European age of Montaigne, from the decade of his early education in the 1530s to the decade of the decline in his status as an author, the 1660s, by when the classicising taste of Louis XIV's court had achieved cultural hegemony? And how, if at all, do other literary narratives and histories of the time relate to that history? *Essais* II 37 develops a very particular example of what Polixenes in Shakespeare's *The Winter's Tale* describes as the addition of 'clerk-like experience' to the process of succession to our 'parents' noble names'. Polixenes' description is itself part of

46 Langer, 'Montaigne's Customs', 81–96, 94–6.

a knowledge transaction: the king is implicitly offering to confirm the counsellor Camillo's noble social status in return for the knowledge that he needs in order not to remain in dangerous ignorance at court.[47]

Montaigne's strategy for adding that experience, for mingling learning and nobility, is very particular, very different from his father's. His sense of his literary and intellectual family, of the social value of vernacular philosophy, is unique. But Kenny's study has shown that this uniqueness was in some ways normal in France across the sixteenth and seventeenth centuries, as literary families began to form across generations. Different individuals within the same families, and across families, constructed their social personae and status, in relation to letters and learning in both Latin and the vernacular, in myriad different ways, with different strategies and schemes for its transmission into the future.[48] They self-identified as noble or gentle via different combinations of succession and clerk-like experience, sought confirmation of their status from different audiences, through different means of communication and different social transactions.

One hypothesis to follow from this might be that the long century from the 1530s to the 1660s, despite many continuities with the late middle ages, was one of tumultuous change, variety, and uncertainty in the relations between letters and learning and social hierarchy across Europe and its global connections. The 1530s and 1540s, as I argued in the beginning of the chapter, see the disputed rise in Europe of a new knowledge society, and of interconnected and rival empires of knowledge, as developments in commerce, faith, and colonialism intersect with new forms of learning and of knowledge networks.[49] The idea that the new learning is the virtue that gives 'man' his 'dignity' and his prerogatives, the virtue that most distinguishes the social and religious elite, both gains force and is forcefully resisted.

The permeation of the arts curriculum by Erasmus's textbooks and editions in many educational institutions is clear by the 1530s, by when 'methodical' learning in written and spoken Latin is influentially associated with moral soundness for the social elite. One had to learn through texts and rhetorical training how to conduct oneself and speak as a Christian gentle person – as long as one was already gentle, without such learning. By 1540 the humanist Latin language turn is underway well beyond Italy; different schemes and curricula for a humanistic education in Latinity are spreading across Europe and its new confessional communities; Ramus rises to notoriety during the 1540s.[50] The Council of Trent (1545–63) revitalises Latin

[47] William Shakespeare, *The Winter's Tale*, ed. Stephen Orgel (Oxford: Oxford University Press, 1996), I.ii.385–92.

[48] Kenny, *Born to Write*.

[49] Paula Findlen, 'Introduction – Early Modern Scientific Networks: Knowledge and Community in a Globalizing World, 1500–1800', in Paula Findlen (ed.), *Empires of Knowledge: Scientific Networks in the Early Modern World* (London: Routledge, 2019), pp. 1–22.

[50] Ann Moss, *Renaissance Truth and the Latin Language Turn* (Oxford: Oxford University Press, 2003); Marino, *The Biography of 'The Idea of Literature'*, pp. 84–150; Anthony Grafton and Lisa Jardine, *From Humanism to the Humanities: Education and the Liberal Arts in Fifteenth- and Sixteenth-century Europe* (Cambridge, MA and London: Harvard University Press and Duckworth, 1986), pp. 140–67.

as the language of Catholic liturgy. Latin is also now available to people from the Americas and Africa. Colleges offering a Latin education are founded in the Spanish Americas, including the Imperial College of Santa Cruz at Tlatelolco (1536), which was intended to foster a gubernatorial class of judges drawn from the Nahua elite. The neo-Latin poet Juan Latino, the son of an African slave, receives his early education in Latin in an aristocratic household in Granada, then his bachelor's degree at the university.[51]

At the same time, and complementarily, the literary and social 'illustration' of the Western European vernaculars on the model of Pietro Bembo's dignification of *trecento* literary Tuscan gains momentum through courts, academies, aristocratic households. The publication and dissemination of Castiglione's *Cortegiano* spread knowledge of the way learning can be dissimulated in the acquisition and performance of 'natural' nobility at court. Modern languages are marketed and taught as a matter of social literacies and competences for those finding their place – and rising – in the social hierarchy.[52] The study of the professional disciplines – theology, law, medicine – at Catholic and Protestant universities is booming across Europe, nourished by a rapidly expanding market of textbooks and learned literature.[53] Humanistic and professional learning is a route to social mobility within social hierarchies based in central institutions such as courts, churches (Reformed and Counter-Reformed), academies, and parliaments.

But these are also the decades when the new evangelical learning, and the vernacular Bible translations and other texts that go with it, enter into demand and dispute even in the valleys and mountains of the Piemontese Alps: the Synod of Chanforan that led to the Olivétan Bible was held near Angrogna in 1532. This learning provides new understandings of church hierarchy and a new language for contesting noble Catholic rule. It can result in some instances in radically egalitarian doctrines. It can blend with existing vernacular languages of popular irreverence and misrule, which now circulate more widely and freely in pamphlet and popular literature. This is the moment of Rabelais' polyglot novels, of the ventriloquising in literary texts both of ancient languages and of popular and anti-hierarchical forms and voices – though Montaigne would prefer the voice of an indigenous person to

---

[51] Baltasar Fra-Molinero, 'Juan Latino and His Racial Difference', in T. F. Earle and K. J. P. Lowe (eds), *Black Africans in Renaissance Europe* (Cambridge: Cambridge University Press, 2005), pp. 326–44, 329; Andrew Laird, 'Colonial Spanish America and Brazil', in Stefan Tilg and Sarah Knight (eds), *The Oxford Handbook of Neo-Latin* (Oxford: Oxford University Press, 2015), pp. 525–40, 530.

[52] Fania Oz-Salzberger, 'Languages and Literacy', in Scott (ed.), *The Oxford Handbook of Early Modern European History, 1350–1750: Volume I*, pp. 192–213, 197–201; Peter Burke, *The Fortunes of the Courtier: The European Reception of Castiglione's 'Cortegiano'* (Pennsylvania: Pennsylvania State University Press, 1996); Jennifer Richards, 'Assumed Simplicity and the Critique of Nobility: Or, How Castiglione Read Cicero', *Renaissance Quarterly*, 54 (2001), 460–86; John Gallagher, *Learning Languages in Early Modern England* (Oxford: Oxford University Press, 2019).

[53] Ian Maclean, *Scholarship, Commerce, Religion: The Learned Book in the Age of Confessions, 1560–1630* (Cambridge, MA: Harvard University Press, 2012); Ian Maclean, *Learning and the Market Place: Essays in the History of the Early Modern Book* (Leiden: Brill, 2009).

that of an evangelical.[54] In the Americas, Europeans are also dealing with what is – from their perspective – a Babel of indigenous vernacular voices.

More broadly, by these decades, the European popularisation through cheaper print and other media of various kinds of learning and knowledge is in full swing. On the Italian peninsula the tradition of women's writing associated with culturally ambitious noblewomen begins to spread through the social ranks.[55] The question of what kind of knowledge is allowable in the hands of the common people and women had never been more paramount, and never more out of the elite's control. Regimes and hierarchies of power and knowledge extend their jurisdiction, both orally and in writing, to previously disconnected 'little states' and diverse religious communities across the plains and valleys of Europe and the Americas. The result can be accommodation and obedience, but it can also be the contestation of authority and open rebellion, followed by violent suppression.

As the century progresses, and as the clerical monarchs Philip II and James I begin their reigns, pressure builds up in the whole European calculus of social esteem. On the one hand, the gentle elite in this period is increasingly identified with higher forms of social literacy such as rhetoric and courtly letters, politico-legal study and bureaucracy, and humanistic command of multiple languages. But the elite male may be expected to acquire and display knowledge and competences from across the whole hierarchised range of arts and sciences, from theology to political intelligence, from physiognomy to duelling. From the perspective of the higher nobility, it means knowledge transactions with learned servants and counsellors who trade information and counsel for wealth, land, and confirmations of social status – as in the case of Camillo and Polixenes. And knowledge is not of course gathered only from books and textual education; a rapidly developing culture of elite male travel in Europe is geared to the gathering of useful knowledge and of tools for social self-differentiation.[56] Itinerant humanistic tutors such as Catharinus Dulcis offer verbal and literary skills across a run of cosmopolitan languages that include Latin, Italian, French, and Spanish, whether inflected for Reformed or Counter-Reformed clientele.[57] The confessionalised European learned book market, supplying study of the professional and philosophical disciplines across the continent, is at its peak, before declining in the 1620s and 1630s.[58]

On the other hand, the well-born, military, landed nobleman is still in many contexts the gold standard, as the case of Montaigne's self-presentation in the *Essais* shows. And from the late sixteenth and early seventeenth centuries, there are

---

[54] Terence Cave, *Pré-Histoires II: langues étrangères et troubles économiques au XVIe siècle* (Geneva: Droz, 2001).

[55] Virginia Cox, *Women's Writing in Italy, 1400–1650* (Baltimore: Johns Hopkins University Press, 2008).

[56] Justin Stagl, *A History of Curiosity: The Theory of Travel, 1550–1800* (London: Routledge, 1995).

[57] Warren Boutcher, 'Vernacular Literature', in Gordon Campbell (ed.), *The Oxford Illustrated History of the Renaissance* (Oxford: Oxford University Press, 2019), pp. 303–37, 321–6.

[58] Maclean, *Scholarship, Commerce, Religion*, pp. 211–19.

the first signs in some regions of the institutionalisation of elite aristocracies along lines of certified purity of blood and depth of noble lineage – such as *limpieza de sangre* in Spain – in order to control social mobility and protect the position of the higher nobility against the lower nobility. Even the wealthy patrician merchants of the seventeenth-century Grand Duchy of Tuscany are in the process of becoming nobles with aristocratic lifestyles oriented towards princely courts.[59] These emergent European elite aristocracies, and those who admired them or aspired to their status, solicited and fashioned their own versions of Latin-and-vernacular learning and letters, whether at court or in print.

Writers responded in many different ways. They responded with historical genealogies, with chivalric and pastoral fantasies of naturally valorous nobility, of – to quote Shakespeare's *Cymbeline* – 'royalty unlearned, honour untaught' discovered amongst ancient forebears.[60] The English stage was a site of social struggle that offered, amongst other forms, tragedies of social mobility.[61] A malignant ensign complains that promotions in the military are now won by the bookish theoric, oratorical bombast and the courtesy of foreigners, not by the suits of the established Venetian families and a reputation for practical soldiership. He sets about to destroy this new hierarchy.[62] A clerk, a household steward, a man learned in astrology, is raised from his writing table to marry a duchess, even though he warns that such noble ambition would be madness – where in the source he talks himself into the unequal marriage with a learned vernacular oration.[63] This steward, Antonio, is written off by the duchess's royal brother, obsessed with preserving the aristocratic purity of his blood in her body, as a 'slave that only smelled of ink and counters' and never looked like a gentleman (III.iv.70). But the play's other educated servant, Bosola, an intelligencer employed to kill Antonio, extinguishes the royal brother's house, and creates the space for Antonio's son to succeed to the Duchy of Malfi. The play is one of many that show 'intelligence' to be a key elite form of social literacy in this period.

From 1580 to 1620 the narratives and histories recounted in imaginative literature offer multiple, ambivalent variations on the story of the relations between acquired or inspired learning, including high vernacular discourse, and the social

---

[59] Ronald G. Asch, *Nobilities in Transition, 1550–1700: Courtiers and Rebels in Britain and Europe* (London: Hodder Arnold, 2003); Gestrich, 'The Social Order', pp. 300–1; Hamish Scott, 'Dynastic Monarchy and the Consolidation of Aristocracy during Europe's Long Seventeenth Century', in Von Friedeburg and Morrill (eds), *Monarchy Transformed*, pp. 44–86; Elisa Goudriaan, *Florentine Patricians and their Networks: Structures behind the Cultural Success and the Political Representation of the Medici Court (1600–1660)* (Leiden: Brill, 2018).

[60] William Shakespeare, *Cymbeline*, ed. Martin Butler (Cambridge: Cambridge University Press, 2005), IV.ii.177.

[61] Jean E. Howard, *The Stage and Social Struggle in Early Modern England* (London: Routledge, 1994).

[62] William Shakespeare, *Othello*, ed. E. A. J. Honigmann and Ayanna Thompson (London: Bloomsbury, 2016), I.i.7–32.

[63] John Webster, *The Duchess of Malfi*, ed. Leah S. Marcus (London: Methuen, 2009), I.ii.331–9, pp. 354–5.

hierarchy. Genres such as romance explore the status inconsistency between social expectations and lived experience, and the modalities of the discursive construction and contestation of honour and social status through wit and knowledge.[64] Consider, if only in outline, two very different but complementary stories at the centre of this moment in Western European literature. One is the story of a nobleman who returns from his university education at the Reformed university of Wittenberg, with his writing tablets and his knowledge of philosophy and theology, but without knowing how to act at court as a prince to reclaim his royal inheritance and persona (Shakespeare, *Hamlet*). The other is the story of a self-made man of disreputable birth, a liar and a rogue who picks up some education in Latin, Greek, and Hebrew in a cardinal's household, and some university education at Alcalà, but whose real learning is the *pícaro*'s everyday art of deception and trickery – a more 'popular' form of social literacy or knowledge. In the end this gets him not acceptance as a noble courtier but a berth on a slave galley and imprisonment – unless, of course, the narrative of his life, including its parodies of learned discourse, regains some honour for him as a gracious entertainer of his prudent, elite readers (Alemán, *Guzman de Alfarache*).[65]

In the remainder of this chapter, I will focus on some further examples of narratives of 'noble ambition' causing the irruption of new social literacies into traditional societies or family histories, to put alongside Lahontan. One obvious example is the most famous of all fictional prose narratives. A poor, mad old *hidalgo* in a village of La Mancha reads too much chivalric fiction, a disreputable form of learned vernacular entertainment revived in a modern, vernacular-humanist form from the 1540s by the French *Amadis* serial. He sets off to live as a knight errant, pursued by local officers of the noble Catholic regime, who would put him back in his place; for a madman, he proves surprisingly learned and wise. His peasant companion acts like a squire, and when set up with a civic office for the purposes of ridicule starts to speak in an elegant vernacular, correcting his peasant wife's diction, and acting in his office with natural wisdom.[66] The episode dramatises, as comedy, the notion that to be an officeholder is naturally to speak a higher vernacular replete with the wisdom of good governance. But Sancho shows an admirable lack of 'noble ambition': he returns willingly back to his proper place, as does Alonso Quijano. The narratives of both protagonists' rise and fall are highly ambivalent.

The same is even more true, perhaps, when the knowledgeable and socially mobile protagonists are female, whether in comedies or histories. In Boccaccio, the

---

[64] Lori Humphrey Newcomb, *Reading Popular Romance in Early Modern England* (New York: Columbia University Press, 2002), pp. 99–100.

[65] Nina Cox Davis, *Autobiography as 'Burla' in the 'Guzmán de Alfarache'* (Lewisburg, London and Toronto: Bucknell University Press; Associated University Presses, 1991).

[66] Miguel de Cervantes, *Don Quijote de la Mancha: Edición del Instituto Cervantes 1605–2005*, ed. Francisco Rico, Joaquín Forradellas, and Fernando Lázaro Carreter, 2 vols (Barcelona: Galaxia Gutenberg Círculo de Lectores, 2004), vol. 1, part two, ch. 5, pp. 730–1.

story of Giletta di Nerbona seems joyously straightforward. She inherits a fortune and medical knowledge from her father and uses it to gain the hand of Beltramo di Rossiglione in marriage by curing the king of France. Beltramo initially rejects his new wife (who is referred to throughout simply as the 'contessa') as a 'medica' unworthy of his noble lineage. But by the end of the story, and partly through her own wit and gifts as a storyteller, she is happily married to the count with two children.[67] In Shakespeare's *All's Well That Ends Well*, this story about a learned woman, especially the ending, famously becomes more ambivalent.[68] And there is no better exploration, in high vernacular rhetoric, of the paradox of noble ambition, than the moment when Helena, a gentle serving woman of humble background, irrupts forward, alone on stage, to reveal she is thinking of wedding the son of her own noble mistress, a countess: 'Th'ambition in my love thus plagues itself'. Her mistress has already tortuously opened up the question of the dispositions her gentlewoman has inherited from her famous physician father, and of how her education might make them good, provided she is not of 'unclean mind'.[69]

When Helena arrives at court, an unknown 'Doctor She' bearing the written prescription resulting from her father's reading and experience, she uses the rhetoric of heavenly inspiration, as though the knowledge she brings comes direct from heaven. The king thinks 'in thee some blessed spirit doth speak' and enters into the desired knowledge transaction: the cure for his fistula in exchange for the hand in marriage of any of the courtiers in his gift (II.i.77–208). The scene might be compared with another involving an unknown woman, a shepherd's daughter, who arrives at court with heavenly inspired knowledge: Joan La Pucelle in *Henry VI, Part One*. Christ's mother has shined on her contemptible estate and willed her to leave her base vocation to free her country from calamity, like a prophetess armed both with visionary knowledge and a sword. The dauphin is astonished by the 'high terms' of her vernacular rhetoric and offers to be her servant rather than her sovereign.[70] Of course, where Helena's comic story ends in a marriage, however unhappy, Joan's ends in the disgrace and death of a false prophetess.

As this already indicates, Shakespeare's histories explore the relationship between letters and learning and social hierarchy in the past, but with an eye on the Tudor present. In *Henry VI Part Two*, a popular rebellion of Kentishmen aims to bring down all literate people – 'scholars, lawyers, courtiers, gentlemen' – and the literate institutions and practices which produce them, in order to restore merry, pre-literate England. Shakespeare's representation of this rebellion and its hatred

---

[67] Giovanni Boccaccio, *Decameron*, ed. Amedeo Quondam, Giancarlo Alfano, and Maurizio Fiorilla (Milan: BUR Classici 2013), III.ix, p. 632.

[68] Lisa Jardine, *Reading Shakespeare Historically* (London: Routledge, 1996), pp. 51–7.

[69] William Shakespeare, *All's Well That Ends Well*, ed. Susan Snyder (Oxford: Oxford University Press, 2008), I.i.81–100 (92), 26–45.

[70] William Shakespeare, *The First Part of King Henry VI*, ed. Michael Hattaway (Cambridge: Cambridge University Press, 1990), I.ii.72–112.

for an elite identified with writing and learning is profoundly ambivalent.[71] But the new men of the Tudor regime who came through grammar school and university must have shifted nervously in their privileged seats during these scenes. In the same play, a queen complains that the young king – somewhat like James VI of Scotland? – is no more than a pupil whose weapons are citations of scripture, and whose study is his tilt-yard (I.iii.53–4).

In the scenes narrating the infamous beheading of Lord Saye by the Kentish rebels led by Jack Cade, the play counterpoints two narratives of noble ambition, of the nobility and its relationship to the common people of Kent: one literary and cosmopolitan, and one war-like and nativist. They are distinguished by different roles for learning and different types of vernacular eloquence. In one of them, to become noble and to perform nobility is to learn foreign tongues and display the foreignness of one's language and behaviour. Lord Saye is the multilingual, Latin-literate administrator and diplomat who has risen by means of his learning to high office. His 'book' preferred him to the king, and he has in turn bestowed gifts on 'learnèd clerks'. His pitch to the rebels who hold him captive is that, since the social hierarchy values knowledge as the wing wherewith 'we fly to heaven' and views ignorance as the curse of God, they cannot but forbear to murder him (IV.vii.60–5).

But his audience does not see the social hierarchy in the same light. Interestingly, but fatally, his version of the county people to whom he is pleading for his life is more literary and learned than true. His Kent is the county of civilised gentry and freeholding, obedient yeomanry addressed and imagined by a near contemporary of Shakespeare's who, like Saye, had risen by learning and office (though nowhere so high) and who had been the first in Tudor England to put Kent's customs on the printed chorographical record: William Lambarde, the author of *The Perambulation of Kent* (1576). Lambarde is most famous for the learned conversation he had in 1601 with Queen Elizabeth, when he presented her with a copy of his *Pandecta*, around the time he was preferred to the office of Keeper of the Records in the Tower of London.[72] Like Saye in his speech, Lambarde begins his text with a citation of Caesar's *Commentarii* 5.14, in which the Roman general declares the Kentish the most humane ('humanissimi') of Britons and more like the French in their customs (*consuetudo*) than the barbarians of the interior.[73]

For Lambarde, Kent is a county of learned new men in the Tudor present.[74] The Kentish gentlemen are not of so ancient stock as elsewhere; courtiers, lawyers and

[71] William Shakespeare, *The Second Part of King Henry VI*, ed. Michael Hattaway (Cambridge: Cambridge University Press, 1991), IV.iv.36; Roger Chartier, 'Jack Cade, the Skin of a Dead Lamb, and the Hatred for Writing', *Shakespeare Studies*, 34 (2006), 77–89.

[72] Jason Scott-Warren, 'Was Elizabeth I Richard II? The Authenticity of Lambarde's "Conversation"', *The Review of English Studies*, 64 (2013), 208–30.

[73] William Lambarde, *A perambulation of Kent: conteining the description, hystorie, and customes of that shyre. Collected and written (for the most part) in the yeare. 1570* (London: Ralph Newbery, 1576), sig. A4r.

[74] John M. Adrian, 'Tudor Centralization and Gentry Visions of Local Order in Lambarde's *Perambulation of Kent*', *English Literary Renaissance*, 36 (2006), 307–34.

merchants are 'continually translated' from London, as from a rich and wealthy 'seed plot'. They are 'acquainted with good letters, and especially trained in the knowledge of the lawes […]' (sig. B1v). Lambarde even claims that, partly because of the Kentish custom of gavelkind, which effectively makes them freeholders not copyholders, the people are freer and happier than elsewhere. There is no 'noble ambition' to corrupt the community. They are so content that even the wealthy yeomanry, who could buy their way to gentle condition, have no desire 'to be apparayled with the titles of Gentrie'. Nowhere in the realm are the common people more willingly governed, more 'civil, just, & bountiful', like the franklins and yeomen of old England (sig. B2r).

So Saye is addressing the same fantasy county, the same civilised place, the same civilised audience as Lambarde – 'the country […] full of riches,/ The people liberal, valiant, active, wealthy', whether the gentle or yeoman sort.[75] But, unfortunately, his real audience is one of illiterate and rebellious artisans and peasants. And Cade convinces them that Saye is personally responsible for the change from the happy society of 'our forefathers', when debts were recorded by scoring and splitting wooden tallies, to an evil society of written transactions, of paper and books, and of grammar taught in newly founded schools – probably an allusion to Saye's involvement at court in the foundation of Eton and King's Colleges. Saye is even held personally responsible for the continued use of the medieval custom of 'benefit of clergy', whereby the ability to recite Psalm 51 in Latin commuted sentences for various crimes for the more socially privileged (IV.vii.25–37).[76]

As a result, when Saye speaks, what his peasant audience hears is someone talking a foreign language, or a number of foreign languages all at once, someone who claims to be noble but has not fought anyone, except with a pen. In the first quarto text of the scene, as a nervous Saye utters a Latin phrase about bad people, the rebels know only that this is a suspiciously foreign and continental tongue – maybe 'French', or 'Dutch', or 'Out-Italian', which is their garbled term for Italian.[77] Saye compounds his error by citing and translating Caesar's Latin commentaries in an elevated English idiom. He also emphasises how his polyglot tongue had 'parlayed unto foreign kings', which once again compounds his error by means of a Gallicism ('parley') that signifies how much political and cultural territory he has conceded to the French (IV.vii.49–50, 66). His tongue is summarily removed, along with the rest of his head. Of course, the off-stage audience is aware that 'noble ambition' is the ultimate cause of this rebellion of the illiterate against the literate: York has made 'John Cade of Ashford' – a shearman and son of a plasterer – minister of his

---

[75] Shakespeare, *The Second Part of King Henry VI*, IV.vii.52.

[76] Joseph A. Nigota, 'Fiennes, James, First Baron Saye and Sele (c. 1390–1450), Administrator', *Dictionary of National Biography* (2008), www.oxforddnb.com/view/10.1093/ref:odnb/9780198614128.001.0001/odnb-9780198614128-e-9411, accessed 1 March 2021.

[77] Shakespeare, *The Second Part of King Henry VI*, pp. 186–7 (note to IV.vii.47).

aristocratic house's royal ambitions, by encouraging him to invent a false noble lineage under the name of Mortimer (III.i.355–9; IV.ii.115–25).

Pleading for his life, Saye points out that, unlike the traditional nobility, he had neither affected 'wealth or honour', nor donned sumptuous apparel, nor indulged in 'guiltless blood-shedding' (IV.vii.83–7). But this more traditional narrative of nobility has much better success in winning over the rebellious commoners of Kent, even if they waver in characteristic fashion. It is put into words by the landed warrior-nobleman Old Clifford, who will later die fighting in the Battle of St. Albans, to be borne aloft by his son like Aeneas bearing Anchises (V.ii). When confronted by Cade's mob in the scene after the confrontation with Saye, he invokes the name of Henry V, who conducted them through the heart of France and made the meanest of them 'earls and dukes' (IV.viii.34). He helps them imagine the 'late vanquished' French crossing the channel to lord it in London streets, '[c]rying "Villiago" unto all they meet' (IV.viii.39, 43). He uses this to rally them to fight again in France, for Henry VI. So instead of performing his nobility as literary for-eignness, and speaking foreign words, Old Clifford uses the spectre of strangers crying in a foreign vernacular (actually Italian – 'vigliacco' for villain, coward) to reconfirm their obedience to the traditional nobility, whose honour is defined by military valour in foreign conquests.

Shakespeare's last English history again features a learned figure who speaks Latin and who rises higher from much lower origins than Lord Saye: Thomas Wolsey.[78] A butcher's son from Ipswich becomes a cardinal and the king's chief minister. In this case, from the perspective of the established, titled nobility, letters/ learning and 'noble ambition' combine in the most extreme fashion to circum-vent the traditional social hierarchy. From the start of the play nobles speak with appalled admiration of the way Wolsey controls the narrative of his own rise, '[o]ut of his self-drawing web'. Wolsey lets it be known that the force of his own merit, a gift from heaven, 'buys' his place next to the king. Not only that, but he controls by 'letter' and 'paper' which of the gentry have the opportunity to gain honour by attending upon the king in his expedition to France for the Field of the Cloth of Gold – a spectacle of noble chivalry they again see as orchestrated by the cardinal, along with the articles of the resulting treaty (I.i.1–80).

It seems Wolsey's control of writing and the documentary sphere outweighs the heroic speech of the traditional nobility. Buckingham aims to cry down 'the Ipswich fellow's insolence' from a 'mouth of honour' or proclaim there is no 'diffe-rence in persons' (I.i.137–9). But he is undone by the written testimony, backed up in speech, of his own surveyor. This is all organised by Wolsey: the 'beggar's book [learning]/ Outworths a noble's blood' (I.i.122–3). And the king ironically turns Buckingham's life into the story of a naturally gifted, learned gentleman, and a rare speaker, whose training enables him to instruct teachers, but whose noble

---

[78] William Shakespeare, *King Henry VIII*, ed. J. M. R. Margeson (Cambridge: Cambridge University Press, 1990), III.i.40.

benefits were ill-disposed by a corrupt mind (I.ii.10–16). Even when Wolsey is caught taxing the aggrieved commons, without the king's knowledge, his control of the letters sent via secretaries to the shires ensures he can claim credit for their revocation (I.ii.103–8).

But Wolsey's downfall appropriately comes by the same means, by his loss of control both of his papers and letters, and of the narrative of his rise. Shakespeare borrows from elsewhere an incident in which he accidentally includes in the papers of state he sends the king an inventory of his enormous private wealth and a copy of a disloyal letter he sent to the pope (III.ii.120–45, 209–22). At this point, with Wolsey undone by one letter, the narrative is reversed by Surrey. He excoriates him for his ambition and personifies him as 'scarlet sin' on behalf of the whole nobility who respect the common good, and who will scarce be gentlemen if he lives (III.ii.292–3). He produces articles against Wolsey written in the king's own hand, including his use of the inscription 'Ego et Rex meus' in his correspondence with Rome and foreign princes (III.ii.314–15) – an inscription which makes the king his servant in writing, and which is answered with a writ of praemunire seizing all his goods to the crown.

King Henry VIII is about a moment in the history of a whole nation when its father, its reigning monarch, calls in the 'doctors learn'd' to cure his conscience of a sickness (II.iv.200–4), but also to facilitate his ambition for a new queen and heir. It also, in passing, marks the surrender of its nobility, 'its travelled gallants', to 'foreign wisdom' from France (I.iii.19,29) at the Field of the Cloth of Gold. Its plot pivots around the replacement of one learned cleric, Wolsey, who is convicted of 'noble ambition', by another, Cranmer, who returns triumphantly from the continent with the right learned opinions about the divorce. It is the Reformed Cranmer's prophetic vernacular oratory that completes the play, and the Reformation, and projects forward from the 1530s moment to the present, *c.* 1612–13, when the foundations of Tudor and Stuart Reformed England have, it seems, been successfully laid by two successive monarchs.

But even the construction of Wolsey's social worth as a learned man remains ambivalent, for he regains nobility in death. The exchange between Katherine and Griffith in act four, scene two demonstrates how epideictic rhetoric could both blame and praise Wolsey, with specific reference to the language arts and their use. Katharine uses the theme of noble ambition – 'a man/ Of an unbounded stomach, ever ranking/ Himself with princes' – and describes how his opinion was law, how he was 'ever double/ Both in his words and meaning', how his promises were false (IV.ii.31–44).

Griffith then responds to this *contra* with his *pro*: though of humble stock, Wolsey was fashioned for honour and for scholarship from birth. He was wise, fair-spoken, and persuading. And he was princely in his patronage of learning: 'ever witness for him/ Those twins of learning that he raised in you,/ Ipswich and Oxford' (IV.ii.48–68). This refers to Wolsey's involvement in the late 1520s in the early stages of the establishment of uniform, humanistic Latin teaching in grammar schools in England,

and their socio-intellectual links with Oxbridge colleges offering the higher arts curriculum. He founded Ipswich grammar school (which did not last) and Cardinal College, which became Christ Church, and published, in 1529, a *Methodus* for the Ipswich school, covering all eight forms and intended as a model for the whole of England.[79] These new pedagogies and institutions irrupted into Tudor society from the 1530s and changed the relationship between learning and social hierarchy, as the new arts of discourse shaped new careers and mentalities in various professions such as law.[80] But the social status of scholars and the status of scholarly skills as foundations of gentility remained unstable throughout our period.[81]

While gesturing towards the social lives of people and a broader historical canvas, this chapter has concentrated on the stories told within vernacular texts of the period about irruptions of new learning, new literacies in communities, courts, families. These irruptions are often represented as being disruptive, damaging, unhealthy, and their protagonists are often described with ambivalence. Beneath such representations is the idea – heavily informed by Old Testament narratives – that new knowledge, new linguistic and social performances and uses of knowledge, in combination with ambition for power and status, could disturb the peaceful reproduction of natural hierarchies and orders, including traditions of ancient and pure religion, and give rise to social malaise and destruction. Of course, what counted as harmful 'new' knowledge, and what safer, traditional knowledge, was itself a matter of great contention. It would only be in the later seventeenth century that the society of orders began to stabilise its relationship with the new, confessionalised knowledge societies and the new forms of linguistic-literary capital that began to take hold in the 1530s and 1540s. At least one can argue it did so in the form of the vernacular polities of France and Britain, with their resurgent, well-educated aristocracies and their social elites defined by superior forms of cultural consumption, including the institutionalised provision of Latin and the civilised vernaculars as noble, unpedantic subjects. Whether it did so in the colonies and outposts of the European powers in the Americas and elsewhere is an open question.[82]

---

[79] William Lily, *Lily's Grammar of Latin in English: An Introduction of the Eyght Partes of Speche, and the Construction of the Same*, ed. Hedwig Gwosdek (Oxford: Oxford University Press, 2013), pp. 72–3, 119.

[80] Lorna Hutson, 'Rhetoric and Law', in Michael John Macdonald (ed.), *The Oxford Handbook of Rhetorical Studies* (Oxford: Oxford University Press, 2017), pp. 397–408.

[81] Richard Kirwan, 'Introduction: Scholarly Self-Fashioning and the Cultural History of Universities', in Richard Kirwan (ed.), *Scholarly Self-fashioning and Community in the Early Modern University* (Burlington: Ashgate, 2013), pp. 1–20.

[82] J. H. Elliott, *Empires of the Atlantic World: Britain and Spain in America, 1492–1830* (New Haven: Yale University Press, 2006); Françoise Waquet, 'Social Status', in Stefan Tilg and Sarah Knight (eds), *The Oxford Handbook of Neo-Latin* (Oxford: Oxford University Press, 2015), pp. 380–92. For social polarisation and patterns of cultural consumption across this period in early modern England see Alexandra Shepard, *Accounting for Oneself: Worth, Status, and the Social Order in Early Modern England* (Oxford: Oxford University Press, 2015).

Stories are not only told within texts. The formats and paratexts, the publication and fortunes of books such as Wolsey's *Methodus* also have multifarious stories to tell about the relationship of learning and letters and social hierarchy in this period. Let us conclude with two brief examples from the period 1580–1620, which has been our principal focus. In his early 1580 and 1582 editions, Montaigne addresses a general reader at the opening of his text, saying he is not adopting a studied posture, not thinking about *service* or *gloire*. He is just writing for the private convenience of relatives and friends. But at the end of this text, and at other dedicatory junctures throughout, it turns out that his friends are women of the high Catholic nobility of his region.[83] And he has studied, in a philosophical vein, to enhance his personal nobility, beyond the transgenerational nobility of his family, while remaining embedded in the vernacular culture of his region and neighbourhood. In 1616, James I and VI, a king whose theatrical company, the King's Men, performed a fantasy (*Cymbeline*) of 'royalty unlearned' around 1610, publishes a folio of learned, vernacular *Works* including everything from scriptural exegesis to political theory. The bishop who introduces it questions both whether a king should be writing at all, and, if he is writing, whether he should enter learned theological and political controversies that expose his honour right across Europe.[84] Never before or since has the mingling of learning and 'noble ambition' been so central and various a phenomenon, the cause of so much ambivalence, uncertainty, and contention in European letters and culture.

[83] Jean Balsamo, 'Montaigne et ses lectrices', *Revue d'études culturelles*, 3 (2007), 71–83.
[84] Jane Rickard, *Authorship and Authority: The Writings of James VI and I* (Manchester: Manchester University Press, 2007), 155–61.

3

Women's Social Status and their Access to Learning in Multilingual Early Modern Italy

HELENA SANSON

IN THE THIRD book of his *Tre libri dell'educatione christiana* ('Three Books on Christian Education') (1584), the theologian Silvio Antoniano (1540–1603) discussed the education of boys according to social status. He advised that 'i fanciulli di qual si voglia conditione, etiandio molto humile, imparassero almeno queste tre cose, cioè leggere, scrivere, et numerare' ('boys of any social status, even very humble, should learn at least these three things, that is, reading, writing, and counting').[1] Those who were destined to become merchants or be part of the major guilds also had to learn some Latin – including speaking it – as it might be a useful skill to possess in their trades with foreign countries. Boys from noble and well-to-do families had to study the 'lettere humane' (i.e. classical studies), be able to speak and write well in Latin, and understand the great orators and historians of the past, even if they did not intend to continue in their studies. Quite different, and much more restrictive, is Antoniano's approach to female education. Social status remains of paramount importance, but what take precedence are considerations linked to gender and morality:

> Quanto poi alle femmine, a me pare che [...] si abbia con esso loro a proceder del tutto diversamente et quanto quelle di humile et povero stato non fa bisogno che sappino neanco leggere; a quelle che sono di mezzana conditione certo non disdice il saper leggere; ma quanto alle nobili, che devono poi essere madri di famiglia di case maggiori, in ogni modo lodarei che [...] apprendessero a leggere et scrivere et numerare mediocremente. Ma che insieme con i figliuoli et sotto la disciplina de i medesimi maestri, imparino le lingue et sappino orare et poetare, io per me non lo approvo, né so vedere che utilità ne possa seguire [...] anzi, io temo che, essendo il sesso femminile vano per natura, non ne diventi tanto più superbo et vogliano le donne far del maestro.[2]

---

[1] Silvio Antoniano, *Tre libri dell'educatione christiana dei figliuoli* (Verona: Sebastiano dalle Donne et Girolamo Stringario, 1584), fol. 153*r*. All translations are mine unless otherwise indicated.
[2] Antoniano, *Tre libri*, fols 153*v*–54*r*.

Proceedings of the British Academy, **246**, 46–70, © The British Academy 2022.

As for girls, broadly speaking, I believe one should proceed in a completely different manner, and for those of humble and poor status it is not even necessary to be able to read; for those of middle status it would not be unbecoming to be able to do so. But for those of noble origin, who will go on to become mothers and matrons of the most prominent household, by all means I would approve that [...] they learnt to read and write and count moderately well. But I cannot at all approve that, together with boys and under the same teachers, they learn the classical languages, are able to recite orations and compose verse. Nor can I see what benefit this could lead to [...], on the contrary, I fear that, since the female sex is vain by nature, they would only become more arrogant and might want to teach others.

From an early age, women were excluded from the 'empire' of knowledge and literary heritage that a prestigious language of culture such as Latin embodied. But in the specific context of multilingual, early modern Italy the majority of women also found themselves excluded from another 'empire' of knowledge and learning that progressively established itself from the beginning of the sixteenth century: the one created by the literary vernacular based on fourteenth-century Tuscan. This process of exclusion cut across social groups: because of their limited educational opportunities, women often found themselves at the margins of this elitist language that had to be learnt from books.[3]

This chapter will discuss, against the background of early modern Italy's linguistic situation, some of the modes of access to literature – and more broadly to learning – that women across social ranks might have been able to experience. It will then also discuss the crucial role played by the translation into the vernacular of works of different genres in opening the doors to knowledge for the female sex.

Linguistic Literacy in Early Modern Italy

Early modern Italy was characterised by political and linguistic fragmentation, a situation that remained unchanged until 1861, when Unification took place. A variety of different vernaculars, all derived from Latin,[4] were in use in everyday life across the peninsula and social groups: cardinals and actors, merchants and dukes, courtly ladies and seamstresses, would have been native speakers of their own local vernacular, with due adjustments according to diatopic, diastratic, diaphasic, and diamesic variations.[5] With the spread of the printing press from the 1460s, authors,

---

[3] On this point see Helena Sanson, 'Women and Language Codification in Italy: Marginalized Voices, Forgotten Contribution', in Wendy Ayres-Bennett and Helena Sanson (eds), *Women in the History of Linguistics* (Oxford: Oxford University Press, 2020), pp. 59–90.

[4] The Italian 'dialects': in the context of Italy, the term refers to that rich range of Romance idioms, still in use in the peninsula, which are indeed languages separate from 'Italian'.

[5] That is to say, variations due to geography, social class, context (and therefore degree of formality and use of different registers), and medium of communication (e.g. spoken or written language).

editors, and publishers felt a growing need for a more homogeneous and standardised literary language. Lively and extensive debates developed at the beginning of the sixteenth century among men of letters and theorists around the nature and definition of this language which was meant to become the new language of culture able to compete with Latin. Among the different currents of thought, the position that ultimately prevailed was the one supported by the Venetian humanist Pietro Bembo (1470–1547), who, in his *Prose della volgar lingua* (1525), promoted fourteenth-century Tuscan as used by Dante, Petrarch, and Boccaccio (particularly Petrarch for poetry and Boccaccio for prose) as the language to be used in literature. Bembo's 'vernacular humanism', as it has been termed, successfully applied the theories of imitation of the best Latin classics (Virgil and Cicero) to the vernacular classics, in line with the spirit of the time.

In recognising the primacy of the works of the great writers of the past, Bembo provided a clear and stable model that could be imitated and reproduced – and could in turn be standardised in a rich body of metalinguistic texts. The competing current of the so-called *lingua cortigiana/cortesiana* pragmatically supported the various types of *koinè* – common language – in use in the smaller and bigger courts of Italy. Largely based on, but not exclusively restricted to, Tuscan, this courtly language thrived in its eclecticism, allowing for contributions from different vernaculars, as well as Latinisms and foreign terms. It had the advantage of being a viable means of communication, but it failed to provide a well-defined and homogeneous model for imitation. This was also the case for another current thought, which was in favour of contemporary Florentine, or a more generically defined Tuscan, which was also innately unstable by its very nature. The process of 'standardisation' of the Italian language, therefore, found its basis and driving force in literature itself – a peculiarity of Italian compared to other linguistic and cultural traditions. Its prescriptive metalinguistic production relied essentially on literary works.[6]

In time, the increasing use of the vernacular over Latin as a language of culture led to an opening up of society and a wider dissemination of knowledge, but in an incomplete manner. The 'symbolic power'[7] created by the literary vernacular, this new, archaising language of culture, had profound and long-lasting consequences in terms of access to learning across the peninsula: for as many advantages as it might have had in terms of clarity and homogeneity, it was, by its very nature, a socially exclusive language, 'created *by* members of the élites, *for* the élites',[8] more specifically by learned (male) scholars for (male) learned users, at the top of the social hierarchy. For those outside Tuscany, in particular, it was *de facto* a foreign language, to be studied in books. For centuries it remained beyond the reach

---

[6] Nicoletta Maraschio and Tina Matarrese, 'The Role of Literature in Language Standardization: The Case of Italy', in Wendy Ayres-Bennett and John Bellamy (eds), *The Cambridge Handbook of Language Standardization* (Cambridge: Cambridge University Press, 2021), pp. 313–46.

[7] Pierre Bourdieu, *Langage et pouvoir symbolique* (Paris: Fayard, 1991).

[8] Brian Richardson, 'The Italian of the Renaissance Elites in Italy and Europe', in Anna Laura Lepschy and Arturo Tosi (eds), *Multilingualism in Italy Past and Present* (Oxford: Legenda, 2002), pp. 5–23 at 13.

of the majority of the dialect-speaking – and widely illiterate – population. Aloof and distant, it became a new Latin of sorts. Due to the clear constraints imposed on their education, women in particular found themselves to be the object of linguistic exclusion and cultural marginalisation.[9]

As for Latin, it was far from being replaced altogether as the language of prestige and culture. It was officially the language of the church and dominated university teaching and all 'high' subjects (e.g. philosophy, theology, medicine, astronomy, and mathematics). With few exceptions (i.e. the *scuole d'abbaco*, for the sons of merchants or artisans), it was also the language of instruction in the traditional school curriculum on which children would learn to read and write. The pervasiveness of Latin in early modern Italy should not be underestimated, nor, as we shall see, should its gender-related implications.

Among the foreign tongues in use in the peninsula at the time, Spanish had the strongest influence, especially, of course, in the Kingdom of Naples and Sicily under the Aragonese, but also owing to the presence of Spanish soldiers across the peninsula during a very turbulent military period in Italian history. From after the Treaty of Cateau-Cambrésis (1559) until the last decades of the seventeenth century, a good part of Italy also found itself directly under Spanish rule. The influence of French was particularly felt in Piedmont, in the Kingdom of Savoy, for geographical and political reasons. Not surprisingly, in his *Libro del Cortegiano* (1528) ('Book of the Courtier'), Baldassare Castiglione (1478–1529) includes knowledge of French and Spanish as a requirement for the intellectual formation of the perfect courtier and courtly lady (II, 37).

In multilingual, early modern Italy a spectrum of linguistic varieties was therefore potentially available to speakers. Several linguistic codes co-existed side by side, with clear differences as to when these should be used, with different levels of comprehension and different geographic and social diffusion. For centuries, Italians across the peninsula lived in a condition of diglossia, with literary Italian as the high variety, used almost exclusively in writing, and the local dialects as the low variety. More specifically, given the nature of these vernaculars – different idioms, not simply diastratic variants of the same language – theirs was a condition of bilingualism. Men and women who were born, or lived, in the peninsula might, or might not, be able to move across these linguistic varieties: their 'linguistic literacy', as we can call it, ranged from the local, native vernacular to the elusive 'lingua cortigiana', from the literary vernacular to Latin, and to foreign idioms.[10] Linguistic literacy is

---

[9] See Helena Sanson, *Women, Language, Grammar in Italy: 1500-1900* (Oxford: Oxford University Press for the British Academy, 2011); Sanson, 'Women and Language Codification in Italy'.

[10] On women's access to sixteenth-century linguistic varieties, with particular attention to the spoken medium, see Helena Sanson, '"Femina proterva, rude, indocta [...], chi t'ha insegnato a parlar in questo modo?": Women's "Voices" and Linguistic Varieties in Written Texts (Italy, 16th–17th Centuries)', *The Italianist*, 34 (2014), 400–17.

taken to mean here an individual's access and ability to use one or more of these different varieties – in speaking and/or writing – which then in turn defined their ability to access different forms of learning, including works of literature.

In this respect, it is worth remembering how, from the 1530s onwards, Italy witnessed an opening up of literary society and some erosion of its hierarchy. The previous decade had seen the progressive disintegration of the Italian court system, culminating with the Sack of Rome (1527), which shook to its foundations those aristocratic ideals that sustained and embodied court culture. The expansion of the printing press and the increased availability of books, alongside the social transformations that took place during the course of the century, also brought about a multiplicity of literary and printed productions aimed at less educated people. The growing expansion of the vernacular as a language of culture crucially allowed more access to learning also to the female sex and, starting from the 1540s, Italy saw a flourishing of women writers of varied social extraction. Yet, one should be wary of overlooking the widespread restrictions that women, across all social ranks, had to face when it came to their access to learning. Indeed, 'events that further the historical development of men, liberating them from natural, social, or ideological constraints' could in fact also 'have quite different, even opposite, effects upon women'.[11] Whether members of the nobility or the growing bourgeoisie, daughters of merchants, wives of artisans or workers, women's place in society was one that the deeply entrenched intellectual infrastructure and pervasive scholarly modes of thought of the sixteenth and seventeenth centuries saw as defined by natural inferiority, and moral and intellectual weakness.[12] Which is why their gender, above everything else, and even before their social status, determined women's access to knowledge and learning.

Women's Access to Vernacular and Latin Learning

Girls were usually excluded from learning in more institutionalised contexts, and their access to literacy would usually take place within the home and by more informal means. A number of factors would contribute to their learning to read (and, perhaps, write), and to how well they acquired such skills. In a cosmopolitan centre like Venice, for instance, in the late sixteenth century 'about 33% of adult males and 13% of adult females could read. The largest part of these literate

---

[11] Joan Kelly-Gadol, 'Did Women Have a Renaissance?', in Renate Bridenthal and Claudia Koonz (eds), *Becoming Visible: Women in European History*, 2nd edn (Boston: Houghton-Mifflin, 1987), pp. 175–201 at 176.

[12] On this point, see Ian Maclean, *The Renaissance Notion of Woman: A Study in the Fortunes of Scholasticism and Medical Science in European Intellectual Life* (Cambridge: Cambridge University Press, 1980).

men and women came from the higher ranks of society'.[13] In urban contexts, girls' access to literacy would have been higher than in rural ones, as social rank would have no doubt increased the possibility of hiring tutors, after girls acquired the first rudiments from their mother. Broadly speaking, 'females who could not read included a majority of the wives and daughters of literate males, and practically all the wives and daughters of illiterate males', whereas we could say that literate females were 'mostly the wives and daughters in the highest social and economic ranks of society, plus a good number of nuns'.[14]

On the issue of female education the family's views – and in particular those of the father, the *pater familias* – were crucial. On this point, opinions varied. In Book III of *La civil conversatione* ('On Civil Conversation') (1574) by Stefano Guazzo (1530–93), we read that so different were the existing customs in raising girls that 'non vi si può dare una determenata regola' ('it is hard to provide a specific rule').[15] Some fathers had their daughters learn to read and write, study poetry, music and painting, sing, compose sonnets; others only accustomed them to the distaff and running the household. The kind of learning young women could have access to depended also on whether they were destined to take the veil, marry, or become courtly ladies.[16] But, whatever their future and their social rank, there was consensus on the fact that they should not have access to works of literature – or of any other kind – that could tarnish their morality.

Women were usually associated with the vernacular and mostly, even though not exclusively, confined to it. Nevertheless, this association did not extend to the *literary* vernacular, which male theorists did not see as the language of 'mothers', or women more broadly. Quite the opposite. In the second edition of his *Dialogo della institution delle donne* (1547), the Venetian polygraph Lodovico Dolce (1508–68) suggested that mothers should make sure their daughters only learnt the native, local vernacular of the civilised part of society.[17] Women who tried to imitate fourteenth-century Tuscan in speaking, just because they believed they had some familiarity with the works of Petrarch or Boccaccio, came across as affected and exposed themselves to ridicule, warned the Tuscan man of letters Agnolo Firenzuola (1493–1543).[18]

---

[13] Paul Grendler, 'Form and Function in Italian Renaissance Popular Books', *Renaissance Quarterly*, 46.3 (1993), 451–85 at 453.

[14] Grendler, 'Form and Function', 454.

[15] Stefano Guazzo, *La civil conversatione* [...] *divisa in quattro libri* (Brescia: Tomaso Bozzola, 1574), fol. 158r.

[16] Guazzo, *La civil conversatione*, fols 159r–60r.

[17] Lodovico Dolce, *Dialogo della institution delle donne* [...] *nuovamente corretto e ampliato* (Venice: Gabriele Giolito, 1547), fol. 30v. The first edition was published in 1545 with the title *Dialogo* [...] *della institution delle donne, secondo li tre stati, che cadono nella vita humana* (Venice: Gabriele Giolito). For a modern edition of the *princeps*, see Lodovico Dolce, *Dialogo della instituzion delle donne, secondo li tre stati che cadono nella vita umana*, ed. Helena Sanson (Cambridge: MHRA, 2015).

[18] Agnolo Firenzuola, *Discacciamento de le nuove lettere, inutilmente aggiunte ne la lingua toscana* (Rome: Ludovico degli Arrighi and Lautizio Perugino, 1524), fol. C4v.

We can see why, when women *did* make use of the literary vernacular in their writings, whether these circulated in manuscript or in print, they felt obliged to include some form of *excusatio* for their limited linguistic abilities. Ippolita Clara (1487–1540), from one of the most prominent families of Alessandria, the wife of a high official at the Sforza court in Milan, besides 300 verse compositions in the vernacular, left a translation in tercets of the first six books of the *Aeneid*. In the letter (dated 10 August 1533) which accompanied the gift of her manuscript to her dedicatee Francesco II Sforza, she apologised for her limited knowledge of Tuscan and the 'forse migliaia d'errori che 'l mio debil occhio non vede' ('the thousands of mistakes that might have escaped my attention').[19] A century later, in 1628, Isabella Sori (before 1614–after 1631), a young woman of letters, also from Alessandria, this time the daughter of a physician, published her *Ammaestramenti e ricordi*, a text on female conduct composed for the benefit of other women. Sori must have received a higher than usual level of education, judging from the sheer range of sources she consulted to compose her work, but felt her knowledge of the literary language was inadequate. When speaking, she wrote, women ought to use their local vernacular according to the 'uso delle bene allevate' ('the manner of well-bred women'), but in writing they had to use Tuscan. She had to concede, though, that she herself was unable to do so: 'io nol so così prontamente fare'.[20]

Yet, even those women who distinguished themselves in the use of the literary vernacular, women of letters who gave their writings to the presses and were able to use the highly stylised Petrarchist model of verse and the literary language, were not necessarily at ease with and fluent in that same language in their everyday life. As a woman of the aristocracy, the poet Vittoria Colonna (1492–1547) found herself by birth at the highest end of the social spectrum.[21] Her sonnets are carefully crafted in fourteenth-century Tuscan, but, since she was born in Marino, in the region of the Colli Albani, not far from Rome, she would have been a native speaker of the local vernacular. The language of her autograph letters differs from her assured poetic language: uncertain and inaccurate, her composite language is an example of *lingua cortigiana*, more specifically *romana*.

At the lowest level of society, access to literacy, to reading and/or writing, was left to chance. This is reflected in the language of extant documents. Born some time in the second half of the fifteenth century in the region of Sabina, the central part of

---

[19] Cited in Simone Albonico, 'Ippolita Clara', in Cesare Bozzetti, Pietro Gibellini, and Ennio Sandal (eds), *Veronica Gambara e la poesia del suo tempo nell'Italia settentrionale: Atti del Convegno (Brescia-Correggio, 17–19 ottobre 1985)* (Florence: Olschki, 1989), pp. 323–83 at 367.

[20] Isabella Sori, *Ammaestramenti e ricordi, circa a' buoni costumi, che deve insegnare una ben creata madre ad una figlia, da citella, d'accasata e da vedova* [...] *con una particolare aggionta di dodeci Difese* [...] *e nel fine un Panegirico*, ed. Helena Sanson (Cambridge: MHRA, 2018), p. 86. Now also available in an Italian edition as Isabella Sori, *Ammaestramenti e ricordi, Difese, Panegirico*, ed. Helena Sanson (Alessandria: Edizioni dell'Orso, 2021).

[21] Helena Sanson, 'Vittoria Colonna and Language', in Abigail Brundin, Tatiana Crivelli Speciale, and Maria Serena Sapegno (eds), *A Companion to Vittoria Colonna* (Leiden: Brill, 2016), pp. 195–234.

rural Lazio, Bellezze Ursini acquired her writing skills against all odds. She came from an impoverished and culturally backwards area, and lived by her wits. At the age of 60 or so, in 1527–8, she found herself before the Inquisition for witchcraft. She left a handwritten confession: expectedly, her writing skills are poor, as is her language. But what matters is that Bellezze was able to write. Intriguingly, along-side her own writing, we also have the transcription made by a notary during the trial against her. The two documents encapsulate the same story, Bellezze's story, with, in principle, the same words. Yet, their different use of language and hand-writing skills, the different phonological and morphological features poignantly capture two worlds apart: that of a marginalised woman of the lowest populace and of a learned notary with a humanist background. Bellezze, tellingly, was well aware of her limitations:

> Al nome de Dio, io Belleze de Agnelo Ursini de Collevecio faccio mano propia questa carta, che me ll'à fatta fà lu pricuratore, e dirrove tutte le mee culpe, che so' stata e so' fatucieta; e la farraio per perdonanza deli granni mali che aio fatto, che me moro de dolore. E mo non guardate ala gnurantia delo scivere.[22]

> In the name of God, I, Bellezze daughter of Angelo Ursini from Collevecchio, am writing this confession in my own hand, as the procurator asked me to do, and I shall tell in it all my sins, because I have been and am a sorceress; and I shall do so to ask for forgiveness for the great damage I have done, that I die of sorrow. And now do not pay heed to my poor writing.

Linguistic inaccuracies and poor handling of the written language were also traits that one can find among nuns in convents who put into words their mystic experi-ence. Caterina Paluzzi, a tertiary Dominican nun from Morlupo (near Rome), was of humble origins. Her writing skills were poor, but she complied with the request of her spiritual father, Alessandro Migliacci, and tried to put into writing her visions and life story. Cardinal Federico Borromeo (1564–1631), with whom she kept an assiduous correspondence, expressed his disappointment at her inadequate use of the written language:

> Vedo che non sai scrivere: non dico quanto al carattere, ma dico quanto alle parole che male sai proferire, né comporre insieme. [...] Vedi, se hai da filare conviene che habbi la conocchia; se hai da cucire devi havere il filo. Se hai da scrivere almeno devi tanto sapere, che possi farti intendere, et scrivere tutte le lettere che vanno in una parola, acciò si intenda. [...] Però [...], figliuola mia, [...] impara bene a scrivere.[23]

---

[22] Pietro Trifone, 'La confessione di Bellezze Ursini, "strega" nella campagna romana del Cinquecento', in *Contributi di filologia dell'Italia mediana*, 2 vols (Perugia: Opera del Vocabolario dialettale umbro, 1987–8), II, pp. 79–136 at 133. See also Michele Di Sivo, *Bellezza Orsini: la costruzione di una strega (1528)* (Rome: Roma nel Rinascimento, 2016).

[23] Cited in Giovanni Antonazzi (ed.), *Caterina Paluzzi e la sua autobiografia (1573–1645): una mistica popolana tra San Filippo Neri e Federico Borromeo* (Rome: Edizioni di Storia e Letteratura, 1980), p. 276. Letter dated 23 August 1611.

I see you cannot write, and I am not referring to your handwriting, but to the words which you are not able to put together well. [...] You see, if you have to spin, you need a distaff; if you have to sew, you need a thread. If you have to write you have to at least be able to write so that people can understand you and write all the letters that compose a work, so that one can understand it. [...] Therefore [...], my dear, [...] make sure you learn how to write well.

Within the convent walls, the degree of linguistic competence in written Italian varied: some nuns mastered the language quite well, others struggled to write even basic shopping lists. Just as outside the convent walls, so also within the local dialect would have prevailed in speaking. The nuns' degree of education reflected their different economic and social background and the kind of upbringing and training they had received *before* entering the convent. A large proportion of convent inhabitants came from privileged and wealthy social groups, but social differences that existed *outside* the convent were maintained also *within*, extending also to variations in linguistic literacy.

In general terms, whether young women were to spend only a limited time there before returning to their homes, or join the ranks of the nuns who took perpetual vows, there was only so much they could aspire to learn in the convent.[24] Sent, aged 11, to the convent of St Anna in Castello against her will, the Venetian nun Arcangela Tarabotti (1604–52) succeeded in carving a name for herself in the literary world, even though she was mostly self-taught. In her writings she recalled the very limited intellectual opportunities young women had access to in the cloisters. The nuns who taught them were often unlearned and could only impart the very basic rudiments of reading: 'Io, che 'l so, il posso liberamente testificare' ('I, who have experienced it, can openly testify to that').[25] Broadly speaking, though, nuns were encouraged to be able to read well so they could appropriately recite the divine office and know the Breviary.[26] New 'professe' were required to own a 'breviario, et altri libri per recitar l'officio' ('the breviary, and other books to recite the office'), as well as 'libri spirituali' ('spiritual books'), to be accepted into the convent.[27]

Within and outside the convent walls, women found themselves the target of the marketing strategies of authors and printers, who, in their quest for a broader

[24] But there were also convents that distinguished themselves as centres of cultural production. See on this, for instance, *Monasteri femminili come centri di cultura fra Rinascimento e Barocco: atti del convegno storico internazionale: Bologna, 8-10 dicembre 2000*, ed. Gianna Pomata and Gabriella Zarri (Rome: Edizioni di Storia e Letteratura, 2005).

[25] Galerana Baratotti (Arcangela Tarabotti), *La semplicità ingannata* (Leiden: Giovanni Sambix, 1554), pp. 148–9.

[26] Luigi Bossi, *Catechismo ad uso delle fanciulle desiderose di farsi monache* (Milan: Pacifico da Ponte e Giovanni Battista Piccaglia, 1621), pp. 62–3, cited in Danilo Zardin, *Donna e religiosa di rara eccellenza. Prospera Corona Bascapè, i libri e la cultura nei monasteri milanesi del Cinque e Seicento* (Florence: Leo Olschki, 1992), p. 126, n. 40.

[27] *Nota di tutto quello, che devono dar i parenti alle zitelle in occasione di monacarle*, cited in Zardin, *Donna e religiosa di rara eccellenza*, p. 126, n. 40. See also Rinaldo Beretta, 'Il monastero delle benedettine di San Pietro di Cremella', *Archivio storico lombardo*, 39 (1912), 293–356 at 355.

and more profitable market, produced their works specifically with a female read-ership in mind. Devotional texts were among the few types of texts considered suit-able for women without concerns for their morality,[28] but publishers also printed a range of other vernacular works, including recipe books and 'libri di segreti', conduct literature texts, works relating to the debate about women – the so-called *Querelle des femmes* – as well as works on obstetrics, travel books, books of songs and madrigals, of needlework and sewing, manuals of model-letters. Women were often included among the users of teach-yourself manuals to learn the rudiments of reading and writing. The title-page of Giambattista Verini's *La utilissima opera da imparare a scrivere varie sorti di lettere* (1530?), for instance, depicts a woman in the act of learning sitting next to her teacher (see Figure 3.1). It is worth keeping in mind that, in light of the existing gap between the vernaculars used in everyday life and the elitist nature of the literary vernacular that authors and publishers strove to adopt in their works, it would be an oversimplification to say that women with limited literacy could access these works without problems. They might have possessed a partial or fully functional ability to read, but that did not necessarily entail immediate access to the archaic, fourteenth-century Tuscan-based literary vernacular. The same issue would have presented itself with refer-ence to the variegated world of popular literature and cheap prints. It comprised calendars and 'almanacchi', pamphlets, broadsheets, chivalric romances, legends of saints, proverbs, 'fogli di aviso' ('newssheets'), devotional texts and texts of basic literacy: these hugely popular outputs of early modern printing presses were not the other side of the coin of higher culture, but rather co-existed side-by-side with it.[29] Women across all social ranks would have been among the consumers of these kinds of works. Often produced in large quantity, in small format and cheap quality, these products of the printing trade were transient and ephemeral in nature, meant for immediate consumption, rather than preservation. They were meant to be 'sold, stuck up or handed out in public spaces, sometimes given away for free' and 'very often read out loud or performed in some way'.[30] They played an important role in offering some form of access to learning to the illiterate and partially literate, because 'people's utilization of the printed word could be col-lective when it was mediated through someone reading aloud'.[31] Street sellers, street singers, street performers, and pedlars could act as intermediaries between

---

[28] Their orthodoxy, however, was at times reason for concern. After the Council of Trent, the axe of some over-zealous censors descended upon some of these works. See on this Gigliola Fragnito, *Proibito capire. La Chiesa e il volgare nella prima età moderna* (Bologna: Il Mulino, 2005), pp. 277–87; Xenia von Tippelskirch, *Sotto controllo. Letture femminili nella prima età moderna* (Rome: Viella, 2011).

[29] See on this Francesco Novati, *Scritti sull'editoria popolare nell'Italia di Antico Regime*, eds Edoardo Barbieri and Alberto Brambilla (Rome: Archivio Guido Izzi, 2004), in particular pp. 110–17 for a list of engravers and printers of popular literature.

[30] Rosa Salzberg, *Ephemeral City: Cheap Print and Urban Culture in Renaissance Venice* (Manchester: Manchester University Press, 2014), p. 4.

[31] Roger Chartier, 'Publishing Strategies and What the People Read, 1530–1600', in *Cultural Uses of Print in Early Modern France* (Princeton: Princeton University Press, 1987), pp. 145–82 at 152.

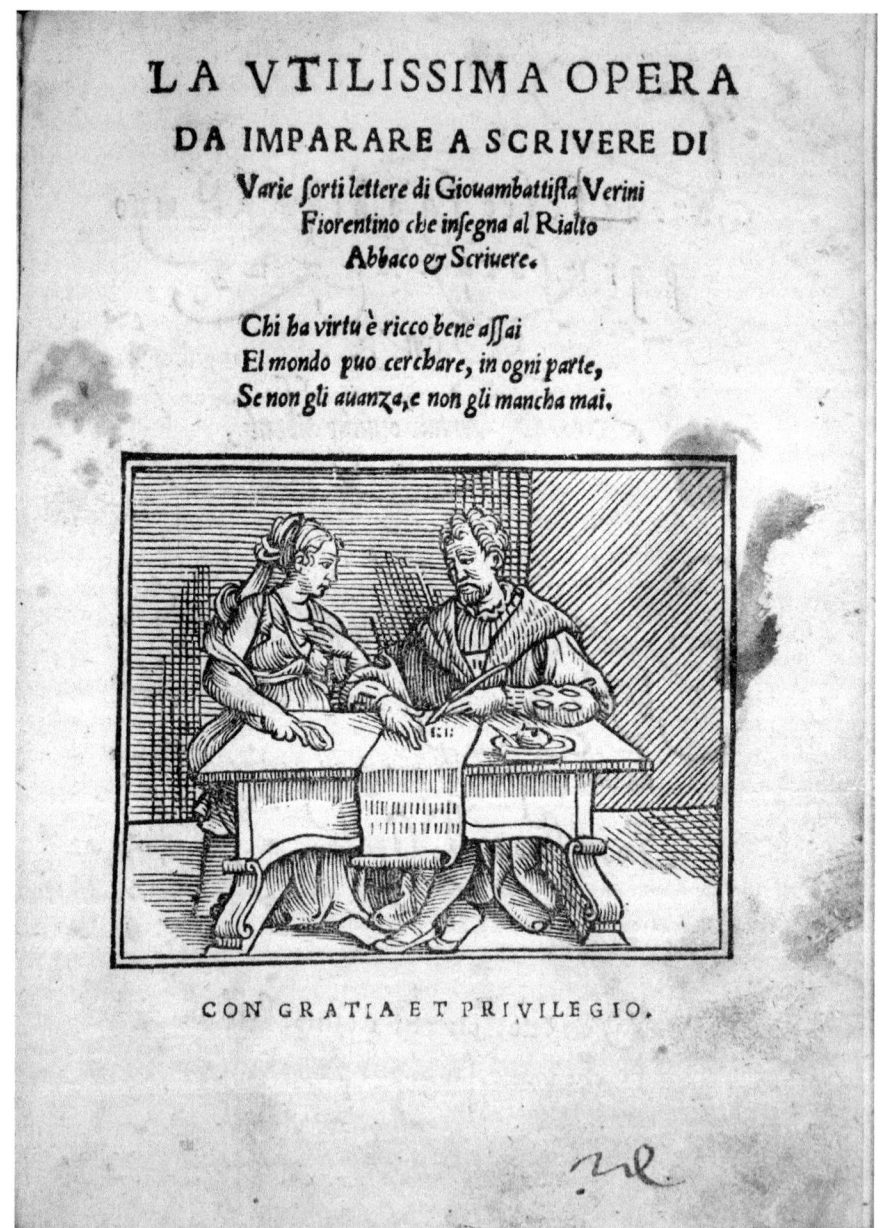

LA VTILISSIMA OPERA
DA IMPARARE A SCRIVERE DI
Varie *forti lettere di Giouambattifta Verini*
Fiorentino che infegna al Rialto
Abbaco e7 Scriuere.

Chi ha virtu è ricco bene affai
El mondo puo cercbare, in ogni parte,
Se non gli auanza,e non gli mancha mai.

CON GRATIA ET PRIVILEGIO.

Figure 3.1 Giovan Battista Verini, *La utilissima opera da imparare a scrivere varie sorti di lettere* (1530?). Biblioteca comunale Passerini-Landi, Piacenza, Fondo Comunale, M.V.39.

the language used in the printed text and the local vernacular: 'Il rito della lettura pubblica [...] fa pensare a una certa diffusione [of printed texts] anche al di là della competenza attiva della lingua' ('the ritual of public reading [...] seem to indicate a certain diffusion of printed texts even beyond an active language competence').[32] Newssheets, the forerunners of modern journalism, informed the public about news and current events – wars and peace treaties, weddings, feasts, processions, travels and explorations, natural disasters and earthquakes – by adopting a language which was closer to the courtly *koinè* discussed earlier, somewhere in-between the literary language and the spoken language, with macro-regional features that tend towards a 'lingua comune' ('common language').[33]

Women across social ranks, and in different contexts, were also keen readers of some of the great vernacular masterpieces, among them the widely successful chivalric poem *Orlando furioso* by Ludovico Ariosto, the quintes-sential example of entertainment reading, with its kaleidoscopic web of love, passion, magic, war, and never-ending adventures. Chivalric poems and all 'libri di batagia' ('books of battles'), as they were called, were usually considered unsuitable – even dangerous – for women. In his *Uffizio della donna maritata* (1583), composed specifically for his young wife Delia Bellanti, the Sienese man of letters Orazio Lombardelli (1545–1608) warned her to avoid 'Rime [...], se non sono spirituali' and 'libri d'amori e di battaglie' ('verse [...] that is not of the spiritual kind [...] books of love and war'),[34] and focus, instead, on spiritual and devotional texts, and lives of saints.[35] Yet, chivalric poems enjoyed great popularity with female readers across social ranks. The *Furioso* also infiltrated the walls of the convents: nuns secretly owned and read copies of the poem.[36] In his *Iconomica* (1552), the Sicilian man of letters Paolo Caggio (first quarter sixteenth century–1562) has his characters Monofilo and Apollonio recall how

---

[32] Laura Ricci, 'La lingua degli avvisi a stampa', in Nadia Cannata and Maria Antonietta Grignani (eds), *Scrivere il volgare fra Medioevo e Rinascimento. Atti del convegno di studi, Siena, 14–15 maggio 2008* (Pisa: Pacini, 2009), pp. 97–114 at 112.

[33] Brian Richardson, 'The Concept of a "lingua comune" in Renaissance Italy', in Anna Laura Lepschy and Arturo Tosi (eds), *The Languages of Italy: Histories and Dictionaries* (Ravenna: Longo, 2007), pp. 11–28.

[34] Orazio Lombardelli, *Dell'uffizio della donna maritata. Capi centoottanta* (Florence: Giorgio Marescotti, 1583), capo 144.

[35] The *Orlando furioso* was not always viewed as an instrument of corruption of women's morality. For instance, Isabella Sori, mentioned earlier, in her *Ammaestramenti* often uses the female characters of the poem as *exempla* of female virtue and interprets specific episodes as positive tales of edifica-tion or strong warnings against the dangers women could face in life, therefore reading the poem as a fruitful combination of 'utile' and 'dilettevole' ('useful' and 'delightful'). See Helena Sanson, 'The *Ammaestramenti e ricordi*, *Difese* and *Panegirico* by Isabella Sori "alessandrina": A Lost Voice from Seventeenth-Century Italy', in Sori, *Ammaestramenti*, pp. 1–70. For a discussion of this edifying reading of Ariosto's poem, see Francesco Lucioli, 'L'*Orlando furioso* nel dibattito sulla donna in Italia in età moderna', *Italianistica*, 47.1 (2018), 99–129.

[36] Gabriella Zarri, *Recinti: donne, clausura e matrimonio nella prima età Moderna* (Bologna: Il Mulino, 2000), p. 94.

certain presumptuous ('superbuzze') nuns were quick to cite lines from the poem to their visitors: 'subito [...] vi saltano con alcune rime del *Furioso*' ('immediately they present you with some lines from the *Furioso*').[37] The Oblate father Carlo Andrea Basso devoted an entire Chapter (VI) of his 1627 *La monaca perfetta* ('The Perfect Nun') to the great perils that 'libri profani et inutili' ('lay and useless books') full of vain and imaginary stories brought to chastity and morality.[38] What good could come from knowing

> il fatto d'Elena, la presa di Troia, i giri d'Enea, i lamenti di Didone, la genealogia de i falsi dei, et le pessime vite loro? Che utilità ponno recarti gli Orlandi, i Rodomonti, i cavalieri erranti, le guerre finte, le prodezze sognate, le virtù dai vitj ammantate [...] le lagrime, gli amori, le pazzie, finzioni et perdimento dei poeti e di tanti vani componimenti ch'escono dalle scole del diavolo per ingannare et intrappolare le anime?[39]

> the story of Elena, the capture of Troy, the adventures of Aeneas, the laments of Dido, the genealogy of fake gods, and their abysmal lives? What good can come from the various Orlandos, Rodomonts, knights errant, fake wars, imaginary feats, vices disguised as virtues [...] the tears, loves, mad gestures, fictions and damnations of poets and the many vain compositions that come out from the schools of the devil to cheat and entrap souls?

Nuns who were found in possession of such books had to be severely punished: these works were a threat to morality, caused resentment towards religious life and hindered spiritual exercises. They could not be excused as some form of innocent, recreational reading, because they only filled the brain with:

> molti fantasmi vani e impertinenti, di pensieri rozzi o d'inutili, et lasciali talmente impressi che nel tempo del divino officio, dell'oratione, del sentire la predica, del legere libri spirituali, [la monaca] non si può raccogliere et non sa trovare attentione; le pare sempre di vedere quei duelli di Rodomonte, quelle pazzie d'Orlando, et altre sciocchezze, onde non si può applicare a cosa buona.[40]

> many vain, impertinent ghosts, with crude and useless thoughts, and they leave such an impression that, while she recites the holy office, when she prays, when she listens to sermons, or reads spiritual books, she [the nun] cannot concentrate and pay attention; she always thinks of Rodomonte's duels, Orlando's mad actions, and other vanities, whereby she cannot devote herself to anything good.

---

[37] Paolo Caggio, *Iconomica* [...] *nella quale s'insegna brevemente per modo di dialogo il governo famigliare* (Venice: al Segno del Pozzo, 1552), fol. 46v [but 47v].

[38] Carlo Andrea Basso, *La monaca perfetta ritratta. Dalla scrittura sacra, auttorità et essempi de' santi padri.* [...] *Opera utilissima a chiunque desidera servir a Dio con perfettione* (Milan: Pacifico Pontio et Giovanni Battista Piccaglia stampatori Archiepiscopali, 1627), p. 426. On Basso's text, see Gabriella Zarri, 'La perfetta claustrale: manuali sei-settecenteschi per l'istruzione delle monache', in Helena Sanson and Francesco Lucioli (eds), *Conduct Literature for and about Women: Prescribing and Describing Life, 1500–1900* (Paris: Classiques Garnier, 2016), pp. 81–102.

[39] Basso, *La monaca*, p. 428.

[40] Basso, *La monaca*, p. 430.

Outside the convent walls, ownership of the *Furioso* could be a sort of status symbol. Isabella Bellocchio, a prostitute tried before the Inquisition in 1589, kept a copy of the poem on display on her mantelpiece, despite being herself illiterate.[41] In his *Dialogo nel quale Nanna insegna a la Pippa* (1536), Pietro Aretino has the prostitute Nanna advise her daughter to make sure she owns and displays a copy of the text: 'fa' vista di leggere il Furioso [...] che terrai sempre in tavola' ('make sure to pretend to read the Furioso [...] which you will always display on your table').[42]

But, here too, we have to remember the important element of the oral circulation and enjoyment of literary works across social ranks, and in particular among the less literate or altogether illiterate. The *Furioso* seemed to inhabit private and public spaces alike. In 1589, the man of letters Giuseppe Malatesta, in his *Della nuova poesia overo delle difese del Furioso*, explained that:

> se voi pratticate per le corti, se andate per le strade, se passeggiate per le piazze [...] non sentite altro che o leggere o recitare l'Ariosto. [...] nelle case private, nelle ville, ne' tugurii stessi et nelle capanne ancora si trova et si canta continuamente il *Furioso* [...]. Onde nasce che infiniti huomini, allettati da questa soavità, non si contentano di assaporar solamente quell'opera che vogliono anco, come convenirsela in propria sostanza, imprimendolasi talmente nella memoria che, se hoggi fusse perduto il *Furioso* del tutto, non mancarebbon le schiere degli huomini che la servano a mente da capo a piede di parola in parola.[43]

> If you frequent the courts, if you walk in the streets, or stroll on the squares [...] you hear nothing but Ariosto being read or recited. [...] in private homes and villas, even in hovels and huts you find and hear the *Furioso* sung all the time [...]. Hence many people, enticed by this suavity, are not simply content to enjoy the work, but also, as if to make it their own, learn it so well by heart that, if the *Furioso* went lost forever, there would still be many who would remember it by heart, from beginning to end, word by word.

Acclaimed as a literary masterpiece, the *Furioso* had an equally strong appeal at the opposite end of the social spectrum, in the refined palaces of gentlemen and ladies engaged in parlour-games that required polished conversational skills.[44] In Girolamo Bargagli's *Dialogo de' giuochi che nelle vegghie sanesi si usano di fare* (1572) the 'gioco delle questioni' ('the game of questions') is described as one that entailed detailed knowledge of literary works, such as the *Furioso* and other chivalric poems. Bargagli recalls an evening in the palace of Countess Agnolina

---

[41] Margaret F. Rosenthal, *The Honest Courtesan: Veronica Franco, Citizen and Writer in Sixteenth-Century Venice* (Chicago and London: University of Chicago Press, 1992), pp. 330–1, n. 89.

[42] Pietro Aretino, *Dialogo nel quale Nanna insegna a la Pippa*, in *Sei giornate*, ed. Giovanni Aquilecchia (Bari: Laterza, 1969), pp. 143–355 at 212.

[43] Giuseppe Malatesta, *Della nuova poesia overo delle difese del Furioso, dialogo* (Verona: Sebastiano Dalle Donne, 1589), pp. 137–8.

[44] See on this George McLure, *Parlour Games and the Public Life of Women in Renaissance Italy* (Toronto and Buffalo: University of Toronto Press, 2013). And specifically with reference to language use, see Helena Sanson, '"Orsù, non più Signora, [...] tornate a segno": Women, Language Games and Debates in Cinquecento Italy', *Modern Language Review*, 105.1 (2010), 103–21.

d'Elci, where 'una bella et ristretta compagnia di donne si ritrovava, lequali, oltre al *Furioso*, questi libri d'*Amadigi di Gaula* et *di Grecia*, et questi *Palmerini* et *Don Floriselli* di leggere si dilettavano' ('there was a pleasant small gathering of women, who, beside this Furioso, also enjoyed reading *Amadis of Gaul* and *Greece*, as well as these *Palmerini* and *Don Floriselli*).[45]

As for the classical languages, Latin was the key that gave access to the great literary heritage of the past and was part of the training necessary to enter public life in adulthood. For women, not having a public role to fulfil, the study of Latin was mostly deemed unsuitable and unnecessary. Besides, certain Latin authors and works were considered lascivious, and knowledge of the language was seen as a liability for women's decency. The language barrier protected their morality. Some men of letters, occasionally, suggested the study of some Latin as a remedy to idleness.[46] Greek, however, was considered to be too much of a burden for the female mind.[47]

Notwithstanding the views of moralists and educationalists, from the four-teenth to the seventeenth centuries 'Italy produced more women who wrote Latin, both in verse and prose, than any other country in Europe'.[48] A number of these women – such as Isotta (1418–66) and Ginevra Nogarola (1418–66), Laura Cereta (1469–99), Cassandra Fedele (1465–1558), and Olympia Morata (1526–55) – had been supported in their studies by the male members of their family, often men of letters themselves. Others acquired knowledge of the classical languages in indirect ways. The Venetian Moderata Fonte (1555–92) (pseudonym of Modesta Pozzo) was able to learn Latin thanks to her maternal grandfather and her elder brother: every day, when he came back from school, he would teach her what he himself had been taught at the 'scuola di gramatica'.[49] Similarly, the Roman Martha Marchina (1600–42),[50] the daughter of a soap-maker, learnt Latin second-hand, from her two brothers who attended the school of the Oratorian Fathers. She went on to become a respected Latin poet.

[45] Girolamo Bargagli, *Dialogo de' giuochi che nelle vegghie sanesi si usano di fare* (Siena: Luca Bonetti, 1572), p. 66. The references are to the well-known Iberian knight-errantry tales of *Amadís de Gaula*, *Amadís de Grecia*, *Florisel de Niquea*, and *Palmerín de Olivia*, published in several volumes, a number of which had been translated into Italian throughout the century to immense success.

[46] Juan Luis Vives, *De l'istitutione de la femina christiana, vergine, maritata, o vedova* (Venice: Vincenzo Valgrisi, 1546), fol. 114*r*. Even then, a careful selection had to be made among suitable and unsuitable authors. Cicero, for instance, was acceptable, but Ovid and Horace were not. See on this Dolce, *Dialogo della instituzion delle donne* (2015), p. 106 [fol. 21*v*].

[47] Dolce, *Dialogo*, p. 106 [fol. 21*v*].

[48] Jane Stevenson, *Women Latin Poets: Language, Gender and Authority from Antiquity to the Eighteenth Century* (Oxford: Oxford University Press, 2005), p. 141.

[49] Giovanni Nicolò Doglioni, 'Vita della signora Modesta Pozzo d'i Zorzi, Moderata Fonte, nominata Moderata Fonte', in Moderata Fonte, *Il merito delle donne* (Venice: Domenico Imberti, 1600), pp. 1–7 at 3.

[50] Marchina is discussed in more detail in Jane Stevenson's contribution to the present volume.

Women of higher social status or the daughters of learned men of letters might have fared better in their access to the classical language, but social status was not a guarantee of in-depth knowledge of the language. We know that Vittoria Colonna studied Latin (but we have no evidence of Greek) at least to the point of being able to use it in her reply poem to the Ferrarese poet Daniele Fini.[51] Words or quotations in Latin, mostly set phrases or biblical quotations, are embedded in the vernacular of her letters, a practice that was nonetheless not unusual at the time.[52]

As the language of prayers and church services, Latin was part of women's lives, especially considering that they were expected to be devout. At the lower end of the social spectrum, knowledge of Latin could have implied a passive, mnemonic, and imperfect knowledge rather than an active one: words, expressions, and set formulae were committed to memory, often repeated mechanically without any proper understanding, and in fact leading to unfortunate mispronunciations and macaronic mingling of Latin and vernacular.[53] Not coincidentally, men of letters played with the implausibility of women's knowledge of Latin in their works.[54] In convents, the nuns' ability to recite prayers and psalms might have still been poor, but nonetheless better than that of women outside the convent. There were also convents in which the nuns had a high level of competence in Latin, both in writing and in speaking: in the convent of Santa Maria delle Vergini in Venice, at ceremonial occasions, canonesses delivered orations in Latin that they had composed themselves,[55] whereas the Benedictine nuns of San Zaccaria in Venice, at the beginning of the sixteenth century, apparently spoke fluent Latin.[56]

But truly accessing the learning embedded in the works of the classical authors or in the works of scientists, philosophers, or theologians required linguistic skills that only few women had. What really made a difference in terms of women's access to this world of learning were the numerous vernacular translations that early modern Italy produced.

Women's Access to Learning: The Role of Translation

Among the many printing centres that existed in Italy, Florence and Venice stood out for focusing upon the production of vernacular books. In the 1550s, between 25 and 31 per cent of the total book production in Venice was of vernacular books,

---

[51] Silvio Pasquazi, *Poeti estensi del Rinascimento: con due appendici* (Florence: Le Monnier, 1966), p. LIII.

[52] Sanson, *Women, Language, and Grammar*, pp. 37–9; Sanson, "'Femina proterva'", 408–13.

[53] See Gian Luigi Beccaria, *Sicuterat: il latino di chi non lo sa. Bibbia e liturgia nell'italiano e nei dialetti* (Milan: Garzanti, 2002).

[54] See Sanson, "'Femina proterva'".

[55] Kate Lowe, *Nuns' Chronicles and Convent Culture in Renaissance and Counter-Reformation Italy* (Cambridge: Cambridge Univerity Press, 2003), p. 29.

[56] Zarri, *Recinti*, p. 93.

a figure which then decreased to 20 per cent in the following decade against the background of the Counter-Reformation.[57] Between 1536 and 1560, for instance, the Venetian printer Gabriele Giolito, responding to market forces and attentive to readers' aspirations, published numerous classical texts in vernacular translation, as well as vernacular literary works by contemporary authors, with Latin books accounting for only 5 per cent of his output.[58] Giolito and his collaborators were among those printers who adopted clear strategies in order to appeal to the growing female readership: translations into the vernacular were among the texts intended for female readers or with women as dedicatees.[59]

In fact, despite the growing importance of the vernacular, throughout the sixteenth century overall more books continued to be published in Latin than in the vernacular. The influence and predominance of Latin as a language of culture and as the language of daily activity of a bilingual (at least in writing, if not in speaking) elite of lawyers, notaries, and clerics continued well into the nineteenth century. Under the sign of Latin, unequal relations and a whole range of mechanisms that hinged on prestige, authority, and manipulation continued to exist.[60] Besides a rich production in prose and poetry, texts on logic, medicine, law, theology, philosophy, alchemy, botany, and virtually any learned discipline were in Latin: one can sense the weight of the exclusion from the world of knowledge for those who had limited or no familiarity with Latin, which, as mentioned earlier, was usually the case for women, even of high social status.

The importance of translations in widening access to culture cannot therefore be stressed enough. Translation from Latin into the vernacular brought the prestigious classical language, and the knowledge associated with it, closer to a socially much wider range of men and women. According to some, Latin works in translation could also provide opportunities for the moral edification of the female sex. In the dedicatory letter of his *L'instrumento de la filosofia* ('The Instrument of Philosophy') (1551), the Sienese man of letters Alessandro Piccolomini (1508–78) stated that vernacular translations of classical texts allowed even those who did not have familiarity with the classical languages to morally improve themselves and not be forced to live 'così imperfetti' ('imperfectly').[61] Women in particular paid the consequences of this situation, since they were not allowed to learn any language other than 'quella che da le nutrici imparano' ('the one they learn from their wet nurses').[62] In the same spirit, a few years earlier, Piccolomini had produced an

---

[57] Paul Grendler, *The Roman Inquisition and the Venetian Press, 1540–1605* (Princeton: Princeton University Press, 1983), pp. 133.

[58] Claudio Marazzini, *Il secondo Cinquecento e il Seicento* (Bologna: Il Mulino, 1993), p. 37.

[59] On women as dedicatees of vernacular translations, see Brian Richardson, *Women and the Circulation of Texts in Renaissance Italy* (Cambridge: Cambridge University Press, 2020), passim.

[60] On this Françoise Waquet, *Latin or the Empire of a Sign: From the Sixteenth to the Twentieth Centuries* (London and New York: Verso, 2002).

[61] Piccolomini, *L'instrumento de la filosofia* (Rome: Vincenzo Valgrisi, 1551), fol. A4*r*.

[62] Piccolomini, *L'instrumento*, fol. A4*r*.

explanation of Ptolemaic cosmography for the benefit of his protégée Laudomia Forteguerri de' Colombini, the treatise *De la sfera del mondo* ('The Sphere of the World') (1540) (Figures 3.2 and 3.3). Keen to study astronomy, the intellectually gifted Laudomia had been unable to do so because she did not know Latin and simply 'per esser nata donna' ('because she had been born a woman').[63] He lamented the fact that women were often unable to distinguish themselves in their studies because so much knowledge was available only in Latin. In early modern Italy, a range of works of literature, conduct, history, astronomy, and philosophy, as well as religious and devotional writings, works of geography, theatre or chivalric romances were translated into Italian. They were translated from the classical languages – or from Spanish and, later, from French – and at times explicitly dedicated to female figures, taken as representative of the kind of readers for whom the work was intended, or otherwise produced with a potential female readership in mind. As one might expect, the paratextual material of these translations often seems to indicate that their intended readership comprised above all women of the middle to higher social ranks, who would have had the kind of skills, means, and leisure needed to be able to devote themselves to reading and learning. In 1540, for instance, the first six books of Virgil's *Aeneid* were published 'in lingua Thoscana' ('in Tuscan') by Niccolò Zoppino, each book dedicated in turn to a different Sienese lady by prominent men of letters.[64] Zoppino, from Ferrara but based in Venice, was among those who championed the use of the vernacular and often explicitly stressed in the prefaces of the works he published the intention to cater more broadly for readers who did not know Latin or Greek.

If translations made an elitist culture more widely available across social ranks, according to some moralists and men of letters they also caused a dumbing down, as it were, of the greatness and richness of the classical tradition. They deplored the fact that these works lost their original force, their qualities of style and content, as well as their moral benefit. Regrettably, they were made available even to the 'donnicciuole' ('lowly women'), of limited education and lower social extraction, who might now have had the presumption to discuss learned matters with men. Even more dangerous in this sense were vernacular translations of the Scriptures. With the Index of Pope Paul IV in 1559, vernacular Bibles could not be printed, read, or kept without the permission of the Holy Office.[65] Not coincidentally, before the Council of Trent the question that women could have been able to approach

---

[63] I quote from the third edition: Alessandro Piccolomini, *Della sfera del mondo* […] *divisa in libri quattro* (Venice: Bartolomeo Cesano, 1553), fol. A2r.

[64] *I sei primi libri del Eneide di Vergilio, tradotti a piu illustre & honorate donne* (Venice: Comin da Trino a istanza di Niccolò Zoppino, 1540); Susanna Braund, in collaboration with Caterina Minniti, 'Female Networks and Virgil Translation in Sixteenth-Century Siena', in Helena Sanson (ed.), *Women and Translation in the Italian Tradition* (Paris: Classiques Garnier, forthcoming).

[65] See on this point Gigliola Fragnito, *La Bibbia al rogo. La censura ecclesiastica e i volgarizzamenti della scrittura (1471–1605)* (Bologna: Il Mulino, 1997). On censorhip more broadly, ead., *Rinascimento perduto. La letteratura italiana sotto gli occhi dei censori: secoli XV–XVII* (Bologna: Il Mulino, 2019).

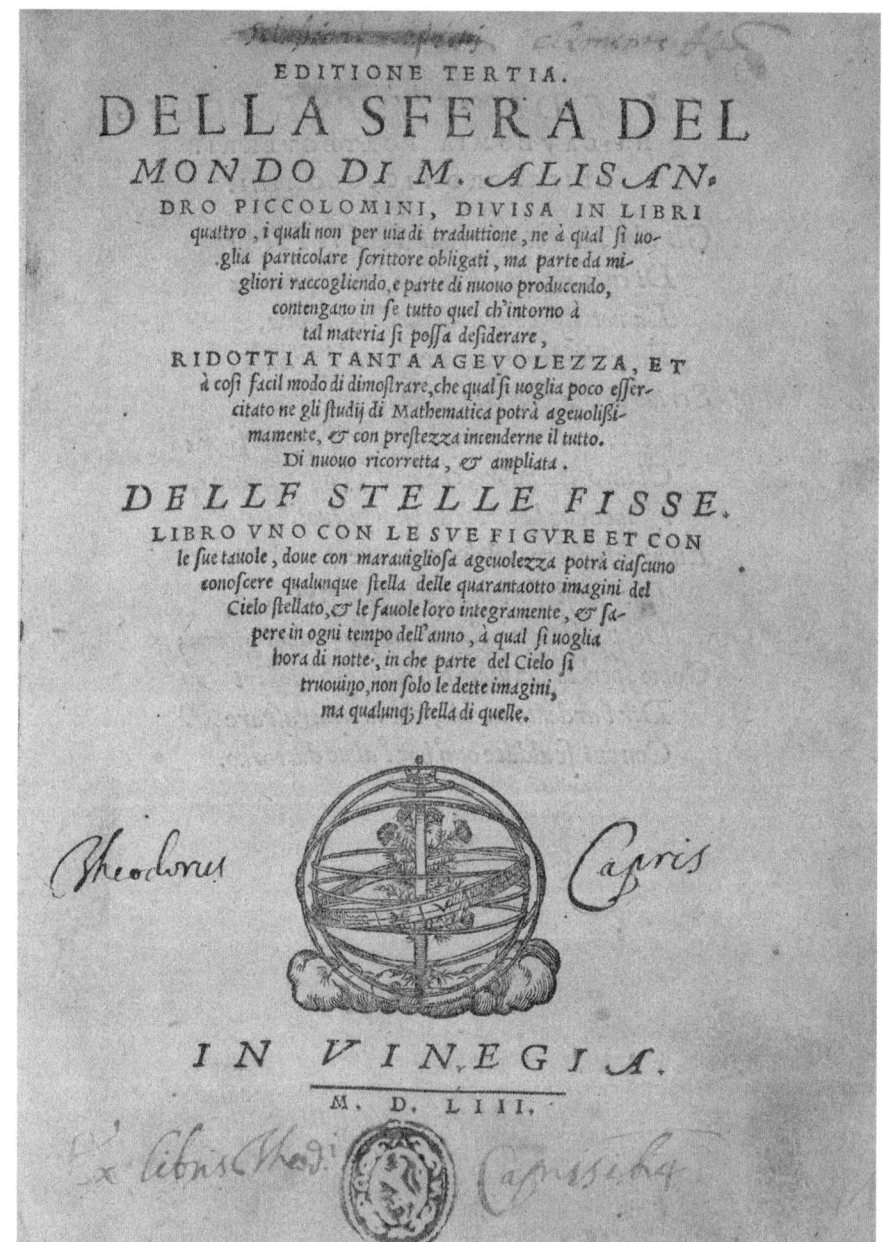

Figure 3.2 Alessandro Piccolomini, *Della sfera del mondo* (1553, 3rd edition), title page. Cambridge University Library, White.c.253.

A LA NOBILISSIM*A* E

BELLISSIMA MADONNA, LA MOLTO GEN-
tile Madonna Laudomia Forteguerri de Colombini, Alifandro
Piccolomini altrimenti, lo ftordito intronato.

S. S. S.

I E' PER *in fin qua uenuto à l'orecchie(Nobi
lißima,e Bellißima Mad.*LAVDOMIA)*che
trouandofi in quefta Primauera paffata la.*S.V.
*un giorno con altre nobilißime Donne in un giar-
dino à folazzo, & effendo tutte infieme ne le piu
calde hore del giorno quafi in un Coro celefte, &
angelico ridutte fotto un Lauro in corona,bellißi-
mi,& molto dotti,e filofofici ragionamenti acca-
der trà uoi. Doue doppò che uarij, & ingegnofi
difcorfi furon hauuti hor da quefta hor da quella,
cadute finalmente in propofito de le cofe diuine,*
come di cofe fimili à uoi, da poi, che per gran pezza fi fu ragionato de la bellezza e
fplendor de i corpi celefti,e del marauigliofo ordine che fenza un minimo fallo tra lor
del continuo s'offerua,e d'altre cofe fimili à quefte,intefi che la.*S.V.*diffe,che oltra'l di-
fpiacer ch'ella ha fempre hauuto,che per effer nata Donna,non le fia ftato conceduto di
poter donare gli anni fuoi à qualche pregiato ftudio,& honorata fcientia, per quefto
ciò le dolea piu che per altro,ch'ella non haueua poffuto pafcer l'animo fuo de le cofe di
Aftrologia,à le quali la fi fentia piu che ad altro inclinata . O nobilißimo e ben purgato
fpirito di Donna,animo ueramente faggio,e fol degno di cofi honorata uefte quanto le
piu rare bellezze,che mai fuffer uifte lo cingon dattorno. Quefta fi può chiamar Donna fenza alcun dubbio immortale,che de l'ardente defio del fapere s'infiamma,e s'accen-
de,ilqual defio de gli huomini fteß i faluo che pochi,con l'acque de l'otio,e de la poca religione d'ammorzar cercan con ogni ftudio, peroche doue ch'effendo egli nel mezzo
pofti di quefta gran Machina,& hauendo d'ogn'intorno infinite cofe, donde poßin con
gran marauiglia,e ftupor conofcer in parte la infinita poffanza di chi l'ha conftrutta in
un punto,nondimeno chiudendo gli occhi de la mente,e ne la lor uiltà oftinati,nel brutto
fango de l'ignorantia dormono gli anni loro.Di che io fpeffe uolte mi fon marauigliato,
e certo è gran cofa,che tutte l'altre fpetie de le cofe create, cofi le piante come gli animali,& ogni altra cofa parimente, operino à punto ciafcheduna per fe fecondo che la
fpinge quella proprietà,ò uer particolar natura,che da l'altre cofe la fa differente,e gli
huomini foli fien quegli che tutto'l contrario facendo fi sforzin di moftrar fegno ne le
lor operationi,piu tofto di quel ch'egli han commune con gli altri animali, che di quel

A ij

Figure 3.3 Alessandro Piccolomini, *Della sfera del mondo* (1553, 3rd edition), dedication
to Laudomia Forteguerri de' Colombini, Piccolomini's protégée, for whose benefit he
claimed to have composed the work. Cambridge University Library, White.c.253.

the Bible without an intermediary had been a reason for concern. Women, especially the *mulierculae* – limited as they were by both their sex and their social status – would inevitably fall into blatant errors and misinterpretations, and lead others astray. But in bigger and smaller centres across the peninsula, there were women who did read vernacular Bibles.[66] Alessandro Strozzi, one of the executors responsible for the implementation of the 1559 Index in Florence and the seizing of full texts of the Bibles and the New Testaments, observed that 'il levar le Biblie volgari alle donne et gli Evangelii dello anno le confonde et quasi si risolvono a non lo poter credere' ('taking away from women vernacular Bibles and Gospel readings for the liturgical year confounds them and they can hardly believe it').[67]

In convents, some nuns acquired at times a remarkable knowledge of the Scriptures. One case in point is that of the Poor Clares of Santa Chiara in Udine. The convent hosted many noblewomen from the town: in 1590, Fra Bartolomeo de Pellegrini, from Vicenza, the nuns' confessor, when interrogated by the ecclesiastical authorities regarding the nuns' possible heretical (anabaptist) positions, admitted that many of them 'parlano della Scrittura et hanno li libri delli evangelii, credo che siano volgari, e la Bibbia, perché parlano più della Scrittura, che non faccio io, et ne hanno molta prattica, adducendola in ogni proposito' ('talk of the Scriptures and possess the Gospels, I believe in the vernacular, and the Bible, because they talk about the Scripture more than I do, and they have a good knowledge of it, and quote from it whenever they can').[68]

Translations for the benefit of other women and the less learned more broadly – both men *and* women – were also produced by women themselves. Whereas scholars have increasingly devoted their attention to the creative production of lay and religious women in early modern Italy, across different literary genres,[69] women's contribution as translators to the circulation of learning across social ranks has been mostly overlooked.[70]

Given that women's handling of the *literary* vernacular was, as we saw, limited by their restricted access to study, translation required a further set of distinctive language skills, given that neither the source language nor the target language were mother tongues. Women engaged in translation as a private form of linguistic or

---

[66] Fragnito, *La Bibbia al rogo*, p. 282.

[67] Cited in Fragnito, *La Bibbia al rogo*, p. 280.

[68] Cited in Giovanna Paolin, 'L'eterodossia nel monastero delle Clarisse di Udine nella seconda metà del '500', *Collectanea franciscana*, 50 (1980), 107–67 at 136.

[69] Besides works dedicated to individual figures and modern editions of texts, studies include also wider surveys of women's writing, such as Virginia Cox, *Women's Writing in Italy, 1400–1650* (Baltimore: Johns Hopkins University Press, 2008) and, by the same author, *Prodigious Muse: Women's Writing in Counter-Reformation Italy* (Baltimore: Johns Hopkins University Press, 2011).

[70] For a first overview of the subject, see Helena Sanson, '"Io che donna indotta e minima sono": Women, Translation and Classical Languages in Early Modern Italy', *Women Language Literature in Italy / Donne lingua letteratura in Italia*, 3 (2021), 29–51. On translations by women in Renaissance Italy, see also Richardson, *Women and the Circulation of Texts*, pp. 2–3, 8, 17–18, 64–5, 108–9, 113, 115, 119.

literary exercise. They translated from Latin, Greek, or Hebrew (or vice versa) and from foreign languages or other vernaculars.[71] As is to be expected, they usually translated texts of a religious nature.[72] At the time, translations or reworkings of the Penitential Psalms were a popular genre, and in 1564, the poet Laura Battiferri Ammannati (1523–89), from Urbino, published in Florence *I sette salmi penitentiali* […] *Tradotti in lingua toscana* ('The Seven Penitential Psalms […] Translated into Tuscan'), each Psalm being dedicated to a nun from a prominent local family.[73] The poet Chiara Matraini (1515–1604), from a modest family of Lucca, offered a similar contribution to rendering the Psalms into Italian. Her *Considerationi sopra i sette salmi penitentiali* (1586) are more than a translation: Matraini expounded on the Latin text, offering also a 'facile e breve dichiaratione' ('easy and brief explanation') for the benefit either of those who did not have the opportunity to read the great theologians who had commented on the Psalms or those who read them, but did not necessarily understand them, 'leggendoli, non l'intendono'.[74]

Women also translated Latin or Greek classical authors. With her translation of the first six books of the *Aeneid*, Ippolita Clara – mentioned earlier – wanted to benefit women: '[l]e indotte donne […] che non intendano la latina lingua' ('those unlearned women who may not understand Latin').[75] Her translation allowed them to gain a moral lesson from each book turned into the vernacular, not least a stern warning against the dangers of conjugal infidelity from the episode of Dido in Book IV. Virgil's *Aeneid* seems to have been a favourite with early modern women translators: we know that a certain Diana Corradini translated at least parts of the poem,[76] and so did the Mantuan Emilia Gonzaga Arrivabene.[77] Other classical authors also received attention: Fiammetta Ubaldina, who flourished around 1585, translated the comedies of Terence.[78] Their translations remained unpublished (and some are lost): despite their reaching a more limited readership, we should not forget the importance of manuscript circulation of knowledge in Renaissance Italy.[79] As for

[71] In this chapter, however, for reasons of space, I shall limit myself to considering translations from Latin and Greek.

[72] I am referring to texts that are explicitly attributed to female translators. A different case would be anonymous translated works that remain unattributed.

[73] *I sette salmi penitentiali del santissimo profeta Davit. Tradotti in lingua toscana da Madonna Laura Battiferra degli Ammannati, con gli argomenti sopra ciascuno di essi, composti dalla medesima; insieme con alcuni suoi sonetti spirituali* (Florence: i Giunti, 1564). On Battiferri's translation, see Jane Tylus, 'Early Modern Women as Translators of the Sacred', *Women Language Literature in Italy / Donne lingua letteratura in Italia*, 1 (2019), 30–43. For a modern edition, see Laura Battiferri, *I sette salmi penitenziali di David con alcuni sonetti spirituali*, ed. Enrico Maria Guidi (Urbino: Accademia Raffaello, 2005).

[74] Chiara Matraini, *Considerationi sopra i sette salmi penitentiali del gran re e profeta Davit* (Lucca: Vincenzo Busdraghi, 1586), fol. 4r. For a modern edition of her *Considerationi*, see Chiara Matraini, *Le opere in prosa e altre poesie*, ed. Anna Mario (Perugia: Aguaplano, 2017), pp. 287–483.

[75] Cited in Albonico, 'Ippolita Clara', p. 368.

[76] Giacomo Filippo Tomasini, *Bibliothecae Patavinae manuscriptae publicae & privatae* (Udine: Nicola Schiratti, 1639), p. 95. The manuscript is now lost.

[77] Maria Bandini Buti (ed.), *Donne d'Italia: poetesse e scrittrici*, 2 vols (Rome: Tosi, 1946), I, 45.

[78] Louis Jacob, *Bibliothèque des femmes illustres par leurs écrits* (Paris: Bibliothèque Nationale de France, Ancien Fonds Français, 22865), fol. 86v.

[79] See on this Brian Richardson, *Manuscript Culture in Renaissance Italy* (Cambridge: Cambridge University Press, 2009).

Greek, the learned Tarquinia Molza (1542–1617), from Modena, also a renowned singer, translated works of Plato, Plutarch, and Aristotle directly from the original language.[80] Olympia Fulvia Morata (1526–55), from Ferrara – daughter of the renowned humanist Fulvio Pellegrino Morato – translated seven Psalms from Greek *into* Latin.[81] Others translated from Greek via Latin, like Matraini who in 1556 brought out her Italian rendering of Isocrates's *To Demonicus* using a Latin intermediary translation (Figure 3.4).[82] Religious women within convent walls also devoted themselves to translation. In his *La nobiltà di Milano* (1595), the historian Paolo Morigia (1525–1604) explained that: 'di presente vivono così nel secolo come nei monasterii molte donne di spirito elevate che posseggono grammatica, et hanno intelligenza bonissima della latinità, et ancora hanno tradotto molte cose nella lingua volgare' ('at present there are many learned women, within and outside the convent walls, who know grammar and understand Latin culture and have translated many things into the vernacular').[83] This was not only the case in Milanese convents. In Florence, in the convent of San Jacopo di Ripoli, the aristocratic Fiammetta Frescobaldi (1518–86) produced an impressive *opus* that comprised also her vernacular translation of 118 saints' lives by Luigi Lippomano and Laurentius Surius (the German Lorenz Sauer). Frescobaldi's upper-rank background would have played an important role in her familiarity with the classical language.[84] Similarly, in 1657 in Brescia, sister Angelica Baitelli (1588–1650), also of aristocratic extraction, rendered from Latin into the vernacular the privileges granted to the convent of S. Giulia throughout the centuries, all the while adding to her translation her own comments, observations – and at times corrections – relative to the original manuscripts. The beneficiaries of her *Annali historici* were the other nuns in the convent and future abbesses 'che rara volta intendono l'idioma latino'

---

[80] These were only published posthumously in the eighteenth century as *Opuscoli inediti di Tarquinia Molza Modenese* […]. *Si premette la vita di Tarquinia compilate dal signor Domenico Vandelli* (Bergamo: Pietro Lancellotti, 1750).

[81] She also translated into Latin the first two *novelle* ('short stories') of Boccaccio's *Decameron*.

[82] Chiara Matraini, *Oratione d'Isocrate a Demonico figliuolo d'Ipponico, circa a l'essortazione de' costumi, che si convengono a tutti i nobilissimi giovani: di latino in volgare, tradotta* (Florence: no pub., 1556). On Matraini's translation, see Eleonora Carinci, 'Chiara Matraini traduttrice l'*Oratione d'Isocrate a Demonico* (1556) e altri scritti', in Sanson (ed.), *Women and Translation in the Italian Tradition* (forthcoming).

[83] I quote from the following edition: Paolo Morigia, *La nobiltà di Milano* (Milan: Giovanni Battista Bidelli, 1619), p. 272.

[84] Elissa B. Weaver, 'Suor Fiammetta Frescobaldi, storica dell'Ordine dei Predicatori e del monastero fiorentino di San Jacopo di Ripoli', in Gabriella Zarri and Gianni Festa (eds), *Il velo, la penna e la parola. Le domenicane: storia, istituzioni e scritture* (Firenze: Nerbini, 2009), pp. 185–91. See also Elissa Weaver, Angelo Cattaneo, and Giovanna Murano, 'Fiammetta Frescobaldi (1523–1586)', in Giovanna Murano (ed.), *Autographa: II. 1 Donne, sante e madonne (da Matilde di Canossa ad Artemisia Gentileschi)* (Imola: Editrice La Mandragora, 2018), pp. 173–81; Laura Saccardi, 'Le lettere in monastero: Fiammetta Frescobaldi OP', in Luisa Secchi Tarugi (ed.), *La donna nel Rinascimento. Amore, famiglia, cultura, potere. Atti del 29. convegno internazionale. Chianciano Terme-Montepulciano, 20-22 luglio 2017* (Florence: Franco Cesati Editore, 2019), pp. 245–64.

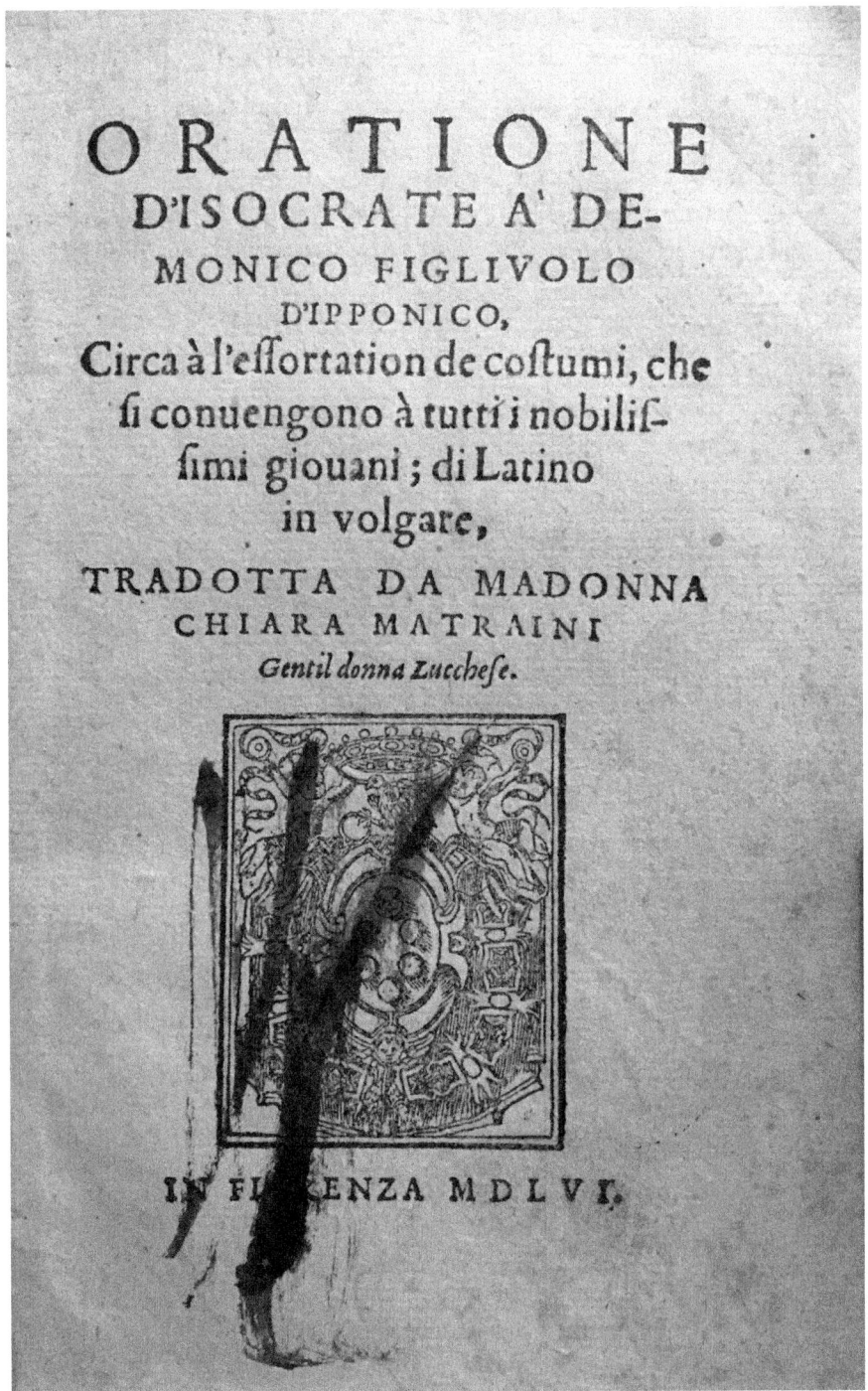

Figure 3.4 Chiara Matraini, *Oratione d'Isocrate a Demonico* (1556). As the title page indicates, Matraini translated Isocrates's oration to Demonicus from Greek via Latin. Biblioteca Marucelliana, Florence, MAG.Misc.592.26.

('who rarely understand the Latin language').[85] Baitelli too, like Ippolita Clara, Isabella Sori, and Arcangela Tarabotti before her, apologised for her limited skills due to her being a 'donniciola ignorante' ('a lowly ignorant woman').[86] Nonetheless in her writings she defied – in more ways than one – the limits imposed by societal restrictions and commonly held prejudices upon women of all social ranks, because of their gender.

In early modern Italy, literacy had many nuances of meaning that had to be carefully intertwined with different degrees of linguistic literacy in a multilingual context. A multiplicity of combinations of these varying degrees determined access to works of literature, and of learning more generally. In the case of women, the overruling factor that determined the outcome of any such combinations was their gender, the very essence of their existence.

[85] Angelica Baitelli, *Annali historici dell'edificatione erettione, & dotatione del Serenissimo Monasterio di S. Salvatore, & S. Giulia di Brescia* (Brescia: Antonio Rizzardi, 1657), p. 6. As a historian, Baitelli has been studied by Silvia Evangelisti, 'Angelica Baitelli, la storica', in Giulia Calvi (ed.), *Barocco al femminile* (Bari: Laterza, 1992), pp. 71–95, and Gabriella Zarri, 'La cultura monastica femminile nel Seicento: Angelica Baitelli', in Gabriella Zarri (ed.), *Libri di spirito: editoria religiosa in volgare nei secoli XV–XVII* (Turin: Rosenberg & Sellier, 2009), pp. 209–29 (orig. in Giancarlo Andenna (ed.), *Arte, cultura e religione in Santa Giulia* (Brescia: Grafo Edizioni, 2004), pp. 145–62). On Baitelli as a translator, see Helena Sanson, 'Two Nun Translators in Seventeenth-Century Italy: Angelica Baitelli and Maria Stella Scutellari', in Sanson (ed.), *Women and Translation in the Italian Tradition* (forthcoming).
[86] Baitelli, *Annali historici*, fol. A2r.

4

English Builders in Translation

CHRISTINE STEVENSON

AMONG THE 'USEFUL and ornamental Sculptures', engravings, in the 'Encyclopedy of the Arts and Sciences' forming the first part of Richard Blome's *The Gentlemans Recreation* (1686) are two dedicated to Sir Thomas Fitch, subscriber to the book and '*Patron*' of these particular plates (Figure 4.1).[1] They illustrate an eight-page chapter about 'Architecture', civil architecture that is, 'Fortification' counting as another art, or science. Each plate takes the form of a three-by-three grid. Most of the cells are filled with details of classical-architectural ornament, lettered from A to R: the bases, capitals, and entablatures belonging to each of the 'five Orders', whose parts are named in the text. Such carved ornament had appeared on English buildings of any pretensions and their fittings for a century and a half, and over the course of the seventeenth century it was applied increasingly systematically, accompanying or replacing older systems derived from heraldry and military architecture.[2] Texts at the foot of each plate identify Fitch and his 'great Knowledge in the Art of Architecture', the second with the aid of his coat of arms, with its leopard heads, and crest.[3]

Fitch, who was baptised in 1637, began as a working builder before he made his fortune as a contractor.[4] The *Gentlemans Recreation* identifies him,

---

[1] Richard Blome, *The Gentlemans Recreation. In Two Parts. The First Being an Encyclopedy of the Arts and Sciences. ... The Second Part, Treats of Horsmanship, Hawking, Hunting, Fowling, Fishing, and Agriculture ...* (London: S. Roycroft for Richard Blome, 1686).

[2] A good introduction in the present context is Nicholas Cooper, 'Rank, Manners and Display: The Gentlemanly House, 1500–1750', *Transactions of the Royal Historical Society*, 6th ser., 12 (2002), 291–310.

[3] That in the first plate reads, 'To the Right Worshipfull S.ʳ Thomas Fitch of Eltham, and Mount-Mascall in Kent, Knight & Baronet; S.ʳ yo.ʳ great Knowledge in the Art of Architecture renders you the Fittest Person to be selected in this Concern, whose name and Countenance will much add to the Reputation thereof, to whose Patronage, this Treatise with the Sculptures of the Severall Orders, is humbly Dedicated, by Richard Blome.'

[4] Except as noted, biographical information is from Joyce Fitch and Roy Stephens, 'Fitch, Sir Thomas, First Baronet (bap. 1637, d. 1688), Building Contractor', *Oxford Dictionary of National Biography*, 23 September 2004, Oxford University Press, www.oxforddnb.com/view/article/37416, accessed 20 February 2016, and Howard Colvin, *A Biographical Dictionary of British Architects, 1600–1840*, 4th edn (New Haven and London: Yale University Press, 2008), pp. 378–9. The former suggests that Fitch began as a bricklayer; the latter identifies him as a 'master carpenter'.

Proceedings of the British Academy, **246**, 71–93, © The British Academy 2022.

Figure 4.1 Richard Blome, *The Gentlemans Recreation*, 1686, plate facing
page 160: details of the classical orders (Call # B3213. Used by permission of the Folger
Shakespeare Library).

not as an expert in marshalling materials and labour on big sites operating, often simultaneously, all over the country but as a landowning baronet with a knowledge of the art of architecture, a knowledge made visible, synecdochally, by 16 illustrations of ornamental parts. What does this representation of Fitch tell us about the relationship between social hierarchy and architectural learning? Nothing new, in fact. However impressive Fitch's social ascent, architecture as an intellectual pursuit, as opposed to the business of construction, was appropriate to a baronet: the 'Art' was an impeccably genteel one. Nor is the selectiveness of Fitch's presentation in the book remarkable. 'Tradesmen', the commonest collective noun for people who worked with their hands, or sold the products of those who did so, came in many social as well as occupational species. Though they might be celebrated for their products (Figure 4.2), other forms of recognition were available when, as was generally acknowledged, old legal and status systems based on land ownership or tenure were significantly compromised, but hardly usurped, by other and sometimes newly prominent criteria: corporate and royal offices, wealth, the production of or involvement with publications like Blome's.

The *Gentlemans Recreation*'s illustrations of the art of architecture do, however, offer an opportunity to extend our appreciation of the complexities involved in defining architectural knowledge and its relation to social status in later seventeenth-century England. The book's dedication to James II explains that it was 'only designed for the *Nobility* and *Gentry*'. More specialised books about the art or business of architecture identify themselves as profitable for wider audiences. Like Blome's, they offer vocabularies, though as a way of bridging the gap between tradesmen and their betters with the aim of making buildings which are durable, convenient (a word then weightier than it is today), and beautiful. John Evelyn went further by writing, in 1664, that a mastery of one specific and very Latinate vocabulary, that of classical ornament, would earn the 'able *Workman*' not only 'applause and satisfaction' but social advancement.[5]

What follows looks first at the implications of Evelyn's suggestion for the careers of building contractors. The chapter then returns to Blome's book and the third of its 'Architecture' illustrations (Figure 4.4) to argue that, while classical ornament was prestigious, its attendant vocabulary was in fact an unstable source of worth, devalued as it was by association with both trade jargons and the pedantry that was antithetical to politeness.

---

[5] *A Parallel of the Antient Architecture with the Modern ... Written in French by Roland Freart, Sieur de Chambray; Made English for the Benefit of Builders*, trans. John Evelyn (London: John Place, 1664), dedicatory epistle to John Denham.

Figure 4.2 'The Elevation or Prospect of the West end of the Steeple of St Bridget als Brides in Fleetstreet …'. Engraving, 627 x 435 mm. © The Trustees of the British Museum.

'S.ʳ Thomas Fitch … Knight & Baronet'

We do not know how much Thomas Fitch worked with his hands before he became a prominent contractor in the national building world and made the money with which to build himself a 'good large and handsome' house, 'with a graceful front towards the *Thames*' at Blackfriars in London, and acquire, and probably build, the seat of Mount Mascall in Kent.[6] The other Kent house mentioned in the Blome illustrations, in Eltham, came with his marriage to Ann Comport, daughter and heir of a gentleman.[7] There is no record of an apprenticeship, and though Fitch was in his lifetime variously described as a bricklayer or a carpenter, occupational affixes could be contract-specific and anyway covered everyone from wage labourers to 'substantial businessmen'.[8]

In October 1674, the architect and natural philosopher Robert Hooke, then beginning work on the rebuilding of London's Bethlem Hospital along with Thomas's younger brother, the master-bricklayer John Fitch, 'Spoke for Mr. Th. Fitch about Knighthood' while dining with the recently knighted Christopher Wren.[9] Discussion about the honour had been prompted by Fitch's recent and successful completion of the task of converting London's Fleet Ditch into a tidal channel (1672–4). It was a huge job: Fitch, who in the end was paid more than £51,000, about 90 per cent of the total cost, regularly had 200 men on site, and more preparing the wharfing elsewhere.[10] It provides our earliest record of a career that would include other civic, and private, commissions as well as contracts all over the English coast for Charles II's Board of Ordnance, often with John Fitch.[11]

---

[6] William Maitland, *The History and Survey of London: From Its Foundation to the Present Time*, 2 vols (London: T. Osborne and J. Shipton, 1756), 2: 924. The Blackfriars house was built sometime between 1676 and 1681: Michael Cooper, *'A More Beautiful City': Robert Hooke and the Rebuilding of London after the Great Fire* (Stroud: Sutton, 2003), pp. 172–3, 219.

[7] Edward Hasted, *The History and Topographical Survey of the County of Kent*, 2nd edn, 12 vols (Canterbury: W. Bristow, 1797–1801), 1: 478.

[8] Lorna Weatherill, 'Consumer Behaviour and Social Status in England, 1660–1750', *Continuity and Change*, 1 (1986), 191–216 at 87. At first with the carpenter John Ball, Fitch contracted for the timber construction involved in the Fleet scheme in August 1671: T. F. Reddaway, *The Rebuilding of London after the Great Fire* (London: Jonathan Cape, 1940), pp. 59, 206. On 4 September 1679 Sir Ralph Verney's correspondent referred to 'Thomas Fitch Esq., bricklayer' in reporting the news about the Kent Sheriff's death: *Seventh Report of the Royal Commission on Historical Manuscripts*, Part I. *Report and Appendix* (London: Her Majesty's Stationery Office, 1870), p. 474.

[9] Walter Adams and Henry W. Robinson (eds), *The Diary of Robert Hooke …* (London: Taylor & Francis, 1935), p. 127 (17 October 1674).

[10] Reddaway, *Rebuilding of London*, pp. 206, 211–16; Cooper, *'A More Beautiful City'*, pp. 164–73; D'Maris Coffman, Judy Stephenson, and Nathan Sussman, 'Financing the Rebuilding of the City of London after the Great Fire of 1666', working paper, 2019, http://eh.net/eha/wp-content/uploads/2019/06/Sussman.pdf, accessed 9 March 2020.

[11] Howard Tomlinson, 'The Ordnance Office and the King's Forts, 1660–1714', *Architectural History*, 16 (1973), 5–25, 72–6 at 16–20; Martin Foreman and Steve Goodhand, 'The Construction of Hull Citadel', *Post-Medieval Archaeology*, 30 (1996), 143–85 at 149, 152, 178–9; Andrew Saunders, *Fortress Builder: Bernard de Gomme, Charles II's Military Engineer* (Exeter: University of Exeter Press, 2004).

Thomas Fitch was eventually knighted at Whitehall Palace in late 1679. The prompt was not the Fleet project or the military contracts, of which the first were then underway, but rather the death of the Sheriff of Kent. Charles II had 'pricked' Fitch to serve as the next one.[12] The hereditable title that was a baronetcy was supposedly conferred in September 1688, only a week or so before Fitch's death and the last of James II's creation before his flight to France at the end of the year.[13] If so, the *Gentlemans Recreation* illustrations anticipate it by referring to him as 'Knight and Baronet' and including the hand-badge of a baronetcy on the chevron of his arms.

The address in Blome's plate to Fitch's 'great knowledge in the Art of Architecture' has been taken as confirmation of his activity as an architect as well as a contractor.[14] More reliable evidence for Fitch's (and his brother's) designs does survive, though no longer much on the ground. An exception is the handsome Guildhall (former town hall) in Windsor, Berkshire (1687–90), a commission which casts more light on Fitch's favour in the royal household: the new town hall was the most important undertaking of a town corporation which had been packed with loyal courtiers immediately after James II's accession in 1685.[15]

It is on the Guildhall's and other accounts that Fitch has been used as an example of how John Evelyn might have imagined '*Architectus Manuarius*', the workman whose skills are 'necessary for the carrying on of a *Building* till it be arriv'd to the perfection of its first *Idea*', achieving a status equivalent to that of '*Architectus Ingenio*', the author of the idea, with the help of publications like Evelyn's.[16] These coinages appear in the 'Account of Architects and Architecture', a 28-page essay attached to Evelyn's translation (1664) of Roland Fréart de Chambray's *Parallele de l'architecture antique et de la moderne* (1650), a comparative study of the orders.[17] Fréart himself had explained few '*Technical tearms* belonging to

[12] *Seventh Report of the Royal Commission*, p. 474. Although sources drawing on the Verney correspondence assume Fitch's service as Sheriff, I can find no other evidence for it.

[13] John Burke and John Bernard Burke, *A Genealogical and Heraldic History of the Extinct and Dormant Baronetcies of England, Ireland and Scotland*, 2nd edn (London: Scott, Webster, and Geary, 1841), s.v. 'Fytche, of Eltham'; Edward Chamberlayne, *Angliae Notitia, or, The Present State of England …*, 18th edn (London: R. Scot, R. Chiswell, M. Gillyflower, and G. Sawbridge, 1694), p. 428.

[14] Colvin, *Biographical Dictionary*, p. 379.

[15] Andrew Barclay, 'The Court, Civic Politics and Architecture in Windsor, 1685–88', *The Court Historian*, 25 (2020), 51–64 at 58–61; Geoffrey Tyack, Simon Bradley, and Nikolaus Pevsner, *Berkshire*, Buildings of England (New Haven and London: Yale University Press, 2010), pp. 702–3. Wren, elected MP for New Windsor in January 1689, agreed to supervise its completion after Fitch's death: Robert Richard Tighe and John Edward Davis, *Annals of Windsor …*, vol. 2 (London: Longman, Brown, Green, Longmans, & Roberts, 1858), pp. 422–3.

[16] Matthew Walker, *Architects and Intellectual Culture in Post-Restoration England* (Oxford: Oxford University Press, 2017), pp. 42–3, 46–7. I do not agree with Walker that Evelyn thought that *Manuarius* could actually become *Ingenio*, but admittedly the text is ambiguous. John Evelyn, 'An Account of Architects & Architecture, Together with an Historical, and Etymological Explanation of Certain Tearms [*sic*] Particularly Affected by Architects', in *A Parallel of the Antient Architecture with the Modern*, pp. 115–42 at 117–18.

[17] On the *Parallele* and this translation, Eileen Harris and Nicholas Savage, *British Architectural Books and Writers, 1556–1785* (Cambridge and New York: Cambridge University Press, 1990), pp. 196–201; Walker, *Architects and Intellectual Culture*, pp. 36–50.

this *Art*', Evelyn wrote, because French '*Workmen* are generally more intelligent in [acquainted with] the proper expressions' than their English counterparts.[18] In proceeding 'from the *Person* to the *Thing*' Evelyn accordingly devoted most of his account of architecture itself to descriptive definitions of the Latin, Italian, and English classical-ornamental vocabulary organised as the parts to which they refer 'succeed one another in *Work*', that is, bottom to top. The '*Cornice*', for example, 'comprehends a small 1. *Regula*, 2. *Cymatium*, 3. *Dentelli*, 4. *Ovolo* or *Echinus*, 5. *Modilions* or Bedding-mouldings with support the *Corona* …', and so on.[19] He imagined a wide readership: 'whilest I seek to gratifie the politer *Students* of this magnificent Art, I am not in the least disdainful of the lowest condescentions to the capacities of the most vulgar understandings'. These understandings were particularly vulnerable to the confusion caused by ad-hoc naturalisations of the foreign vocabulary, the 'complemental and impertinent *Phrases*' which found their built equivalents in 'mischiefs and absurdities … busie and *Gotic* triflings' with the orders.[20]

Evelyn was attempting to clarify a vocabulary that was necessarily a shared one, though it is doubtful how far the *Parallel of the Antient Architecture with the Modern* filtered down the artisanal ranks (it was not cheap).[21] William Winde wrote to his client, and cousin, Lady Mary Bridgeman in 1698 about the mouldings for the gallery at Castle Bromwich Hall, Warwickshire. He reminded her that it would be better to leave the cornice plain than have it made by 'an Indiferent Carver' and suggested that she have Mr Anscough, a local person she had proposed, send him samples: 'I would have but two of the members Carved, wch is the cyma reverse, under the ogee, and the ovelo undr ye planceres [planceer], ye first withe Lace & ye second with Eyes & ankers.'[22] This was a common language. Castle Bromwich's remodelling had been underway for 13 years and Lady Bridgeman had conducted the entire correspondence with Winde during that period. She may or may not have needed to translate 'ovelo' (ovolo) into something like 'bulging quarter-circle moulding' for Mr Anscough; that was maybe one test of his competence.

As the form of Evelyn's account of 'Architecture' suggests, the historical relationship between classical ornament and its vocabulary ran deeper than that between signified and signifier. The ornament's prestige derived in part from being analogised with the Latin language: we 'have fewer Judges of a Latine

[18] Evelyn, 'Account', p. 113.
[19] Evelyn, 'Account', pp. 113, 135.
[20] Evelyn, 'Account', p. 113; *Parallel of the Antient Architecture with the Modern*, dedicatory epistle to John Denham.
[21] Felicity Henderson, 'Faithful Interpreters? Translation Theory and Practice at the Early Royal Society', *Notes and Records of the Royal Society*, 67 (2013), 101–22 at 116–17. The 'Account's' cross-references to the book's illustrations are so scanty that one wonders how any reader made sense of the definitions.
[22] Geoffrey Beard, 'William Winde and Interior Design', *Architectural History*, 27 (1984), 150–62 at 155.

style in building than in writing', Wren, a superb Latinist, wrote jokily to the Dean of St Paul's Cathedral about its repair a few months before London's Great Fire of 1666, 'but I hope you will goe to the charges of trew latine'.[23] The prestige was reinforced through the external discourses provided by new English-language publications and translations of Italian- and French-language treatises on the orders, as well as by the habit of using this ornament to epitomise an entire art.[24]

'Carpenters (as Carpenters)'

Evelyn presented four *architecti* in the 'Account of Architects and Architecture'. To *Manuarius* and *Ingenio* he added '*Architectus Sumptuarius*', 'a full and overflowing *Purse*: since he who bears *this* may justly also be styled a *Builder* … the *Primum mobile*', and '*Architectus Verborum*', who like the modest author writes about the subject.[25] *Verborum* is Evelyn's own contribution to the analysis of a difficulty latent in writing about European architecture since the mid-fifteenth century: who are the builders? Those who actually do build, those who pay for the building, or those who execute their independent '*Judgment*' when it comes to its planning and other dispositions (*Ingenio*)?[26]

All the *architecti* are valid within the analysis of any architectural culture, but as descriptions of roles, not individuals. Certainly static patronal and occupational identities simply do not work for a period and a place when design – and for that matter writing about architecture – was an 'ad-hoc … activity dictated by opportunity rather than full-time commitment' for the vast majority of practitioners.[27] 'Carpenters (*as* Carpenters)' work to the architect's direction, wrote Fitch's

[23] Arthur T. Bolton and H. Duncan Hendry (eds), *The Thirteenth Volume of the Wren Society. Designs and Drawings by Sir Christopher Wren for St. Paul's Cathedral, the Residentiaries' House and the Deanery* (London: Wren Society, 1936), p. 44. Christy Anderson, 'Learning to Read Architecture in the English Renaissance', in Lucy Gent (ed.), *Albion's Classicism: The Visual Arts in Britain, 1550–1660* (New Haven and London: Yale University Press, 1995), pp. 239–86 at 276.

[24] Christy Anderson, 'Monstrous Babels: Language and Architectural Style in the English Renaissance', in Georgia Clarke and Paul Crossley (eds), *Architecture and Language: Constructing Identity in European Architecture, c.1000–c.1650* (Cambridge: Cambridge University Press, 2000), pp. 148–61 at 160–1. On external systems of meaning see also Bert De Munck, 'The Agency of Branding and the Location of Value: Hallmarks and Monograms in Early Modern Tableware Industries', *Business History*, 54 (2012), 1055–76 at 1068–9; Bert De Munck, 'Artisans, Products and Gifts: Rethinking the History of Material Culture in Early Modern Europe', *Past & Present*, 224.1 (2014), 39–74 at 65–7, 73–4.

[25] Evelyn, 'Account', pp. 117–18, 121; Walker, *Architects and Intellectual Culture*, pp. 37–9.

[26] On the difficulty as inaugurated by Leon Battista Alberti, Tim Anstey, 'Authorship and Authority in L. B. Alberti's *De Re Aedificatoria*', *Nordisk Arkitekturforskning*, 4 (2003), 19–25 at 21–2.

[27] Hentie Louw, 'The "Mechanick Artist" in Late Seventeenth-Century English and French Architecture: The Work of Robert Hooke, Christopher Wren and Claude Perrault Compared as Products of an Interactive Science/Architecture Relationship', in Michael Cooper and Michael Hunter (eds), *Robert Hooke: Tercentennial Studies* (Aldershot: Ashgate, 2006), pp. 181–99 at 181.

contemporary Joseph Moxon.[28] The parenthetical insertion is there because some-times carpenters acted as architects, with all the activation of different cultural competences that might entail: conversing about volutes, perhaps, as well as about roof trusses.[29]

Evelyn's scheme can accommodate Fitch's climb up the social ladder: in Italy, he wrote approvingly, the knowledge of architecture '(and to speak properly in its *tearms &c.*) is universal' to the extent that even '*Manuary*' architects of 'obscure extraction' have been 'rewarded with *Knighthood*'. Yet it cannot quite bring itself to recognise the difference between individuals and their roles: even Gian Lorenzo Bernini, who had a craft training, appears as one of the manuaries so rewarded (with a papal knighthood), which makes makes one realise quite how rarified the *Ingenio* category is.[30] Evelyn was definitely not, in 1664, in a position to appreciate the way in which building contractors and property developers (*Architectus Pecuniarum?*) would after London's Great Fire two years later come to dominate a construction industry which after textiles and clothing was likely the second biggest in the metropolis.[31]

Such undertakings demanded robust credit, in both the financial and personal senses, but it could be grown. Samuel Fulkes (Fulks, Foulkes) was first recorded as a mason working for 2*s*.6*d*. a day at Whitehall Palace in 1664.[32] He 'took small contracts of '£9, £14, £117, and £613 in the 1670's and much larger contracts for £1,888, £1,946, £3,204 and £3,335 in the 1680's', including at parish churches rebuilt after the Fire, and in 1683 together with William Wise contracted to employ a total of 42 masons, rough-setters, sawyers and labourers at the Winchester Palace site. In 1687 Fulkes took on nothing less than the west end of Wren's St Paul's Cathedral (begun 1675); he also added the steeple (1701–4), designed by Wren, to the tower of St Bride off Fleet Street (Figure 4.2).[33]

---

[28] Joseph Moxon, *Mechanick Exercises, or, The Doctrine of Handy-Works* (Scarsdale: The Early American Industries Association, 1979), p. 148 (my emphasis): a facsimile of the third edition (1703) of Moxon's book, first published in parts in 1678–9.

[29] On such competences, Lawrence E. Klein, 'Politeness and the Interpretation of the British Eighteenth Century', *Historical Journal*, 45 (2002), 869–98 at 872–3.

[30] Evelyn, 'Account', pp. 120 (quotations), 119.

[31] Peter Earle, *The Making of the English Middle Class: Business, Society and Family Life in London, 1660–1730* (Berkeley: University of California Press, 1989), p. 22. On building in London, Elizabeth McKellar, *The Birth of Modern London: The Development and Design of the City, 1660–1720* (Manchester: Manchester University Press, 1999); Judy Z. Stephenson, *Contracts and Pay: Work in London Construction 1660–1785* (London: Palgrave Macmillan, 2019).

[32] Judy Stephenson kindly informs me that this is almost certainly the charge-out rate levied by the contractor; Fulkes probably took home 26–28*d*. daily. The fact that he was named in the Office of Works record suggests but does not prove that he had finished an apprenticeship; he took the freedom of the Haberdashers Company by redemption in 1671.

[33] Douglas Knoop and G. P. Jones, 'The Rise of the Mason Contractor', *Journal of the Royal Institute of British Architects*, 3rd ser., 43 (17 October 1936), 1061–71 at 1063 (quotations); Douglas Knoop and G. P. Jones, *The London Mason in the Seventeenth Century* (Manchester: Manchester University Press, 1935), pp. 33–4, 51–2, 57, 77–8; James W. P. Campbell, 'Building a Fortune: The Finances of the Stonemasons Working on the Rebuilding of St Paul's Cathedral 1675–1720', in *Proceedings of the Third*

Fulkes became a specialist mason-contractor; fortunes were more typically made, or maintained, on the basis of a wider product range. Edward Marshall (*c.* 1598–1675) acted as mason-contractor, architect, and carver of architectural ornament and church monuments: John Aubrey drew upon Marshall's copies of epitaphs in compiling what would become known as his *Brief Lives* of notable contemporaries. Edward's son Joshua Marshall (1628–78), who succeeded him as Master Mason to the crown in 1673, became one of the St Paul's contractors, dealt in stone, made funerary monuments, and speculated in house-building.[34] Joshua was worth around £14,000 at the time of his death, which made him the richest manufacturer among Peter Earle's sample of 375 London citizens who died between 1665 and 1720.[35]

We know nothing specific about the Fitch brothers', Fulkes's, and the Marshalls' learning, but during their apprenticeships and for the rest of their working lives they certainly watched and talked with people at work as well as with others like Aubrey and John Webb, friend of and collaborator with Edward Marshall and the most experienced, as well as intellectually ambitious, specialist architect of the mid-seventeenth century.[36] They studied the existing buildings and monuments to which their patrons regularly referred in commissioning their own; and collected prints, drawings, and notebooks, perhaps through bequests. They bought or borrowed books offering to help them address patrons (including defaulting ones) in person and in letters; calculate quantities of materials, or mouldings carved; keep their accounts; assess investments in property rights – and learn about the classical orders.[37] Even men like Samuel Fulkes, with no apparent interest in adopting the *Ingenio* role or in selling funerary monuments or chimney-pieces adorned this way, were overseeing the production and placement of classical ornament like the pilaster capitals on the famously diminishing stages of St Bride's steeple. That said,

---

International Congress on Construction History, vol. 1 (Cottbus: Brandenburg University of Technology, 2009), unpaginated; Paul Jeffery, *The City Churches of Sir Christopher Wren* (London: Hambledon, 1996), pp. 224–5.

[34] Adam White, 'A Biographical Dictionary of London Tomb Sculptors *c.*1560–*c.*1660', *Walpole Society*, 61 (1999), 1–162 at 86–7 and Colvin, *Biographical Dictionary*, pp. 679–80 (Edward); Ingrid Roscoe, Emma Hardy, and M. G. Sullivan (eds), *A Biographical Dictionary of Sculptors in Britain, 1660–1851* (New Haven and London: Yale University Press, 2009), pp. 808–13 (both Marshalls).

[35] Earle, *Making of the English Middle Class*, p. 33.

[36] In 1655 Webb, considering the chimneypiece at Lamport Hall, Northants, wrote that 'because of ye enrichments I would wish it [the lower part] were wrought here in Towne by Mr Marshall': John Bold, *John Webb: Architectural Theory and Practice in the Seventeenth Century* (Oxford: Clarendon Press, 1989), p. 85.

[37] See, for example, [Antoine de Courtin], *The Rules of Civility; or, Certain Ways of Deportment Observed in France ... Translated out of French* (London: J. Martyn and John Starkey, 1671); Stephen Primatt, *The City & Country Purchaser and Builder* (London: S. Speed, 1667); Stephen Monteage, *Debtor and Creditor Made Easie, or, A Short Instruction for the Attaining the Right Use of Accounts* (London: J. R., 1675). On property agreements, William C. Baer, 'The Institution of Residential Investment in Seventeenth-Century London', *Business History Review*, 76.3 (2002), 515–51.

whatever Thomas Fitch's aspirations and how he set about realising them he was unlikely to have thought that studying classical detailing alone would do the trick.

'Books of *Architecture*'

Fitch trained, probably by apprenticeship, as either a carpenter or a bricklayer, and then became rich by building wharves and citadels. In this way (as Evelyn might have imagined the trajectory) he acquired the leisure to read about what Moxon called 'Architecture' in his list of available English-language books on the subject: all but one are translations, with emphasis on the orders.[38] Moxon, writing in the late 1670s, thought that there were plenty of such books. Fifteen years earlier Balthazar Gerbier had described 'this refined Age, which abounds in Books, with the Portractures of the Out and Inside of the best Buildings', but at the same time Evelyn lamented the 'few assistances which our *Workmen* have of this nature'.[39] His translation of Fréart de Chambray's *Parallele* was to fill the dangerously wide gap between the ignorant pretensions and 'busie and *Gotic* triflings' of English artificers and the indifference of their betters, on the one hand, and the distinguished practitioners and well-informed nobility of France and Italy on the other.[40] In any case, we assume, Fitch graduated to a condition of *un*-trainedness through autodidacticism, the self-education which writers and publishers claimed was necessary for a mastery of 'architecture', that 'noble Art'.[41]

Fitch's social elevation was both flagged and propelled by the titles, land ownership, at least two splendid portraits (Figure 4.3),[42] and the appearance of his and his wife Ann's names and arms on the 'Architecture' plates and other prints published by

[38] Moxon, *Mechanick Exercises*, pp. 117, 156 (he understood architecture itself as a broader practice: pp. 130, 144, 148); Bold, *John Webb*, pp. 19–20.

[39] Moxon, *Mechanick Exercises*, p. 117; Balthazar Gerbier, *Counsel and Advise to All Builders for the Choice of Their Surveyours, Clarks of Their Works, Bricklayers, Masons, Carpenters, and Other Work-Men Therein Concerned ...* (London: Thomas Mabb, 1663), sigs g2v–g3, p. 7 (quotation); *Parallel of the Antient Architecture with the Modern*, dedicatory epistle to John Denham.

[40] *Parallel of the Antient Architecture with the Modern*, dedicatory epistle to John Denham, and Evelyn, 'Account', p. 120.

[41] 'An Account of Two Books. I. Cours d'architecture, enseigné dans l'Academie Royale d'Architecture, Premiere Partie; par M. Francois Blondel ...', *Philosophical Transactions*, 10.122 (30 March 1675), 549–50 at 549 (quotation); the review is usually attributed to Henry Oldenburg, the Secretary of the Royal Society. Autodidacticism in architectural learning forms a major theme in Walker's *Architects and Intellectual Culture* (pp. 25–7, 40–2, 46–50).

[42] Peter Lely, to whom the Norfolk portrait illustrated is attributed, died in 1680, when Fitch was about 43. It has been assumed that the painted 'S.ʳ Thomas Fytch Barᵗ' was added later: see Richard Johns's entry on the National Inventory of Continental European Paintings database, https://vads.ac.uk/large.php?uid=85382&sos=3, accessed 2 August 2018. Another portrait, in the collection of the University of Leicester, is attributed to Michael Dahl, who during Fitch's lifetime resided in London between 1682 and 1684.

Figure 4.3 Portrait of Sir Thomas Fitch attributed to Peter Lely. Oil on canvas, 126.2 x 102.4 cm. Norwich Castle Museum & Art Gallery (Norfolk Museums Service).

Blome, including illustrations for a sumptuous pair of biblical 'histories' (1688–90), translations of the so-called Bible de Royaumont (1670).[43]

[43] Fitch's arms (as a knight) appear on at least one edition (c.1680?) of a map of Scandinavia which Blome began publishing in 1669–70 (www.raremaps.com/gallery/detail/23780/a-generall-mapp-of-scandinavia-where-are-the-estates-and-ki-blome, accessed 1 March 2020) and another of Kent (www.mapmogul.com/en-GB/english-counties/a-mapp-of-kent-with-its-lathes-and-hundreds/prod_78034, accessed 9 April 2020). He and Ann each sponsored an Old and New Testament illustration in Nicolas

This kind of 'dispersed sponsorship' of book illustrations was unique to Britain. It was conventionally understood as a 'disinterested act of patronage', free from the taints of commercial advantage or even recompense, the costs outweighing the returns.[44] More tacitly, it signalled common cause with other subscribing 'members of the armigerous classes', right up to the royal family, in a generally celebrated but vaguely defined programme of national improvement to be achieved, in part, through translations.[45] Even more tacitly, subscribing to an improving book and patronising its illustrations connoted a wholesome breadth of voluntary obligation and investigation: another kind of translation, across the boundaries set by narrow commercial interests. In 1667, Thomas Sprat explained that gentlemen, by definition not obliged to be 'peculiarly conversant about any one sort of *Arts*, may often find out their *Rarities* and *Curiosities* sooner, than those who have their minds confin'd wholly to them'. Theirs is necessarily a kind of knowledge different from that of those who 'chiefly labor for present livelyhood, and therefore cannot defer their *Expectations* so long, as is commonly requisit for the ripening of any *new Contrivance*'.[46]

Yet commercial interest regularly prompted the accommodation of Sprat's wider and higher aims. Thomas Fitch was just one of 231 'Benefactors' to the *Gentlemans Recreation*. Typically for its date, it found no place for economic topics among its 25 subject headings, but like several of Blome's publications it represented a substantial undertaking commensurate with one of Fitch's own.[47] It is an excellent example of the book-object 'whose making, keeping and use brings people and objects into distinctive types of social relations with one another', especially when it came to the making.[48] Though this book was ostensibly no simple commodity, framed as its subscription proposals surely were (they do not survive) to foreground the patronage and not the cash extended, it formed part of what Craig Clunas has

---

Fontaine, *The History of the New Testament* ..., trans. Joseph Raynor (London: Samuel Roycroft for Richard Blome, 1688) and Nicolas Fontaine, *The History of the Old Testament* ..., trans. John Coughen, Anthony Horneck, 'and other Orthodox Divines' (London: Samuel Roycroft for Richard Blome, 1690): see the list of subscribers in the latter. Lady Fitch was a widow by 1690.

[44] Antony Griffiths, *The Print before Photography: An Introduction to European Printmaking 1550–1820* (London: British Museum Press, 2016), pp. 314–15 (quotation), 356–7.

[45] M. C. W. Hunter, 'The Crown, the Public and the New Science, 1689–1702', *Notes and Records of the Royal Society of London*, 43 (1989), 99–116 at 109 (quotation); Henderson, 'Faithful Interpreters?', 111–12.

[46] Thomas Sprat, *The History of the Royal-Society of London for the Improving of Natural Knowledge* (London: J. Martyn and J. Allestry, 1667), p. 391; Malcolm Oster, 'The Scholar and the Craftsman Revisited: Robert Boyle as Aristocrat and Artisan', *Annals of Science*, 49 (1992), 255–76 at 265.

[47] Julian Hoppit, 'The Contexts and Contours of British Economic Literature, 1660–1760', *Historical Journal*, 49 (2006), 79–110 at 81–2. The best account of Blome's book publishing remains Sarah L. C. Clapp, 'The Subscription Enterprises of John Ogilby and Richard Blome', *Modern Philology*, 30 (1933), 365–79; see also Hunter, 'The Crown, the Public and the New Science', 107–9.

[48] Warren Boutcher, 'Literary Art and Agency? Gell and the Magic of the Early Modern Book', in Liana Chua and Mark Elliott (eds), *Distributed Objects: Meaning and Mattering after Alfred Gell* (New York and Oxford: Berghahn, 2013), pp. 155–75 at 159.

called the commoditisation of knowledge itself.[49] Writing about late sixteenth- and early seventeenth-century (late Ming) China, Clunas describes the 'growth in the acceptability and use of objectified, fact-centred methods of cultivation among the elite'.[50] Blome's *Gentlemans Recreation* is also a notable manifestation of this growth as it showed itself in later seventeenth-century England, and one all the more notable for his presentation of it as the focus of an exceptionally wide 'community of practice' among subscribers, contributors, translators, draughtsmen, and engravers.[51] This suggested the construction metaphor that was then nearly inescapable in accounts of any kind of collaborative project, or polity. The Preface describes Blome's 'Building up of this elaborate *Work*'; the lettering on the first of the Fitch's plates explains that he was the 'Fittest Person to be Selected in this Concern', as if Fitch were a successful bidder for a contract.[52] Blome was the 'undertaker'-architect.

The ornamental details illustrated in Fitch's plates are the 'expression of structural components', representations of tectonic relationships that are ultimately dictated by gravity.[53] Beams need supports; rain falls down, and walls need protection from it (Figure 4.1, 'L' and 'O'). Of course, even the humblest buildings have beams and supports and eaves. The difference between them and buildings in a classical style is made by the articulation or animation of the statics, and of the joints between parts, through the use of ornament like a scotia (concave moulding) between two tori (convex mouldings) at the bottom of a column where it meets the plinth (Figure 4.1, 'Q').[54] Though the finer proportional relationships among these parts, or sub-parts are not readily apparent, treatises made them the subjects of keen attention: Blome's plates do so by showing each part's height in relation to a standard and in theory arbitrary module ('Model').[55] That, in essence, is architectural classicism.

---

[49] Blome's *Proposals for the Printing Le Grand's Histories of Nature, Being an Entire Course or Body of Philosophy ...* (London, s.n., 1693), p. [2] explain that regular subscriptions, 50*s.*, yielded a copy in sheets; an additional 5 guineas brought a '*Memorial*' of arms and titles '*Engraven* to a *Sculpture* as *Patron* thereof' and a display of one's arms 'amongst the *Benefactors*'. See also the *Proposals for the Printing of Guillim's Heraldry* ([London]: [Richard Blome], 1674): subscribers of 26*s.* would have their coat armour '*Registred ...* with some Honourable remarks of their *Family*, to remain to posterity'. The plates in the architecture section of the Royal Institute of British Architects Library's copy of the *Gentlemans Recreation* have been coloured.

[50] Craig Clunas, *Superfluous Things: Material Culture and Social Status in Early Modern China* (Honolulu: University of Hawai'i Press, 2004), pp. 118, 167 (quotation).

[51] On the communities, Terttu Nevalainen, 'Social Networks and Language Change in Tudor and Stuart London: Only Connect?', *English Language & Linguistics*, 19 (2015), supplement: *Sense of Place in the History of English*, 269–92 at 271.

[52] See note 3.

[53] Christy Anderson, 'A Gravity in Public Places: Inigo Jones and Classical Architecture', in Louise Durning and Richard Wrigley (eds), *Gender and Architecture* (Chichester: John Wiley, 2000), pp. 7–28 at 20.

[54] Edward R. Ford, *The Architectural Detail* (New York: Princeton Architectural Press, 2011), p. 178. Of course, costlier materials generally accompanied the investment in workmanship that this like other kinds of ornament announces.

[55] Mario Carpo, 'Drawing with Numbers: Geometry and Numeracy in Early Modern Architectural Design', *Journal of the Society of Architectural Historians*, 62 (2003), 448–69.

The third plate illustrating Blome's 'Architecture' chapter, which had another patron, is quite different in its approach to the subject and unique as a presentation of it (Figure 4.4).[56] Blome explained that he had borrowed the format of the 'Eliptical Tables' which diagram each of his Encyclopedy's arts and sciences from Christophe de Savigny's *Tableaux accomplis de tous les arts liberaux* (1587).[57] An oval frame decorated with builders' and surveyors' tools contains free-form bubbles, whose links diagram the relationships between building types and sub-types (fortification creeps in here), materials, and the considerations of 'Duration' (durability, involving the choice of materials), 'Healthfullness & conveniency', and 'Beauty'. The last ropes in the classical orders (via 'Stateliness, & Unniformity'). They are introduced in the second-highest bubble, though a little awkwardly: the lists of the five orders, beginning with the Tuscan, and then of their constituent parts are squashed against the edge of the frame (upper right, in Figure 4.4).

One sympathises with the table's designer, who had nothing to go on – de Savigny's *Tableaux* do not include architecture – and who was grappling with a peculiar relationship. Blome's readership would have recognised architecture as both a (high-end) product and as a branch of knowledge, as the 'result of two overlapping and necessary practices': those of solid and convenient construction on the one hand and conveying 'Beauty' through ornament on the other.[58] We might take for granted the distinction between a building's structure and its ornament, but it is a relatively modern one in the Western world. What Jacques Derrida called the 'logic of the supplement', whereby (in the words of Donald Keith Hedrick) 'that which is the "supplement" or dependent category [beauty, ornament] on the one hand appears *superfluous* and on the other appears *necessary for completion*' has become an important analytical tool in art and architectural history.[59]

Solidity, convenience, and beauty must be united, and the latter must not be confused with mere words. Surveyors, wrote Gerbier in 1663, referring to a role that could involve design, are sometimes 'minded more to show that they were

[56] The donor was John Speccot of Penheale in Cornwall (1665–1705), on whom see *The History of Parliament: The House of Commons 1690–1715* (2002), www.historyofparliamentonline.org/volume/1690-1715/member/speccot-john-1665-1705, accessed 12 March 2020.

[57] *Gentlemans Recreation*, Preface; Steffen Siegel, *Tabula: Figuren der Ordnung um 1600* (Berlin: Akademie Verlag, 2009), pp. 168–71.

[58] Anne-Marie Sankovitch, 'Structure/Ornament and the Modern Figuration of Architecture', *The Art Bulletin*, 80 (1998), 687–717, especially 687, 711 (quotation); Antoine Picon, *Ornament: The Politics of Architecture and Subjectivity* (Chichester: John Wiley and Sons, 2013), p. 38; Jonathan Hay, 'The Passage of the Other: Elements for a Redefinition of Ornament', in Gülru Necipoğlu and Alina Payne (eds), *Histories of Ornament: From Global to Local* (Princeton: Princeton University Press, 2016), pp. 62–9, 357–8, at 64.

[59] Jacques Derrida, *The Truth in Painting*, trans. Geoff Bennington and Ian McLeod (Chicago: University of Chicago Press, 1987), p. 64; Donald Keith Hedrick, 'The Ideology of Ornament: Alberti and the Erotics of Renaissance Urban Design', *Word & Image*, 3 (1987), 111–37 at 125 (emphases in the original).

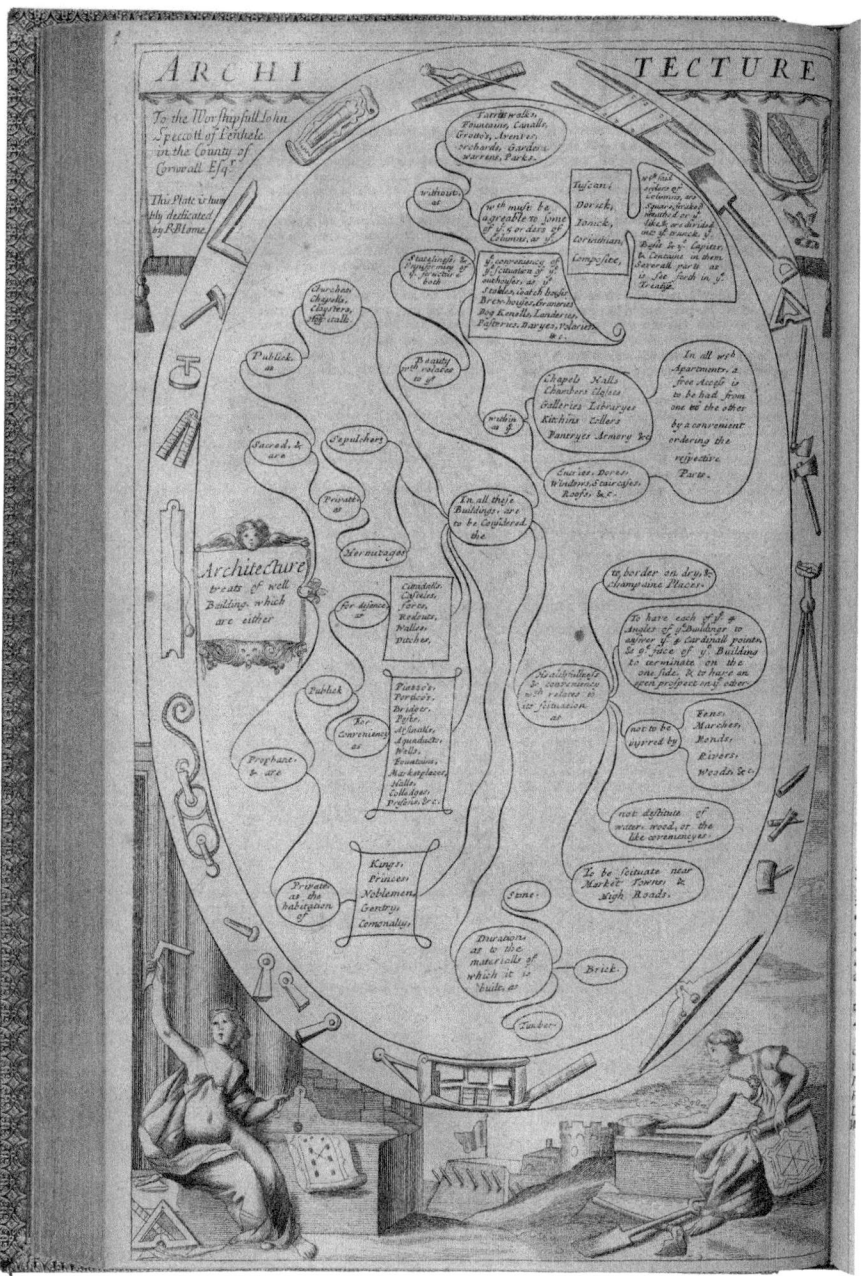

Figure 4.4 Richard Blome, *The Gentlemans Recreation*, 1686, plate facing page 157: 'Architecture' (Call # B3213. Used by permission of the Folger Shakespeare Library).

skill'd in *describing* of Columns, Pilasters, Cornishes and Frontispices, (though for the most part placed as the wilde *Americans* are wont to put their Pendants at their Nostrils) then to have studied Conveniency, and what most Necessary'.[60] The identification of terminological extravagance with ludicrous results was already old: 'when I hear our Architects thunder out their Bombast words of *Pillasters*, *Architraves* and *Cornonices*, of the *Corinthian* and *Dorick* Orders, and such like stuff, my imagination is presently possess'd … when after all, I find them but the paltry peices of my own Kitchin Door', wrote Michel de Montaigne, in Charles Cotton's translation (1685–6) of the *Essays*.[61] Gerbier's observation was only the beginning of a regular critique of jumped-up tradesmen anxious to promote, not the timeless and beautiful verities of the orders, but their own careers. '*Gentlemen-Mechanicks*', Evelyn called them, contemptuously.[62]

These complexities do not ruffle Blome's 'Architecture' chapter's text, which was written by Sir Henry Hobart, 4th baronet of Blickling Hall in Norfolk, whose interests in the subject are otherwise unknown.[63] It is an undistinguished product of autodidacticism, beginning with a terse résumé of the diagram which prefaces it: 'ARCHITECTURE is the *Art* of *Building*. *Buildings* are either *Sacred*, or *Prophane*. … *Prophane Buildings* are also Publick or Private; … Private or particular *Buildings* are the *Habitations*, as well of the *Nobles* and *Gentry*, as of the *Pesant*.'[64] (The implication that English society could, via its houses, be satisfactorily categorised under three headings would have struck many readers as comical.) Overall, however, the text is dominated by lists, keyed to the illustrations, of the discrete parts of the orders shown.

The text does not draw attention to its use of perhaps-unfamiliar words but sometimes supplies equivalents: 'the *Voluta* [volute] or *Scroll*', a defining feature of Ionic and Composite capitals (Figure 4.1, middle row), for example.[65] By contrast, Joseph Moxon's English-language version of Giacomo Barozzi da Vignola's *Regola delli cinque ordini d'architettura* (1562), called *Vignola: Or the Compleat*

---

[60] Gerbier, *Counsel and Advise*, p. 4 (my emphasis of 'describing'). The wildness of the Americans is an allusion to an ill-fated Dutch expedition to the Guianas, during which Gerbier's daughter was killed by mutinous sailors. Jeremy Wood, 'Gerbier, Sir Balthazar (1592–1663/1667), Art Agent, Miniature Painter, and Architect', *Oxford Dictionary of National Biography*, 23 September 2004, Oxford University Press, www.oxforddnb.com/view/article/10562, accessed 19 April 2016.

[61] *Essays of Michael, Seigneur de Montaigne …*, trans. Charles Cotton, 3 vols (London: T. Basset, M. Gilliflower, and W. Hensman, 1685–6), 1: 597.

[62] Evelyn, 'Account', p. 119.

[63] Blome, *Gentlemans Recreation*, 'Preface to the Reader'. On Hobart (c.1657–1698), *The History of Parliament: The House of Commons 1690–1715* (2002), www.histparl.ac.uk/volume/1690-1715/member/hobart-sir-henry-1657-98, accessed 7 March 2020.

[64] Blome, *Gentlemans Recreation*, p. 157.

[65] Blome, *Gentlemans Recreation*, p. 160. 'Voluta', like so many other classical-architectural terms, was introduced to English-language publication in 1563, in Shute's *First and Chief Groundes of Architecture* ('voluta, n.', *OED Online*, March 2020, www.oed.com/view/Entry/224593, accessed 12 March 2020); it seems not to have become the modern 'volute' until the 1690s ('volute, n.', *OED Online*, March 2020, www.oed.com/view/Entry/224596, accessed 17 April 2020). Peter Burke, 'Translating the Language

Architect (1655), from which the pictures in the plates dedicated to Fitch were copied, is prefaced by a list explaining the 'hard words' – '*Voluta* the same that *Scroll* is' – which might be puzzling. 'Hard' words was a customary way of labelling borrowings from other languages.[66]

Unlike Blome's fat folio 'for the *Nobility* and *Gentry*', Moxon's *Vignola* is a compact octavo (a translation from the Dutch [1650], itself taken from a heavily abridged French version [1631] of Vignola's text) addressed to the 'Ingenuous Artist', that is, artificer, and specifically the 'young Practitioner'.[67] Though it is tempting to scrutinise the difference in phrasing between '*Voluta* the same that *Scroll* is' (Moxon) and '*Voluta* or *Scroll*' (Hobart) – the one suggests a need, as perceived, to explain through translation, and the other, to show delicacy in the face of consumers who might not care to think that they *need* the translation – the evidence does not bear such a weight of interpretation. Lists of 'hard' classical-ornamental words were customary; what is interesting is the way they seem to have been considered as one of the regular cultural competences, not of the educated patron, but of the artificer.[68]

Metaphorical, though not necessarily classical, architecture permeates seventeenth-century English writing. Foundations, pinnacles, and pillars dot a landscape roamed by churchmen, natural philosophers, and polemicists; in this respect, the language of architecture was itself an 'intellectual accomplishment'.[69] The specific vocabulary of the orders was something different. It was likely available for oral use in English before it began to appear in print in the later sixteenth century,[70] and it is also likely that the next century's printed lexicons were catching up with trade practice at least as much as they were informing it. In 1672 the joiner John Symes (Symms) agreed to wainscot and make the screen for the hall at London's Brewers Hall, rebuilt after the Fire, for £355. The panelling was to be 17 feet high, 'with Archetrive frees & Cornish &: 6 frontispeces', the screen 'to bee maid with

of Architecture', in Jane Tylus and Karen Newman (eds), *Early Modern Cultures of Translation* (Philadelphia: University of Pennsylvania Press, 2015), pp. 25–44 at 43.

[66] D. T. Starnes, 'English Dictionaries of the Seventeenth Century', *Studies in English*, 17 (1937), 15–51 at 20, 24, 27, 30, 39.

[67] Carolina Mangone, 'Vernacular Vignola', *Art in Translation*, 10 (2018), 30–54 at 45 (which mistakenly identifies the translator as 'John' Moxon); Harris and Savage, *British Architectural Books*, pp. 352, 458–60.

[68] Wider architectural-historical questions have come to the fore in scholarship on the uses of the vernacular in seventeenth-century translations of treatises, particularly those published in the north Netherlands. Mangone, 'Vernacular Vignola'; in addition to the sources she cites see Andrew Hopkins and Arnold Witte, 'From Deluxe Architectural Book to Builder's Manual: The Dutch Editions of Scamozzi's *L'Idea della Architettura Universale*', *Quaerendo*, 26 (1996), 274–302.

[69] Anthony Geraghty, *The Sheldonian Theatre: Architecture and Learning in Seventeenth-Century Oxford* (New Haven and London: Yale University Press, 2013), p. 53; Christine Stevenson, *The City and the King: Architecture and Politics in Restoration London* (New Haven and London: Yale University Press, 2013).

[70] David Cast, 'Speaking of Architecture: The Evolution of a Vocabulary in Vasari, Jones, and Sir John Vanbrugh', *Journal of the Society of Architectural Historians*, 52 (1993), 179–88 at 181.

frontispeces & Corenthan Colloms', 'ye upper end of ye hall to bee done with palasters with theare Capitalls & fustoans'.[71] 'Cornish' is a phonetic spelling of the usual 'corniche' (cornice); 'palaster' for pilaster is a spelling of the previous century; 'festoon' ('fustoan') had not yet made it into English print.[72] The Brewers' agreement with Symes suggests that no one bothered, or needed to, consult a lexicon when composing it.

Who, therefore, used the explanations of 'ovolo', etc., that appear in Blome's Encyclopedy, Evelyn's 'Account' and Moxon's *Vignola*? (Possibly no one, of course: the fact that the book-object is manufactured does not mean that it made any difference to anyone's conduct or competences.) Though Henry Wotton had casually suggested in his *Elements of Architecture* (1624) that he might as well use the word 'columne' instead of 'piller' 'for the word among Artificers is almost naturallized', it was Balthazar Gerbier, writing 40 years later, who was the first to point out that successful construction management requires a degree of bilingualism.[73] Sir Balthazar, knighted by Charles I, was the most inventive of the operators supplying the market of those interested in civil construction after 1660.[74] His *Counsel and Advise to All Builders* (1663), that is, owners of buildings or future buildings, advises that if they are to 'have more credit with the several Master Workmen', the latter 'must be spoken unto in plain intelligible terms', which meant adopting their vocabularies for the sake of credit, and harmony: they 'do love to be spoken unto in their own phrases'. Such condescension might be a trial which his 'manual' tried to ameliorate: it 'doth both now and then proffer a word or two to cherish the Readers patience, for that bare names of materials, of forms, and several parts of works will too soon tire noble Persons'.[75] Similarly, Randle Holme's richly illustrated *Academy of Armory* (1688), an astonishingly ambitious and ultimately truncated attempt to subsume knowledge of 'trades and sciences' through their representations on heraldic devices, offers 'for the better understanding of all the parts of a Pillar, or Column ... the several terms, which Artists have given to the diverse Mouldings about the same ... by which any Gentleman may be able to discourse a Free-mason, or other workman, in his own terms'.[76]

---

[71] Anya Matthews (to whom thanks for permission to cite), 'The Architectural Development and Political Uses of London's Livery Halls, 1603–1684' (PhD diss., Courtauld Institute of Art, University of London, 2015), p. 240, quoting London Metropolitan Archives CLC/L/BF/G/135/MS05502.

[72] 'pilaster, n.' *OED Online*, Oxford University Press, March 2020, www.oed.com/view/Entry/143809, accessed 21 April 2020. 'festoon, n.' *OED Online*, Oxford University Press, March 2020, www.oed.com/view/Entry/69573, accessed 21 April 2020.

[73] *The Elements of Architecture: Collected by Henry Wotton Knight ...* (London: John Bill, 1624), p. 29.

[74] Jason Peacey, 'Print, Publicity, and Popularity: The Projecting of Sir Balthazar Gerbier, 1642–1662', *Journal of British Studies*, 51 (2012), 284–307, especially 305.

[75] Gerbier, *Counsel and Advise*, sigs g2v–g3.

[76] Randle Holme, *The Academy of Armory, or, A Storehouse of Armory and Blazon ...* (Chester: Printed for the author, 1688), 3: 466. Andrew Gray, 'The World on a Shield: The Encyclopaedic Vision of Randle Holme', in Fiona Robertson and Peter N. Lindfield (eds), *Semy-de-Lys: Speaking of Arms, 1400–2016* (Oxford and Stirling: The Heraldic Imagination, 2016), 43–50, https://heraldics2014.wordpress.com/publication-semy-de-lys/, accessed 1 March 2020.

In this way the terms of the building site were identified as having joined the 'new world of Words' which in 1656 the lexicographer Thomas Blount advised his readers that they would encounter, in books about Turkish history, for example (*'Janizaries'*, *'Turbants'*, and *'Seraglio's'*), or indeed in the course of conversation and consumption.[77] 'In the mouths of common people, I heard of *Piazza, Balcone*, &c. in London'; 'Nay, to that pass we are now arrived, that in London many of the Tradesmen have new Dialects ... The Shoo-maker will make you Boots, *Whole Chase, Demi-Chase*, or *Bottines*, &c.'.[78] Boot-buyer beware: though Blount detected nothing worse than affectation in the new dialects, it was in his spirit that Elisha Coles included 'Canting Terms' in his dictionary published 20 years later. ''Tis no disparagement', Coles wrote, to understand them. 'It may chance to save your throat from being cut, or (at least) your Pocket from being pickt.'[79] One sign of what William Winde called 'Indiferent' artificers might be their very fluency in bamboozle, and we read approving references to those whose very inarticulacy was a sign of true, hands-on expertise built over the generations. In March 1668 Evelyn described the launch of the *Charles* at Deptford, 'built by old *Shish*, a plaine honest Carpenter (Master builder of this Dock) yet one that can give very little account of his art by discourse, as hardly capable to reade, yet of greate abilitie in his calling: They <have> ben Ship-Carpenters in this Yard above 100 yeares'.[80]

Signs and Substances

In late 1675, Wren wrote to Isaac Barrow, the Master of Trinity College, Cambridge, about the new library which he was designing for it: 'I suppose you have good masons, how ever I would willingly take a farther paines to give all the mouldings in great', that is, in drawings to scale: 'wee are scrupulous in small matters & you must pardon us, the Architects are as great pedants as Criticks or Heralds'.[81] The reference to the notoriously pedantic heralds is witty, and apposite. Like that of mouldings, the language of blazon was the subject of many publications (many of them by Blome), and like that of mouldings it was threatened by devaluation in the hands of those

---

[77] Peter Burke has commented on the difficulties presented by the Ottoman empire when it came to translations into Latin: 'The Renaissance Translator as Go-Between', in Andreas Höfele and Werner von Koppenfels (eds), *Renaissance Go-Betweens: Cultural Exchange in Early Modern Europe* (Berlin and Boston: De Gruyter, 2005), pp. 17–31 at 30.

[78] Thomas Blount, *Glossographia, or, A Dictionary, Interpreting All Such Hard Words, Whether Hebrew, Greek, Latin, Italian, Spanish, French, Teutonick, Belgick, British or Saxon, as Are Now Used in Our Refined English Tongue* ... (London: Humphrey Moseley and George Sawbridge, 1656), sigs A2–A3; Starnes, 'English Dictionaries', 30–3.

[79] Elisha Coles, *An English Dictionary Explaining the Difficult Terms That Are Used in Divinity, Husbandry, Physick, Phylosophy, Law, Navigation, Mathematicks, and Other Arts and Sciences*. ... (London: Samuel Crouch, 1676), 'To the Reader'; Starnes, 'English Dictionaries', 48.

[80] Jonas Shish (1605–80): E. S. De Beer (ed.), *The Diary of John Evelyn*, 6 vols (Oxford: Clarendon Press, 1955), 3: 506–7 (3 March 1668).

[81] David McKitterick (ed.), *The Making of the Wren Library, Trinity College, Cambridge* (Cambridge: Cambridge University Press, 1995), pp. 144–5. The Library was completed internally in 1690.

who thought that mere words and not a comprehensive understanding of what they stood for would suffice. The result would be more of 'those irregular *congestions*, rude and brutish inventions, which generally so deform and incommode' English gentry houses (Evelyn), and coats of arms which show only too clearly their delineation by 'Common Painters and such Mechanicks' (the *London Gazette*, commenting in 1715 on one of Blome's books of heraldry).[82] Do not, Edmund Bolton's *Elements of Armories* (1610) tells us, 'foolishly suppose' that the 'Termes, & use of *Blazon* which ... comprehends but the description of the mechanicall parts, were all'. That is 'as far from the thing ... as signes from substances'.[83] Wotton's *Elements of Architecture*, published 14 years later, is equally alert: it will 'say no more concerning Columnes and their Adjuncts, about which Architects make such a noyse in their Bookes, as if the very tearmes of Architraves, and Frizes, and Cornices, and the like, were enough to graduate a Master of this Art'.[84] Pedantry, which connoted an inability to distinguish sign from substance, was in 'radical opposition' to gentility and Wren, sensibly, offered drawings instead of words.[85]

The difficulties of describing a 'society whose legal system and status system were based on possession of land at a time when non-landed skills, wealth and power were increasingly significant' was entirely evident in early modern England even if no one, then or now, has entirely resolved it.[86] In her study of Elizabethan popular literature, Laura Stevenson concluded that writers praising merchants and artificers, and the civic oligarchies which they comprised, could do so only within an existing system to which commercial initiative and craft skill were irrelevant: 'there was not even a language that described capitalistic virtues'.[87] Questions inevitably followed (must the virtues be capitalistic ones, as opposed to those grounded in 'engagement with the growing significance of credit relations'?) but Stevenson's suggestion that a new, tradesman- and entrepreneur-specific language of values and virtues had emerged in England by the end of the seventeenth century reflects a consensus among historians.[88]

---

[82] Evelyn, 'Account', p. 120; *London Gazette* 5348 (19 July 1715), in a notice mentioned but misdated in Clapp, 'Subscription Enterprises', 374 n. 27.

[83] *Edm. Bolton His Elements of Armories* (London: George Eld, 1610), p. 92.

[84] Wotton, *Elements of Architecture*, p. 42.

[85] Steven Shapin, '"A Scholar and a Gentleman": The Problematic Identity of the Scientific Practitioner in Early Modern England', *History of Science*, 29 (1991), 279–327 at 290 (quotation), 301–3. I am indebted to an anonymous referee for the point about the substitution, as well as many others.

[86] David Cressy, 'Describing the Social Order of Elizabethan and Stuart England', *Literature and History*, 3 (1976), 29–44 at 29.

[87] Laura Caroline Stevenson, *Praise and Paradox: Merchants and Craftsmen in Elizabethan Popular Literature* (Cambridge: Cambridge University Press, 2002), pp. 91, 210 (quotation), 212; see also Ian Anders Gadd, 'Early Modern Printed Histories of the London Livery Companies', in Ian Anders Gadd and Patrick Wallis (eds), *Guilds, Society & Economy in London, 1450–1800* (London: Centre for Metropolitan History, 2002), pp. 29–50 at 38 on such 'social hybrid forms' as 'merchant prince'.

[88] Stevenson, *Praise and Paradox*, p. 157; Mark Hailwood, '"The Honest Tradesman's Honour": Occupational and Social Identity in Seventeenth-Century England', *Transactions of the Royal Historical Society*, 6th ser., 24 (2014), 79–103 at 94.

How could the new 'language' work with the specific technical and commercial competences of the builder? Answers might be found, not in texts, but in pictures, though admittedly in a tiny sub-group of a print genre that emerged in London after the Fire: celebratory depictions of a tall new building which name both architect and builder-contractor. The engraving of the west end and steeple of St Bride (Figure 4.2), '235 feet high', which names Wren as 'Architect' and Samuel Fulkes as 'Mason', is a good example just because it is a strange one. The section is drawn in perspective, not the conventional orthogonal projection. Alongside the unorthodox rendering of the section planes themselves to show brick and stone masonry, not neutral blanks, the print impresses the viewer with the sheer complexity of this product of the mason's and carpenter's art.[89] Its boast of 'Shewing the Inside and outside', together with its rendition of the inside's sophisticated masonry, can stand for an attempt to show that like beauty, the contractor's art is both supplementary and necessary to architecture.

The intellectual formation of the early modern English architect has attracted significant scholarly attention, and understandably so.[90] During the later seventeenth century a previously somewhat fuzzy role came into sharper focus thanks to the extraordinary organisational and design activity demanded in the aftermath of London's Great Fire, and the publications prompted by that activity, as well as by the restoration of the monarchy six years earlier. Architectural knowledge was itself a commodity and a prestigious one, as Blome's *Gentlemans Recreation* and its recourse to the construction metaphor suggests.

This chapter has used Blome's three 'Architecture' illustrations and Thomas Fitch's patronage of two of them to explore the status of the language of classical ornament. In print, it took up a disproportionately large amount of space compared to other branches of (or, bubbles comprising) the discipline. This vocabulary was highly Latinate, which was one source of its prestige and by extension of that which it represented. At the same time, however, the vocabulary's value was destabilised by the recognition that it was not, in fact, one that artificers necessarily needed to be taught. One response to this suggestion, apparent in Evelyn's 'Account of

---

[89] Bernard Adams, *London Illustrated, 1604–1851: A Survey and Index of Topographical Books and Their Plates* (London: Library Association, 1983), p. 42, no 22/36. The engraving was included in the second volume (1714 or 1715) of the *Nouveau Théâtre de la Grande Bretagne* but judging from its style it is unlikely to have been prepared especially for it. John Strype praised this 'good cut': John Stow, *A Survey of the Cities of London and Westminster: Containing the Original, Antiquity, Increase, Modern Estate and Government of Those Cities*, ed. John Strype, 6 books in 2 vols (London: A. Churchill, J. Knapton, R. Knaplock etc., 1720), 1: 265. Fulkes had also taken over the mason's contract for the church's body after Joshua Marshall's death in 1678: Paul Jeffery, *The City Churches of Sir Christopher Wren* (London: Hambledon, 1996), pp. 224–5.

[90] Anthony Gerbino, Stephen Johnston, and Gordon Higgott, *Compass and Rule: Architecture as Mathematical Practice in England, 1550–1750* (New Haven and London: Yale University Press in association with the Museum of History of Science, Oxford, and Yale Center for British Art, 2009); Kimberley Skelton, *The Paradox of Body, Building and Motion in Seventeenth-Century England* (Manchester: Manchester University Press, 2015); Walker, *Architects and Intellectual Culture*.

Architects & Architecture', which exhorts language training for the entire social hierarchy, was to link artificers' casual naturalisation of the vocabulary with their equally 'rude and brutish' ornamental inventions.

Evelyn's encouragement of a separate-but-equal form of social advancement for the 'able *Workman*' as opposed to the *Ingenio* architect might be said to have been realised with prints of the sort just described. Of course the prescription drastically misrepresents the historical realities of the artisanal and architectural roles, but that was and is a common problem in writing about buildings and their construction.

Part II

Roles of Cultural Production
in Social Status

5

The Social Status of Publishers of Learned Texts in Europe, 1560–1630

IAN MACLEAN

EARLY MODERN HUMANISTS and authors whose social status might have been expressed through (or defined by) the books they produced had to rely on publishers in the world of literature and learning to which they aspired. These publishers came from diverse social origins, underwent very different levels of training, ranging from the most demanding scholarly preparation for dealing with sophisticated ancient and humanist texts, to a modest grasp of their own vernacular, together with a familiarity with the commercial aspects of their trade, and nothing more. They might also have been authors and scholars in their own right. They might have been printer-publishers or just publishers. As creators of books, it fell to them to fulfil the functions of choosing copy, liaising with its author or editor, ensuring the material production of the book, storing it, advertising it, selling it, and distributing it. This involved them in occupying an uncomfortable intermediate position between three areas of activity: the *artes mechanicae* or *illiberales* of the printshop; 'correction' or the scholarly vetting of books; and profit-making commercialism that was traditionally seen as ideologically incompatible with the objects of learning and culture that their authors produced. In this chapter, I set out to investigate how they balanced these competing functions, and what effect their efforts had on their own social status and the practice of their trade. I shall limit myself to considering only the publishers of learned materials (principally humanist texts, natural philosophy, medicine, law, and history). Even with this limitation, the disparate nature of these figures means that it is otiose to try to establish an average type of publisher or engage in a quantitative analysis of the field. A description based on family resemblance (i.e. one which is couched in such a way as not to postulate any essential feature possessed by all early modern publishers) will not generate a very strong model or ideal type. For these reasons, I have chosen to examine the status of publishers using materials and information I have accumulated through my various studies

Proceedings of the British Academy, **246**, 97–120, © The British Academy 2022.

on the history of continental books.[1] I shall use what at first will seem to be an alien model of analysis (one that is certainly very different from the categories the social actors themselves would have used): Pierre Bourdieu's theory of 'habitus', 'field', and 'capital', which I shall discuss in turn, even though they are manifestly interdependent.[2]

For Bourdieu, 'habitus' connotes a mental disposition that structures the experience of a human agent by incorporating objective social conditions in him or her in the form of custom, but does not determine his or her nature. It is associated with a collective identity, and manifests itself in symbolic elements such as skills, clothing, material belongings, aesthetic preferences, and taste. I have argued elsewhere in a broad sense that Renaissance lawyers and physicians have a 'habitus', allowing one to use such phrases as 'to think like a lawyer' or 'to think like a physician'.[3] I believe that the same is true of publishers, or at least of the sub-class of publishers – those active in the production of new, conserved, or revived knowledge – that I have singled out in this chapter, who were active in the period following on from the heroic first generation of printing entrepreneurs. By that time (roughly, the turn of the sixteenth century), the principal features of the new technology had coalesced, and the trade or profession had taken on a stable character. This 'habitus' was quite broad. In its most limited sense, it was determined by the copy delivered to them by a third party, their own selection of copy *sua sponte*, and their promotion of their product in the book market, involving material and editorial choices, production, advertisement, distribution, and warehousing. But their activities did not stop there: they were also postmen, and communicators of international news through *avvisi*; they acted as agents or commissioners for others on their travels; they looked after the patrons and relatives of the persons for whom they published books, and they were very active correspondents with authors, scholars, and their professional colleagues, and their premises could act as their *poste restante*. These have been described as 'veritable homes to cultural and social exchange between passing scholars, correctors

---

[1] Ian Maclean, *Learning in the Marketplace: Essays in the History of Early Modern Books* (Leiden and Boston: Brill, 2009); Ian Maclean, *Scholarship, Commerce, Religion: The Learned Book in the Ages of Confessions, 1560–1630* (Cambridge, MA: Harvard University Press, 2012), esp. ch. 4 (pp. 97–133): 'Labor, Impensa, Emolumentum: The Publisher of Learned Books'.

[2] See Ian Maclean, 'Bourdieu's Field of Cultural Production', *French Cultural Studies*, 3 (1993), 283–9 (a review essay of Pierre Bourdieu, *The Field of Cultural Production: Essays on Art and Literature*, ed. and introd. Randal Johnson [Cambridge: Polity, 1993]); John B. Thompson, *Books in the Digital Age* (Cambridge: Polity, 2005). See also, for a modern overview of the uses of Bourdieu, Johan Lindell, 'Bourdieusian Media Studies: Returning Social Theory to Old and New Media', *Distinktion: Journal of Social Theory*, 16 (2015), 362–77.

[3] Ian Maclean, *Interpretation and Meaning in the Renaissance: The Case of Law* (Cambridge: Cambridge University Press, 1992); Ian Maclean, *Logic, Signs and Nature in the Renaissance: The Case of Learned Medicine* (Cambridge: Cambridge University Press, 2001); on the 'habitus' of a theology, see Johann Joachim Weidner (1672–1732), [praeses], *Dissertatio theologica inauguralis [...] an theologia sit habitus practica* (Rostock: typis Jo. Jac. Adleri, 1732).

and print shop workers'.[4] It is generally assumed that there was a golden age of such humanist printer-publishers which came to an end at the end of the six-teenth century, with the disappearance of figures such as Henri II Estienne, Paulus Manutius, and Andreas Wechel; I shall return to this assumption in the conclusion.

Bourdieu's term 'field' refers to a 'separate social universe', an area of the social world characterised by hierarchical organisation and by internal relations of force and regulatory mechanisms, physically located in the agents who both bring it into being by their struggle to dominate it, and modify it by their actions. Its structure is objective, and is related by homology to the general field of society (which includes the political, religious, and economic fields). Each field has a distinctive logic that defines the conditions under which agents and organisations can participate in the field and flourish or falter within it. Did the sub-class of early modern publishers under consideration here live in such a field? And how did such a field relate to their practice as publishers and their social status vis-à-vis others members of society? The issue of their membership of a mercantile community is clearly very relevant to these questions, and to the question of how they related to the political and religious forces around them and the scholarship that they sponsored.

Bourdieu's sociological concepts are informed by a sustained analogy with eco-nomics and 'capital'. The publishing chain in his account is a supply chain leading from author to reader, and a value chain, in which each passage to the next link adds value. For the modern publisher, it represents economic capital (money), human cap-ital (editorial staff), symbolic capital (prestige), and intellectual capital (ownership of copyright). In Bourdieu's account, culture is mapped onto a vocabulary of commerce: authors have 'specific capital' (the recognition of their peers), which they 'invest' in order to derive maximum benefit from it. They employ 'strategies of accumulation', and rely on 'cultural bankers' (publishers) as 'producers' of sym-bolic goods to be enjoyed by 'consumers' (readers). This analysis works particu-larly well when applied to nineteenth-century cultural and literary production, as it is constructed on a conflictual model of human social interaction. The field of cul-tural production was then inversely related to economic and class interests. It was situated between the field of power whose values it inverted, and the 'habitus' of those who contributed to it as artists and writers. It was subdivided into a field of restricted production (high art) and a field of large-scale production (mass literature and popular literature). In the former of these, what was at stake was 'symbolic cap-ital' which could take the form of prestige, celebrity, honour, or consecration; the

---

[4] Henri-Jean Martin and Roger Chartier (eds), *Histoire de l'édition française, vol. 1: Le livre conquérant du moyen âge au milieu du 17e siècle* (Paris: Promodis, 1982), pp. 228–9: 'entrepreneurs et savants tous ensemble, leurs ateliers sont de véritables foyers de l'échange culturel et social entre auteurs de passage, correcteurs d'épreuves et artisans du livre'. See also see Jean Balsamo and Michel Simonin, *Abel L'Angelier et Françoise de Louvain* (Geneva: Droz, 2002), on the activities of Françoise de Louvain in Paris; and Shanti Graheli, 'How to Build a Library across Early Modern Europe: The Network of Claude Espilly', in Matthew McLean and Sara Barker (eds), *International Exchange in the Early Modern Book World* (Leiden and Boston: Brill, 2016), pp. 171–213 (183) on some of these functions.

most successful artists or writers in this sub-field might be those who earned the least. I shall ask here what were the honours (the 'symbolic capital') to which early modern publishers of learned books aspired, and whether it is possible to detect in their case a clash of values and interests similar to that which pertained in the nineteenth century.

Social Origins and Education

I turn now to a description of the publishers' world in terms that they themselves could have recognised. It is to be expected that the first entrepreneurs to embrace the new technology of printing should have come from very diverse sectors of society: artisans who had mastered the material challenges of printing; merchants who saw its potential to open up entirely new markets; scholars, political figures, and religious administrators who grasped its potential for the dissemination of knowledge and its relationship with power. One spectrum on which these publishers of this generation can be placed is that ranging from hard-headed mercantilism to humanistic scholarship; among the early practitioners, Anton Koberger of Nuremberg (1440/5–1513) could be placed at one end of this spectrum, and Aldus Manutius of Venice (1449/52–1515) on the other. The former of these figures, the son of a prominent family of bakers, employed up to 100 print workers and 24 presses, owned two paper mills, and created a network of outlets in Venice, Milan, Paris, Lyon, Vienna, and Budapest. The latter came from a patrician background, had a high-level humanist education in Rome, and became a very distinguished scholar of Greek texts whose printed production included the complete works of Aristotle, Hippocrates, and many other such authors. We would naturally associate the dictum 'knowledge is a gift of God and so cannot be traded' ('scientia donum Dei est, unde vendi non potest') with Manutius.[5] It seems natural that he should have published a translation of Alcinous's *Introduction to Platonic Philosophy* in 1497, with its praise of the moral character of philosophy and the 'libertas philosophandi' that came to be a slogan of the Republic of Letters.[6] But he was also a very shrewd book merchant who launched a new typeface and portable format on to the market.[7] Conversely, we should have expected Koberger to have included only books with good sales potential in his list, but it is noteworthy that he too published Alcinous's text at the very beginning of his career, in November 1472.

---

[5] G. Post, K. Giocarnis, and R. Kay, 'The Medieval Heritage of a Humanist Ideal: Scientia donum Dei est, unde vendi non potest', *Traditio*, 9 (1955), 195–234. An excellent example of the rhetoric by which *marchands libraires* portrayed themselves as the disinterested servants of the Republic of Letters is to be found in the preface of the *Communium opinionum syntagma* (Lyon: Symphorien Beraud, 1581),*2r-v, written by Béraud about his deceased associate and godfather Filippo Tinghi.

[6] See Ian Maclean, 'The Sceptical Crisis Reconsidered: Galen, Rational Medicine and the *libertas philosophandi*', *Early Science and Medicine*, 11 (2006), 247–74.

[7] Alcinous, *De doctrina Platonis liber*, trans. Marsilio Ficino, published with Iamblicus, *De mysteriis Aegiptiorum* (Venice: in aedibus Aldi, 1497); *Disciplinarum Platonis epitome*, trans. Pietro Balbi (Nuremberg: Koberger, 1472).

This neatly demonstrates that survival as a publisher of learning in all its guises required knowledge of both learning and the market.[8]

Subsequent generations of such publishers came from quite diverse backgounds. There are university graduates who become publishers, as one might expect, but also persons who are founders of dynasties from much less literate beginnings: Christophe Plantin of Antwerp was a book-binder; Louis Elzevier of Leiden the same, beginning his career in that capacity with Plantin; Sigmund Feyerabend a typecutter.[9] In many cases where these figures founded a dynasty, the next generation was sent to a university, but not all: Robert Estienne had his son privately tutored by very distinguished humanists, for example, and the same probably happened to Andreas Wechel. Other fathers, uncles, or godfathers had their children learn the trade of publishing as apprentices to themselves or to colleagues: this was the case of the Feyerabend and Schönwetter families of Frankfurt, the Plantin-Moretus of Antwerp, and Symphorien Beraud of Lyon, the godson of Filippo Tinghi.[10] It was common also for less exalted figures in the printing house, often correctors, factors, or agents, but also occasionally compositors,[11] to rise to the dignity of publisher through promotion or marriage to a daughter of their employers, as did Josse Bade (who married a daughter of Jean Treschel); or by marriage to his employer's widow (as Henri I Estienne did by marrying Johannes Higman's widow in Paris, or Dr Zacharias Palthen did by marrying the widow of Johann Wechel in Frankfurt); or by being bequeathed the print shop, as was Sébastien Beraud of Lyon by Filippo Tinghi; or taking it over with a sponsor on the employer's death, as did Peter Fischer from Jonas Rhodius.[12] It is also the case that wives and widows could, and did, take on the role of publisher without the matrimonial support of another member of the printing trade.[13] Some of those who achieved the status of publisher

[8] On the Koberger dynasty, see Oscar von Hase, *Die Koberger: eine Darstellung des buchhändlerischen Geschäftsbetriebes in der |Zeit des Übergangs vom Mittelalter zur Neuzeit* (Leipzig: Breitkopf and Hartel, 1885); on Manutius, the classic study is by Martin Lowry, *The World of Aldus Manutius: Business and Scholarship in Renaissance Venice* (Oxford: Blackwell, 1979).

[9] Alphonse Willems, *Les Elzevier: histoire et annales typographiques* (Brussels: van Trigt et al., 1880); Leon Voet, *The Golden Compasses: A History and Evaluation of the Printing and Publishing Activities of the Officina Palntiniana in Antwerp*, 2 vols (Amsterdam: Vangendt, 1969–72); Heinrich Pallmann, *Sigmund Feyerabend: sein Leben und seine geschäftlichen Verbindungen nach archivalischen Quellen* (Frankfurt: Völcker, 1881).

[10] See note 8 and Hildegard Starp, 'Das Frankfurter Verlagshaus Schönwetter 1598–1726', *Archiv für Geschichte des Buchwesens*, 1 (1958), 38–113; Henri-Louis and Julien Baudrier, *Bibliographie lyonnaise*, 13 vols (Paris: de Nobele, 1964–5), 4.125, V.40–52, VI.442.

[11] *Histoire de l'édition française*, 1.228, suggests that this is not a feature of the French book trade.

[12] Josef Benzing, 'Die deutschen Verleger des 16. Und 17. Jahrhunderts', *Archiv für Geschichte des Buchwesens*, 5–6 (1977), cols. 1077–322 (1246). There are many other similar cases recorded in this article.

[13] Annie Parent-Charon, 'A propos des femmes et des métiers du livre dans le Paris de la Renaissance', in Dominique de Courcelles (ed.), *Des femmes et des livres, France et Espagne, XVIIe–XVIIe siècle* (Paris: Ecole des Chartes, 1999), pp. 137–48. An outstanding case is that of Françoise de Louvain, widow of Abel L'Angelier: see Balsamo and Simonin, *Abel L'Angelier et Françoise de Louvain*. See also Deborah Parker, 'Women in the Book Trade in Italy, 1475–1620', *Renaissance Quarterly*, 49 (1996), 509–41.

graduated from a role in the print shop to setting out on their own, often with financial help from someone else: this is the case of Sebastian Gryphius (an agent and a corrector before becoming a publisher) and Etienne Dolet (who began as a corrector).[14]

Publishers did not all possess the same degree of learning and education. At one end of the spectrum we find Sigmund Feyerabend, a publisher of massive legal tomes in Latin, yet who was unable to read that language; at the other, figures such as Henri II Estienne and Franciscus Raphelengius who wrote in fine humanist Latin and Greek.[15] One might be inclined to believe from the printed remains of publishers that this linguistic sophisication was fairly widespread, but the florid dedications that they signed in the paratext of their books were quite often not their work, but rather that of their corrector or another learned figure of their acquaintance. Many founders of dynasties had their children learn the trade by travelling and acting as agents for their print shops. As a result, most publishers acquired a number of modern foreign languages: at the Frankfurt Book Fair, for example, in the late sixteenth century, Italian, Dutch, French, and German were all spoken by attendees, very often fluently if imperfectly. The surviving correspondence of publishers to their foreign clients testify to this as late as the eighteenth century. Such knowledge of modern languages was a feature of the merchant class as a whole, as was the practice of letterwriting; so extensive was this that one recent study has attributed to them a 'furor scribendi'.[16] It has been claimed that their 'psychology' (what I am here calling their 'habitus') can be seen both in their private correspondence and their private accounts, to which I shall return (p. 104); publishers not only shared with them the need to establish trust with others of their profession through these means, but also the trust of their clients, the learned authors.[17]

---

[14] Raphaële Mouren, *Quid novi? Sébastien Gryphe à l'occasion du 450ᵉ anniversaire de sa mort* (Villeurbanne: Presses de l'ENSSIB, 2008); Michèle Clément, *Etienne Dolet, 1509–2009* (Geneva: Droz 2012). In Geneva, all publishers had to undergo an apprenticeship: see Elena Muceni, *'Genevae apud Johannem Ludovicum Dufour*: A Genevan Printer in the History of Malebranchism', *Quaerendo*, 48 (2018), 1–16 at 3. See also Jacques Guignard, 'Imprimeurs et libraries parisiens 1525–36', *Bulletin de l'Association Guillaume Budé*, 2 (1953), 43–73, and Heinrich Schrörs, 'Der Kölner Buchdrucker Maternus Cholinus', *Annalen des historischen Vereins für den Niederrhein*, 85 (1808), 147–65, for data on Parisian and Cologne publishers.

[15] Johann Goldfriedrich, *Geschichte des deutschen Buchhandels vom Westfälischen Frieden bis zum Beginn der klassischen Litteraturperiode (1648–1740)* (Leipzig: Verlag des Börsenvereins der deutschen Buchhändler, 1908), pp. 413–15 makes the point that booksellers needed to know Latin, but not publishers.

[16] Sophus Reinert and Robert Fredona, 'Merchants and the Origins of Capitalism': Harvard Business School 2017 Working Paper 18-021.

[17] Robert S. Lopez and Irving W. Raymond, *Medieval Trade in the Mediterranean World: Illustrative Documents Translated with Introductions and Notes* (New York: Columbia University, 1955), p. 378. See also Armando Sapori, *Le marchand italien au Moyen Age* (Paris: Librairie Armand Colin, 1952). I take these references from Francesca Trivellato, 'Discourse and Practice of Trust in Business Correspondence during the Early Modern Period', working paper, Economics History Workshop, Department of Economics, Yale University, 2004, https://economics.yale.edu/sites/default/files/files/Workshops-Seminars/Economic-History/trivellato-041013.pdf, accessed 22 November 2021.

The Publisher as Merchant

The general term 'publisher' covers a quite broad spectrum of commercial activity. In Latin legal documents of the time, it was usually rendered as 'typographus' and distinguished from 'bibliopola' or bookseller and 'impressor' or printer.[18] At the one end of the spectrum of 'typographi' we find the printers who never took initiatives themselves, but produced copy for others. Above them were master printers, who sometimes acted only for others, but on other occasions arranged finance, or themselves provided it, to allow speculative printing to take place. The printer-publishers who took on few or no commissions were yet grander figures, who might or might not have had printing skills or even linguistic competence in various languages. Some printer-publishers were also retail booksellers, and engaged in all levels of printing, as did Christophe Plantin.[19] Some booksellers were publishers but not printers, as was, for example, Peter Kopf of Frankfurt, but even he used the name 'typographus' as well as 'bibliopola' to describe himself in official documents.[20]

The primary social identity of a publisher was as a merchant.[21] The theoretical *degré zéro* of mercantile activity was the unscrupulous pursuit of profit and the accumulation of wealth at the expense of others.[22] In the medieval and early modern period, such activity was rarely if ever divorced from religious considerations, especially the aspiration to achieve salvation in the afterlife. In one famous surviving case, a merchant's account books began with the formula 'nel nome di Dio e del guadagno'. The element of profit could make merchants feel morally uneasy, given the church's prohibition of usury and its doctrine of a 'just price' (which was not meant to be the price determined by the market, although it often ended

---

[18] See for example the Pope Gregory XIII's privilege of the *Corpus juris canonici* (Rome: in aedibus Populi romani, 1582), which refers to 'Typographi, librorum impressores, ac bibliopolae'.

[19] *Histoire de l'édition française*, 1.228, offers the following threefold division: *marchand-libraire*; *marchand-imprimeur*; *imprimeur-libraire*.

[20] Hans-Joachim Koppitz (ed.), *Die kaiserlichen Druckprivilegien im Haus- Hof- und Staatsarchiv Wien* (Wiesbaden: Harrassowitz, 2008), p. 292: applications to the Imperial Chancery for privileges dated 14 April 1597 and 11 April 1608. Wilfried Enderle 'Die Druckerverleger des katholischen Deutschlands zwischen Augsburger Religionsfrieden 1555 und Westfälischen Frieden 1648', in Gert Kaiser, Heinz Finger, and Elisabeth Niggemann (eds), *Bücher für die Wissenschaft: Bibliotheken zwischen Tradition und Fortschritt. Festschrift für Günter Gatterman zum 65. Geburtstag* (Berlin: de Gruyter Saur, 1994), pp. 37–60, has produced a five-fold categorisation of Catholic book producers in Germany between 1555 and 1648 which focuses on the scale of their professional activities: 'Grossdrucker' who employed other printers; printer-publishers who received privileges from the Court and other official establishments; publishers who operated by themselves in middle-sized towns and cities; printers who were mainly dependent on contracting out their labour to 'Grossdrucker', but occasionally financed a modest book; and learned publishers who operated in the sphere of universities, high schools and were at the service of humanist scholars.

[21] Not infrequently, publishers also had interests in other areas of the mercantile world: the spice trade, jewellery, linen, wool, property: all much more rewarding mercantile activities than publishing: see Maclean, *Scholarship, Commerce, Religion*, pp. 287–8, and the references cited there.

[22] Werner Sombart, *Der moderne Kapitalismus* (Munich and Leipzig: Duncker and Humboldt, 1928), sees this approach as the origins of capitalism.

up being identical to it).[23] Merchants quite often went to some lengths to disguise the money that they extracted from others in the form of profit through vehicles such as letters of exchange (which, of course, had other functions as well). Their wills sometimes record discreetly sums to be restored to those from whom they had obtained money in this way.[24] They also were at pains to distance themselves from the image of a bad merchant, and in their private correspondence and their private accounts they strove to persuade their clients and each other of the integrity of their behaviour, their commitment to hard work, their *bona fides*, their fairness, and the quality of their goods.[25] This moral component of their behaviour, which they themselves saw as essential to their social status, was to lead to the recommendation by social thinkers such as Caspar Barlaeus in his *Mercator sapiens, sive oratio de coniungendis mercaturae et philosophiae* of 1632 that merchants should espouse philosophy itself and integrate classical wisdom into their lives.[26] The publishers of learned books clearly shared these views, sought to establish trust not only with others of their profession but also with the authors who were their clients, and aspired to be treated as members of the Republic of Letters. They hoped no doubt to receive descriptions of themselves by the authors they served similar to that written by the astronomer Francesco Giuntini about the Florentine publisher Filippo Tinghi in the edition of Sacro Bosco's *De sphaera emendata* of 1577: 'a man, who beside his superlative probity of mind, shows also a very precise diligence in publishing books of the highest degree of accuracy'.[27] Private descriptions of their behaviour by authors were however often much less elogious.[28]

Publishers' private accounts, like those of other merchants, usually began with a invocation to the deity; in more public documents (prefaces, applications for privileges), they were at pains to point out that what they did involved risk, and was driven by their desire to be of service to others, in the name not only of God, but also of learning and scholarship. They often linked the anti-commercial rhetoric of the gift to their protestations of the hard work and the personal commitment of financial resources that their trade entailed (features shared with

---

[23] Selma Hagenauer, *Das 'justum pretium' bei Thomas von Aquino: ein Beitrag zur Geschichte der objektiven Werttheorie* (Stuttgart: Kohlhammer, 1931).

[24] Francesco Galassi, 'Buying a Passport to Heaven: Usury, Restitution, and the Merchants of Medieval Genoa', *Religion*, 22 (1992), 313–26. For a contemporary discussion in the context of Canon Law, see Juan de Medina, *Tractatus utilissimi de rerum dominio, earum restitutione, et reliquis contractibus. De usuris, cambiis et censibus* (1st edn 1550) (Cologne: apud Petrum Cholinum, 1607).

[25] Iris Origo, *The Merchant of Prato: Francesco di Marco Datini* (New York: Knopf, 1957).

[26] *Oratio de coniungendis mercaturae et philosophiae* (Amsterdam: Athenaeum, 1632). The locus classicus of this recommendation is in Cicero, *De officiis*, 3.15.

[27] Johannes de Sacro Bosco, *Sphaera emendata* (Antwerp: Joannes Bellerus, 1582) a2r: 'vir praeter summam animi probitatem, etiam in libris castigatissime excudendis exquisitae diligentiae'; for an earlier example see the scholar-printer Jodocus Badius's description of Anton Koberger in the dedicatory letter to Angelo Poliziano's *Illustrium virorum epistole* (Lyon: in officina Nicolai Wolf, 1499) as 'clearly the prince of book dealers, and not the last in the ranks of faithful and honorable merchants' ('librariorum facile princeps et inter fideles et honestos mercatores non inferiori loco positus').

[28] Maclean, *Scholarship, Commerce, Religion*, pp. 43–6.

all other mercantile enterprises).[29] The use of protective measures and monopolistic provisions such as privileges, the practice of piracy and unauthorised reprinting of the copy of their clients evince on the other hand the hard commercial realities which went together with these more lofty aims. Equally, the advertisements of their wares on title-pages could be seen as a purely commercial act. Even so, for some of them, 'guadagno' did not necessarily mean surplus profit or mercantile expansion. While it was possible to become rich and to accumulate goods, it is also true that many publishers harboured no more than the ambition to stay in business and to survive crises caused by the many external dangers (war, plague, economic downturns) and internal ones (saturated markets, unredeemed credit, problems of cash flow, persistent debt). Many of these risks were found also in the community of merchants. Some risks were not, notably the problem of unsold stock whose potential purchasers were a far broader and less measurable constituency than that targeted by a wool merchant, for example, whose clients were mainly wholesalers. A specific feature of the early modern economics of publishing was its main mode of wholesale dealing: it consisted in barter ('Tauschhandel'), swapping printed sheet against printed sheet with colleagues rather than purchasing their wares. These acquisitions made most publishers willy-nilly into booksellers.[30] This had the effect of making their problems with cash flow yet worse.

The normal mode of being of a medieval merchant was to travel with his goods to a fair; they sold to other wholesale merchants, kept factors and warehouses in fair cities, located their headquarters in a centre on a prominent trade route having good local artisanal resources, and licensed itinerant salesmen to sell their goods. The early generations of publishers such as the Kobergers did the same. They were based in Nuremberg, but had strong trade connections all over Europe. Their activities were contemporary with the emergence of a new figure: that of the sedentary merchant, who directed his commercial empire through managers and agents established in other centres of trade.[31] This was the branch system, copied from Italian banks and the practice of wool and silk merchants, using shops whose identity was recognised by a shop sign which in the case of publishers was often related to their printer's mark, about which I shall have more to say later (see pp. 109–18). Some publishers (the Giunti, the Manutius press, and two expatriate family presses, the de Gabiano and Portonari in Lyon) calqued themselves on this model of trade and came to use

---

[29] On this see Natalie Zemon Davis, 'Beyond the Market: Books as Gifts in Sixteenth-century France', *Transactions of the Royal Historical Society*, 33 (1983), 69–88; Natalie Zemon Davis, *The Gift in Sixteenth-century France* (Oxford: Oxford University Press, 2000).

[30] In a letter dated 4 October 1634 to his colleague Willem Blaeu, Balthasar II Moretus of the Plantin-Moretus firm made clear the problems of Tauschhandel: 'I admit that we are not engaged in printing to exchange books for books, but to make money from them' ('ich bekenne dat wy niet en drucken om boecken met boecken te manghelen maer om geldt daer van te maecken'): Museum Plantin Moretus, Archiev 142, f. 423.

[31] Sophus Reinert and Robert Fredona, 'Merchants and the Origins of Capitalism': Harvard Business School 2017 Working Paper 18-021, and the bibliography cited there.

agents and factors or factors whom they commissioned to act on their behalf in crucial places abroad such as the Frankfurt Book Fair.[32] Publishers of learned books were international in outlook, and involved in close financial relations with fellow publishers which crossed confessional and national divides. This tended, in the case of publishers of learned material, to create if not equality, then at least solidarity, whereas the local status of publishers of different confessional allegiances could differ quite widely.

The status of publishers in their place of residence was clearly that of citizen and merchant, and they shared with merchants in other lines of business a fiscal relationship to the town or city in which they were located, often involving a set of concessions relating to specific taxes and municipal duties such as the watch, and a set of social practices such as fulfilling municipal offices, owning their own property, investing in other properties in the town, having household servants, and having portraits painted of themselves: in some collections, portraits of printers and publishers exist in the same proportion as those of other early modern merchants of similar standing.[33] This status was not the same in all locations: in Lyon, for example, they were often appointed to the high civic office of 'échevin', and bene-fited from their close association with the Italian banking sector, whereas in Basel and Geneva, two towns closely linked to Lyon's publishing trade, their main link was to the local institution of higher learning rather than the municipal patriciate. They were affiliated to the non-mercantile world of cities through titles such as 'libraire juré [de l'université]', 'academiae typographus', or 'imprimeur du roi', or through contracts with ecclesiastical figures or institutions. Confessional allegiance could be, but was not always, an impediment to local advancement. In Paris and later in Frankfurt, where Andreas Wechel fled to after the St Bartholomew's Day massacre in 1572, he belonged to a religious minority which excluded him from municipal office; he had to struggle to regain status in the German Imperial city. His son-in-law Jean Aubry, however, when sent to Reformed Basel in the interests of the firm, achieved status more easily by being elected to the prominent guild known as the Safranzunft.[34]

Not all publishers chose to be active in town councils, confraternities, and guilds (these were often not specific to the printing industry, especially in the early years of the sixteenth century), and the taxation that was levied on them did not always reflect their real wealth, which they were able to conceal by simply agreeing

---

[32] Angela Nuovo, *The Book Trade in the Italian Renaissance* (Leiden and Boston: Brill, 2015): Voet, *The Golden Compasses* (on Plantin's use of his son-in-law Jan Moretus).

[33] Maclean, *Scholarship, Commerce, Religion*, p. 97 (a reference to the Porträtsammlung of the Herzog-August Bibliothek, Wolfenbüttel). These items are one source of their 'status externus', the other depending on the esteem in which they were held by other persons: Michael Christophorus Hanovius, *Philosophiae civilis sive politicae pars tertia* (Magdeburg: Renger, 1758), p. 526, para 568.

[34] R. J. W. Evans, 'The Wechel Presses: Humanism and Calvinism in Central Europe, 1572–1627', *Past and Present Supplement*, 2 (1975), 4.

to pay a high sum or by not declaring the true extent of their assets.[35] In cities where they were numerous, they often lived in close proximity to each other: in Paris, this resulted in there being two very distinct areas in which there were print shops, one near the university and its associated conventual houses, where Latin and other learned languages were published, the other being in the Palais near the law courts, which was the centre of vernacular productions.[36] Location was associated with prestige: in Frankfurt, various publishers (Nicolas Bassée, Andreas Wechel) who had fled there to avoid religious persecution disposed of sufficient wealth to buy themselves premises in the best part of the city: a fact much deplored by the Lutheran municipal council.[37] The upward social mobility evinced by such purchases was a feature of the whole merchant class: but what publishers possessed that their fellow-merchants did not was a publicly visible involvement with their product through the imprint of their books, and close ties to different social groups, that is, the humanists and authors who wrote for them, and local religious or educational centres. The patrons for whom they produced books could also bring them very visible social promotion: a number of them were even ennobled for their services to scholarship, the empire, or the church (as were Heinrich Petri of Basel, Horace Cardon of Lyon, and Paulus Manutius of Venice and Rome).[38]

Publishing was a trade that in one respect embodied a new conception of mercantilism. It involved a number of separate proto-industrial processes (paper-making, printing, binding) and was characterised by 'putting out', that is, the separation of artisans into independent contributors to the completed end product.[39] The print shop itself was a well-defined and collaborative space, where alien social structures co-existed, crossing the boundary between illiberal and liberal arts: unskilled manual labour (the pressmen); skilled labour performed by apprentices who rose

[35] Richard MacKenney, *Tradesmen and Traders: The World of the Guilds in Venice and Europe, c. 1250–c. 1650* (New York: Barnes and Noble, 1987); Alexander Dietz, *Frankfurter Handelsgeschichte*, 4 vols (Glashütten im Taunus: Verlag Detlev Auvermann, 1970), 3.17, 37 records the tax paid by the Feyerabend and Wechel houses, but it is not clear that this is a very reliable indication of wealth as a publisher: Matthias Meyn, *Die Reichsstadt Frankfurt am Main vor dem Bürgeraufstand von 1612 bis 1614, Struktur und Krise* (Frankfurt: Kramer, 1980), p. 90 points out that many merchants paid a high sum to avoid declaring the extent of their wealth. Filippo de Vivo has informed me that Roberto Meietti was one of the lowest-assessed publishers in Venice, but on the evidence of his international trade, he does not seem to justify this position. Publishers could be lured to other cities by the promise of tax concessions or even goods (for example food staples such as wheat, and fuel for heating, as were offered to Wechel's heirs by the Count of Hanau to attract them to his city): Evans, 'The Wechel Presses'.

[36] Ian Maclean, 'La querelle des femmes en France et en Angleterre de 1615 à 1632: conjoncture et structures', *Littératures classiques*, 81 (2013), 149–71 (and the references given there).

[37] Evans, 'The Wechel Presses'; Dietz, *Frankfurter Handelsgeschichte*, 3.33, 37.

[38] On Petri, see Alfred Hartmann and Beat Rudolf Jenny (eds), *Die Amerbachkorrespondenz* (Basel: Universitätsbibliothek, 1973), 7.177–82; on Cardon, see Jean-Irenée Depéry, *Biographie des hommes célèbres du département de l'Ain* (Bourg: Bottier, 1835), 1.393–4; on Manutius's printer's mark and the details of his elevation see below, p. 116, and Nuovo, *Book Trade*, pp. 181–2.

[39] On the association of the print trade with emergent capitalism, see Benedict Anderson, *Imagined Communities: Reflections on the Origins and Spread of Nationalism* (London: Verso, 1991).

to be journeymen and in some cases masters; mercantile practices of production, advertisement, and distribution performed by the publisher; and intellectual expertise, located in the corrector (and sometimes also in the publishers themselves).[40] In one important respect, it was also at odds with the politico-economic context in which it operated, through the extension of literacy to compositors, the illiberal members of the print shop. Clive Griffin's excellent study *Journeymen Printers: Heresy and the Inquisition in Sixteenth-century Spain* reveals that they were not necessarily from literate backgrounds, but often acquired literacy through apprenticeship; and their ability to read and write in the vernacular (it was rare that they possessed ancient languages to the same degree) gave them a privileged place in their societies, and an intimate awareness of the politico-religious context in which they found themselves that led them often to become radical in their views, and predisposed them to heterodoxy if not heresy.[41] The apprentice-journeyman-master sequence recalls the role of guilds and mysteries in medieval mercantile practice, which did not threaten the regimes in which they operated in the same way as did literacy. The close alliance of publishers and scholars, and the association of scholars with the clergy, excluded them from all but the lesser version of ennoblement that came from holding office: merchant 'échevins' in Lyon, for example, were all made members of the 'noblesse de cloche' in this way, and quite a number of them were *marchands-libraires*. In France they could also aspire to the acquisition of land which bore a noble title, which many of them achieved; this would allow subsequent generations to climb the social ladder by undertaking military service.[42]

The corrector or correctors in the print shop had a very high status, and did not come cheap.[43] They were responsible for ensuring that the text was as free from error as possible (in the case of very sensitive texts such as the Elzevier New Testament, there were as many as eight re-readings), and were often very serious scholars in their own right. Friedrich Sylburg, for example, who corrected texts for the Wechels of Frankfurt and for Hieronymus Commelinus of Heidelberg, was among the foremost Greek scholars of his generation. It is not unusual to find in the colophon of a work a quite distinguished corrector named (a certain Angelus Cantinus, Doctor of Laws, corrected widely for Venetian printers in the 1620s; as did Enrico Clerici, a professor of humanities in Venice).[44] The role of correctors in the workshop provided a very direct link to the world of scholarship. They may

---

[40] Robert W. Scribner, *Germany: A New Social and Economic History*, 3 vols (London and New York: Arnold, 1996–2000), I.13–23, 160–6.

[41] Clive Griffin, *Journeymen Printers: Heresy and the Inquisition in Sixteenth-century Spain* (Oxford: Oxford University Press, 2005).

[42] Françoise Bayard and Pierre Cayez, *Histoire de Lyon du XVIe siècle à nos jours* (Roanne: Horvath, 1990), p. 84; Benoît Garnot, *Société, cultures et genres de vie dans la France moderne XVIe-XVIIIe siècle* (Paris: Hachette, 1991). A good example of social advancement and ennoblement through the acquisition of land is given in Baudrier, *Bibliographie Lyonnaise*, 7.28 ff. (Lucimborgo da Gabiano).

[43] See Maclean, *Scholarship, Commerce, Religion*, p. 122.

[44] See Anthony Grafton, *The Culture of Correction in Renaissance Europe* (London: British Library, 2011).

have been the promoters of scholarly texts, but as far as I know they were never financiers. Publishers received either direct (if they were themselves correctors) or reflected glory from this, and were themselves often participants in the production of scholarship, as promoters of copy as editors of difficult texts; Henri II Estienne, Franciscus Raphelengius, and Hieronymus Commelinus were among the foremost editors of humanist texts of their day. This led them in some but not all parts of Europe to be formally recognised for their service to the liberal arts (and the university) in the titles they bore ('academiae typographus', 'libraire juré', 'messagier de l'université', for example).[45]

The Mark of the Printer/Publisher

I come finally to a locus of symbolic capital in the publisher's world: the printer's or publisher's mark to be found almost universally on the title-pages of learned books.[46] I have already mentioned that the branch system produced shop signs bearing the merchant's chosen mark. The standard example of this is the vine bush, that in the ancient world was hung outside a wine shop to indicate what sort of shop it was. This has a small element of symbolism; as the emblematologist Jacobus Masenius points out, it operates through a metonymy (the vine that supplied the wreath of Bacchus), giving rise to the ancient saying 'vino vendibili non est opus suspensa hedera' ('If your wine is saleable, it is not necessary to advertise it') (i.e. hang a vine bush outside your shop).[47] Such signs were known as 'insigna ignobilia' ('non-noble signs') or 'insignia mercatorum et artificum' ('the signs of merchants and artisans').[48] In the age before copyright, they could be chosen at will by a merchant or tradesman (though their appropriation by others could be contested), and were distinguished from 'insigna nobiliora' ('Wappen' or coats of arms), the form of which was regulated and could be only displayed and used with the authority of the state.[49] Bartholus's treatise *De insigniis et armis* of 1335 contained the classic

[45] In Italy, the title of university accredited printer was almost unknown; if it is found, it is usually attributed by the printer-publisher to himself: Maclean, *Scholarship, Commerce, Religion*, p. 103.

[46] On this topic, see two important recent studies: Nuovo, *Book Trade*, pp. 143–94; Anja Wolkenhauer and Bernhard F. Scholz (eds), *Typographorum Emblemata: the Printer's Mark in the Context of Early Modern Culture* (Berlin and Boston: de Gruyter, 2018), esp. the following chapters: Bernhard F. Scholz, 'The Truth of Printer's Marks: Andrea Alciato on "Aldo's Anchor", "Froben's Dove", and "Calvo's Elephant". A Closer Look at Alciato's Concept of the Printer's Mark', pp. 269–96, and Valérie Hayaert, 'The Legal Significance and Humanist Ethos of Printers' *Insignia*', pp. 297–314.

[47] Jacobus Masenius, *Speculum imaginum veritatis occultae* (Cologne: Kinchius, 1681), p. 459.

[48] Barthélemy de Chasseneuz, *Catalogus gloriae mundi* (1st edn 1529) (Geneva: apud Philippum Albertum, 1617), p. 25; Pierre Rebuffi, *In titulum Digestorum de verborum et rerum significatione commentaria* (1st edn 1576) (Lyon: apud Gulielmum Rovillium, 1586), p. 4; Hanovius, *Philosophiae civilis sive politicae pars tertia*, paras. 597–604 (where there is a category of 'insignia mixta' as well as 'vulgaria seu ignobilia' and 'nobiliora').

[49] For examples of contestation, see Nuovo, *Book Trade*, pp. 153–4; the use of a prestigious mark could also be conceded for money to a colleague (p. 150).

discussion of the nature of merchants' marks, which the jurist saw as providing a defence against competition and a guarantee of the quality of a given product. These functions, together with the desire for political regulation, were also paramount in early modern legislation, such as François I's *Ordonnance* of 1539.[50]

Insignia in learned books cover a broad spectrum: purely decorative elements or playful allusions to the name of the publisher (as is the millet ('meio') in Roberto Meietti's mark); allusions to the hard work of the publisher (in the mark chosen by Christophe Plantin, whose motto was 'labore et constantia' ('by hard work and persistence'), and that of Jean Maire, simply 'labore'); evocations of the place of publication (as in the mark of the Cholinus family of Cologne); finally, complex images carrying information about the aspirations of the book producer in a complex visual language, with scholarly, political, and religious messages, often reinforced by an allusive text, which are of interest here.[51] Among the objects chosen to convey these messages are animals from the medieval bestiary, religious imagery, and the full range of symbolic material and mythological and human representations that found their way into emblems. As Angela Nuovo points out, heraldry furnished the archetype for the very first device in a printed book, that adopted by Johann Fust and Peter Schöffer in 1457 (Figure 5.1). It depicts two shields hanging from a branch, as would have been the shield of a medieval knight taking part in a tournament.[52] A sequence can be detected in the use of shields and trees; the military metaphor of the 'scutum' can be seen as a device to ward off fraud, and the tree was adapted to carry not a shield but a message on a banderolle.[53] Robert Estienne's mark of a man under a tree bearing the apostolic injunction 'noli altum sapere' ('be not high-minded': Rom. 11:20) refers to the limits of legitimate scholarly enquiry, and implicitly to the responsibility of both publisher and author to respect these (Figure 5.2).[54] The image clearly influences the choice of various Elzeviers, one of whom chose to use the representation of Minerva and her shield under an olive tree with the motto 'ne extra oleas' ('don't stray beyond the olive tress'), again referring to the limits of

---

[50] Hayaert, 'Legal Significance', p. 310.

[51] Lorenzo Carpanè, 'Roberto Meietti', www.treccani.it/enciclopedia/roberto-meietti, accessed 22 November 2021; Nuovo, *Book Trade*, pp. 151–2 (Christophe Plantin); Paul Hoftijzer, '*Pallas Nostra Salus*: Early Modern Printers' Marks in Leiden as Expressions of Professional and Personal Identity', in Wolkenhauer and Scholz (eds), *Typographorum Emblemata*, pp. 169–96 (181) (Jean Maire). The Cholinus family also made liberal use of the mark of the Society of Jesus: see Ian Maclean, 'Sacrobosco at the Book Fairs, 1564–1624: The Pedagogical Marketplace', in Matteo Valleriani and Andrea Ottone (eds), *Publishing Sacrobosco's 'De Sphaera' in Early Modern Europe: Modes of Material and Scientific Exchange* (Springer, forthcoming 2022).

[52] Nuovo, *Book Trade*, p. 147; Heinrich Grimm, *Deutsche Buchdruckersignete des sechszehnten Jahrhunderts* (Wiesbaden: Pressler, 1965), p. 13, points out that commoners such as printers had to be cautious in concocting devices in the form of coats of arms.

[53] Hayaert, 'Legal Significance', p. 308.

[54] Elizabeth Armstrong, *Robert Estienne Royal Printer* (Cambridge: Cambridge University Press, 1954), p. 10, sees the text as 'a manifesto of intellectual humility in the presence of revealed truth, directed alike at excessive dogmatism on the part of Christians and of excessive presumption on the part of "humanist" rationalism'.

Figure 5.1 The mark of Fust and Schoeffer from Juan de Torquemada, *Expositio brevis et utilis super toto psalterio* (Mainz: per petrum Schoyffer, 1476), sig. v7ʳ: shelfmark LR.3.h.7. Courtesy of All Souls College, Oxford.

Figure 5.2 The mark of Robert Estienne from Juvenal, *Satirarum libri v* (Paris: ex officina Rob[erti] Stephani, 1516), title-page: shelfmark e.4.13(2). Courtesy of All Souls College, Oxford.

Figure 5.3 The mark of Louis Elzevier from Louis Cappel, *Diatriba de veris et antiquis literis* (Amsterdam: apud Ludovicum Elzevirium, 1645), title-page: shelfmark 12:SR.68.d.14. Courtesy of All Souls College, Oxford.

legitimate enquiry (Figure 5.3); another member of the family adopted the depiction of a solitary man under an elm tree wound round with a vine, with the motto 'non solus' ('not alone') which has been taken to refer to the mutually beneficial alliance of the sturdy practical (wooden) input of the publisher with the (vinous) inspiration of the scholar (Figure 5.4).[55] These images are relevant to the issue of social status

---

[55] Willems, *Les Elzevier*, xci–iii: 'ne extra oleas [ferri]' is discussed in Erasmus *Adagia*, 2.2.10. The association of elms and vines is found in Ovid, *Metamorphoses*, 10.15 and in Alciato's emblem 159 'amicitia etiam post mortem durans'; see also Hoftijzer, 'Early Modern Printer's Marks', pp. 180–1.

Figure 5.4 The mark of Abraham and Bonaventura Elzevier from Claude Saumaise, *Commentarius de Hellenistica* (Leiden: ex officina Elseviriorum, 1643), title-page: shelfmark f.9.10(1). Courtesy of All Souls College, Oxford.

in that they affirm strongly the association of publishers with their scholar-clients, as Valérie Hayaert points out: 'Emblematic creations bring to the fore the liveliness of *aemulatio* and *inventio* in Humanist circles. Renaissance printers created much more than lexica of trademarks: their refined use of an emblematic grammar provides a vivid picture of the learned friendship between men of letters, printers, publishers and authors of the sixteenth century.'[56]

---

[56] Hayaert, 'Legal Significance', p. 312.

Printers' marks may include text, and are similar to emblems in all respects, except for the absence of commentary. A very famous mark, which is an enriched version of one of Alciati's emblems from the innovative collection of these that he published in 1531, is that of Andreas Wechel and his successors. Wechel's uncle Christianus was an early publisher of the *Emblemata*, and the 1535 edition that he produced of Alciato's work carries as part of its printer's mark Emblem 119 (sometimes numbered 118) without the motto 'Virtuti fortuna comes' ('good fortune is the companion of virtue') (Figure 5.5). The image is of a caduceus, crossed by two cornucopiae and mounted with a second set of wings. The mark (Figure 5.6) is surmounted by Pegasus (the sign Wechel adopted at around this time for his second Parisian premises): this is also illustrated in Alciato's Emblem 14, under the title 'consilio et virtute Chimaeram superari, id est, fortiores et deceptores' ('the monster Chimaera (i.e. the mighty and the deceitful) is defeated by judgement and virtue').[57] To the bottom of the staff are added two clasped right hands emerging from clouds, which signify 'concordia' and collaboration in another emblem (39 'unum nihil, duos plurimum posse': 'two can do many things, one alone none'). We can detect here references to two aspects of the status to which the publisher aspired: not only high humanist content, with the strong connotations of the value of collaboration and rejection of error, together with allusions to the commercial risks involved in publishing that will be reduced if the path of virtue (i.e. respect for the truth and accuracy in representation) is followed. Wechel was at this point in his career a protestant sympathiser: his nephew Andreas, a Calvinist, was to become in 1572 a victim of Parisian Catholic intolerance and a refugee. The 'Chimaera' to which the Alciato Pegasus emblem refers could therefore be seen to have a radical religious message (the monster of theological error), but this is more speculative than the associations with scholarship and economic risk.

When Andreas Wechel developed his own printer's mark after 1574 (Figure 5.7), he added only one repeated element, placed symmetrically on either side of the caduceus: this was his monogram (AW) surmounted by a 'sign of four', which appears on other marks, most notably that of the Parisian printer Jean Granjon (fl. 1504–22), who, like Andreas, placed his monogram underneath it. The 'sign of four' is symbolic of Christ and the cross, and therefore is an indication of Andreas's personal piety. Like Jean I de Tournes in Paris in 1555–6, Andreas's heirs in Hanau, where at some time after 1596 they as Calvinists had fled to escape the intolerance of the Lutheran regime in Frankfurt, had this mark engraved in stone and set above the entrance to their premises where a coat of arms would be in a college or a noble house (Figure 5.8).[58] By this act, the 'insignium ignobile' became very visible, was

---

[57] Michael Pexenfelder, *Ethica symbolica et fabularum umbris in veritatis lucem varia erudtiione, noviter evoluta* (Munich: Rauch, 1675), p. 128 describes Pegasus as the 'ingenii et eruditionis symbolum'.
[58] Hayaert, 'Legal Significance', p. 299.

Figure 5.5 Andrea Alciato, *Emblemata* (Leiden: ex officina Plantiniana apud Franciscum Raphelengium, 1596), p. 437: Emblem 118: 'Virtuti fortuna comes' (mea).

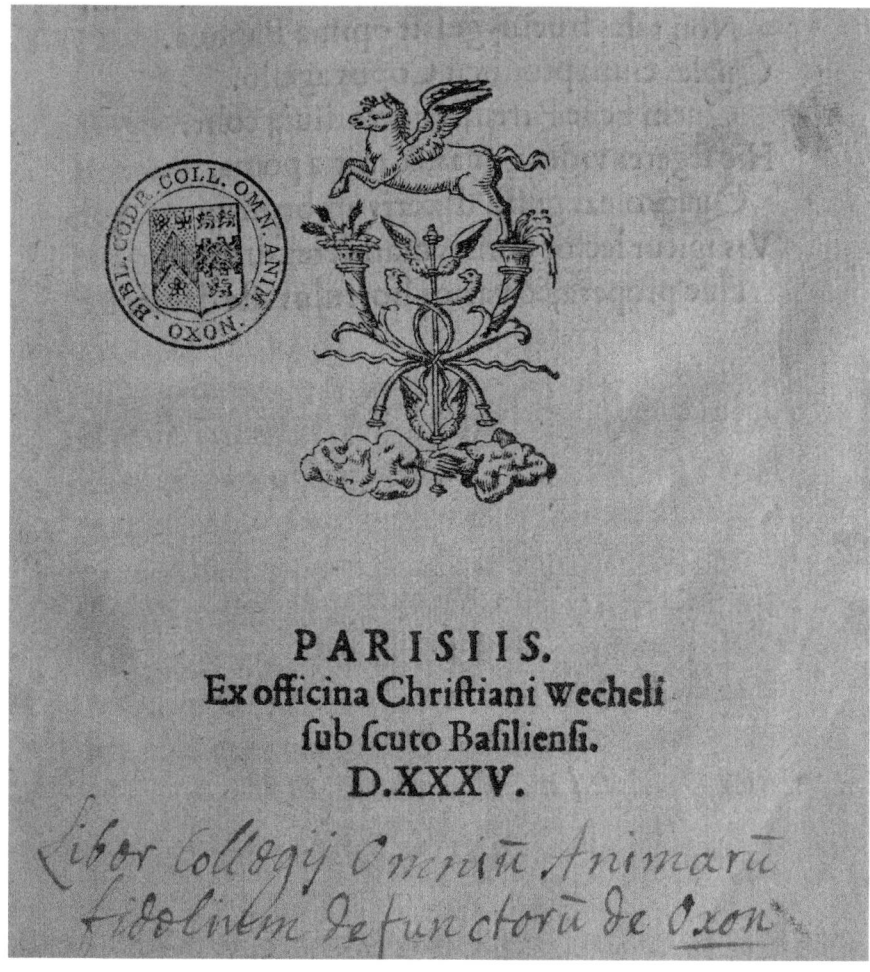

Figure 5.6 The mark of Christianus Wechel from Joannes Copus, *De fructibus libri quatuor* (Paris: ex officina Christiani Wecheli, 1535), title page: shelfmark cc.infra.1.21(1). Courtesy of All Souls College, Oxford.

ennobled, by implication publicly sanctioned, and set in stone.[59] Marks could become noble in another way, too: after 1572, Aldus Manutius the Younger chose as his mark the grant of arms made to his father Paulus as an imperial knight (incorporating the famous Dolphin and Anchor device and reinforced by an imperial eagle).[60]

[59] Walter Martin Fraeb, *Hanau in der Geschichte des Buchhandels und Druckschriften* (Hanau: Verlag des Vereins, 1931), p. 19 (with an image).
[60] Nuovo, *Book Trade*, pp. 181–2 (with an image).

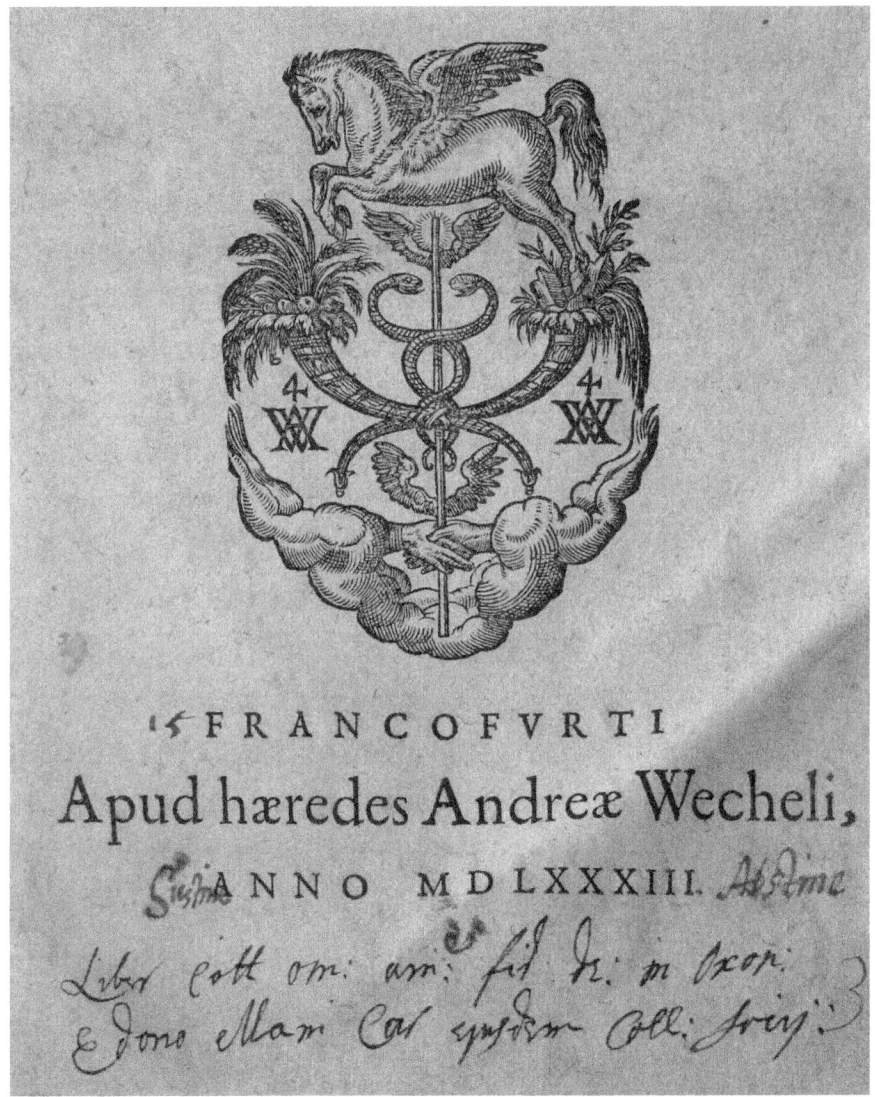

Figure 5.7 The mark of Andreas Wechel from Pausanias. *Tēs Hellados periēgēsis* [*Accurata Graeciae descriptio*] (Frankfurt: apud haeredes Andreae Wecheli, 1583), title-page: shelfmark g.infra.2.14. Courtesy of All Souls College, Oxford.

Figure 5.8 The lintel of the house of the Wechel Presses in Hanau from Walter Martin Fraeb, *Hanau in der Geschichte des Buchhandels und Druckschriften* (Hanau: Geschichtsverein, 1931), p. 19: shelfmark Hist.Bg.57. Courtesy of All Souls College, Oxford.

Habitus, Field, Capital

This brief survey of features of the social status of publishers of learned books has not addressed a number of pertinent questions. Did they perceive themselves as having all the same status? How was it defined in legal terms? Did their status change over the course of their careers? To what extent did it depend on where they practised their trade in Europe? And did they all relate in the same way to the community of authors which they served? It is also pertinent to ask whether publishing was a locus of social mobility in the early modern world. These are very broad and complex questions, and it might be objected that even if I could answer them, no general picture would emerge, because the circumstances of each case would be unique. What I shall now try to do on the basis of the limited and somewhat disparate evidence I have produced is to give a Bourdieusian account of their status using the interrelated categories of habitus, field, and capital.

Except for the reference to labour and expense, there is little evocation of the specific mode of thinking linked to the artisanal side of the publisher's role in producing books. It seems to me rather that there are two versions of 'habitus' or mental dispositions that apply to a publisher; that of the merchant, and that of the scholar. They share a number of characteristics with their counterparts in, say, the wool or spice trades: hard work, fidelity as financial and fiscal accuracy, and fidelity as an element of the ethics of exchange (i.e. *bona fides*). Merchants have as part of their habitus a 'mercatoria prudentia' (as distinguished from other forms of prudence) which will ensure profit and the continuity of their trade; publishers who are merchants have in addition a cultural role that makes them 'witnesses to the truth' ('testes veritatis'), and obliges them to reproduce (as far as their knowledge and conscience will permit) the truth, the whole truth, and nothing but the truth. In Adrien Baillet's terms, the best of them 'have distinguished themselves by their knowledge, their fidelity, their accuracy and their impartiality, which are the four principal qualities necessary for books to be well produced'.[61] These virtues (especially that of impartiality) are potentially in conflict with the confessional world in which they find themselves. But even if they believe that they can operate in a confessionally free world of scholarship, they have to excuse themselves from the taint of profit-making, and present themselves as the servants of the Republic of Letters whose 'priests' are the scholars that they publish.[62] They bring to these scholars the promise of textual accuracy through their employment of correctors; they also deploy on their behalf the trade secrets of the international zone of scholarship (marketing, manipulation of international markets, collaboration with

---

[61] Adrien Baillet, *Jugemens des savants sur les principaux ouvrages des auteurs*, vol. 1, ed. Bernard de la Monnaye (Paris: Charles Moette et al., 1723), p. 345: '[ils] se sont signalés par leur savoir, par leur fidelité, par leur éxactitude [*sic*], et par leur désintéressement, qui sont les quatre principales qualités nécessaires pour les bonnes impressions des Livres.'

[62] On authors as the 'priests of the republic of letters', see Maclean, *Scholarship, Commerce, Religion*, p. 246.

colleagues that transcends confessional differences, the use of legal protection for their products which benefited also their authors, and networks of distribution) and the strategies necessary for financial survival. These features of their activity as publishers are partially disguised by their rhetorical self-presentation as subscribers to the ideology of knowledge as a gift.

The field in which they operate is that of the city. This excluded them from all but the kind of nobility that in some places was conferred by municipal office. They did not have to be implicitly at odds with the philistine values of bourgeois existence, as Bourdieu claims they were in the nineteenth century, and indeed, those early modern publishers of learned books who were financially successful did not deny themselves the comforts of urban existence. In order-based societies where the *premier état* were the clergy, they could even benefit from close association with this class, and from institutions such as universities. But the threat of the confessional allegiances and divisions which impinged on the world of scholarship was omnipresent, and could affect their status and even survival in conflictual environments. The confessionalised European world after 1560 can be compared in this respect to the culturally conflicted environment of nineteenth-century France.

The capital that they deployed came in various guises: economic capital (money), human capital (editorial staff), symbolic capital (prestige), intellectual capital (the exclusive rights to publication in a given jurisdiction). Their system of barter with colleagues, and the uncertainty of locating clients, often produced severe problems of cash flow and storage which justified in part publishers' frequent threnodies about money, and made them look to diversification as a partial remedy. Their human capital consisted in the workers in the print shop; of these, the corrector brought them the greatest prestige, tying them very closely to the world of scholarship. They themselves expressed their symbolic capital most clearly through their marks, which conveyed various messages: their allegiance to the values of humanism, their essential role in the Republic of Letters, their piety, their accuracy, and the financial risks they took on behalf of their authors and others, which they sought to mitigate by procuring privileges for their books in certain markets. This range of messages neatly reveals the faultline that characterises their status as members of two orders (that of scholarship and that of commerce) whose fundamental values were in the end irreconcilable. It may also allude more widely to the potential faultline within scholarship itself: the boundaries of legitimate intellectual study will in the early years of the Enlightenment become a moral and conscientious issue in the free application of historical enquiry to religious texts and subjects that had previously been exempt from such scrutiny. Perhaps this is the area where Bourdieu's insights into the internal contradictions of class in nineteenth-century France most clearly have a parallel in the early modern world.

6

Literary Collaboration and Social Legitimacy in an Actor's Oeuvre: The Peculiar Case of Francesco Andreini (d.1624)

SARAH GWYNETH ROSS

NEVER TRUST AN actor. Had the Mantuan notary Sinforiano Forti heeded this advice, he might not have ended up an abettor in an act of theatrical self-representation perpetrated by Francesco Andreini (d.1624), a commedia dell'arte star recently turned author. On 9 June 1607, Andreini appeared at Forti's offices to register his final will and testament. In this document, Andreini claimed to be, and Forti registered him as, 'M[agnifi]cus D[ominu]s Franc[iscu]s f[uit] q[uondam] D[omini] Antonij de Andreinis de Pistoia, et civis Mant[uae] p[er] dec[re]tu[m] ducalem' ('His Magnificence, Lord Francesco, son of Lord Antonio de Andreini from Pistoia, and citizen of Mantua by ducal decree').[1] Citizen of Mantua Andreini was, but the ink had scarcely dried on that paperwork. Three days earlier (6 June 1607), Andreini had secured his honorary citizenship in Mantua, a fact recorded by Ercole Marliani, Duke Vincenzo I Gonzaga's secretary. In Marliani's attestation, however, he described the supplicant for citizenship as a respectable man, but not a member of the landed nobility; in this case, the actor was described not as 'His Magnificence, Lord Francesco' but as 'M[esse]r Franc[es]co Andreini da Pistoia' ('Mister Francesco Andreini from Pistoia').[2] Honourable commoner to nobleman in three days? Now that would be quite a case of social mobility! Far more likely, it was another fascinating instance of a phenomenon increasingly familiar to scholars, following the work of Natalie Zemon Davis; it was another fiction in the archives.[3]

---

[1] Testament of Francesco Andreini, Archivio di Stato di Mantova (ASMn), atti Sinforiano Forti, b.4460, unfoliated. All translations from the Italian and Latin are my own unless otherwise noted.

[2] Attestazione del Cancelliere Ducale Ercole Marliani (6 June 1607), ASMn, Notarile, Atti Sinforiano Forti, b.4460, unfoliated.

[3] Natalie Zemon Davis, *Fiction in the Archives: Pardon Tales and their Tellers in Sixteenth-Century France* (Stanford: Stanford University Press, 1987).

Proceedings of the British Academy, **246**, 121–138, © The British Academy 2022.

This fiction had an even more improbable script than most, however, since two millennia of clerical and legal anti-theatricalism relegated performers like Andreini to society's margins. To the best of my knowledge, no other performer before Francesco amassed these levels either of cultural or of literal capital. How had he managed this feat?

Scholars these days do work on the understanding that people could change social categories before the modern era. Following recent work by John Padgett, we have even begun to speak with more confidence about social mobility in Renaissance Italy.[4] If wealth accumulation, network building, and advantageous marriages offered clear routes to social betterment, did professional success or a humanistic education work similarly? The peculiar case of theatrical social mobility analysed in the present chapter answers that question in the affirmative. We will consider here how Francesco Andreini's turn from performances of vernacular humanism on the stage to those on the page made his real-world performance as 'His Magnificence' more compelling, and the special power that his publications drew from Francesco's posthumous collaboration with his celebrated wife, Isabella (d.1604). Then as now, Isabella enjoyed wider fame than her husband both as a performer and as a poet; her posthumous reputation constituted an indispensable asset for her husband's authorial career.

Francesco retired from acting immediately following Isabella's death in the summer of 1604. His first literary work was that of an editor, publishing posthumous editions of his wife's work in service to her reputational posterity, while also paving the way for his own first solo-authored publications. Our primary analytical quarry here will be analysis of this first phase of Francesco's entrance into the world of print, and especially the way he interwove his authorial identity with Isabella's. Contextualising this discursive manoeuvring will lead us to consider the social and moral obstacles faced by everyone involved with the commedia dell'arte, as well as how atypical his strategies look from the perspective of gender. The peculiar case of Francesco Andreini shows us literary ambitions and pursuits reshaping not only social categories but even patriarchal norms. Above all, Andreini's machinations reveals the interplay of social, moral, and literary assets in the complex calculus of 'status' in early modern Italy.

Spotlight on Isabella

A captivating performer, and author of a popular pastoral fable, and a collection of poetry impressive enough to earn her membership in the Accademia degli Intenti of Pavia, Isabella's too-short career did important preliminary work in raising

---

[4] John Padgett, '"Open Elite": Social Mobility, Marriage, and Family in Florence, 1282–1494', *Renaissance Quarterly*, 63 (2010), 357–411. On cultural approaches to social positioning, see especially Renata Ago, *Il gusto delle cose. Una storia degli oggetti nella Roma del Seicento* (Rome: Donzelli Editore, 2006); Brian Maxson, *The Humanist World of Renaissance Florence* (Cambridge: Cambridge University Press, 2014); Sarah Gwyneth Ross, *Everyday Renaissances: The Quest for Cultural Legitimacy in Venice* (Cambridge, MA: Harvard University Press, 2016).

the profile and status of the commedia dell'arte. Her example had convinced the literary elite, including a few clerics, that the commedia, even inclusive of its women performers, might be understood as a type of vernacular humanism and a platform for delivering both Christian virtue and classical polish to the masses.[5] Not surprisingly, Isabella's kin and colleagues affiliated with her. Her first-born son, Giovan Battista, eagerly cultivated his image as 'Isabella's son' well into his dotage.[6] Isabella's daughter-in-law, Virginia Ramponi, got the tag 'Isabella reborn'.[7] But Francesco Andreini, Isabella's co-star and co-director of the Compagnia dei Gelosi, connected himself to her legacy in the most distinctive and collaborative mode.

Francesco Andreini's first two ventures in print constituted ongoing collaborations of different kinds with his erstwhile wife and co-star: a republication of Isabella's popular *Rime* (1605; first edition 1601 and second in 1603), now ornamented with eulogies and elegies from other prominent literati, including the luminary Giovan Battista Marino; an edition of Isabella's unpublished *Lettere* (1607); and a collection of his original compositions elaborating upon the semi-improvised speeches delivered in his signature role of Capitan Spavento da Val Inferna (Captain Shellshock from Hell's Valley), the *Bravure del Capitan Spavento* (first edition, 1609), which he claimed to have published 'per lasciar qualche memoria di me, e per seguitare l'honorato grido della moglie mia, la quale haveva lasciato al mondo, con tanta sua gloria, e con tanto suo honore il suo bellissimo Canzoniero, la sua bellissima Mirtilla Favola Boscareccia, & il Compendio delle sue bellissime Lettere' ('in order to leave some memory of myself, and to follow the honorable celebrity of my wife, who bequeathed to the world her ravishing *Rime*, her marvelous *Mirtilla* (a pastoral fable), and the Compendium of her lovely *Lettere*').[8] Scholars have hardly overlooked this instance of apparent literary chivalry; on the contrary, we (myself included) have repeated the story of Francesco stewarding Isabella's reputational posterity so often that I fear we have unintentionally normalised this wildly atypical situation.

---

[5] On Isabella's career and reception, see especially Anne MacNeil, *Music and Women of the Commedia dell'Arte* (Oxford: Oxford University Press, 2003); Julie Campbell, *Literary Circles and Gender in Early Modern Europe: A Cross-Cultural Approach* (Aldershot: Ashgate, 2006), ch. 2; Meredith Ray, *Writing Gender in Women's Letter Collections of the Italian Renaissance* (Toronto: University of Toronto Press, 2009), ch. 5; Sarah Gwyneth Ross, *The Birth of Feminism: Woman as Intellect in Renaissance Italy and England* (Cambridge, MA: Harvard University Press, 2009), ch. 5; Rosalind Kerr, *The Rise of the Diva on the Sixteenth-Century Stage* (Toronto: University of Toronto Press, 2015), especially ch. 5.

[6] Even in a late patronage plea of 1651, Giovan Battista Andreini signs 'figlio d'Isabella'. See Giovan Battista Andreini's letter to Carlo II Gonzaga, doc. 76 in Claudia Burattelli, Siro Ferrone, Domenica Landolfi, and Anna Zinanni (eds), *Comici dell'Arte Corrispondenze*, 2 vols (Florence: Casa Editrice Le Lettere, 1993), vol. 1, pp. 166–7, quotation at 166; contextualised, p. 167 n.3.

[7] See Emily Wilbourne, 'Isabella ringovinita: Virginia Ramponi Andreini before "Arianna"', *Recercare*, 19 (2007), 47–71.

[8] Francesco Andreini, *Bravure del Capitan Spavento* (Venice: Giacomo Antonio Somasco, 1609), sig. ++2v.

The traditional benchmarks of womanly excellence constituted that starchy trip-tych of chastity, silence, and obedience, undergirded by Christian piety. Humanistic texts and conduct books also emphasised that a wife should be frugal, observe her maternal duties punctiliously, and serve her husband's interests unquestion-ingly.[9] Renaissance feminism had cut a discursive path for women intellectuals and writers; but the operational paradigm of wifely excellence had not shifted much.[10] Francesco Andreini hybridised normative and Renaissance feminist modalities, presenting Isabella as a paragon of traditional wifeliness and innovative literary leadership. The widower announced this new conception of excellence already in the Latin epitaph that he placed on her (now destroyed) grave in the Church of Sainte-Croix in Lyon, then reproduced in the prefatory material for the 1605 edition of her *Rime*. On the normatively feminine side, Francesco insisted that Isabella had been 'magna virtute praedita, honestatis ornamentum, maritalisque pudicitiae decus' ('outstanding for her great virtue, an ornament of integrity, paragon of marital modesty'); he also specifies that she went down on 9 June 1604 in the line of maternal duty 'from a miscarriage (*ob abortum*)'. Yet readers also learn that Isabella was 'ore facunda, mente fecunda ... Musis amica, & artis Scenicae caput' ('fertile in her speech, and fertile in her mind ... a friend to the Muses, and head of the theatrical art').[11]

The humanistic canonisation of Isabella continued apace in Francesco's editorial work for the 1607 edition of Isabella's *Lettere*. While he did not claim his contributions to this volume explicitly, he left strong hints of his hand. First, the dedicatory letter, although signed with the name Isabella Andreini, nonethe-less is dated 4 March 1607, that is, nearly three years after Isabella's death. In her 1601 correspondence with Erycius Puteanus, a Dutch humanist turned Professor of Rhetoric in Milan, Isabella had mentioned working hard on a volume of letters; so, most of the collection likely came from her hand.[12] Yet the standard practice of writing a dedication just before a volume went to press, and the dating of the letter in this case, point to Francesco as the probable author of this piece.[13] Indeed, Meredith Ray has read both this editorial work and Francesco's references to his literary stewardship peppered through his oeuvre as evidence of him taking up a

[9] A representative text is Francesco Barbaro's treatise 'On Wifely Duties'; see Benjamin Kohl and Ronald Witt (eds), *The Earthly Republic: Italian Humanists on Government and Society* (Philadelphia: University of Pennsylvania Press, 1978), pp. 179–230.

[10] On theories and practices of Renaissance feminism, see especially Constance Jordan, *Renaissance Feminism: Literary Texts and Political Models* (Ithaca: Cornell University Press, 1990); Virginia Cox, 'The Single Self: Feminist Thought and the Marriage Market in Early Modern Venice', *Renaissance Quarterly*, 48 (1995), 513–81; and Ross, *The Birth of Feminism*.

[11] Isabella Andreini, *Rime d'Isabella Andreini, Comica Gelosa, & Academica Intenta detta l'Accesa* (Milan: Bordone and Locarni, 1605), sig. A7r.

[12] Quoted in Ray, *Writing Gender*, pp. 296–7 n.19. For the full letter, see Charles Reulens, *Erycius Puteanus et Isabelle Andreini: Lecture faite à l'Académie d'Archéologie le 3 février 1889* (Antwerp: n.p., 1889), pp. 25–6.

[13] Ray, *Writing Gender*, p. 162.

position as 'Isabella's historian and hagiographer, the promoter of her impeccable image'.[14] I follow Ray in this reading, as well as in the conviction that two of the letters in the collection itself, those framed as husbands lamenting the loss of their wives, were Francesco's original compositions. What I wish to stress in the following analysis of these artefacts are the ways Francesco signalled his presence, his ongoing collaboration with Isabella, to readers at the time.

The widowers' letters, one of which appears midway through the volume, and the other at its conclusion, would have jolted contemporary readers. The other letters do adopt a wide range of voices to discourse on philosophical and social topics such as honour, friendship, and love – topics that had animated Isabella's speeches in her eponymous character of the ingenue, as well as the dialogues in her pastoral fable, *Mirtilla* (first edition, 1578). To that point in the volume, however, we find no letters of mourning or condolence. Not only does that persona seem out of keeping with the rest, the virulence of misery expressed in this instance represents a departure as well. 'Nel perderti hò perdut'ogni cosa', the widower claims, adding, 'anzi sopravivo contra ma voglia à me stesso, il viver m'è proprio un flagello d'esser vissuto troppo' ('In losing you, I have lost everything […] I have actually, and against my will, outlived myself; for me, being alive is truly a scourge, a goading awareness that I have lived too long').[15] Isabella certainly could have thought her way into an old man's headspace, but nothing she published while alive adopted that voice. The speaker's observation that he has 'lived too long', more-over, seems only too fitting as a poignant self-reference from Francesco. Given that the real-life widower was about 20 years Isabella's senior, it would surely have seemed a cruel irony that he should have been the one to survive and mourn.

Other clues in these letters nudged readers to think of Francesco collaborating with Isabella. A second widower's lament closes the collection as a whole. In this case, the widower regrets, 'non posso pianger sopra le tue ossa honorate quanto vorrei' ('I cannot weep over your honored bones as I would wish'). The letter gives no context for that remark, but it fits the well-known circumstance that Isabella had been buried in Lyon, where a commemorative coin had also been struck on the occasion, but Francesco thereafter returned to Italy.[16] The widower-speaker continues to dwell upon the image of the now-inaccessible grave, addressing the letter's fictitious recipient, an unnamed male friend, and begging, 'pregate Iddio, che mi consoli, permettendo, che quanto prima quel Sepolcro, che la mia carissima donna rinchiude, ancor me accolga. Sia col suo cenere unito il mio' ('pray to God that he console me, granting that, as soon as possible, the Tomb which now encases my dearest lady contain me. And let my ashes be mixed with hers').[17] The ways in

---

[14] Ray, *Writing Gender*, pp. 162–5; quotation at p. 163.
[15] Isabella Andreini, *Lettere d'Isabella Andreini Padovana, comica Gelosa et academica Intenta nominata l'Accesa* (Venice: Marc'Antonio Zaltieri, 1607), sig. 136v.
[16] *Lettere*, sig. 154v.
[17] *Lettere*, sigs. 155r-v.

which the widower construes the excellences of the deceased make plain why this widower's paroxysms of grief should be forgiven, and in so doing strongly echo Francesco's epitaph for Isabella, indicating to readers that in these letters it is the departed actor and poet upon whom we are meditating. The widower addresses his deceased wife directly, calling her a credit to their age, and beseeching her, 'ch'io possa imitarti nell'altezza dei pensieri. Tu benche mortale sempre havesti pensieri immortali. L'istesso anch'io vorrei, e senz'altro l'havrò, poiche dalla tua bontà mi verrà la gratia' ('that I might imitate you in the loftiness of my own thoughts. You, although mortal, always had immortal thoughts. I would like the same myself, and certainly I'll have that grace, since from your bounty it will come to me').[18] Part of the message here doubtless is the typical theme in mourning literature that a loved one's loss should spur survivors to abandon worldly concerns and turn to things divine. Still, as the last word in a volume of erudite letters attributed to a celebrated woman intellectual, I think the image of the widower receiving from his dead beloved 'the same immortal thoughts' should be understood to be Francesco positioning himself as the primary heir and beneficiary of Isabella Andreini's literary and cultural estate.

Reading these letters as the product of the widower Francesco's budding authorship, we see him do more than steward Isabella's memory; he collaborates with it, and in a manner of speaking with her. If Francesco wedged himself only obliquely into Isabella's *Lettere*, two years later he would bring Isabella explicitly and even jarringly into the first work published under his own name, the *Bravure del Capitan Spavento* (1609). In one prefatory letter, as we have seen, Francesco in his own voice explicitly positions the work as an homage to the author who was once his wife. A second prefatory letter, in the guise of a shepherd named Corinto, almost overdetermines the *Bravure* as a monument to Isabella. In Corinto's mourning for the death of his beloved nymph Fillide, Francesco rehearses again concepts from the second widower's lament of Isabella's *Lettere*, including the wish for entombment with the dead beloved: 'O quanto volentieri haverei le mie ossa con le sua ossa, la mia cenere con la sua cenere, rinchiuse in un medesimo tempo, & in un medesimo sepolcro?' ('O how willingly would I have my bones with her bones, my ashes with hers, enclosed at the same time, in the same tomb?')[19] Distorting pastoral conventions, Francesco even gives the bereaved shepherd children to protect; Corinto states that, as much as he craves to share Fillide's grave, 'la pietà congiunta con l'amore de' nostri teneri Fanciulli, e nostri communi Figli, mi ritiene il corso' ('piety, joined with the love of our tender little ones, the children we made together, keeps me on course').[20] Pastorals did not typically get into the weeds of childrearing, still less the responsibilities of a survivor to care for a family even in the face of suicidal grief. Francesco once again jostles genres, temporalities, and

---

[18] *Lettere*, sig. 155r.

[19] Andreini, *Bravure*, sig. ++r.

[20] Andreini, *Bravure*, sig. ++v.

the boundaries between his characters and his own identity to create a space in which he and Isabella may still somehow be in the scene together.

The incongruous disquisitions on Isabella that Francesco shovels into the dialogues themselves seem similarly designed to draw readers' attention. The *Bravure*, while showcasing Capitan Spavento's verbal gymnastics, are structured as dialogues between Francesco's signature character of the cowardly braggart and his acerbic servant, Trappola, modelled in part on Cervantes's Sancho Panza. While comedy thrived on convoluted interactions and relationships, the Captain, a summation of all failed virilities, *never* got the girl. Accordingly, Isabella's periodic appearances in the *Bravure* as the Captain's lost beloved relied on the reader's recognition of the present work's writer with his former stage character.

Direct references to Isabella abound in the *Bravure* but let us consider only the most extensive example. Capitan Spavento and Trappola inhabit the world of social satire, so whiplash ensues when the Captain abruptly turns in this case from a ribald boast about kissing the goddess Venus to praise in lugubrious tones the departed Isabella; and his servant, instead of one of his usual tart ripostes, joins in the fawning – even rattling off Isabella's literary CV! Such a shift offered another way in which Francesco, in Meredith Ray's terms, played Isabella's 'historian and hagiographer' while at the same time, in the terms I am suggesting, he maintained a collaborative relationship with her that legitimised his own endeavours:

CAPITAN: Dapoi il ricevuto bacio dalla rosata bocca di Venere, e data la libertade a' Cupido, ella mi disse, Capitano Spavento, va', & ama mentre, che tu haverai, e spirito, e vita, Isabella Andreini, Academica Intenta detta l'Accesa, ornamento, e splendor de secol nostro. Ilche fu' fatto: Amai, amo, & amero', se bene hor posso dire, che in un punto la viddi, e ne fui privo; essend'ella passata a' miglior vita.

TRAPPOLA: Padrone la vostra Amata Donna si puo' dir viva, e non morta; Se viva e' colei, che gloriosa rimane al Mondo per mezo della Virtù. Io l'hò più, e più volte sentita lodare da Nobilissimi ingegni; Hò vedute l'Opere sue alla Stampa, cioè il suo Canzoniero, la sua Mirtilla, Opera Boscareccia, & il Compendio delle sue Lettere, che tutte insieme m'hanno fatto stupire, come stupisce chiunque le vede.

CAPITAN: La mia Carissima Donna fù tanto ammiratrice delle antiche, e gloriose Donne, che superando tutti gli humani affetti, sempre di loro trattava, e sempre cercava d'imitarle; adoperando per Rocca il Libro, per Fuso la Penna, e per Ago lo Stile.

TRAPPOLA: Platone chiamò Minervo [*sic*] Dea Filosofante, bellicosa, e Tritogenia, volendo significare la Donna essere il vero Albergo dell'Armi, e delle Lettere, e tale credo, che fusse la vostra Signora Isabella; Attendete dunque ad honorarla morta, si come viva caldamente l'amaste.

CAPITAN: Così sarà per certo.

CAPITAN: After I received that kiss from Venus's rosy mouth, and after I'd freed Cupid, Venus said to me: 'Captain Spavento, go now; and so long as you have breath and life, love Isabella Andreini, member of the Academy of the Intenti and called by them The Burning One, ornament and splendor of our age.' So I did: I loved, I love, and I will love her, though now I could say that almost in the same moment as I saw her I lost her, seeing that now she has passed to the better life.

TRAPPOLA: Padrone, one might also call Your Lordship's Beloved Lady alive, and not dead,since she remains present and glorious in this World by means of her Virtues. I have many, many times heard her praised by the Most Noble geniuses. I have seen her Works at the Presses, that is: her *Rime*, her *Mirtilla* (a Pastoral Fable), and the Compendium of her *Letters*, all of which together have made me marvel, just like everyone else who sees them.

CAPITAN: My Dearest Lady was such an admirer of the ancient and glorious Ladies that, passing beyond every human concern, she was always talking about them, and always trying to imitate them, holding a Book instead of a Distaff, a Pen instead of Spindle, and Literary Style instead of a Needle.[21]

TRAPPOLA: Plato called Minerva the Philosophic Goddess, warlike, and Tritoness, wishing to construe that Lady as the true abode of both Arms and Letters, and such I think was Your Lordship's Lady Isabella. Take care, then, to honour her dead, as much as you loved her passionately while she lived.

CAPITAN: That will certainly be the case.[22]

This out-of-place encomium reminded readers particularly of Isabella Andreini's academic and literary prestige. Note that neither Capitan Spavento nor Trappola refers to her success on the stage. If in the few years before her death Isabella identified both as a *Comica Gelosa* (actor with the Gelosi company) and as an *Academica Intenta* (member of the Accademia degli Intenti), only the literary credentials get explicit citation in this case. Through connection with his celebrated wife's authorship, Francesco Andreini refigured his Capitan, transforming the buffoon's nonsensical classicising, formerly played for laughs, to an earnestly humanistic register. In so doing, the mendacious braggart became a virtuous character, at least for the moment. This form of breaking the fourth wall did critical work for Andreini in socio-cultural terms. Aiming at respectability for himself and his art, he stressed here his Captain's, and by extension his own, humanistic and moral credentials, augmenting them by association with the unimpeachable cultural model he followed not only as a husband but also as an author. Social aspirations, for him, clearly required leveraging literary credentials.

---

[21] On this trope of Renaissance feminism, see especially Lisa Jardine, '"O Decus Italiae Virgo": or The Myth of the Learned Lady in Renaissance Italy', *The Historical Journal*, 28 (1985), 799–819; and Margaret King, *Women of the Renaissance* (Chicago: University of Chicago Press, 1991), pp. 180–1.

[22] Andreini, *Bravure*, sigs. I6v-I7r.

This strange manifestation of Isabella's ghost, then, authorised Francesco's turn from the stage to the page, and legitimised his maiden voyage in the world of print – a gutsy debut at that. *The Bravure*, while drawing on millennia of dialogic conventions, constituted the first literary elaboration on speeches given in an actor's signature role. This collection served as a prelude to what would become a cohesive project of defending and ennobling the commedia dell'arte that occupied Francesco for the rest of his life, and many of his colleagues and kin for decades to come. It made a great deal of sense, then, to keep the spotlight at intervals on the virtuous literary icon Isabella, even in a ludic space like the *Bravure*, where neither Isabella's eponymous character nor the erudite poet herself belonged.

The Heroic Widower

In situating himself as Isabella's designated mourner, affiliating his literary career to hers and burnishing her reputation even to the (partial) effacement of his own identity, Francesco Andreini undertook some unprecedented self-fashioning for a man of his time. This stewardship, as Meredith Ray notes, served '[Isabella's] benefit and his own'.[23] I would like to take that idea, offered as part of the context within which Ray situates her splendid analysis of Isabella Andreini's epistolary writing, and make it our next object of inquiry.

If Francesco had fashioned himself as the designated mourner and literary steward of a famous male author, that would require little explanation, being a typical accumulation of status points through association with an established humanist. Since that humanist happened to be a woman, however, and Francesco's own wife at that, that choice demands further analysis. In patriarchal terms, a husband subsuming his personhood into his wife's made very little cultural sense. Frame that personhood in the normatively masculine terms of intellectual and literary leadership, rather than piety or some other attribute conceivably applicable to both sexes, and one moved into the realm of the bizarre and even transgressive. Francesco's role as the heroic widower had no stable precedent, and should be considered one of his innovations, forged in the unusual conditions of his need to position Isabella as at once his former wife, his current muse and the font of his authorial legitimacy, and as an emblem of his profession's potential for humanistic excellence.

What other husband, even mythological, ever situated his wife as the founding parent of his intellectual or literary genealogy? What other male author interwove his own writings with his wife's, while leaving her with the byline, thereby moving into the territory of literary transvestism? Orpheus might be considered a model for the widower, his irredeemable loss the precondition for his sublime poetry.

---

[23] Ray, *Writing Gender*, p. 164.

Yet Eurydice seems only to have been beautiful, not brilliant. As for Orpheuses in the historical world, we think immediately of Dante and Petrarch. Here, too, however, Laura and Beatrice only got the attributes of beauty and, in the case of Beatrice, optimal piety as well. The geniuses in these poetic couples remained the male parties. The learned Heloise would be another possibility, and Abelard certainly stresses his lover and eventual wife's intelligence. Yet this was no model marriage; rather, that intellectual love story stood as a cautionary tale, and besides that Abelard never credited Heloise with cultural leadership. Closer to Andreini's own time, we do find the Quattrocento poet Malatesta Malatesti expressing his desire to self-immolate at his wife Elisabetta's grave; but it was his love, not her genius, that remained the point in that case, too.[24]

The closest precursor I am aware of comes from Andreini's own context: Adriano Valerini's 1570 funerary oration for the performer Vincenza Armani. This lengthy eulogy emphasised to the *literati* of Cremona, the city in which Armani had died the previous year, that she had possessed every human excellence, including a complete mastery of Latin by the age of 15.[25] Valerini's model doubtless inspired Andreini, but could not be a mere template for him. Valerini and Armani seem to have been lovers, but they were not married; accordingly, Valerini leaves the type of love he had for Armani vague, somewhere in the zone of poetic chivalry. Francesco, in positioning himself as the steward not of an ideal beloved but of his actual wife and the mother of his eight children, needed to write a different script. As a husband and father, he was supposed to exude patriarchal authority, not defer to a wife in the knightly mode permissible in the context of courtly (non-marital) poetics.

Indeed, even the poetic tradition set some boundaries on how much grief a man might express. For all his moon-calfing about Laura, Petrarch stuck to abstractions; we find in the *Canzoniere* no models for Francesco Andreini's disquieting suicidal ideations or reflections on his own advancing age. And small wonder: Petrarch situated the *Canzoniere* less as an archive of experience than as a bid for poetic fame. In particular, his frequent play on the tangencies of the Italian name Laura and the Latin word for laurel tree (*laurea*) marked the cycle as an application for the laurel crown traditionally bestowed on poets in the ancient world. Lovelorn poetics were also a side hustle for Petrarch, a civic-minded humanist by day, in which capacity he sometimes even attacked overflowing feeling as a public menace.

---

[24] See Shannon McHugh, *The Gender of Desire* (New York: New York University Press, 2015), pp. 204–5. For a helpful survey of approaches to marital love and its literary representation, see also Perrine Galand-Hallyn and John Nassichuk (eds), *Aspects du Lyrisme conjugal à la Renaissance* (Geneva: Droz, 2011).

[25] *Orazione d'Adriano Valerini Veronese, In morte della Divina Signora Vicenza Armani, Comica Eccellentissima, 1570*, ed. Ferruccio Marotti and Giovanna Romei, in *La commedia dell'arte: storia, testi, documenti; La professione del teatro*, 2 vols (Rome: Bulzoni Editore, 1991), pp. 31–41; on Armani's mastery of Latin, p. 33.

In one striking excursus on good government from his later years, for instance, Petrarch urged Francesco da Carrara, Lord of Padua, to ban wailing women from public spaces, because their cacophonous funerary lamentations had no place in a well-ordered patriarchal society.[26]

In a similar spirit of curbing the (patently gendered) social danger of strong emotions, premodern conduct literature, conventions of consolation, and even civil law had long construed the type of boundless grief Francesco Andreini expressed as blameworthy in men. For a start, since antiquity histrionic lamentation constituted women's work. As we have learned from Anna Wainwright, the Renaissance widow continued in that vein; she remained the one expected to grieve profoundly, sincerely, piously, and at great length; many women writers, paradigmatically Vittoria Colonna, even made literary careers for themselves out of that traditional expectation.[27] Men might also weep, of course, but soberly – and preferably at the death of a male leader, male friend, or male child. As much as they loved Cicero, Renaissance humanists sometimes got uncomfortable about the moral philosopher's loss of composure at the death of his daughter, Tullia. Even in the case of the death of a male child, moreover, a father who admitted to a sorrow so profound that it led to thoughts of suicide got tart reminders about manly restraint from at least a few of his humanist well-wishers.[28] Still more pointedly regarding the male bereaved, Carol Lansing's extraordinary book on the processes and policies driving the transition from commune to republic in the later medieval period includes the striking example of Orvieto, where she found over 200 cases in which residents faced stiff fines for performative grief at funerals. Out of these hundreds of fines, only *two* were levied against women![29] Had he lived in medieval Orvieto, then, Francesco Andreini's style of mourning might have brought him a fine for criminally effeminate emotionalism.

What inspired such a departure, then? Like all commedia types, Francesco Andreini's heroic, histrionic widower constituted an improvised figure incorporating elements from different genres. In this case, the invention offered Francesco a means to maintain the tightest possible connection to Isabella. That connection brought him, by association, a powerful literary, and thereby also social, authorisation.

---

[26] An excellent discussion and translation of Petrarch's letter appears as 'How a Ruler Ought to Govern His State' in Kohl and Witt (eds), *Earthly Republic*, pp. 25–80.

[27] Anna Wainwright, '"*La città vedova*": Widowhood and Politics in Italian Renaissance Literature', PhD thesis (New York, 2017).

[28] Margaret King, *Death of the Child Valerio Marcello* (Chicago: University of Chicago Press, 1994), pp. 146–8. For a broader treatment of mourning conventions, see George McClure, *Sorrow and Consolation in Italian Humanism* (Princeton: Princeton University Press, 1991).

[29] Carol Lansing, *Passion and Order: Restraint of Grief in the Medieval Italian Communes* (Ithaca: Cornell University Press, 2008), especially ch. 3, 'Laments and Male Honor'; for the data on Orvieto, pp. 2 and 98.

The heroic widower's atypical deference to a wife as a literary model made a significant contribution to Renaissance feminist discourse, but the more I learn about Francesco the more convinced I become that this was not his aim. There is not space here to address the lack of praise Francesco offered for any woman other than Isabella (not even his own daughters), let alone the misogynous conceits he toyed with in dialogues penned in the 1620s.[30] Suffice it to say that Francesco Andreini drew from the scripts of Renaissance feminism exclusively for Isabella. This, too, suggests that the character of the heroic widower, however sincere it may have been, constituted a strategic mask serving his objectives in 1604, as he left the stage and took up his pen. Gaining through affiliation with Isabella's literary honour sufficient cultural capital to move smoothly into the world of humanistic publication, he might as an author rather than a 'mere' player put down stable social roots for his children, and set about further ennobling the family business of the commedia dell'arte.

Comedy Is Hard

The Shakespearean actor Edmund Keane (d.1833) is sometimes credited with the deathbed quip, 'Dying is easy; comedy is hard'. The attribution may be apocryphal, but comedy *is* hard – and no matter the era. Still, the stakes of performance in Francesco Andreini's day were higher than in Keane's, let alone in ours. Considering the murky place of actors in the early Seicento helps us better understand why Francesco deemed it worthwhile to leverage creatively all the literary cachet he could get to lend himself and his still-embattled profession some class.

From a practical standpoint, Raimondo Guerriero reminds us that, occasional gifts from courtly service aside, commedia dell'arte performers earned their livings through 'daily (public) performance'.[31] This gruelling work, involving constant and dangerous travel city-to-city in Italy and, for headliners like the Andreini family, tours of war-torn France and the Holy Roman Empire as well, brought an income whose insufficiency and instability we may judge by the fact that even the celebrated actor, friend of Francesco Andreini, and eventual dramaturge Flaminio Scala (d.1624) for years at a time gave management of his perfume shop in Venice, with its far more stable and reliable income, priority over touring with his theatrical companies.[32]

---

[30] On the latter point, see Julie Campbell's introduction to and translation of Andreini's dialogue 'On Taking a Wife' in Campbell and Maria Galli Stampino (eds), *In Dialogue with the Other Voice in Sixteenth-Century Italy: Literary and Social Contexts for Women's Writing* (Toronto: Centre for Reformation and Renaissance Studies, 2011), pp. 265–87.

[31] Raimondo Guarino, 'Commedia dell'Arte and Dominant Culture', in Christopher Balme, Piermario Vescovo, and Daniele Vianello (eds), *Commedia dell'Arte in Context* (Cambridge: Cambridge University Press, 2018), pp. 149–64; quotation on p. 152.

[32] Robert Henke, *Performance and Literature in the Commedia dell'Arte* (Cambridge: Cambridge University Press, 2010), p. 183.

Beyond the physical stamina required, daily public performance also entailed a socially damaging tangency to street peddling and prostitution. This taint may be one reason why, for all the claims of some actors to noble parentage, not a single Italian performer of the premodern era seems to have maintained ties to their birth kin. Testaments are scarce for premodern theatre people, but in the case of two celebrities whose testaments do survive, Francesco Andreini and Flaminio Scala, neither mentions kin of their own generation. Scala's will of 1616 provides for funerary masses that would include remembrance of his father, Giacomo Scala, but does not mention his mother; nor does he name any other relations, only his executor Curzio Vesi (relationship unspecified), a Pietro Baldanzini who had been serving as shopkeeper at the perfumery, and his servant, Marco Olmo.[33] Andreini's will claims his father as Lord Antonio of Pistoia, as we have seen, but does not name his mother; and, also in the context of commemorative masses, Andreini sets up an annual gift for the Cantelma in Mantua in exchange for saying 'ogni mese due messe et un offitio per l'Anima et suffragio di esso testatore et m[adonn]a Isabella Canali Venitiana gia sua consorte et luoro [*sic*] padre et madre' ('every month two masses and an Office [of the Dead] for the soul and divine refuge of the testator and for madonna Isabella Canali who was once his wife, and for their [*sic*] father and mother').[34] Since neither man mentions a mother by name, they may have been illegitimate. Whatever the case, neither Scala nor Andreini signal any blood kin with whom they remained in contact.

A historian could run mad trying to specify the social and economic place of early modern Italian actors with much more precision than what I have just offered. Considering the most famous of the first two generations of theatrical stars – Vincenza Armani (d.1569), Adriano Valerini (d.1590s), as well as Isabella and Francesco Andreini, and Flaminio Scala – archival and published documents abound, but only for the years after their professional lives were well underway. Frustratingly, we do not have a shred of evidence about the lives of these *comici* that pre-dates their wildly successful careers pretending to be other people. Francesco Andreini, for instance, among the most effective and energetic of self-presenters, never discussed his youth. Even in prefatory material, a literary space tailor-made for an author to signal any useful connections, especially familial, to which they might lay reasonable claim, he fell silent. The narrative we (myself included) have hitherto parroted about him – the young solider taken captive, who spent eight years in a Turkish prison, then by some unspecified mechanism escaped, thereafter to take up a second career as an actor – comes not from any archival evidence, or even from Francesco's own publications. Rather, this tale derives from a potted family history that Francesco's son Giovan Battista included in a rhetorical showpiece,

---

[33] Testament of Flaminio Scala, Archivio di Stato di Venezia, Notarile Testamenti (Atti Beacián), b.58, n.363.

[34] Testament of Francesco Andreini, Archivio di Stato di Mantova, Notarile Testamenti (Atti Sinforiano Forti), b.4460, unfoliated.

the most elaborate of his many defences of the commedia, *La ferza* (*The Scourge*, 1625).[35] This representation of his father's indomitable spirit may have reflected some larger truth about Francesco's past; but the details of the plot sound suspiciously like a theatrical scenario. In any event, Francesco himself never claimed any such thing; the only past he actively engaged was his time performing with the honourable Compagnia dei Gelosi, 'il cui grido non vedrà mai l'ultima notte' ('whose acclaim will never have a closing night'), and above all his relationship to Isabella.[36]

Whatever their backstories, then, it seems that comics (re)created their social worlds whole cloth when they began their careers. Those created worlds rested in practical terms on the unreliable income of street performing, shouting down popular preachers, fishwives, fruit-vendors, and peddlers of dubious panaceas all the while. There were occasional windfalls from elite patrons, but benefactors (or their secretaries) might also forget their promises. Even Isabella Andreini resorted to the gift stationery she received from the Queen of France to make heavy-handed follow-up requests for payment from the Medici factotum, Belissario Vinta.[37] Even if we cannot trace their social origins with precision, in short, evidence abounds for *comici* working hard in socio-economic terms.

Comedy was even harder from a cultural and religious standpoint. I do not mean to conjure a vision of Counter-Reformation censorship killing Renaissance creative ferment.[38] Yet I am concerned that we may have in recent years begun painting somewhat too rosy a picture of the latitude for expression during the later sixteenth and seventeenth centuries.[39] If supporters of theatricals eventually got their way in Catholic Italy, that would not happen until at least 20 years after Francesco Andreini's final exit from the earthly stage in 1624.

Consider, for instance, the 1597 prohibition *De comicis spectaculis tollendis* (*On the removal of comic performances*) commissioned by Federico Borromeo, who had only two years before been appointed Archbishop of Milan. While Borromeo, among whose legacies stands the Ambrosiana Library, deserves his

---

[35] Giovan Battista Andreini, *La Ferza: Ragionamento secondo contra l'accuse date alla Commedia* (Paris: Nicolao Callemont, 1625), sig. F1r.

[36] Andreini, *Bravure*, sig. ++2v.

[37] Discussed in MacNeil, *Music and Women*, p. 48.

[38] Representative cases of twentieth-century scholarship in this vein include Paul F. Grendler, *The Roman Inquisition and the Venetian Press, 1540–1605* (Princeton: Princeton University Press, 1977) and Gino Benzoni, *Affani della cultura. intellettuali e potere nell'Italia della Controriforma e barocca* (Rome: Feltrinelli, 1978).

[39] Those setting wide boundaries for theatre in particular include Michael Zampelli, 'Incarnating the Word: Giovan Battista Andreini, Religious Antitheatricalism and the Redemption of a Profession', PhD thesis (Boston, 1998); and Gianvittorio Signorotto, 'La Scena Pubblica Milanese al tempo del Cardinale Federico e del Conte di Fuentes', in Danilo Zardin and Maria Luisa Frosio (eds), *Carlo Borromeo e il cattolicesimo dell'età moderna* (Rome: Bulzoni, 2011), pp. 25–71. A nuanced but still rather sanguine approach to the broader dialectic between censorship and expressivity appears in Marco Cavarzere, *La prassi della censura nell'Italia del seicento. Tra repressione e mediazione* (Rome: Edizioni di Storia e Letteratura, 2011).

reputation as a humanist, I join Roberta Arcaini in stressing that some of his cultural policies extended the (in)famous censorship of Carlo Borromeo, Federico's cousin, patron, and predecessor as Archbishop of Milan.[40] *De comicis*, written by Antonio Seneca, Carlo Borromeo's longtime colleague and former Vicar General of Milan, reproduces the elder Borromeo's prohibitions against comic theatre in a palpably vitriolic spirit: 'Multa ubique sunt in universa Christiana Republica ad fidelium animos pravis moribus imbuendos, astutis Satanae artibus adinventa, sed illud sine ulla dubitatione censeri praecipuum videtur, quo hominibus honestae voluptatis specie ad omnem obscenitatem, & turpitudinem Comicis spectaculis via monstratur' ('There are many things found throughout the Republic of Christendom that have been devised by the cunning schemes of Satan to infect souls with wicked habits, but without a doubt one to be taken most seriously is comic theatre, by which (under the guise of innocent pleasure) the path to all obscenity and filth is revealed').[41] Here we find copious citation of ancient hardliners such as Trajan and Justinian, as well as the early Christian killjoys Tertullian and Cyprian, a gingerly exposition of a few passages from Thomas Aquinas (who had a soft spot for theatre), and a wide platform for contemporary haters such as Cardinal Gasparo Contarini (d.1542). This exposition of nearly 1,200 words minces none of them. All of the evidence stacks up to make one overarching point: comedy constitutes a mortal sin for performers and audience members alike. The final paragraph does state that the authorities may at their discretion allow a performance if its content has been reviewed by censors and determined to be tame; if the performance does not take place during any holy days; and of course so long as none of the performers happen to be in holy orders. Still, Seneca's heart lay more in his wholesale condemnation than in the minutiae of its implementation or the exceptions that might be, and in fact often were, made.

Lambasted here we find, unsurprisingly, the presence of lubricious and violent material in comedy. Beyond this, however, Seneca expresses a subtler anxiety about comic performances misdirecting audience members' creative imaginations, which should be trained to visceral meditations on the saints, construing popular theatre as roughly akin to demonology. Despite what we today might see as the commedia dell'arte's manifest artifice, with its distorted masks, silly codpieces, unlikely plots, and broad caricatures, Christian anti-theatricalists of the premodern period found comedy dangerous for making things that were not real seem real, thereby scrambling viewers' faculty of discernment. Noting that some might question how harmful it could be to watch at least tame comedies, Seneca insists that comedies create a world of confused values in which sin may easily breed.

[40] Roberta Giovanna Arcaini, 'I comici dell'Arte a Milano: accoglienza, sospetti, riconoscimenti', in Annamaria Cascetta and Roberta Carpani (eds), *Scena della gloria. Drammaturgia e spettacolo a Milano in età spagnolo* (Milan: Vita e Pensiero, 1995), pp. 256–326; p. 319 for this particular concern.
[41] *De comicis spectaculis tollendis*, ed. Giovan Battista Castiglione, in *Sentimenti di S. Carlo Borromeo intorno agli spettacoli* (Bergamo: Pietro Lancellotti, 1759), p. 172.

Confused by comedy's higgledy-piggledy storylines, and the pleasurable toying with the expected boundaries between right and wrong at least until the final resolution, viewers would become more vulnerable to their own sensual fantasies, and ultimately to the wiles of demons.[42]

It would be wrong to set too fine a line between the worlds of clerics and performers, as Michael Zampelli has shown.[43] Yet even those orders that embraced aspects of theatre for teaching and preaching, above all the Jesuits, certainly did not stage funny plays; the protagonists were saints and figures from the Bible. And we need also to bear in mind that Jesuits also became some of the most virulent anti-theatricalists of the later seventeenth century. Gian Domenico Ottonelli, for one, published not one but two door-stopper treatises in the 1640s that attacked the commedia dell'arte from every side, though most often in a misogynist vein, lambasting its women performers as whores and succubae.[44] Another Jesuit, Paolo Segneri, offered a sequel to Ottonelli: *In detestazione delle commedie scorrette* (1687). Segneri's invective situates *comici* 'in ritual courtship with Satan' along with magicians, enchanters, witches, wizards, prostitutes, gypsies, idolaters, Jews, and heretics.[45]

Francesco Taviani long ago claimed that debates on theatre in the post-Tridentine world constituted a 'story of words, not of facts' and, echoing him, Bernadette Majorana has recently stressed that anti-theatrical discourse 'did not result in actual prohibitions and sanctions, though it did produce clear-cut normative boundaries that, in practice, seemed to allow room for interpretation'.[46] Zampelli shows more caution, but still reframes clerical anti-theatrical discourse less as censorship and more as a lively competition with popular theatre. While all this may be true overall, I would resist discounting the effects of clerical vitriol. A play might inspire the ire of a censor at any moment, which *could* result in a jail term, fine, or even capital punishment. One unfortunate thespian in Naples even seems to have been sentenced to galley service, apparently for his work making people laugh.[47] Less tragically, Flaminio Scala, even at the height of his own fame, faced a serious prohibition: Cardinal Bonifacio Caetani announced that the actor had given him 'the

---

[42] *De comicis*, p. 175.

[43] Zampelli, 'Incarnating the Word', especially ch. 2 on 'Religious Antitheatricalism'.

[44] Gian Domenico Ottonelli, *La pericolosa conversatione con le donne, o poco modeste, o ritirate, o cantatrici, o accademiche* (Florence: Luca Franceschini & Alessandro Logi, 1646); and *Della moderatione Christiana moderatione del theatro* (Florence: Giovanni Antonio Bonardi, 1649).

[45] Sengeri's treatise discussed and quoted in Bernadette Majorana, 'Commedia dell'arte and the Church', in Christopher Balme, Piermario Vescovo, and Daniele Vianello (eds), *Commedia dell'arte in Context* (Cambridge: Cambridge University Press, 2018), pp. 133–48 at 142. I am grateful to Virginia Reinburg for suggesting the language of combating demonology in anti-theatrical treatises; this is a line of inquiry I hope to pursue hereafter.

[46] Majorana, 'Commedia dell'arte and the Church', p. 135.

[47] See Joe Connors, 'Chi era Ottonelli?', in Christoph Frommel and Sebastian Schütze (eds), *Pietro da Cortona, Atti del convegno internazionale, Roma/Firenze 12-15 novembre 1997* (Milan: Electa, 1998), pp. 29–35.

greatest disgust that anyone of his condition could ever have induced in me', and forbade Scala from performing in the duchy of Modena.[48] All actors were vulnerable to censure that had serious implications. As we have just seen, moreover, moral hard-liners made performing and even watching bawdy theatre a mortal sin, as well as paying the actors who performed it. Technically speaking, then, comic actors and anyone abetting them should be denied Communion; so, spiritual anathema forever loomed, even if it seldom landed.

Beyond the realities of specific sanctions or punishments, moreover, I take the position that discourse conditions our perceptions, the meaning we make out of the world; accordingly, it conditions our lived experience. Spiritual authorities had marked the genre of the commedia dell'arte as unfit for Christian performance or consumption. That marking mattered to actors, even if not a single priest ever denied them the Eucharist; it mattered, even if an actor's own productions tended to pass censorial muster and even earn the occasional clerical plaudit, as did those of the Andreini troupes, apparently even in Milan.[49] Indeed, some testament to actors' perception of anti-theatrical discourse as a very real liability may be found in the vigour with which the most erudite among them defended their art in print, starting with Francesco's *Bravure* in 1609 and continuing at least through his son Giovan Battista's later theoretical works (1650s). Doing comedy in the Seicento was clearly no laughing matter.

Conclusion

How far could literary positioning could go in reshaping perceptions of men, like Francesco Andreini, whose professions might otherwise have placed them low on the social (and moral) hierarchy? Lateran canon Tomaso Garzoni's *Piazza universale di tutte le professioni del mondo* (first edition, 1585) gives us a few hints. On the one hand, Garzoni rehearses anti-theatrical tropes with relish, stressing that in the ancient world actors 'furono tenuti per persone vili' ('were considered vile persons'), a designation with pejorative social *and* moral valences, reminding us once again of the tight connection between moral qualities and social position; extending the connection, Garzoni stresses that ancient actors held 'niuna riputatione presso a tutti, onde furono cacciati molte volte (come narra Suetonio) fuor di Roma vergognosamente, & ripulsi da gli honori de' cittadini, e de' soldati, come attesta Cicerone' ('no good reputation with anyone, hence they were shamefully thrown out of Rome many times (as Suetonius tells us) and denied the honours of citizens,

---

[48] See discussion in Henke, *Performance and Literature*, p. 183.

[49] Roberta Arcaini has found nearly two dozen instances of Andreini companies appearing even in Milan; see 'I comici dell'arte a Milano' and the appendix to the volume, pp. 733–54. She notes that appearances do not necessarily mean performances, but that theatrical companies faced danger and expense in travel, so would not have made so many trips had there not been significant profit (and thus most likely performances) involved.

and soldiers, as Cicero attests').[50] Garzoni also indicates that bad comics of his own time, going for the cheapest laughs in the piazza, warrant similar treatment. Yet he also points to the emergent category of good comics who, 'non recitando, ma scrivendo, hanno di moralissimi costumi ripieni gli' lor scritti, ponendosi avanti a gli occhi quel fin lodevole d'insegnar l'arte del viver sapientemente, come al Comico si conviene' ('not in performing, but in *writing*, have filled their works with the best examples of comportment, setting as their praiseworthy goal teaching the art of living wisely' [emphasis mine]).[51] Among Garzoni's models for the good comic stands Isabella Andreini, whose literary fame saved her from the category of the prostitute to which her status as a public performer might otherwise have relegated her.

The peculiar case of her husband, Francesco Andreini, bears out Garzoni's formulation as well as Isabella's, and even more tangibly. Let us return to the first week of June in the year 1607, when 'Mister' Francesco received his deed of honorary citizenship from the ducal secretary at the Mantuan court, and then 'His Magnificence' Lord Francesco, now citizen of Mantua, registered his final will and testament. The Compagnia dei Gelosi that Francesco headlined and ran with Isabella from the 1580s to her death in 1604 had enjoyed Mantuan, Florentine, and even Milanese patronage for all those years. Yet Francesco's citizenship and estate building did not crystallise until 1607, that is, *after* he had retired from performing and begun to amass literary honour as his celebrated wife's cultural executor. The timing of this former actor's unusual coup reinforces that the relationship explored in this volume between literature, learning, and social hierarchy could be very tight indeed in Seicento Italy.

---

[50] Tomaso Garzoni, *Piazza universale di tutte le professioni del mondo* (Venice: Roberto Meghetti, 1605), sig. Aaa 3r.

[51] Garzoni, *Piazza*, sig. Aaa 4v.

7

Marta Marchina, Poetry, and Social Mobility in Baroque Rome

JANE STEVENSON

IN THE LATE fourteenth century, humanistically educated women start to appear in many of the great cultural centres of Renaissance Italy, such as Venice, the Veneto, and Florence.[1] Axel Erdmann lists no fewer than 210 Italian women who ventured into print in the sixteenth century alone; which compares with a norm in other European countries of 20–30.[2] Additionally, scribal publication remained an important mode of circulating texts, and large numbers of women left writings in manuscript.

Many of these women could be described as prodigies, and as such, the point about them was that they constituted cultural capital for their city. It followed that they were public figures; aristocrats for the most part, or the daughters of famous humanists.[3] Their learning therefore did not alter their place in the social hierarchy.

The seventeenth century in Italy has received relatively little attention. Literary historians have tended to present it as an era of intellectual and artistic decadence.[4] Virginia Cox writes of 'the showy, brilliant and erudite poetic language of the Italian Baroque', and suggests that it marginalised women writers.[5] Some, however, could cope with this cultural turn, and Marta Marchina was one of them.

Though the view that 'the tradition of female humanism … had died everywhere in Europe by the seventeenth century' is still held,[6] learned women in fact continued

---

[1] For example, M. L. King and Albert Rabil, Jr. (eds), *Her Immaculate Hand: Selected Works By and About the Women Humanists of Quattrocento Italy* (Binghamton: Center for Medieval and Early Renaissance Studies, 1983).

[2] France comes nearest, with 30. Axel Erdmann, *My Gracious Silence: Women in the Mirror of Sixteenth Century Printing in Western Europe* (Luzern: Gilhofer & Rauschberg, 1999), pp. 206–23.

[3] Jane Stevenson, 'Women Prodigies', in Philip Ford, Jan Bloemendal, and Charles Fantazzi (eds), *Brill's Encyclopaedia of the Neo-Latin World* (Leiden and Boston: Brill, 2014), pp. 1200–1.

[4] Domenico Sella, *Italy in the Seventeenth Century* (London and New York: Longman, 1997), p. 188.

[5] Virginia Cox, 'Fiction, 1560–1650', in Letizia Panizza and Sharon Wood (eds), *A History of Women's Writing in Italy* (Cambridge: Cambridge University Press, 2001), pp. 52–64 at 63.

[6] Margaret L. King, *Women of the Renaissance* (Chicago: Chicago University Press, 1991), p. 211.

Proceedings of the British Academy, **246**, 139–160, © The British Academy 2022.

to play an active part in Italian culture. A noble Venetian of the seventeenth century, Elena Piscopia (1646–84), was the first woman to be unequivocally awarded a PhD, at Padua in 1678;[7] and she had several female contemporaries who were almost as learned. In fact, the role of female prodigy was so firmly established in Italy 1600, that it had become somewhat stereotyped. Such a woman learned languages, the more the better, played at least one musical instrument, and orated in Latin on suitable occasions. Piscopia, for example, can be found performing in this fashion. When Cardinal César d'Estrées paid her a formal visit in 1681, she read to him from Isocrates, commented on the passage, spoke Hebrew, French, Spanish, and Latin to him, and gave a recital on the organ and clavicymbal. That evening they met at the academy of the Ricovrati, of which she was a member, where she orated in his praise.

Piscopia, like most of her predecessors as women prodigies, was a noble-woman. The subject of this paper, Marta Marchina, was not; and she does not conform to this well-established stereotype. At no time did she orate in public, or act as any kind of public figure. Nor was she a member of an academy.[8] However, her life was materially changed by her unusual learning, and there is certainly a sense in which her poetry constituted cultural capital for her patrons, and to some extent, for herself. Both her own career and those of her principal patrons illustrate aspects of the relationship between social mobility and education.

The Life and Times of Martha Marchina

Marchina was an artisan-class woman Latin poet associated with some of the most intellectually active circles of Baroque Rome, and the object of enlightened, even affectionate, patronage from senior Catholic clerics. In order to understand this, it is probably best to begin by outlining her life, while remembering that the only sources are Giovanni Vittorio Rossi's *Pinacotheca imaginum illustrium*, a collection of biographical notices of interesting Italian contemporaries, first published in 1648,[9] two years after Marchina's death, a *Life* in her collection of verse, *Musa Posthuma*, published 14 years after her death, largely based on Rossi corrected in some details

---

[7] Her works were printed, *Helenae Lucretiae (quae et Scholastica) Corneliae Piscopiae virginis pietate, et eruditione admirabilis, ordine S. Benedicti privatis votis adscriptae, Opera* (Parma: Hippolytus Rusati, 1688), and there were two contemporary biographies, Antonio Lupis, *L'eroina Veneta, overo la vita di Elena Lucretia Cornara Piscopia* (Venice: per il Curti, 1689), and Massimiliano Deza, *Vita di Helena Lucretia Cornara Piscopia* (Venezia: Antonio Bosio, 1686).

[8] Patrizia Bettella, 'Women and the Academies in Seventeenth-Century Italy: Elena Lucrezia Cornaro Piscopia's Role in Literary Academies', *Italian Culture*, 36.2 (2018), 100–19. In the seventeenth century, three Roman academies, the Arcadi, Infecondi and Humoristi, elected Queen Christina, Elena Piscopia, and Margherita Sarrocchi respectively, so this was by no means an unheard-of honour for an educated woman.

[9] Ianus Nicius Erythraeus [Rossi], *Pinacotheca Imaginum Illustrium, doctrinae vel ingenii laude, virorum*, 3 vols (Köln: Judocus Kalcovius [Kalkhoff], 1643–8) III, 234–48. This third volume appeared posthumously, since he died in 1647.

by information from Fathers of the Oratory, and transcriptions of her monument in the Chiesa Nuova in Rome, which is no longer extant. We can see of her only what her patrons saw, and of that, what they chose to pass on.

Marchina was originally from Naples – Niccolò Toppi is proud to claim her for his 1678 *Bibliotheca Napoletana* – but she was Roman by formation.[10] Macedo and Rossi agree that she was only a few years old when her family moved to Rome. She was one of four children, with two brothers, one older, one younger, while a baby sister died in infancy. Rossi states that her father manufactured brooms and tablets of scented soap, and sold them in a little shop near the church of Santa Maria della Pace.[11] The family 'sustained life by the work of their hands, but respectably, and this side of the squalor of manual work'; they were not the lowest of the low, Macedo suggests, but decent artisans.[12]

But Marchino must evidently have been a man of some social ambition, since he was prepared to encourage the education of his sons. According to her epitaph, Marchina was barely seven when she developed a burning desire to study. This ambition might have seemed doomed to inevitable frustration, but at about the same time, her mother died. This family calamity turned out to be something of a blessing in disguise, because her father put her in charge of her brothers. He presumably could not afford domestic help. The family were in the habit of attending Santa Maria in Vallicella – otherwise known as the Chiesa Nuova – a new church, which had been recently founded by St Philip Neri and was the centre of his new order, the Oratorians. It was situated in what was then quite a poor working-class district, so it is quite possible that the Marchino family were simply living in its immediate vicinity: certainly, Marchino's shop was about five minutes' walk away.

The Oratorians are crucial to this story. The order is generally associated with church music – the 'Oratorio', so popular as a musical form in the eighteenth century, takes its name from them – but as St Philip Neri originally conceived it, and for its first half century, the mission of the Oratory was to the urban poor rather than the rich.[13]

St Philip Neri himself ministered to the poor in a variety of ways. According to the rules of his order, individual Oratorians were supposed to devote themselves to works of charity of their own choice, so a number of them concerned themselves with education, though they did not, at this early stage of their history, run formal schools as the Jesuits did.[14] It is possible that Marchina's father had got wind of

---

[10] Niccolo Toppi, *Bibliotheca Napoletana, et apparato a gli Huomini illustri in lettere di Napoli e del Regno, delle Famiglie, Terre, Citta e religioni, che sono nello stesso regno dalle loro origini, per tutto l'anno 1678* (Naples: Antonio Bulifon, 1678), 208–9. His source is Giovanni Rossi.

[11] Rossi, *Pinacotheca Imaginum Illustrium*, III.235: 'haud procul ab Aede Deiparae virginis de pace, quam vocant, officinam orbiculorum ex odorato sapone, et scopularum, instituit, eoque artificio se suosque tuebatur'.

[12] 'Labore manuum, sed honesto, & citra sordes artis sedentariae, vitam tolerarunt' (sig. §§§1ᵛ).

[13] John Patrick Donnelly SJ, 'The Congregation of the Oratory', in Richard L. De Molen (ed.), *Religious Orders of the Catholic Reformation* (New York: Fordham University Press, 1994), pp. 189–216.

[14] Louis Ponnelle and Louis Bordet, *St Philip Neri and the Roman Society of his Times (1515–1595)*, trans. R. F. Kerr (London: Sheed & Ward, 1932).

this. Certainly, one of their number, Fr Ludovico Santolino, offered to educate the Marchino boys. Interestingly, in Rossi's account of her life, he assigns the brothers' education to the Jesuits, not the Oratorians.[15] This is probably because by the mid-century, Jesuit schools were increasingly well understood to be vectors of social mobility.[16]

Since it was now Marchina's business to look after her brothers, this gave her a heaven-sent opportunity to develop her own intellectual interests. When they came home each day, she insisted that they tell her everything they had learned, and by that means, managed to pick up a Latin education at second hand – as an incidental result, this process ensured that her brothers' homework was phenomenally well prepared by ordinary schoolboy standards.

Interestingly, a Venetian near-contemporary, Modesta da Pozzo, later the author of a defence of women (1600),[17] acquired the beginnings of her considerable education by similar means. The orphaned family was left in the charge of their grandparents. She learned Latin from her older brother from the age of nine. Every day when he came home from his Latin school, he taught her what he had learned. Like Marchina, she learned in this second-hand way to read Latin very well and write it adequately.[18]

In any case, Marchina was successful in mastering the first stages of Latin. Furthermore, after Santolino had taught the Marchino brothers for a while, Marchina's own intellectual ambitions evidently also became known to him. Since she was working on her own at home, she became desperate for books, and asked if she could borrow some. Santolino, at first, demurred, since he thought Latin poetry unsuitable for a young working-class girl whose future was necessarily domestic. But all the same, perhaps intrigued, he began to be interested in the family, and went to see their father. Possibly, since the Marchino boys had begun to appear extraordinarily earnest and well-trained due to their sister's efforts, though Macedo does not directly say so, Santolino was beginning to think that the Oratorians might sponsor one or other of them through seminary. To Santolino's surprise, their father disclaimed all knowledge of his sons' attainments and declared that it was all due to Marchina. He showed Santolino an epigram she had composed, and the Oratorian

[15] *Pinacotheca* III.235.

[16] Judi Loach, 'Revolutionary Pedagogues? How Jesuits Used Education to Change Society', in John W. O'Malley SJ, Gauvin Alexander Bailey, Steven J. Harris, and T. Frank Kennedy (eds), *The Jesuits: Cultures, Sciences, and the Arts, 1540–1773* (Toronto and London: University of Toronto Press, 1999), 5–23.

[17] Modesta Pozzo, writing as Moderata Fonte, *The Worth of Women: Wherein is Clearly Revealed their Nobility and their Superiority to Men*, ed. and trans. Virginia Cox (Chicago: University of Chicago Press, 1997).

[18] Paul F. Grendler, *Schooling in Renaissance Italy: Literacy and Learning 1300–1600* (Baltimore and London: Johns Hopkins University Press, 1989), pp. 94–5. See now Paola Malpezzi Price, *Moderata Fonte: Women and Life in Sixteenth-century Venice* (Madison: Fairleigh Dickinson University Press, 2003).

was rather impressed: he capitulated to her original request, and allowed her to start borrowing books from the Fathers' library. She began working at home on Latin, poetic composition, and the beginnings of Greek and Hebrew studies, with Santolino as her guide. He was also her confessor, and consequently her spiritual director.[19]

Santolino's interest in her increased as she began to show her obvious ability. He showed her work to Antonio Querenghi, an elderly and distinguished poet and scholar from Padova,[20] and to Iacopo Volpone, another of the Oratorian Fathers, and brought some of her verses to a chapter-meeting of the Oratory. Following discussion at this meeting, a demonstration was staged. She was brought in person to a meeting of the Oratorians, and asked to compose extempore on a subject given her by Querenghi (Jacob's fight with the angel). She was allowed pen and paper, and after reflection, composed an elegant little epigram, which she gave to Father Volpone, who gave it to Querenghi.

At some point, some of her verse was read by another very cultivated Oratorian, Virgilio Spada (it may be relevant that he was a collector of curiosities).[21] Through him, she also became known to his still more distinguished brother, Cardinal Bernardino Spada, because Virgilio encouraged her to write to him. She was sufficiently within Spada circles to participate in a literary game: when Cardinal Spada found his copy of Caesar's *Commentaries* had been gnawed by a mouse, he wrote an epigram, which was duly imitated by his literary associates, including Alexander Pollinus (who subsequently contributed an encomiastic poem in Greek and Latin in the front matter of *Musa Posthuma*) and Marchina.[22]

This quiet life was cut short when, like many Romans of all social classes, Marchina died of a fever, aged only 46.

It might seem that, as a working-class woman, Marchina would have lived a life without choices. In fact, a variety of possible futures were presented to her as a direct consequence of her learning. Santolino's first thought was to offer her a job, teaching a Latin school in his native *comune* of Santa Sofia,[23] 250 miles from Rome, an option which Rossi says she found daunting.[24] She obediently set off, with her younger brother as chaperone, but he fell ill *en route* in Foligno, so she went alone to Loreto to pray for his recovery, and wrote to Santolino to explain the situation.

---

[19] Donnelly, 'The Congregation of the Oratory', p. 192, '[Neri] rarely served as director to women, but many other Oratorians did'. The informal services held at the Oratory were open to women and children on Sundays and feast days (p. 194). Rossi, *Pinacotheca*, III.236.

[20] Uberto Motta, *Antonio Querenghi (1546–1633): Un letterato padovano nella roma del tardo Rinascimento* (Milano: Vita e pensiero, 1997).

[21] G. Finocchiaro, *Il Museo di curiosità di Virgilio Spada: una raccolta romana del Seicento* (Roma: Palombi, 1999).

[22] *Musa Posthuma*, 61–4.

[23] In Emilia-Romagna near the border with Tuscany: the nearest place of any size is Forlì. The detail that it was to be a Latin school is from Rossi, *Pinacotheca*, III.237.

[24] Rossi, *Pinacotheca*, 237. Macedo says, 'the province seemed uncultivated to Marchina'; 'acerbe ac dura Marthae prouincia visa est' (*Musa Posthuma*, sig. §§§ 5r).

He allowed her to return. Subsequently, according to Macedo (but not Rossi), an unnamed powerful patron, referred to as 'Romae Princeps' suggested that she should be given a professor's chair in the Sapienza (Rome's university, founded 1303).

> There was a grandee of Rome who wanted her to have a chair in the Sapienza of the beloved city, and to teach openly among the other masters. But she resisted through maidenly shame and by her bashfulness caused the gentleman to drop this proposition.[25]

A variety of Italian women had held, or at least, were believed to have held, university chairs by the 1620s, so this detail may be supplied by Macedo as a grace note.[26] Meanwhile, and more certainly, since it is confirmed by Rossi, Cardinal Francesco Barberini interested himself in her fate (nephew of Urban VIII, he was a major patron of the arts in seventeenth-century Rome). He offered to sponsor her into a good convent, the new Carmelite house of St Teresa (who had been canonised in 1622), founded by Caterina Cesi, widow of Giulio della Rovere, in 1627.[27]

The Barberini were the most powerful family in the Rome of the 1620s and 1630s, so in their own rise, the Spadas were competing with them; and Marchina was a Spada protégée. Consequently, she was potentially a part of their cultural capital. Cardinal Spada, perhaps not wishing to see Marchina annexed by the Barberini, offered to place her in a convent in his native *comune*, Brisighella, most probably the observant Franciscan house of Santa Maria degli Angeli, since this was Brisighella's most notable convent.[28]

But from Marchina's point of view, to take up either of these offers would have meant enclosure, since in 1563, the Council of Trent had ruled that all female convents must be in strict *clausura*. Though life as a nun would have given her economic security, it would have been hard for her to continue her studies. Seventeenth-century Italian convents were not centres of advanced humanist culture,[29] though many nuns wrote, and even published, in Italian, or studied music.[30] Theresa of Avila's reform of the Carmelite order stressed contemplative

---

[25] 'Ac fuit Romae Princeps, qui optavit, ut in almae urbis Sapientia Cathedram haberet, et inter reliquos Magistros palam doceret. Sed Virginalis obstitit verecundia, et pudore obtinuit, ut ille Princeps a proposito desisteret' (sig. §§§§ 1ᵛ).

[26] Jane Stevenson, *Women Latin Poets: Language, Gender and Authority from Antiquity to the Eighteenth Century* (Oxford: Oxford University Press, 2005), 149–52.

[27] Carolyn Valone, 'Women on the Quirinal Hill: Patronage in Rome, 1560–1630', *The Art Bulletin*, 76.1 (1994), 129–46 at 140.

[28] *Musa Posthuma*, sig. §§§§ 2r.

[29] There are exceptions to this generalisation: Santa Maria delle Vergini in Venice, was noted for its learning (Mary Laven, *Virgins of Venice* (London: Viking, 2002), p. 76), and in San Salvatore and Santa Giulia, Brescia, Angelica Baitelli became a historian (Silvia Evangelisti, 'Angelica Baitelli: A Woman Writing in a Convent in Seventeenth Century Italy', in Els Kloek, Nicole Teeuwen, and Marijke Huisman (eds), *Women of the Golden Age: An International Debate on Women in Seventeenth-century Holland, England, and Italy* (Hilversum: Veroloren, 1994), pp. 157–65). But normally, nuns could not pursue humanist studies.

[30] See Craig A. Monson, *Disembodied Voices: Music and Culture in an Early Modern Italian Convent* (Berkeley and London: University of California Press, 1995); Robert L. Kendrick, *Celestial Sirens: Nuns and their Music in Early Modern Milan* (Oxford: Clarendon Press, 1996).

prayer rather than the life of the mind, and female Franciscans were not scholarly. Another probably relevant factor in her deliberations was that her own spiritual life was formed by the Oratorians, for whom religion belonged in the workaday world.

The usual alternative to a convent for an early modern woman was matrimony, though not inevitably so: Gabriella Zarri has explored the 'third state' for women which began to develop in post-Tridentine Italy, a condition of voluntary celibacy allowing both religious dedication and secular participation, sometimes within dedicated but uncloistered institutions.[31] It is easy to think of reasons why Marchina would have preferred such a 'third state' to seeking a husband. She was exceptionally devout, and marrying a fellow artisan would almost certainly have put paid to the study which was so important to her. There was little chance of making an upwardly mobile match, since, as Carlo Dionisotti has pointed out, half of early modern Italian intellectuals were in one way or another dependent on the church, and there were in any case, strong cultural barriers against cross-class marriage.[32]

Historians of women have tended to treat paid employment as a desirable prize, particularly employment in a profession as opposed to manual labour, but if Marchina had taken Santolino's well-meant offer, she would have been isolated in the mountains, away from all her friends, while accepting a chair at the Sapienza, if one were indeed offered to her (by Cardinal Barberini?), would have put her in a horribly exposed position,[33] and convents were prisons.[34] As her father's housekeeper-assistant in Rome, she was within reach of intellectually stimulating company at the Chiesa Nuova, she enjoyed independence and physical mobility, and she could spend her leisure hours as she chose, even if there were few of them.

It is also worth noticing what Macedo says about her adult work life:

> She performed the work of making soap of perfumes, making tablets out of it, spinning, sewing, weaving, and woolwork. She had studied the greater Phrygian art [gold embroidery] from birth, and practised it almost miraculously. Silent, she wove from gold and silken thread, and painted with a needle, [things] she was accustomed to dedicate to sacred uses.[35]

---

[31] Gabriella Zarri, *Recinti. Donne, Clausura e matrimonio nella prima età moderna* (Bologna: Il Mulino, 2000), pp. 459–77.

[32] Carlo Dionisotti, 'Chierici e laici', *Geografia e storia della letteratura Italiana* (Torino: Einaudi, 1967), pp. 47–71.

[33] Humanism was aggressively competitive. See Lauro Martines, *Strong Words: Writing and Social Strain in the Italian Renaissance* (Baltimore and London: Johns Hopkins University Press, 2001), esp. pp. 14–15, 24–36.

[34] Elissa Weaver, 'The Convent Wall in Tuscan Convent Drama', in Craig Monson (ed.), *The Crannied Wall: Women, Religion and the Arts in Early Modern Europe* (Ann Arbor: University of Michigan Press, 1991), pp. 73–86, 75.

[35] 'Saponem odorarum conficere, pilulas ex eo componere, nere, suere, texere, lanificio operam dare. Phrygionicam artem grandior natu iam edidicit, et prope miraculum exercuit. Multa ex aureo, et serico filo texuit, et acu pinxit, quae sacris usibus dicare solita' (sig. §§§§ 2v).

As an adult, Marchina was working with her hands, but somebody else was scrubbing the floors and fetching the water by the time she was adult. The nature of the Marchinos' handiwork needs to be nuanced. Making coarse, soft soap out of caustic lye and animal tallow was notoriously smelly and unpleasant work, but hard tablets of perfumed soap were made out of olive oil for the most part, were pleasant to handle even in the course of manufacture, and expensive to buy.[36] It is not physically possible to sew silk and gold thread with nails broken by coarse housework and lye-roughened fingers. Marchina's daily tasks, as described here (Rossi confirms her activity as a gold-embroiderer)[37] required her to have clean, smooth hands, and at a hobbyist level, would have been eminently suitable for a gentlewoman: Isabella Cortese's *Secreti*, for example, includes recipes for soap.[38]

It is also relevant that gold and silk thread were extremely expensive. If she was doing this textile work as an offering to the church, then the Marchinos had really gone a very considerable way up in the world by the time Marchina reached adulthood. But it seems more than possible that the Oratorians ended up taking a different way of giving Marchina and her family a helping hand, and what she was actually doing was making gold-embroidered textiles such as altar-frontals and chalice veils for the Chiesa Nuova on a commission basis.

With respect to what this might have meant to Marchina herself, embroidery can be a form of self-expression; and religious embroidery in particular can be a form of meditation. She was far from being the only educated Italian woman to practise this art.[39] Marchina's epigrammatic verses are brief meditations on religious topics, for the most part; they could very well have been composed while stitching. The Anglo-Latin poet William Alabaster, who had converted to Catholicism, highlights a relationship between Catholic religious meditation and versification in a document he wrote in 1599 after his conversion:

> I was wont often to walke into the feildes alone, and (being then summer) ther I wold sett me downe in certaine coerne feldes, where I could not be seene nor heard of others, and here passe the tyme in conferences between almightie God and my soule, sometimes with internall meditation uniting my will to god, somtimes forming and contryving the same meditations into verses of love and affection, as it were hiding of the fyer under ashes, with the reding wherof I might afterwardes kyndle my devotion at new tyme againe.[40]

[36] John A. Hunt, 'A Short History of Soap', *The Pharmaceutical Journal*, 263 (1999), 985–9.

[37] *Pinacotheca* III.239.

[38] Isabella Cortese, *Secreti* (Venezia: appreso G. Bariletto, 1565), pp. 114–16.

[39] Laura Cereta, an excellent Latinist born in Brescia in 1469, wrote at night, and embroidered in the dawn hours, for pleasure. Diana Robin, 'Women, Space and Renaissance Discourse', in Barbara K. Gold, Paul Allen Miller, and Charles Platter (eds), *Sex and Gender in Medieval and Renaissance Texts: The Latin Tradition* (New York: SUNY, 1997), pp. 165–87, at 176–7 gives a full translation of the letter, no. II in Iacopo Filippo Tomasini (ed.), *Epistolae* (Padua: Sebastiano Sardi, 1640).

[40] In ch. 5 of the 1599 autobiographical document entitled 'Alabaster's Conversion', Rome, Venerable English College, Liber 1394 (available at www.philological.bham.ac.uk/alabconv/text.html, accessed 20 November 2021).

His practice might illuminate Marchina's composition of her brief, intense, religious poems. A workroom in which a solitary woman sat embroidering fulfilled the same requirements as Alabaster's cornfield, since the work was in itself of a kind to support rather than disrupt composition.

Marchina was by no means unique among the women of her century in trying to carve out the life she wanted by making intelligent use of friendly churchmen. Elena Piscopia, whose father was determined that she should marry, took vows as a Benedictine tertiary, which tied her father's hands, but allowed her to continue living in the Palazzo Cornaro surrounded by her own books. Massimiliano Deza comments on her essentially paradoxical and liminal status: 'To sum up, the Lord wanted her to live as a hermit in the city, a nun in her father's house, and an Idea of virtue for women in the world.'[41] The same could have been said of Marchina, though her way of life was very much more humble.

Though in offering Marchina a teaching job, possibly a lecturing job, or a convent dowry, her patrons were clearly trying to do their best for her, if she had been a boy, they could have done a great deal more. The Spada family themselves are an instructive example of how an enterprising boy could make his and his families' fortune through education in Counter-Reformation Italy. Early in the seventeenth century, Paolo Spada, a coal merchant allegedly descended from colliers, was nominated treasurer for the Romagna region by Pope Clement VIII, and became sufficiently wealthy through tax farming to allow his sons Bernardino and Virgilio to study philosophy, theology, and law at Jesuit colleges and take positions at the papal court.[42] Bernardino's rise was swift, and he quite clearly continued to build on his father's achievements and become richer and richer. He also became a diplomat, apostolic nuncio to the court of Louis XIII, and political spokesman for Pope Urban VIII, positions which testify to his education rather than his wealth. His brother Virgilio, the Oratorian, was also impressively upwardly mobile. He excelled at secretly collecting funds for the successive popes Innocent X and Alexander VII, and was Superintendent of the Works on the fabric of St Peter's.

With the aid of fecund siblings, the Spada brothers succeeded in establishing a clerical dynasty: Bernardino and Virgilio's relations included cardinal Giambattista Spada (1597–1675), cardinal Fabrizio Spada (1643–1717), and Sigismondo Spada (1622–75), a papal chaplain. Two others of Bernardino's nephews, Gregorio and Orazio, were virtually adopted by him, following him about as he moved between Paris, Bologna, and Rome, educated as refined gentlemen, and groomed for

---

[41] 'Mà in fine il Signor le voleva Romita nella Città, Religiosa nella Casa Paterna, et Idea di Virtù alle Donne del Secolo'. Massimiliano Deza, *Vita di Helena Lucretia Cornara Piscopia* (Venezia: A. Bosio, 1686), p. 43.

[42] Sandra Cavallo and Tessa Storey, *Healthy Living in Late Renaissance Italy* (Oxford: Oxford University Press, 2013), pp. 49–52.

good marriages. Gregorio married the Marchesa Camilla Fantuzzi, daughter of a prestigious senatorial family of Bologna, while Orazio married Maria Veralli in 1636, an heiress with three cardinal uncles and four more among her more distant relations: as Irene Fosi and Maria Antonietta Viseglio comment, 'marriage alliances and the Curia went hand in hand'.[43] The Spadas were commoners, and new to the Curia, but Orazio's marriage gave them links to more established figures at the papal court, and thus reinforced their position, while Gregorio's netted him a noble wife, confirming the extent to which the family had risen from their provincial origins. Cardinal Fabrizio Spada, Secretary of State to Innocent XII, was one of Orazio's children.

Bernardino Spada was nominated as cardinal in 1626, and from 1631 lived permanently in Rome. He bought the Palazzo Capodiferro in 1632, and turned it into a major palace – complete with special effects by Borromini – which he shared with Orazio and his wife.[44] Most of his considerable personal wealth was invested in his collection: he died in 1661, at which point he owned 20 major sculptures and several hundred paintings.[45]

Thus when they encountered Marchina, Bernardino and Virgilio Spada were second-generation *nouveaux riches*, who had used education, cultivation, and the church as weapons for the collective social advancement of their family. Through Virgilio, they also had a special connection with the Chiesa Nuova.[46] This is witnessed by the creation of a no-expense-spared private chapel there, now dedicated to St Carlo Borromeo, which was built between 1663 and 1679.[47] It was originally conceived by Virgilio Spada as a celebration of the Spada family and dedicated to the Virgin, though at some point it metamorphosed into the Borromeo chapel which exists today.

The Marchino brothers' Latin studies should probably be understood as the first tentative stages of a similar attempt at social advancement through education and the church. The older brother, never named, is not mentioned in Marchina's writings, and perhaps died young. But Giuseppe, the younger, continued to study Latin intensively, on the evidence of Marchina's letters to him, and it seems very likely that he took holy orders. The closeness between Marchina and Giuseppe Marchino may be suggested by the fact that it was he who went with her on her

---

[43] I. Fosi and M. A. Visceglia, 'Marriage and Politics at the Papal Court in the Sixteenth and Seventeenth Centuries', in T. Dean and K. J. P. Lowe (eds), *Marriage in Italy, 1300–1650* (Cambridge: Cambridge University Press, 1998), pp. 197–224, 203. See also C. Casanova, 'Le donne come "risorsa": le politiche matrimoniali della familia Spada', *Memoria*, 21 (1987), 157–95

[44] Carlo Cresti and Claudio Rendina, *Palazzi of Rome* (Köln: Könemann, 1998), pp. 2–12.

[45] See Roberto Cannatà, *La Galleria di Palazzo Spada, genesi e storia di una collezione* (Rome: Edizioni d'Europa, 1993), pp. 25–70, which covers the collection of Bernardino Spada.

[46] See Antonella Pampalone, *La Capella della famiglia Spada nella Chiesa Nuova* (Rome: Ministero per i beni cultuali e ambientali, 1993).

[47] Borromeo had given a much-needed boost to the nascent Oratorians by visiting the Chiesa Nuova in 1579. Donnelly, 'The Congregation of the Oratory', p. 191.

abortive journey to Santa Sofia. There is a somewhat older-sister note in a poem she wrote to him:

> You appear to be a straitlaced fellow, and too severe,
>   My brother, since none of my verses ever please you.
> This one is silly, you say, this is harsh, the others are wordy,
>   This is flat, these are tumid, this one has a hole in it, those others collapse—
> You criticise innumerable faults in my verses —
>   And yet it is I who compose poems, albeit bad; you compose none.[48]

Despite her modest and retired way of life, Marchina's fame travelled abroad in a way that suggests that both the Oratorian Fathers and the Spadas held her in genuine regard. The third volume of Rossi's *Pinacotheca* suggests that by 1647 at the latest, her life-story was being told within Rome. This was 14 years before the publication of her book of verses. Rossi gives Antonio Querenghi as his source of information.[49] All he knows is that she wrote epigrams: it will be remembered that Querenghi was given one at the exhibition of her talents which has already been mentioned.

There is, however, evidence that her verses were put into circulation. Toppi, in his Neapolitan bibliography of 1678, knew of her only from a transcription of her tombstone, and had no idea how to access any of her work. But the Piarist Fr. Carlo di S. Antonio in his book on the modern epigram, *De Arte Epigrammatica* published in Cologne in 1650 (12 years before *Musa Posthuma*) quotes four of her poems as models of style.[50] This suggests that Cardinal Spada or Virgilio Spada was showing her poems around to interested parties, years before they were eventually published. I find it interesting that di S. Antonio does not present the verses he quotes as curiosities, of interest for being the work of a woman, or indeed, for being the work of a member of the lower orders. Many women writers have suffered from being presented essentially as prodigies, and consequently, objects of patronising curiosity.[51] In *De Arte Epigrammatica*, the poems are simply offered as examples

---

[48] Esse videris homo rigidus, nimiumque severus,
        dum, germane, tibi carmina nulla placent.
      Desipit hoc, inquis, dura isthaec, illa redundant,
        hoc iacet, ista tument, hoc hiat, illa cadunt.
      Innumeras notas in nostro carmine mendas:
        atqui ego non bona, tu carmina nulla facis.

[49] 'There are epigrams by her composed in an elegant style, finished with pleasing and lively ideas, which Antonio Quaerengo, who has read her, and whose veracity cannot be doubted [says] were elaborated and perfected by her.' 'Erant ea epigrammata adeo eleganti stylo confecta, adeo venustis argutisque conclusa sententiis, ut Antonio Quaerengo, qui ea legerat, fides fieri non posset, fuisse ab ipsa elaborata atque perfecta' (III.236).

[50] Carlo di S. Antonio, *De Arte Epigrammatica sive de ratione epigrammatis rite conficendi, libellus* (Coloniae Ubiorum: E. Egmond et socios, 1650), pp. 81, 81–2, 87, 88 (the second edition, Firenze, sub signo Stellae, 1673, includes two more epigrams; on St Philip Neri, 63, and 'votum Urbis Florentiae', 163. The other four are on 123, 124, 135, 136).

[51] See for a truly egregious example, the account of the black American Phyllis Wheatley in *The Critical Review* 21 (1766), 282.

of excellence, and no exclamation is made over the author's unusual gender and background. Subsequently, Fr. di S. Antonio contributed a poem in Marchina's praise to *Musa Posthuma*.[52]

The Oratorian Paolo Aringhi, who knew her personally and exchanged verses with her, wrote about her at some length in 1651, saying 'her poems excited admiration among learned men, and were eventually put in the hand of Pope Urban VIII himself' (a poem in *Musa Posthuma*, asking a favour for Cardinal Spada, is addressed to the pontiff).[53] He adds, 'her compositions were collected together by the work of pious men, and put forth into the light, lest they should lie in the tomb of oblivion together with their author'. Again, his admiration is genuine, and shows that the collection was passing around in manuscript. He quotes a letter to her from Cardinal Spada, and elsewhere, two poems on St Peter in the Mamertine prison.[54]

A witness that her work was circulated beyond Rome is a book published in Spain in 1680. Her self-deprecating *distichon ad lectorem* (on p. 91 of *Musa Posthuma*), and her epigram on St Laurence were quoted in an anthology of Spanish verse and Latin verse (mostly by Italians) with Spanish translations, printed in Valencia.[55] As in *De Arte Epigrammatica*, the editors present her work simply on its merits. No other women's verse is included. Twenty years later, two epigrams are quoted by Sebastian Kortholt in his *Disquisitio de Poetriis Puellis* of 1700.[56] She is also mentioned in Aringhi's *Triumphus poenitentiae* (1670) as an example of virtuous life. Considerably later, Domenico Martuscelli's *Biografia degli uomini illustri del Regno di Napoli* gives an account of her, based mainly on Rossi, but including a Latin epigram on the death of her baby sister from *Musa Posthuma*.[57]

The circulation of information about Marchina is therefore distinctly different from the way in which learned women's names with some attached gossip were copied from one reference book to another from the fourteenth century onwards.[58]

---

[52] *Musa Posthuma*, sig. §§ 8r. Another Piarist (they were a teaching order) also contributes a poem, sig. §§ 8v.

[53] 'Cuius carmina eruditissimis quibusque viris admirationi extitere, et ipsimet Vrbano Octauo Pont. Max. vbi ad eius manus aliquando delata sunt. ... Huius autem elucubrationes paulo post piorum virorum studio in unum collectae, ne una eum auctore obliuionis tumulo interceptae iacerent, in lucem evocatae prodibunt'. Paolo Aringhi, *Roma Subterranea Novissima*, 2 vols (Rome: Vitale Mascardi, 1651), vol. 1, p. 157 (Lib. I, Cap. 29, §§ 17–18), *Musa Posthuma*, pp. 51, 84, 87.

[54] Aringhi, *Roma Subterranea*, vol. 1, pp. 200–1 (Lib. II, Cap. 1, §32), *Musa Posthuma*, letter, pp. 60–1, 'Petrus Apostolus', p. 26.

[55] *Varias, hermosas flores del Parnaso, que in quatro floridos, visitos quadros, plantaron iunto a su cristilina fuente D. Antonio Hurtado de Mendoza ...y otros illustres poetas de España* (Valencia: en casa de Francisco Mestre, 1680), the title shows that it was taken from the 1662 edition, indicating that the latter was in circulation (distich sig. ¶¶4v, epigram on 39).

[56] Sebastian Kortholt, *Disquisitio de Poetriis Puellis* (Keil: Barthold Reuther, 1700), pp. 26–7. Paolo Aringhi, *Triumphus poenitentiae* (Roma: Philippus Maria Mancini, 1670), pp. 359–52

[57] Domenico Martuscelli (ed.), *Biografia degli uomini illustri del Regno di Napoli*, 5 vols (Napoli: Nicola Gervasi, 1813–18), IV, no pagination; *Musa Posthuma*, 78.

[58] Jane Stevenson, 'Inventing Fame', in Patricia Philippy (ed.), *A History of Early Modern Women's Writing* (Cambridge: Cambridge University Press, 2018), pp. 348–630. She does sometimes appear in such lists, such as the vague accounts of Benito Jerónimo Feijoo 'Defensa de las mujeres', which is

Five of these books quote her work, and the things that the authors know about her are different. Additionally, *Musa Posthuma* in its entirety was reprinted in Naples in 1701. It is clear that she was by no means an entirely obscure figure in the half-century or so after her death, though after 1701, the only scholar to mention her was Benedetto Croce.[59]

The funerary arrangements which were made for her are also very striking. She was buried in the Chiesa Nuova, in the nave, on the right, by the chapel of St Philip Neri, founder of the Order. As Macedo comments, this was a most honourable place. Her epitaph was by Gaspar de Simeonibus, who was like Virgilio Spada, one of Innocent X's secretaries, and fortunately, the inscription over her tomb was copied by Rossi and Macedo, since the tomb is no longer *in situ*. I once went to look for it, with the help of a friendly and obliging Oratorian, but the Chiesa Nuova underwent extensive rebuilding in its first hundred years, particularly in the side chapels,[60] and there was also a fire in the early seventeenth century,[61] so the inscription must at some point have been destroyed.

The inscription was long enough to constitute a summary of her life, and read as follows:

> In memory of Martha Marchina, virgin Neapolitan by origin, brought up in Rome, to whom a wonderful love of wisdom came at only seven, for her pursuit of notable piety and chastity. Thereupon, with an equal cultivation of morality and learning, she studied the humanist arts and first, the rules of ancient Latin poetry, and she was wonderfully talented in imitation, having taught herself. She was learned in Hebrew and Greek letters and the sterner disciplines ... she went at last to immortality on the fifth of the ides of April 1646, aged 46. The fathers of the company of the Oratory, who were witnesses of her diligent and upright life, and her guardians after her death, raised this well merited monument.[62]

The fact that she was an artisan's daughter is not mentioned: in fact, it sounds almost as if she was a sort of honorary female Oratorian: it's worth noting that the Oratorians were responsible for placing the memorial, which cannot have been

---

unaware of her published work, in his *Teatro crítico universal*, 9 vols (Madrid: Imp. Lorenzo Francisco Mojados/ Francisco del Hierro, 1726–40), I.325–98, 378, or Georg Christian Lehms, *Teutschlands Galante Poetinnen*, 2 vols (Frankfurt am Mayn: Anton Heinscheidt, 1715), II.137–40.

[59] 'Appunti di letteratura secentesca inedita o rara', *La Critica*, 3rd ser., 28 (1929), 468–80.

[60] Pampalone, *La cappella della famiglia Spada*.

[61] *Santa Maria in Vallicella, Chiesa nuova* (Roma: Tipi Centenari, 1974), and see further Pampalone, *La Capella della famiglia Spada*. The fire destroyed St Philip Neri's original quarters, so since Marchina's tomb is said to have been by his chapel, it may also have fallen victim to the fire.

[62] DOM. Marchinae Marchinae, ortu Neapolitanae, Virgini, educatione Romanae: cui, ad insigne pietatis ac pudicitiae studium, mirus sapientiae amor, vel septenni accessit. Eoque deinceps pari morum, atque ingenii cultu Humaniores artes, ac Latinam, in primis Poesin ad veterum normam, atque aemulationem suo ipsa instructo, eximiè calluit exercituque; Hebraicis Graecisque literis docta, Severiores disciplinas, fastu procul, religiosè attigit Animi quaesito magis ornatu, quam nominis: cuius gloriam sponte latius in Urbis luce, dum plane abiecit. In finum transmisit immortalitatis. obiit v. Idus Aprilis. Ad MDCXXXXVI, aetatis XXXXVI. Patres congregationis Oratorii, quos illa vitae probae accurandae habuerat monitores, Curatores post funeris, monumentum benemerenti, pos[uerunt] (*Musa Posthuma*, sig. §§§§6r).

cheap: the sheer number of words implies a fair-sized tablet. There is something quite unusual in the way that a woman whose claim to fame is entirely dependent on her individual talent is being put forward for the interested attention of posterity.

Marchina's Verse

Macedo suggests why her work was admired by contemporaries when he describes it as 'nitidus et facilis, non fucatus, non neglectus'. That is, it was graceful and distinguished, with a strong sense of the appropriate, neither over-ornamented, nor lax. Her chosen form was the epigram, very fashionable in the seventeenth century. Daniel Russell observes, 'while it is common to associate epigrammatic wit with satire, it could also be turned to the needs of religious expression when the intention was to inspire awe or astonishment'.[63] Her verses are elegant, often a little melancholy, and display a characteristically Baroque taste for paradox and contrast, as we see in 'The Visitation of the Blessed Virgin to Elizabeth', where Mary at once carries and is carried:

> The Virgin climbs the rocks of the mountain with eager steps
>   And her journey equals the paths of the winds.
> No wonder; she is not delayed by the weight of her womb
>   For willingly, the omnipotent boy ascended to the heights.
> Love adds swift wings to the virginal feet
>   So she can bear the irksomeness of the journey for a long time.
> So, go, Virgin mother, climb the mountains – but alas,
>   The child you carry in your womb, all too soon, will himself carry the Cross.[64]

Orazio Spada, one of Cardinal Bernardino's hand-picked nephews, contributed to a slim volume of Latin verse and prose on the Visitation, which suggests how in tune Marchina is with the aesthetics of the Spada circle.[65] Another poem similarly reveals a heroic vision of Mary, 'The Sun Speaks to the Virgin':

---

[63] Daniel Russell, 'The Genres of Epigram and Emblem', in Glyn P. Norton (ed.), *The Cambridge History of Literary Criticism*, 9 vols (Cambridge: Cambridge University Press, 1989), III.278–83, 282.

[64]
> Sedula saxosi superat fastigia montis
>   Virgo, et ventorum gressibus aequat iter.
> Nec mirum; nullo tardatur pondere ventris,
>   Nam sponte omnipotens tendit ad alta puer.
> Virgineis pedibus celeres amor addidit alas
>   Ut possit longe taedia ferre viae.
> Ergo age Virgo parens, montes conscende, sed heu! Quem
>   Fers utero natus, mox feret ipse Crucem. (p. 20)

[65] *Viatores, sive Laudes Deiparae Virginis in Montana ut Elisabetham inviseret abeuntis latina et graeca, soluta et vincta numeris oratione celebratae a … Horatio Spada, Pompeio Eugenio, Francisco Maria Rho* (Rome: apud F. Caballum, 1630).

Enter, O Virgin and do not despise my chariot,
  Or scorn to take the reins in your snow-white hand.
Lo, the Sun is more splendid, while he companions you, praising you:
  Our brightness yields to your radiance.[66]

Here, the Virgin is 'the woman clothed with the sun' (Revelations 12), or Our Lady of Victory (a popular Counter-Reformation devotion, in which she is often represented in a whole-body halo of rays). While this Sun is Apollo in his chariot, the Virgin herself is a goddess; an anti-Phaethon as well as an anti-Eve; cancelling a mythic act of primal disobedience as the Sun willingly gives her the reins. In this poem, the reward of perfect obedience is empowerment.

These poems of Marchina's are classic example of the seventeenth-century taste which Mario Praz describes:

> Seventeenth-century men saw instances of *argutezza* (wit) in every aspect of the universe. All the phenomena of the surrounding world, all the categories of learning, supplied them with suggestions for this mental idiosyncrasy of theirs: they discovered mysterious witticisms in the aspects of the earth and the sky, heroical devices and symbols in all the creatures; animals and plants possessed a witty language for them; and full of wit was the language of God.[67]

Marchina also enjoyed clever structures, such as epigrams of this form:

> Iesus, Christus, Amor docuit, superavit, adussit
> Terram, Erebum, Venerem: lege, cruore, face.[68]

The form is *versus rapportati*: the cleverness lies in the way that the appositional structure sets up complex resonances between the triads (for example, Christ instructs and conquers, as well as kindles, human love): it is also, of course, as three-in-one, a representation of the Trinity. A *fax* is often a wedding-torch, a meaning which the use of 'Venus' as a word for love seems to support, but it is also the light of the sun. The third term of the epigram is therefore a twist, evoking in four words the highly affective, quasi-erotic pietism of the Baroque. It is not easy to translate, but a possible rendering is

> Jesus teaches the world with his law;
> as Christ, he conquers Hell with his blood,
> as Love, he kindles Desire with his light.

---

[66]   Ingredere, et nostros Virgo ne despice currus
          Nec pigeat nivea flectere lora manu
      En Sol splendidior, dum te comitantur ovantem;
        Luminibus cedunt lumina nostra tuis.(p. 21)

[67] Mario Praz, 'The Flaming Heart: Richard Crashaw and the Baroque', in *The Flaming Heart: Essays on Crashaw, Machiavelli, and other Studies in the Relations between Italian and English Literature from Chaucer to T.S. Eliot* (New York: Doubleday, 1958), pp. 204–63 at 206.
[68] *Musa Posthuma*, p. 5.

'Amor' and 'ignis' are words which resonate through Marchina's writing; very characteristic of Baroque piety.[69]

One poem which is more interesting than it appears at first sight is apparently the beginnings of a hymn: Macedo thinks there is some of it missing, though he does not say why, but the fact that it is a classic, iambic dimeter verse like the hymns of St Ambrose strongly suggests that, like them, it ought to have eight verses. It begins:

> Jesus, eternal joy
> Hope, life and love of the heart
> Given to us mortals
> As a pledge of future glory.[70]

The reason why it is interesting is that it is recalls the hymns of a somewhat earlier woman, the Dominican nun Laurentia Strozzi; and that therefore it seems possible that the Oratorians had introduced her to the work of another woman Latinist.[71]

Macedo also suggests that a poem on p. 17 of *Musa Posthuma* is an imitation of Horace's *Epode* 16, not in terms of content, but of metre, which again suggests that she is acquainted with Strozzi, who had an unusually strong interest in metrical experiment. However, there are also distinct points of contact between this poem on the Virgin and Martial's epigram IX.43; Marchina's first line is 'Prome tuas jam Gange comas, quid Phoebe moraris?', while Martial's similarly opens with Apollo lingering in his pleasure grounds, and his last line is 'Nata est hostia, Phoebe; quid moraris?'/'the victim is born, Apollo, why do you delay?' Martial's 'hostia' is merely a thank-offering; Marchina's thought has taken another path: her principal subject is the birth of the Virgin, who will outshine the sun, but who might also be thought of as a consecrated creature.[72] The inevitable cycle of the heavens mirrors, for her, the equally certain birth of a Redeemer.

The importance of this poem is that it demonstrates that Marchina's Latin reading was not confined to Christian texts. It might seem surprising that Santolino would put as obscene a poet as Martial in his protégée's hands, but Marchina's talent, like Martial's, expressed itself in epigrams, and Justus Lipsius had created

---

[69] For example, Durante Alberti's altarpiece for the chapel of the Venerable English College in Rome (1580) shows Christ's blood falling onto a map of England, while an angel holds a banderole with the motto 'I come to set the world on fire'. Peter Davidson, 'Recusant Catholic Spaces in Early Modern England', in Ronald Corthell, Frances E. Dolan, Christopher Highley, and Arthur F. Marotti (eds), *Catholic Culture in Early Modern England* (Notre Dame: University of Notre Dame Press, 2007), pp. 19–51 at 23.

[70]
> Iesu perenne gaudium
> Spes, vita amorque cordium
> Nobis datum mortalibus
> Pignis futurae gloriae. (p 16)

[71] *Venerabilis Laurentiae Stroziae Monialis S. Dominici in monasterio divi Nicholaie de Prato, in singula totius Anni solemnia, Hymni* (Firenze: Filippo Giunta, 1588). See Jane Stevenson, 'The Latin Poetry of Suor Lorenza Strozzi', in Laurie Churchill, Phyllis R. Brown, and Jane E. Jeffrey (eds), *Women Writing Latin From Roman Antiquity to Early Modern Europe*, 3 vols (New York and London: Routledge, 2002), III, 109–32.

[72] *Musa Posthuma*, p. 17.

an expurgated Martial, of which there were eight Italian editions between 1597 and 1628. This is presumably the version she read.[73]

Musa Posthuma

Having sketched what is knowable of Marchina's life, and suggested that she was perceived in her own century in Counter-Reformation circles as a poet of talent rather than a female prodigy, which was a distinct phenomenon, I now wish to turn to a consideration of how her surviving work reached print, and of what this has to tell us about literature and social advancement in the context of the family politics of Baroque Rome.

A sizeable number of her Latin poems were printed 16 years after her death in 1646, together with a number of her letters, mostly in Latin, and a brief biography. The resulting book, *Musa Posthuma*, was published in Rome by Filippo Maria Mancini in 1662, edited by a Portuguese Franciscan called Francisco Macedo, and dedicated to Christina, ex-queen of Sweden. Macedo was a Counter-Reformation hack, a reliable defender of orthodoxy.[74] Like most of Macedo's publications, *Musa Posthuma* was aimed at a particular contemporary moment.[75]

The first question to be asked is the reason why it was put together. This seems to be due to one of the major *causes célèbres* of the mid-seventeenth century, the abdication and spectacular conversion of Christina, ex-queen of Sweden, who left her native land in 1655, and fled to Rome. She was received in December 1655 by Pope Alexander VII, then in the first year of his pontificate,[76] in a manner which fully reflected the diplomatic importance of the occasion. Alexander VII had been born Fabio Chigi, a member of an important Roman family, which doubtless made all the capital it could from the extraordinary spectacle of an erstwhile Protestant monarch seeking refuge with the pope.

However, it was another major Roman family, the Barberini, as Stefanie Walker and Frederick Hammond have shown, who were central to the extraordinarily

---

[73] *M. Val. Martialis Epigrammata expurgata. Iusti Lipsi, aliorumque adnotationibus illustrata. Omnia recens emaculata, vt emendatiora hactenus non prodierint* (Verona: haeredes Andreae Bochini, 1597) is the earliest.

[74] Francisco Macedo, born Coimbra, Portugal, 1596; died Padua, 1 May 1681, was a Portuguese Franciscan theologian. He entered the Jesuit Order in 1610, which however he left in 1638 in order to join the Discalced Franciscans. These also he left in 1648, for the Observantines. In Portugal he sided with the House of Braganza. Summoned to Rome by Pope Alexander VII, he first taught theology at the College of the Propaganda, and subsequently church history at the Sapienza, and as consultor to the Inquisition. At Venice in 1667, during the week beginning 26 September, he held a public disputation, against all comers, on nearly every branch of human knowledge, especially the Bible, theology, patrology, history, law, literature, and poetry. He named this disputation 'Leonis Marci rugitus litterarii' (the literary roaring of the Lion of St. Mark); this obtained for him the freedom of the city of Venice and the professorship of moral philosophy at the University of Padua.

[75] 'Appunti di letteratura secentesca inedita o rara', 468–80.

[76] 'The Creation of a Roman Festival: Barberini Celebrations for Christina of Sweden', in Stefanie Walker and Frederick Hammond, *Life and the Arts in the Baroque Palaces of Rome* (New Haven and London: Yale University Press, 1999), pp. 53–70.

elaborate festival *adventus* which greeted the erstwhile queen in 1655. Christina, however, left Rome shortly after, paid an interim visit to the city in 1658, and decided to return for a third time in 1662. Pope Alexander VII had taken against her in the meantime, due to her erratic conduct, in particular, her ordering the assassination of her Master of the Horse on grounds of treason. Christina considered she had passed a legitimate sentence, refusing to accept that as an ex-monarch, she no longer possessed judicial authority.

The sensitive social antennae of Rome's leading families evidently registered the queen's diminished status. Though the queen's travels in 1662 produced festival volumes recording entertainments offered to her, none record an event in Rome.[77] This gave the Spada family an opportunity. The existence of the works of the virtuous and talented Marchina gave this relatively parvenu family an opportunity gracefully to advertise their own significance, at no great expense, with the aid of the versatile Francisco Macedo, who was an admirer of Queen Christina.[78] Cardinal Bernardino Spada died in 1661, but his nephew Giambattista had received his red hat in 1654, and the family was still very much a presence in Rome.

Musa Posthuma is dedicated to Queen Christina, and the introductory poem, by Cardinal Bernardino Spada, is addressed to her. His contributions in fact may suggest that the publication was originally his idea, though in the event, he didn't live to see it appear. His poem is on the subject of heresy, addressed to Christina and given in both Latin and Italian versions. After this introduction, and a dedication to Christina which compares Marchina to Cornelia, mother of the Gracchi, and Polla Argentaria,[79] there is an address to the reader, followed by a poem in Marchina's praise by Alexander Pollinus, one of seven poets known as the 'Pleias Alexandrina', an international group of Latin poets whose poetry appeared under the auspices of Pope Alexander VII, and were also associated with the Spadas.[80] Macedo's biography comes next, the poems, then finally, some letters.

---

[77] *Balletto a cavallo fatte nella piazza di Naiburgo* [Neuburg] *dal sereniss. Duca di Giuliers ... per il passagio della invitissima ... Christina Alessandra regina di Suetia ...* ([Neuburg], 1662); Francesco Sbarra, *La magnanimità d'Alessandro dramma musicale rappresentato in Insprugg alla maesta d'Alessandra Christina regina di Svetia* ([Innsbruck]: appresso Michele Wagner, 1662)

[78] He published *Elogium Christinae Heroinae Optimae* (Lisbon, s.n., 1650) – when she was still a Protestant – also *Descriptio Coronationis Christinae auctore fratre Francesco Macedo* (Lisbon, s.n., 1651) (the coronation took place October 1650). It may be worth noting that the Jesuit who converted Queen Christina was Antonio Macedo, perhaps a relative. Francesco also published *Christina Pallas togata Alexandri VII. auspicijs Romae triumphatrix* (Romae: Ex Typographia Reu. Camerae Apostolicae, 1656); and *Christina regina Alexandro papae; Alexander Christinae reginae*, distichs, no place, no date [Rome, probably 1656], which ends 'canebat Macedo'. The year before *Musa Posthuma*, he published *In obitum ... card. Spadae, naenia lyrica* (Roma: Philippus Maria Mancini, 1661), which suggests that he was a Spada protégé.

[79] Classical Roman women remembered as writers and almost invariably mentioned in lists of learned ladies.

[80] Alexander Pollinus, Augustus Favoritus, Ferdinandus de Furstenberg, Joannes Rotgerus Torckius, Natalis Rondininus, Stephanus Gradius, and Virginius Caesarinus, *Septem illustrium virorum poemata* (ed. altera) (Amsterdam: Elsevier, 1672). Most of the addressees of these verses were Jesuits.

The relevance of Queen Christina to *Musa Posthuma* is witnessed by the Vasa coat of arms which decorates the title-page, and by the dedication, which is couched in quite interesting terms:

> Nor is it improper that you, who are an embodiment of Pallas [Athena], should take this virgin's conception, which talent gave birth to, to your royal breast, whiter than any snow, purer than any star, whom Lucina [goddess of childbirth] will never trouble.[81]

The message is that the work of a virgin poetess is a suitable gift for a virgin queen: Christina, though not herself a Latin poet, was a highly educated woman, and such a gift was not only graceful, but highly appropriate.[82]

The idea that the publication of Marchina's work was in some way connected with the self-advancement of the Spadas is strengthened by the book's contents. *Musa Posthuma* contains some 91 pages of letters and shortish Latin poems. The first 56 pages consist of religious poems, but pp. 57–61 contain both letters and poems, mostly to or about Spadas and other patrons, including three on Paolo Spada, the patriarch, one on Gregorio Spada, the cardinal's nephew and protégé, and one on the cardinal's older brother Francesco, who had made his career in the army.[83] As an oeuvre, it has an obvious utility from a Spada viewpoint. This is verse and prose from a grateful client who was also that unusual thing, a virgin poetess, which praised Spada virtue and Spada magnificence in poem after poem.

Perhaps the most probable explanation for the book is that Bernardino Spada gave the fair copy of Marchina's work to Francisco Macedo, told him to read the entry on her in Rossi's *Pinacotheca*, and to put the materials together into a book, with the aid of whatever the Fathers of the Oratory remembered about her. There may possibly have been a presentation manuscript to be given to the ex-queen (though if so, it does not survive among her manuscripts, which are in the Biblioteca Apostolica), since the printed book is a poorly produced and poorly proofread little volume, and even in a bespoke binding, it can never have looked very impressive. However, in 1662, currying favour with ex-Queen Christina herself had ceased to be important. What she provided was an extraneous *reason* for issuing a book which, as it circulated among the literary-minded within and without Rome, would have advertised the virtues of the Spada family to good effect. Festivals, events, and other kinds of news were often supported by small books; though this one does not record a festival as such, it is evidently a response to the ex-queen's return to Rome.[84]

---

[81] 'Nec dedecet Regium tuum sinum Virginius foetus, quem ingenio peperit, suo, omni nive candidiorem, omni astro puriorem, cuius tu Lucinam agere ne graveris, quae Palladem repraesentas.'

[82] For a discussion of Christina's intellectual life, see Susanna Åkerman, *Queen Christina of Sweden and her Circle: The Transformation of a Seventeenth-Century Philosophical Libertine* (Leiden, New York, København, and Köln: E. J. Brill, 1991). Christina certainly used Latin fluently; since Latin letters survive in some number. She seems to have preferred French for her personal writing.

[83] *Musa Posthuma*, pp. 70, 76, 82–3.

[84] Laurie Nussdorfer, 'Print and Pageantry in Baroque Rome', *The Sixteenth Century Journal*, 29.2 (Summer, 1998), 439–64.

Macedo's praise of Marchina seems at first simply to deploy the well-worn tropes for describing learned women: for example, like the nun-poet Laurentia Strozzi, she is described as 'Another Sappho, but different from the first in her moral character and religion'.[85] But on closer inspection, his choice of comparanda is interesting. She is also compared to Strozzi, Margherita Sarrochi, Tarquinia Molza, and Veronica Gambara. A very far from random list.

Laurentia Strozzi was a Dominican nun of San Niccolò in Prato in the second half of the sixteenth century. Her book of 104 Latin hymns, heavily indebted to the odes of Horace, was published at the Giunta Press in Florence in 1588, and as I have argued, Marchina may well have read them.[86] In any case, like Marchina, she was an Italian woman writing Christian poetry in Latin which was published as a book. Margherita Sarrocchi was like Marchina in another respect, since she was born in Naples (in 1559), and died in Rome in 1617. Like Marchina, she used her education to maintain a public position as a woman of letters; and was an associate of Torquato Tasso and Galileo Galilei. She published poetry in Italian, notably *La Scanderbeide, poema eroica*, published in Rome in 1626.[87]

Tarquinia Molza, a native of Modena, wrote extensively in Italian and Latin, and translated from Greek, notably Plato's *Charmides*. She published little during her lifetime except poetic contributions in Italian and Latin to various gratulatory and memorial volumes, but her work circulated extensively in manuscript, and gave her a public position. After her husband's death, she was invited to the court of Ferrara in 1582 as a singer, and in 1583, became officially a court lady with a salary, so she used her education for self-advancement.[88] Francesco Patrizi wrote a series of neo-Platonic dialogues, *L'amorosa filosofia*, in which he gives her biography, and presents her as a 'new Diotima' (with reference to the woman philosopher in Plato's *Symposium*) and 'philosopher of love'.[89] By decree of the S.P.Q.R., Dec. 8, 1600, she and her family were granted Roman citizenship, and she was given the title of *Unica*. Therefore, though she seems actually to have spent her time between Modena and Ferrara, she was another woman Latinist who had been a public intellectual in Rome within recent history.

---

[85] Rossi, *Pinacotheca Imaginum Illustrium* I.250 says of Strozzi: 'While the one is very expert in pagan religion, the other is infused with Christian mysteries. The one burns with the flame of shameful love, and is convicted as a tribade by her own confession, the other burns, kindled with the purest and most holy fire of divine love' ('si quidem fuit illa vere expers religionis, haec Christianis sacris imbuto; illa impurissimorum amorum flamma exarsit, quae, suas etiam confessione, Tribas fuisse convicitur; haec purissimo sanctissimoque divini amoris igne succensa flagravit').

[86] See n. 73 above.

[87] María Bayarri, 'Universos poéticos femeninos: las amigas de Galileo Galilei', *Revista de la Sociedad Española de Italianistas*, 2 (2004), 19–27. Her epic poem *Scanderbeide* is edited and translated by Rinaldina Russell (Chicago: Chicago University Press, 2006).

[88] Charles Castleman, 'Three Musical "Virtuose di Ferrara": Lucrezia Bendidio, Laura Peperara and Tarquinia Molza', *Anuario Musical*, 23 (1968), 191–8.

[89] Ed. John Charles Nelson (Firenze: Felice le Monnier, 1963). The MS of *L'amorosa filosofia* is Parma, Biblioteca Palatina, MS Pal. 418.

The last of Macedo's comparanda, Veronica Gàmbara, was a rather earlier figure, since she died in 1550. She was the great-niece of the famous Isotta Nogarola,[90] and a literary figure: her surviving writings consist of some 50 poems and over 130 letters, all in Italian except for a handful of verses in Latin. She also had strong connections with the church via her brother Uberto, a churchman and diplomat: he was governor of Bologna from 1528 to 1533 and became a cardinal in 1539: as a widow and with his countenance, she held court as a woman of letters in Bologna, visited by Pietro Bembo, Tarquinio Molza (grandfather of Tarquinia), and many others: his official position perhaps meant that her activity as a salon hostess was seen as an aspect of the city's reception of distinguished guests.[91]

Thus, to sum up, the context into which Marchina is put is one of highly visible, entirely respectable, and praiseworthy women Latinists, all Italian, and relatively recent. Two of the four have clear associations with Rome itself, and three of the four published Latin verse of one kind or another. Three of them used their writing to make themselves a position as public intellectuals, and one of them as a stepping stone to employment. The result is to render Marchina's work admirable rather than freakish, a very different strategy from most writing about women prodigies, which tends to represent them either as unique, or as 'the second Sappho'.

So, what does the story of Martha Marchina herself, of how her poetry reached publication, and of her principal patrons, tell us about literature and social class? For Marchina herself, the ability to compose a Latin epigram enabled her to better her life. Though her physical circumstances did not change very materially, her talent gave her friends and patrons who lent her books, offered her protection, and gave her a recognised and dignified place with respect to a new religious order, the Oratorians, and an arriviste clerical dynasty. She was able to resist interventions in her life which did not accord with her wishes; and the evidence from anthologies suggests that her poems were taken seriously by the literary-minded.

For men such as the Spadas, the capacity to write a Latin epigram on a mouse gnawing a copy of Caesar, with all that entails, was a significant aspect of their social positioning. The shift from ancestors rumoured actually to be colliers to the status of a rich coal-merchant and tax farmer, achieved by Paolo Spada, required guile, opportunism, and numeracy. However, the move from the obscurity of Brisighella to the papal court, and socially advantageous marriages for carefully chosen, groomed and educated heirs, which was achieved by his sons Bernardino and Virgilio, was entirely facilitated by education. Bernardino Spada did not publish

---

[90] She was the daughter of count Gianfrancesco da Gàmbara and Alda Pia, so her father was the brother of Ginevra Nogarola's husband Brunoro da Gàmbara.

[91] Gaetano Giordani (ed), *Della venuta e dimora in Bologna del sommo pontifice Clemente vii. per la coronazione di Carlo v. imperatore celebrata l'anno mdxxx* (Bologna: fonderia e tip. Gov., 1842), pp. 77–8, C. H. Clough, 'Pietro Bembo, Madonna G., Berenice and Veronica Gàmbara', *Commentari dell'Ateneo di Brescia per l'anno 1963*, 162 (1965), 209–17.

books of verse; he received dedications.[92] And, as a baroque poet might have put it, humble literary mice could aid Spada lions. In this instance, Francisco Macedo, who had been putting his fluent pen at the service of Catholic orthodoxy and many individual patrons for some 20 years, and Marchina herself, grateful, humble, talented, and because of her gender, intriguing.

---

[92] Such as Onorio Domenico Caramella, *Museum illustriorum poetarum, qui ad hæc vsque tempora latino carmine scripserunt* (Venice: Typis Omnibenij Ferretti, 1651); Omobono de Bonis, *Commentarii resolutorii de examine ecclesiastico et disquisitionibus moralis* (vol. III) (Bologna: apud Nicolaum Tebaldinum, 1627).

Part III

Representing Social Status:
Genres and Discourses

8

The *Idiota*'s Authority: Fifteenth-Century Hierarchies in Dialogue

RICHARD J. OOSTERHOFF

Idiotae rapiunt caelos.[1]

THE OPENING SCENE of Nicholas of Cusa's *Idiota de sapientia* begins with its hero, a poor *idiota* who walks across the Roman forum and nearly bumps into a rich lawyer, trained in the arts of Cicero. The man smiles, greets the orator, and says mildly: 'Your pride astounds me. You are exhausted from always reading so many books, yet the experience doesn't humble you. It must be because the science of this world, in which you think you're the best, is foolishness with God and puffs people up with pride. True knowledge humbles. I hope to find true knowledge, because it is a treasury of joy.'

Stunned, the orator splutters. 'How dare you, you ignorant pauper of an idiot? How can you deride letters, since no one learns without them?'

The idiot mollifies without retreat. 'Great orator, it is not presumption which makes me speak, but love. For I see that you've given yourself to the search for wisdom by hard, hollow labour. If I call you back so that you weigh your mistake, I think you'll rejoice escaping a worn trap. Authority's opinion holds you; you're like a horse free by nature but tied up by art to a fence, only able to eat what others give it. Your mind, tied to the authority of writers, feeds on strange, unnatural food.'

Despite his shock, the orator is intrigued and begins to probe. 'If the food of wisdom cannot be found in the books of the wise, where then?' And so the idiot begins to teach. He knows he is an idiot, and this true knowledge of himself makes him at once humbler and wiser than those learned in books. It is not that books contain no wisdom, but that it cannot be found there *by nature* (*naturale ibi*). Rather, wisdom cries out in the streets, and knowledge is to be found in the books of nature,

---

[1] 'The unlearned grasp the heavens'. Jacques Lefèvre d'Étaples (ed.), *Contemplationes Idiotae. De amore divino. De Virgine Maria. De vera patientia. De continuo conflictu carnis et animae. De innocentia perdita. De morte* (Paris: Henri Estienne, 1519), fol. 96v.

Proceedings of the British Academy, **246**, 163–180, © The British Academy 2022.

those God wrote with his finger. He teaches the orator from first principles, how counting, weighing, and measuring in the streets leads to understanding of mathematics and other conceptual realities, an intellectual chain leading from nature without to nature within.[2]

This passage introduces three dialogues that Nicholas of Cusa wrote in 1450 as a talented church lawyer who had been made a cardinal in Rome barely a year earlier. Most commentators are quick to observe that it is Nicholas' own views that come from the *Idiota*'s mouth, as he teaches how human ability to craft is exercised through acts of measurement: human minds project themselves onto the world, unfolding diverse approximations of nature, and through nature stretch towards the very mind that created nature, God. The *idiota* is an artful conceit, alluding to this author's central preoccupation with 'learned ignorance', by which one can know God better by recognising how little we know of God – that truer ignorance becomes the basis for truer knowledge. Thus the mode of unlearning is itself a trope, as Cusanus puts himself in the role of Socratic questioner. Even more significantly, Nicholas of Cusa echoed St Paul, for whom Christian salvation was a kind of 'foolishness to the Greeks' (1 Cor. 1.23). Indeed, the governing metaphor of the 'book of nature', where the solid truths of *res* could be untangled from illusory *verba*, was a learned commonplace of its own.[3]

---

[2] In the foregoing I have paraphrased Nicolaus Cusanus, *Idiota de sapientia*, in *Opera omnia* (Hamburg, 1940–2002), vol. 5, pp. 3–10. 'Convenit pauper quidam idiota ditissimum oratorem in foro Romano, quem facete subridens sic allocutus est: Miror de fastu tuo, quod, cum continua lectione defatigeris innumerabiles libros lectitando, nondum ad humilitatem ductus sis; hoc certe ex eo, quia "scientia" "huius mundi", in qua te ceteros praecellere putas, "stultitia" quaedem "est apud deum"et hinc "inflat". Vera autem scientia humiliat. Optarem, ut ad illam te conferres, quoniam ibi est thesaurus laetitiae. ORATOR: Quae est haec praesumptio tua, pauper idiota et penitus ignorans, ut sic parvifacias studium litterarum, sine quo nemo proficit? IDIOTA: non est, magne orator, praesumptio, quae me silere non sinit, sed caritas. Nam video te deditum ad quaerendum sapientiam multo casso labore, a quo te revocare si possem, ita ut et tu errorem perponderes, puto contrito laqueo te evasisse gauderes. Traxit te opinio auctoritatis, ut sis quasi equus natura liber, sed arte capistro alligatus praesepi, ubi non aliud comedit nisi quod sibi ministratur. Pascitur enim intellectus tuus auctoritati scribentium constrictus pabulo alieno et non naturali. ORATOR: Si non in libris sapientum est sapientiae pabulum, ubi tunc est? IDIOTA: Non dico ibi non esse, sed dico naturale ibi non reperiri. Qui enim primo se ad scribendum de sapientia contulerunt, non de librorum pabulo, qui nondum erant, incrementa receperunt, sed naturali alimento "in virum perfectum" perducebantur. Et hi ceteros, qui ex libris se putant profecisse, longe sapientia antecedunt. ORATOR: Quamvis forte sine litterarum studio aliqua sciri possint, tamen res difficiles et grandes nequaquam, cum scientiae creverint, per additamenta. IDIOTA: Hoc est quod aiebam, scilicet te duci auctoritate et decipi. Scripsit aliquis verbum illud, cui credis. Ego autem tibi dico, quod "sapientia foris" clamat "in plateis", et est clamor eius, quoniam ipsa habitat "in altissimis". ORATOR: Ut audio, cum sis idiota, sapere te putas. IDIOTA: Haec est fortassis inter te et me differentia: Tu te scientem putas, cum non sis, hinc superbis. Ego vero idiotam me esse cognosco, hinc humilior. In hoc forte doctior exsisto. ORATOR: Quomodo ductus esse potes ad scientiam ignorantiae tuae, cum sis idiota? IDIOTA: non ex tuis, sed ex dei Libris. ORATOR: Qui sunt illi? IDIOTA: Quos suo digito scripsit. ORATOR: Ubi reperiuntur? IDIOTA: Ubique.'

[3] Augustine, e.g. *En. Ps.* 45.7: 'Liber tibi sit pagina divina, ut haec audias: liber tibi sit orbis terrarum, ut haec videas. In istis codicibus non ea legunt, nisi qui litteras noverunt: in toto mundo legat et idiota' ('Let the divine page be a book for you, so that you might hear these things; let the whole world be a book for

For the historian, the mere presence of enduring tropes about hierarchies of knowledge and knowers says little. More telling is their use at specific times and places. Cusanus, to use the name customary among specialists, is often read as a philosopher whose powerful originality authorises his standing within intellectual culture. The trope of the *idiota*, I shall argue, in part establishes this view – the dialogue *is* a remarkable work of philosophy. But it also shows Cusanus responding to intensifying pressure from unlearned classes in upper Germany, insistent that learning was not the only way to authority. Roughly similar arguments have been made as a way to explain the irrepressible 'common man' of the later Reformation.[4] More precisely, other scholars have probed some of the biographical links of Cusanus to late medieval religious movements with prominent lay components.[5] My own effort will set Cusanus in relation to literature written by rather less learned contemporaries, thereby re-evaluating more common scholarly narratives about the relation of intellectual elites to spiritual authority. In what follows the *idiota* may help us see tensions distinct to fifteenth-century Europe around the authority of unlearned sorts.

Fifteenth-Century Options

Cusanus was a canny operator in the new bureaucracies that knit fifteenth-century Europe together. He ended life as an ecclesiastical prince-bishop of Brixen, who some thought might be pope – his brilliant career makes it difficult to see him as an *idiota* in any sense. He was a cardinal well schooled in the universities, an expert collector of

---

you, so that you may seem them. Those who do not know how to read, do not read those books, while the unlearned read all the world'). Ernst Robert Curtius, *European Literature and the Latin Middle Ages*, trans. Willard R. Trask (Princeton: Princeton University Press, 1953), pp. 319–26; Hans Blumenberg, *Die Lesbarkeit der Welt* (Frankfurt a.M.: Suhrkamp, 1981). For the significance of book metaphors in relation to social standing, see Klaus Schreiner, 'Laienbildung als Herausforderung für Kirche und Gesellschaft: Religiöse Vorbehalte und soziale Widerstände gegen die Verbreitung von Wissen im späten Mittelalter und in der Reformation', *Zeitschrift für Historische Forschung*, 11.3 (1984), 257–354, at 262–3. For useful qualifications, see Lodi Nauta, 'A Weak Chapter in the Book of Nature: Hans Blumenberg on Medieval Thought', in Arjo Vanderjagt and Klaas van Berkel (eds), *The Book of Nature in Antiquity and the Middle Ages* (Leuven: Peeters, 2005). Blumenberg also supplied an evocative and widely read account of Cusanus (though not linked to the book metaphor), in *The Legitimacy of the Modern Age*, trans. Robert M. Wallace (Boston: MIT Press, 1983), pp. 359–60, 534.

[4] See Peter Blickle's earlier works, summed up in *Der Bauernkrieg: Die Revolution des gemeinen Mannes* (Munich: Beck, 1998); cf. Lyndal Roper, '"The Common Man", "The Common Good", "Common Women": Gender and Meaning in the German Reformation Commune', *Social History*, 12 (1987), 1–21.

[5] Nikolaus Staubach, '*Cusani laudes*. Nikolaus von Kues und die Devotio Moderna im spätmittelalterlichen Reformdiskurs', *Frühmittelalterliche Studien*, 34 (2000), 259–337; Nikolaus Staubach, 'Cusanus und die Devotio Moderna', in Inigo Bocken (ed.), *Conflict and Reconciliation: Perspectives on Nicholas of Cusa* (Leiden: Brill, 2004), pp. 31–51; Inigo Bocken, 'The Language of the Layman: The Meaning of the *Imitatio Christi* for a Theory of Spirituality', *Studies in Spirituality*, 15 (2005), 217–49; Inigo Bocken, 'Visions of Reform: Lay Piety as a Form of Thinking in Nicholas of Cusa', in Christopher M. Bellitto and David Zachariah Flanagin (eds), *Reassessing Reform: A Historical Investigation into Church Renewal* (Washington, DC: Catholic University of America Press, 2012), pp. 214–31.

manuscripts, and the author of a steady flow of tracts at the highest levels of theological and philosophical abstraction. Cusanus defined the profile of the learned churchman. Yet if he was a typical churchman, he was typical also in having a life that reveals moments of instability in the hierarchy of lay and priestly, unlearned and erudite.

For his origins did not guarantee such power. Cusanus came from a merchant family, up and coming in the shipping business along the bustling Rhine river, with a local network of low-level magistrates and officials. The young Nicholas pursued ambition by way of the universities, an option chosen by a growing cadre of men from merchant families in late medieval Europe.[6] He studied first at Heidelberg, and then at Padua, where he became a doctor of laws, a canon lawyer. In the 1420s, presumably while at Padua, Nicholas made a name in budding humanist circles. Poggio Bracciolini recognised the young man's talent, asking him to report copies of Cicero's *Republica* and Pliny in his visits to northern monasteries. Nicholas' reputation as a scholar was confirmed when he found 12 previously unknown plays of the Roman comic writer Plautus, news that Poggio swiftly transmitted to his friends. His merchant origins put Cusanus in a rising class of notaries and a bureaucratic elite that spanned merchants and clerics, from Petrarch to acquaintances such as Leon Battista Alberti. The young Rhinelander's skill with old texts stood him in good stead at the Council of Basel, which overflowed with opportunity for a talented, ambitious young lawyer like Cusanus. Whether or not his move to the papal camp was motivated by opportunism, as enemies claimed, it was certainly rewarded. The pope sent him on important missions, first to Constantinople in the entourage of Cardinal Bessarion, and then later as a papal nuncio throughout the German lands. And Cusanus did see the unified papacy as a solution to the schisms of Christendom. Much of Cusanus' manuscript hunting was for patristic and medieval sources on the unity of the church – a humanist's effort to find legal mechanisms for holding Christendom together.

We can therefore see Cusanus operating in what John Van Engen has called a 'world of multiple options'.[7] Late medieval Europe was unified through political means, which meant a daily experience of thickening Europe-wide networks.[8] By 1400, the mendicant orders of the thirteenth century had set up administrative centres in most towns, linking local parishes one to another through news and cycles

---

[6] Jacques Verger, *Men of Learning in Europe at the End of the Middle Ages*, trans. Steven Rendall (Notre Dame: University of Notre Dame Press, 2000); Rita Copeland, *Pedagogy, Intellectuals, and Dissent in the Later Middle Ages: Lollardy and Ideas of Learning* (Cambridge: Cambridge University Press, 2001); Daniel Hobbins, *Authorship and Publicity Before Print: Jean Gerson and the Transformation of Late Medieval Learning* (Philadelphia: University of Pennsylvania Press, 2009).

[7] John Van Engen, 'Multiple Options: The World of the Fifteenth-Century Church', *Church History*, 77 (2008), 257–84. For another portrait of fifteenth-century religion as rich in options, see Matthew Champion, *The Fullness of Time: Temporalities of the Fifteenth-Century Low Countries* (Chicago: University of Chicago Press, 2017).

[8] On these political means, compare Robert Bartlett, *The Making of Europe: Conquest, Colonization and Cultural Change, 950–1350* (Princeton: Princeton University Press, 1993) and R. I. Moore, *The Formation of a Persecuting Society* (Oxford: Blackwell, 1987).

of preaching and confession. Lawyers devised frameworks that compared and normalised local status and customs, applying regulation through expanding realms, offering new linkages between the local parish, its practices and preoccupations, and the larger worlds of empire and the papacy. The fastest growing institution of the fifteenth century was the university, as every prince preferred to have lawyers and theologians trained in his own lands.[9] Indeed, university men made church councils the instrument that linked the rising temperatures of Europe ever more tightly to local, regional concerns.

One should not overplay the suddenness or uniformity with which either university-educated bureaucrats or local diocesan concerns arose, yet there are clear marks of tension. The crusades against Cathars and Albigensians, recurrent peasants rebellions, Lollardy in England, Hus in Prague, and Joan of Arc in France all were flashpoints of local concern ever more acted out on the pan-European stage. Late medieval local concerns often took on the language of anticlericalism, resisting the arrogation of spiritual authority to educated men and religious orders.[10] The 'spiritually intense' members of these communities were increasingly lay. As André Vauchez and Richard Kieckhefer have shown, saints in earlier centuries had normally been bishops, hermits, and great men. By the fifteenth century, saints were more than ever lay persons, often women, who had become the focus of local veneration – papal inquests of canonisation tried not so much to stimulate local fervour as to restrain and contain popular piety.[11]

This context made hierarchy an important but tricky topic. Cusanus remained aware of his bourgeois origins, and when he learned he had been made cardinal, he noted that 'ut sciant cuncti sanctam Romanam ecclesiam non respicere ad locum vel genus nativitatis, sed esse largissimam remuneratricem virtutum' ('so that all may know the holy Roman church does not consider the place of birth or ancestry, but most generously rewards abilities').[12] Intellectually, he was especially attracted to a certain kind of writer who stood outside the university and legal establishments. Ramon Llull, the Catalan merchant-turned-missionary to the Muslims, believed that new intellectual tools were necessary for converting the broader Mediterranean world to Christianity. He is famous now for inventive approaches to combinatorics, along lines that would influence early modern philosophers such Leibniz. He positioned

---

[9] Jacques Verger, 'Patterns', in H. de Ridder-Symoens (ed.), *A History of the University in Europe, Vol. 1: Universities in the Middle Ages* (New York: Cambridge University Press, 1992), pp. 35–74.

[10] Out of many studies, see Peter A. Dykema and Heiko Augustinus Oberman (eds), *Anticlericalism in Late Medieval and Early Modern Europe* (Leiden: Brill, 1993).

[11] André Vauchez, *Sainthood in the Later Middle Ages*, trans. Jean Birrell (1st edn 1981; Cambridge: Cambridge University Press, 1997); Richard Kieckhefer, *Unquiet Souls: Fourteenth-Century Saints and Their Religious Milieu* (Chicago: University of Chicago Press, 1984).

[12] Hermann Hallauer and Erich Meuthen (eds), *Acta Cusana: Quellen zur Lebensgeschichte des Nikolaus von Kues* (Hamburg: Meiner, 1983), vol. I.2, no. 849 (21 October 1449). I slightly modify the translation of Donald Duclow, 'Life and Works', in Christopher M. Bellitto, Thomas M. Izbicki, and Gerald Christianson (eds), *Introducing Nicholas of Cusa: A Guide to a Renaissance Man* (New York: Paulist Press, 2004), pp. 25–56 at 25.

himself, however, outside the university, an autodidact in Latin and the philosophical arts. His claim to artlessness served his message: nature offered truths immediately available to the human mind, including truths about God's triune nature.[13] Llull's own dialogues, therefore, present him as an *idiota* directly reading the book of nature, inferring divine truths with a kind of natural, untutored logic. This is the feature of Llull's thought that seems to have attracted Cusanus, possibly already in his student days at the University of Heidelberg, and certainly in 1428, when he spent time rifling through the large corpus of Lullian texts in the Sorbonne's library.[14]

Scholars of Cusan thought agree that the *Idiota* dialogues of 1450 show him at the *apogee* of his accomplishment.[15] They were written during the first year of his cardinalate. They also bear the traces of Cusanus' response to the Dominican Johann Wenck, who opposed the papal party that Cusanus had joined in the 1430s during the Council of Basel. When Cusanus wrote his long *De docta ignorantia*, Wenck found it permeated with heresy, ultimately linking him with several late medieval lay movements: Waldensians, followers of Eckhart and Wyclif, and beguines and beghards.[16] All shared the same error, in Wenck's view, claiming a direct union with God that denied the Creator's distinction from the creation. Cusanus first answered with an *Apologia doctae ignorantiae* in 1449, and especially the first of the *Idiota* dialogues reformulates Cusan philosophy around the refrain that true knowledge requires first-hand experience.[17]

Wenck was right to be worried, in a sense. In fact, Cusanus himself later became – like Jean Gerson, Johannes Nider, and other churchmen – careful and wary of the excesses that could arise in popular devotion.[18] Yet when Cusanus wrote the *Idiota* dialogues in 1450, the worries and compromises of real pastoral experience were still

---

[13] Mark D. Johnston, *The Evangelical Rhetoric of Ramon Llull: Lay Learning and Piety in the Christian West Around 1300* (Oxford: Oxford University Press, 1996).

[14] Eusebius Colomer, 'Heimeric van den Velde entre Ramón Llull y Nicolás de Cusa', in Johannes Vincke (ed.), *Gesammelte Aufsätze zur Kulturgeschichte Spaniens* (Münster: Aschendorff, 1963), pp. 216–32.

[15] Theo van Velthoven, *Gottesschau und menschliche Kreativität* (Leiden: Brill, 1973), pp. 15–29; Kurt Flasch, *Nikolaus von Kues: Geschichte einer Entwicklung* (Frankfurt a.M.: Vittorio Klostermann, 1998), p. 273; David Albertson, *Mathematical Theologies: Nicholas of Cusa and the Legacy of Thierry of Chartres* (Oxford: Oxford University Press, 2014), ch. 9.

[16] Johannes Wenck, *De ignota litteratura*, ed. Edmonde Vansteenberghe (Munster: Aschendorff, 1910), pp. 29–30. This debate has been studied in detail by K. M. Ziebart, *Nicolaus Cusanus on Faith and the Intellect: A Case Study in 15th-Century Fides-Ratio Controversy* (Boston: Brill, 2013); see also Matthew T. Gaetano, 'Nicholas of Cusa and Pantheism in Early Modern Catholic Theology', in Simon J. G. Burton, Joshua Hollmann, and Eric M. Parker (eds), *Nicholas of Cusa and the Making of the Early Modern World* (Leiden: Brill, 2019), pp. 199–227.

[17] For a close reading, see Ziebart, *Cusanus on Faith and Intellect*, pp. 105–34.

[18] A famous example is his reaction to the blood cult at Wilsnack; see Caroline Walker Bynum, *Christian Materiality: An Essay on Religion in Late Medieval Europe* (New York: Zone, 2011), pp. 15–17. See further John Van Engen, 'Friar Johannes Nyder in Laypeople Living as Religious in the World', in *Vita Religiosa im Mittelalter: Festschrift für Kaspar Elm zum 70. Geburtstag* (Berlin: Dunker & Humblot, 1999), pp. 583–615; Daniel Hobbins, 'Gerson on Lay Devotion', in Brian Patrick McGuire (ed.), *A Companion to Jean Gerson* (Leiden: Brill, 2006), pp. 41–78.

months into the future. (Moreover, until his death, Cusanus remained a supporter of the 'in between' kinds of spiritual life pursued by the *Modern Devout*, also like Gerson. In his will he left a curious charter for the *Bursa Cusana*, a school to be set up on the model of the Brothers of the Common Life at Deventer.[19]) As an answer to Wenck, the dialogues of 1450 take on a defiant tone, because they mirror a genre increasingly used among such late devout movements.

Naming the *Idiota*

Some readers will have already bristled at my translation of the Latin *idiota* as 'idiot'.[20] Modern historians take pains to use 'layman', framing the matter as one between Latinity and not.[21] Take the Orator's outburst against the 'ignorant' (*ignorans*) pauper, which Hopkins renders in typical fashion as 'utterly unschooled', a choice of word that steers away from our associations of 'idiocy' with mental disability, stupidity, irrationality, and even social failure.[22] The *idiota* is first a matter of education, and historians of medieval Europe make the *idiota* the obverse of 'literate' ('lettered', *litteratus*) clergy.[23]

One can find in the history of the word *idiota* a reliable genealogy of these senses. The Greek ἰδιώτης primarily referred to a 'private person', one who does not hold public or professional office – a layperson.[24] Transplanted into classical Latin, the word described those lacking culture, especially the culture of Roman elite soaked up through the study of letters. It was hardly a neutral descriptor, of course. Without training, the *idiota* was cognitively handicapped. Cicero aligned the *idiota* with rude understanding, to be contrasted with the 'ingenious (*ingeniosus*) or comprehending (*intelligens*)' man.[25] In Roman culture, always cosmopolitan, the term *idiota* also carried a social judgement against the rustic, a figure of boorish stolidity.

---

[19] Staubach, '*Cusani laudes*' and '*Cusanus und die Devotio Moderna*'.

[20] Perhaps there is some comfort in the fact that I have a seventeenth-century English precedent: Nicholas de Cusa, *The Idiot in Four Books: The First and Seconde of Wisdome, the Third of the Minde, the Fourth of Statick Experiments, or Experiments of the Ballance*, trans. John Everard (London: William Leake, 1650).

[21] The usual translations are: Nicholas de Cusa, *Idiota de Mente, The Layman: About Mind*, trans. Clyde Lee Miller (New York: Abaris, 1979); Jasper Hopkins (ed. and trans.), *Nicholas of Cusa's Complete Philosophical and Theological Treatises* (Minneapolis: Arthur J Banning Press, 2001).

[22] The *OED* offers two current definitions, a legal or technical one on disability, and a colloquial definition, what we might call a social judgement: 'A person who speaks or acts in what the speaker considers an irrational way, or with extreme stupidity or foolishness.'

[23] Herbert Grundmann, 'Litteratus – illiteratus: Der Wandel einer Bildungsnorm vom Altertum zum Mittelalter', *Archiv für Kulturgeschichte*, 40 (1958), 1–65 at 2, 6. A study which applies this approach to Cusanus is Jan-Hendryk de Boer, 'Plädoyer für den Idioten. Bild und Gegenbild des Gelehrten in den Idiota-Dialogen des Nikolaus von Kues', *Concilium Medii Aevi*, 6 (2003), 195–237.

[24] Henry George Liddell and Robert Scott, *A Greek-English Lexicon*, rev. and augmented by Sir Henry Stuart Jones (Oxford: Clarendon Press, 1940), s.v.

[25] ' … quae non modo istum hominem ingeniosum atque intelligentem, verum etiam quemvis nostrum, quos iste idiotas appellat, delectare possent' (' … [statues] which not only could delight that clever and comprehending man, but even one such as us, whom he calls *idiotae*'). Cic. Verr. 2, 4, 2, §4.

Although the word retained such meanings throughout the middle ages, it developed new connotations too. Some were simply about language. As local vernaculars grew away from the Latin of antiquity, *idiota* gained new shades of meaning as 'monoglot' or specifically lacking Latin. Already in the early fifth century Augustine used the word this way in his sermons.[26] As the Venerable Bede explained by way of a specious etymology: 'they call *idiotae* those naturally limited to only their own language and knowledge, who lack the knowledge of letters. These the Greeks call *proprium* or ἴδιον'.[27] Isidore of Seville, who mapped the world of words for medieval Europe, likewise presented the word as a matter of skill: 'Idiota, inperitus, Graecum est. Inperitus, sine peritia'.[28]

More distinctively Christian meanings accrued too. It was Christian authors who made the *idiota* stand in for the common run of humanity, the Christian masses. Tertullian had already described the 'simple or even foolish and *idiotae*, who make up the majority of believers'.[29] This sense of *idiotae* as the masses merged with the notion of illiteracy in Gregory the Great's fierce interventions on behalf of images as books for the 'laity' – or, as he wrote 'books for the *idiotae*'.[30] Regularly used in this sense, the *idiota* now also meant non-clergy – a meaning that paralleled Cicero's rustic, but now part of the specifically Christian dyad of priest–people.

Thus European Christians applied the term with much deeper ambiguity than had the Romans. The chief reason was the Latin New Testament, which linked the *idiota* to apostolic witness in three places. In the *Acts of the Apostles*, the priests of Jerusalem marvel at Saint Peter and Saint John, both 'sine litteris et idiotae' (unlettered and unlearned), as they use the Jewish scripture to preach the resurrected Christ. The founding apostles of Christianity – one of them the bishop of Rome – are here simple folk, inspired to preach and teach by the gospel they witness to. The motif of inspiration returns in 1 Corinthians 14, where Saint Paul speaks of the Holy Spirit 'who gives space to the *idiota*', giving voice to the voiceless in prayer (v. 16).[31] Paul also links such inspiration to madness or insanity, urging the church not to prophesy in tongues all at once, for if 'an unbeliever or an *idiota* enters,

---

[26] Above n. 3.

[27] 'Idiotae enim dicebantur qui propria tantum lingua naturalique scientia contenti litterarum studia nesciebant, siquidem Graeci proprium ἴδιον vocant' ('Those who only knew their own language, not understanding natural knowledge or literary studies; in fact, the Greeks called their own tongue an *idiom*'). The Venerable Bede, *Expositio Actuum Apostolorum*, ed. M. L. W. Laistner, CCSL 121 (Turnhout: Brepols, 1983), p. 26, and see pp. 36–42. Cited by de Boer, 'Plädoyer für den Idioten', 208.

[28] Isidore of Seville, *Etymologiarum sive Originum libri XX*, ed. W. M. Lindsay (Oxford: Oxford University Press, 1911), vol. 2, p. 405 (X.144).

[29] He uses 'idiota' for the '*simplices*' or even '*imprudentes et idiotae, quae maior semper credentium pars est*'. *Tertulliani Opera*, Corpus christianorum series latina, 2 (Turnhout, 1954), p. 1161.

[30] Gregory the Great on pictures as books for the laity (idiotae): Registr. 9, 208, in MGH *Epistulae* 2. p. 195.21, cit. Grundmann, 'Litteratus – illiteratus', p. 7.

[31] 1 Cor 14:16. 'Ceterum si benedixeris spiritu, qui supplet locum idiotae, quomodo dicet: Amen, super tuam benedictionem? quoniam quid dicas, nescit' ('Else when thou shalt bless with the spirit, how shall he that occupieth the room of the unlearned say Amen at thy giving of thanks, seeing he understandeth not what thou sayest?').

will they not think you mad?' (v. 23).[32] In the New Testament scriptures, the word *idiota* draws together fundamental themes of apostolic piety: Christian simplicity, the teaching of the unlearned, the outsider.

The Christian simplicity of the *idiotae* supplied the leitmotif of medieval dissent. Simple folk were fundamental to the waves of monastic reform beginning in the eleventh century with the Benedictine reformer Peter Damian. He linked the *idiota* closely to apostolic piety in his treatise on *The holy simplicity that should precede puffed up knowledge*, in which he included a section on 'Cur deus per viros idiotas ac simplices mundum instituit' ('why God teaches the world through *idiotae* and simple folk'). There he observed that God could have sent philosophers and orators, but chose to send 'simple men and fishermen' to sow the seeds of the faith.[33] Late medieval models of apostolic simplicity drew on this vocabulary too. Perhaps the most paradigmatic case is that of St Francis of Assisi, whose followers sweated over his letters and hagiography to divine a charter of holy vocation for the Franciscans, not least in the violent debates over poverty and learning.[34] In such writings, Francis protested repeatedly – in Latin – that his example was not that of the learned elite, but that his simplicity of life made him an *idiota*.[35]

So if *idiota* does not straightforwardly translate to 'idiot', neither does it simply mean 'layman' or simply lacking Latin letters. To read 'layman' misses this range of tones. A good fifteenth-century example comes from a textbook by the Brothers of the Common Life, where the author distinguishes the *idiota* from the *laicus*, noting that a *laicus* certainly can be a man of letters, while a cleric can indeed be illiterate.[36] In other words, Cusanus had access to a perfectly good word for 'layman': *laicus*. In my paraphrase of Cusanus' *Idiota*, I chose 'idiot' for two reasons. In part I hoped to jog us out of the familiarity that 'layman' offers. More importantly, however, 'idiot' suits the way Cusanus plays with overtones of idiocy and folly. Cusanus deploys irony deliberately, as his craftsman accuses the orator of prideful knowledge (*scientia*), which in fact is folly (*stultitia*). This passage introduces a playful series of dichotomies that upturn the usual categories

---

[32] 1 Cor 14:23. 'Si ergo conveniat universa ecclesia in unum, et omnes linguis loquantur, intrent autem idiotae, aut infideles: nonne dicent quod insanitis?' ('If therefore the whole church be come together into one place, and all speak with tongues, and there come in those that are unlearned, or unbelievers, will they not say that ye are mad?').

[33] Peter Damian, *De sancta simplicitate scientiae inflanti anteponenda*, ch. 3, ed. Migne, *Patrologia Latina*, vol. 145, p. 697.

[34] David Burr, *The Spiritual Franciscans: From Protest to Persecution in the Century After Saint Francis* (Pittsburgh: Pennsylvania State Press, 2003).

[35] Francis of Assisi, *Écrits. Texte latin de l'édition de K Esser* (Paris: Éditions du Cerf, 1981), 206, 252. See further Johannes Schneider, 'Das Word idiota im mittelalterlichen Latein', in Elisabeth Charlotte Welskopf (ed.), *Untersuchungen ausgewählter altgriechischer sozialer Typenbegriffe und ihr Fortleben in Antike und Mittelalter* (Berlin: Akademie-Verlag, 1981), pp. 132–57 at 137.

[36] Johannes Synthen, *Dicta Sinthis super prima parte Alexandri* (Strassburg: Martin Schott, 1487), sig. a2r.

of learned and ignorant, books and natural world, the poor and the rich. The moral and social here cannot be unlaced from the epistemic.

Authority in Devout Dialogue

I want to recover this dappled language of moral, epistemic, and social hierarchy, because it alerts us to the cultural possibilities of Cusanus' own time. One thread of evidence is the genre of dialogue in which Cusanus wrote. The philosophical dialogue was nothing new, reaching back to Plato and Cicero, as well as Augustine.[37] Moreover, an enormously wide range of pedagogical texts used dialogue to transmit information – only a very small number of these exploited dialogue's polyvocal capacity to keep dissenting views in play.[38] Yet within the devotional literature of fifteenth-century Upper Germany, one can detect a groundswell of dialogue that plays with hierarchy.

It helps to remember that Cusanus lived in a time of media change. Around 1400, new paper-making technology encouraged the outpouring of cheap, short, manuscript tracts, a revolution in media a full 50 years before the printing press, a turn Daniel Hobbins has summarised with special care.[39] The very cloisters that Cusanus and Poggio Bracciolini and others scoured for ancient manuscripts were, in the eyes of most contemporaries, far more important as sites of manuscript production. This was above all true for the renewed religious orders of Germany and the Low Countries, Carthusians, reformed Benedictines, Brothers and Sisters of the Common Life, and Augustinian canons. In particular, Modern Devotion and groups like them produced an overflowing stream of texts and practices: before all else, written and preached sermons, but also 'collations' (vernacular addresses delivered by lay people), Lollard Bibles, books of hours and other vernacular liturgies, 'exercises', and mirrors for the discretion of souls.[40]

---

[37] Rudolf Hirzel, *Der Dialog: Ein literarhistorischer Versuch* (Leipzig: S. Hirzel, 1895); Vittorio Hösle, *The Philosophical Dialogue: A Poetics and a Hermeneutics*, trans. Steven Rendall (Notre Dame: University of Notre Dame Press, 2012). Cusanus is situated in this context by Tilman Borsche, 'Der Dialog—im Gegensatz zu anderen literarischen Formen der Philosophie—bei Nikolaus von Kues', in Klaus Jacobi (ed.), *Gespräche lesen. Philosophische Dialoge im Mittelalter* (Tübingen: Gunter Narr Verlag, 1999), pp. 407–33.

[38] E.g. the bibliography in Carmen Cardelle de Hartmann, *Lateinische Dialoge, 1200–1400: Literarhistorische Studie und Repertorium* (Leiden: Brill, 2007). For an early example of dialogue to address hierarchical dissent consider Norma N. Erickson, 'A Dispute between a Priest and a Knight', *Proceedings of the American Philosophical Society*, 111.5 (1967), 288–309. Although this is not the point here, university disputation can be seen as dialogic in this sense: Anita Traninger, *Disputation, Deklamation, Dialog: Medien und Gattungen europäischer Wissensverhandlungen zwischen Scholastik und Humanismus* (Stuttgart: Franz Steiner Verlag, 2012); Alex J. Novikoff, *The Medieval Culture of Disputation: Pedagogy, Practice, and Performance* (Philadelphia: University of Pennsylvania Press, 2013).

[39] Hobbins, *Authorship and Publicity before Print*, pp. 7–10, and notes.

[40] Mary A. Rouse and Richard H. Rouse, 'Backgrounds to Print: Aspects of the Manuscript Book in Northern Europe of the Fifteenth Century', in their *Authentic Witnesses: Approaches to Medieval Texts and Manuscripts* (Notre Dame: University of Notre Dame Press, 1991), pp. 449–66; Koen Goudriaan, *Piety in Practice and Print: Essays on the Late Medieval Religious Landscape* (Hilversum: Verloren, 2016).

Here we find the origins of Cusanus' *idiota*. Inigo Bocken has argued that we find already in the celebrated *Imitatio Christi* of Thomas à Kempis a kind of lay epistemology, in which the humble farmer is presented as better suited for the spiritual life than a vain philosopher.[41] But there are many further links. Late medieval devout movements along the Rhine circulated a genre of vernacular dialogues featuring a cleric learning from an *idiota*, one of the 'poor in spirit' who often presents Eckhartian statements about radical unity with God as a source of theological knowledge.

Perhaps the most telling of such dialogues are those featuring a woman as the *idiota*. A well-known example is the *Schwester Katrei*, a tract that circulated under the name of the great German Dominican mystic Meister Eckhart. The title character is a beguine who develops a state of perfect detachment, to the point that she can teach the 'master', a process which takes up the largest part of the text.[42] Another short story circulated under the title 'Meister Eckhart's Daughter', with a similar device; a young girl asks for Eckhart at the Dominican convent, saying she is 'neither girl nor woman, nor husband nor wife, nor widow nor virgin, nor master nor maid nor manservant'. When she meets Eckhart, he asks for explanation of the riddle, and she tells him that to be any one of those things would distract her from God: 'but I am none of all these things: I am just a thing like anything else and go my way'. In the dialogue, the character Eckhart reports that 'I have just heard the purest person I have ever met'.[43]

In fact, Eckhart never wrote these works. Nevertheless, in this textual tradition, Eckhart was thought to teach that the prevalent hierarchy of men over women did not apply; that spiritual authority instead derived from the directness of one's relationship to God. Eckhart's sermons circulated in Dutch translation among the Modern Devout; particularly *Beati pauperes* (sermon 87), on poverty in spirit as the posture *all* Christians must adopt for God to work in them.[44] The same mechanism takes up a much longer book found among the Modern Devout, *Meister Eckhart and the Layman*, which puts lay people on a level by using Eckhart's steps to union with God through *Abgeschiedenheit*, or 'detachment'.

Cusanus' debt to Meister Eckhart was already obvious in his own time. In fact, since Eckhart was associated with the 'Free Spirits' and other lay heretical movements, affinities to Eckhart were Johannes Wenck's main charge against

---

[41] 'Melior est profecto humilis rusticus, qui Deo servit, quam superbus philosophus qui se neglecto cursum caeli considerat' ('The humble rustic who serves God is entirely better off than the proud philosopher who neglects himself while theorising the movements of heaven'). *Imitatio Christi* 1.2.2, cit. Bocken, 'The Language of the Layman', 230.

[42] Kurt Ruh, 'Eckhart-Legenden', in *Die deutsche Literatur des Mittelalters Verfasserlexicon* (Berlin: Walter de Gruyter, 1980), vol. 2, pp. 350–3.

[43] Franz-Josef Schweitzer, *Der Freiheitbegriff der deutschen Mystik* (Frankfurt a.M.: Peter Lang, 1981), pp. 322–70, translated as an appendix in Bernard McGinn, Frank Tobin, and Elvira Borgstadt (trans.), *Meister Eckhart, Teacher and Preacher* (New York: Paulist Press, 1986), pp. 349–84.

[44] R. A. Ubbink, *De Receptie van Meister Eckhart in de Nederlanden gedurende de middeleeuwen: een studie op basis van middelnederlandse handschriften* (Amsterdam: Rodopi, 1978), who deals with the sermon at pp. 62–95.

Cusanus' treatise *On Learned Ignorance*. But the topos of the lay person teaching the learned master went beyond these works. In 'Die fromme Müllerin', a miller's wife teaches two Dominicans. They ask her the traditional questions of learned theology: what is a godly life? What is godly love? What is an angel? What is God? She answers with a question that reveals the poverty of their academic approach, cutting to the core: What must one do to be worthy of heavenly joy?[45] In similar stories, the benchmark figure of mysticism, a monk, prays that God show him whom to emulate in devotion, and God answers by showing a child; in other variants, the monk is shown a beggar or a humble nun.[46]

For nineteenth-century German historians, eagerly searching for the bourgeois origins of their own national figure of the farmer, the temptation was to see these stories as an index of the vernacular Volk. In reaction, scholars of the last century tended to explain away these stories as *topoi*, restrictive tools of an elite. Between these poles, we can take a middle path. In a tale called 'The Young Woman of 22 Years', we find the title character come to a theologian, a 'maÿster der göttlichen geschrifft'. She asks him what she should do, in order to approach the highest perfection and truth, to become a friend of God. The master asks about what spiritual exercises (*übungen*) she has practised up to this point. She offers three outward exercises, as well as three inward ones. The outward *übungen* are what we might expect: (1) to reflect on the life of Jesus, (2) to consider the birth of the divine Word in Mary, and (3) to rely on Christ's blood with full confidence. In these three exercises we can see the late medieval turn towards a Christocentric piety, strongly emphasising both Christ's incarnation and its attendant focus on the materiality of blood – as Caroline Walker Bynum has shown to special effect, blood cults became hugely popular in Germany at the time. For our purposes, however, the three inward exercises are more interesting. Here the young woman describes staying separated, 'alle dage', from all other creatures. Second, she describes keeping herself away from all unnecessary things that might come between God and her soul. Third, she tells of her habit of finding ten feet of space whenever she enters the church, and then 'I unify myself to my God in such a way that I think no one is there but God and me alone'.[47]

By now the Meister's response is unsurprising to us: he exclaims 'you have the right way', and that in 50 years of wearing a religious habit he has never found anyone

[45] Here I paraphrase one MS: 'Die prester fassen neder und vereyngiten sich mit er in gotlicher liebe und frag[ten] sie in dem ersten mall was eyn emfangen were gotlichen lebens. Sie fragten sie aber was die gotliche liebe were … Sie fragten sie was eyn engell were … Sie fragten sie was ist got … [Sie fragten] Noe gebent myr auch eyn lere und sagent myr was soll eyn mensche thun das er wurdich were der clarer gotlicher freude?' Gotha, Thür. Landesbücherei, Chart. B.237, fols. 171v–172v (urn:nbn:de:urmel-ec8bced2-a977-4d1c-bfc9-85764298432f5). I have not been able to compare transcriptions listed in Kurt Ruh, 'Die fromme (selige) Müllerin', in *Die deutsche Literatur des Mittelalters Verfasserlexicon* (Berlin: Walter de Gruyter, 1980), vol. 2, pp. 974–7.

[46] F. P. Pickering, 'Notes on Late Medieval German Tales in Praise of *Docta Ignorantia*', *Bulletin of the John Rylands Library*, 24 (1940), 121–37 at 123. See also the larger literature on the 'geistliche hausmagd'.

[47] I have used Version A, found in Pickering, 'Notes'; see also the bibliography in Kurt Ruh, 'Das Frauchen von 22 (21) Jahren', in *Verfasserlexicon* (Berlin: Walter de Gruyter, 1980), vol. 2, pp. 858–60.

reach such perfection. At first glance, this appears to be the kind of egalitarianism that fascinated nineteenth-century nationalists. But this is not about *equality* of status, much less democracy. Rather, the levelling move turns on *humility*. When the Meister asks the young woman 'what is your state?' (*was ist uwer staet?*), he refers to her religious status – is she 'secular' and 'in the world' or is she under vows?[48] She answers immediately that she is 'bound to the world'.[49] Yet what justifies her questions, at each stage, is her 'meek' (*oetmodenclichen, demütiglich*) manner. Hungering for immediate experience of God, the soul's direct access to God, the mystic pursues cognitive purity not by raising themselves up, but by emptying themselves. This move has a profound social effect: the common denominator of humanity is lowered to simply being, in order to establish a common claim on divinity, to emphasise what all creation shares from God. This is vividly so for 'Eckhart's Daughter', who insists not that she is equal to other people, but the opposite, that she is 'like any other thing'. This stance, the complete separation of the soul (*Abgeschiedenheit*) is precisely what puts these texts in the Eckhartian tradition.[50]

This is also what opened up these texts to critique, as we saw in Wenck's charges against Cusanus. Yet these texts circulated widely along the Rhine, in various vernacular dialects. And Nicholas was hardly the only interested cleric. Multiple axes of hierarchy run through such examples. The most obvious is that of gender, and indeed these fit alongside a growing late medieval group of texts written by women, such as the 'Sister-books' circulating in Dominican women's houses.[51] These and similar 'lives of sisters' (*vitae sororum*) adopt tropes of humility similar to those I have outlined in this chapter.[52] Scholars once limited these to being exemplars of an ecstatic 'female' spirituality, using visionary power to dissent from the constraints of male clerical power; the feminine here is visual, vernacular, and ecstatic, to be contrasted with the male textual, latinate, and rational.[53] Recent studies have found this dichotomy too strong. In a closer examination of

---

[48] 'Syt ir in der ee, und hait ir geut und ere dere in der werelt?' in Pickering, 'Notes', p. 126.

[49] 'Ich byn in der ee gebunden', in Pickering, 'Notes', p. 126.

[50] To explore this commonplace further, see Amy Hollywood, *The Soul as Virgin Wife: Mechthild of Magdeburg, Marguerite Porete, and Meister Eckhart* (Notre Dame: University of Notre Dame Pess, 1995), ch. 6, and Bernard McGinn, *The Harvest of Mysticism in Medieval Germany* (New York: Crossroad, 2006), pp. 167–71.

[51] For an overview, see John Van Engen, 'Communal Life: The Sister-Books', in A. J. Minnis and Rosalynn Voaden (eds), *Medieval Holy Women in the Christian Tradition c. 1100–c. 1500* (Turnhout: Brepols, 2010), pp. 105–31. More closely: Gertrud Jaron Lewis, *By Women, for Women, about Women: The Sister-Books of Fourteenth-Century Germany* (Toronto: Pontifical Institute of Mediaeval Studies, 1996); Rebecca L. R. Garber, *Feminine Figurae: Representations of Gender in Religious Texts by Medieval German Women Writers 1100–1375* (New York: Routledge, 2003).

[52] For an overview of *mulieres religiosae*, see relevant chapters of Bernard McGinn, *The Flowering of Mysticism: Men and Women in the New Mysticism: 1200–1350* (New York: Crossroad, 1998) and his *The Varieties of Vernacular Mysticism (1350–1550)* (New York: Crossroad, 2012).

[53] Gerda Lerner, *The Creation of Feminist Consciousness: From the Middle Ages to Eighteen-Seventy* (New York: Oxford University Press, 1993); Hollywood, *The Soul as Virgin Wife*; Jeffrey F. Hamburger, *The Visual and the Visionary: Art and Female Spirituality in Late Medieval Germany* (New York: Zone, 1998).

the Sister-Books, for instance, Claire Jones has shown that cloistered nuns were more responsible than once thought for bookish copying and for the ordered lives of Latin liturgy, as they earned deeper (if limited) respect for their writings from their male counterparts.[54]

The overriding concern in this late medieval surge of devotional material is a distinctively Christian approach to the *idiota*, as the word history of the previous section suggests. The goal was not to make nationalist revolutionaries, as nineteenth-century historians would have argued. Herbert Grundmann, looking at medieval dissenting movements, argued that the evidence did not support a materialist account of revolutionary change: 'titles of *rusticani, rustici, idiotae*, and *illiterati* tell us nothing at all about the social position of the heretics ... a weaver was not made into a heretic, but rather a heretic became a weaver'.[55] Likewise, these dialogues do not fit best with concerns about gender hierarchies, but rather with concerns about Christian virtues, the standing of a human soul in God's presence. Therefore *idiota* dialogues constantly use the humble to critique worldly power, pride, and self-regard. The leading spiritual writers of the Brothers and Sisters of the Common Life wrote their own versions, often borrowing similar language, sometimes translating them into Latin. One bestseller of the period, Gerhard Zerbolt of Zutphen's *De reformatione virium*, borrows artisanal metaphors to assemble various exercises – much like the *übungen* of the Jungefrau of 22 years – that are intended to transform one's inner senses.[56] A layman in the Groenendaal community, Jan van Leeuwen, became known as the 'good cook', whose writings were widely read by monks and lay devout alike.[57] Cusanus' *idiota* emerged in a world where exemplary knowledge belonged to the humble – rich or poor, cleric or lay, male or female.

Cusanus' Authority

Cusanus wrapped his *idiota* in learned layers. In the *idiota*, Christian folly converges with Socratic idiocy, much as would happen in Erasmus' *Praise of Folly*.[58] One could easily find other versions of these themes in twelfth-century Platonists, whom

---

[54] Claire Taylor Jones, *Ruling the Spirit: Women, Liturgy, and Dominican Reform in Late Medieval Germany* (Philadelphia: University of Pennsylvania Press, 2017). On literacy among women religious more generally, Rabia Gregory, 'Authority and Authorship in Late Medieval Women's Religious Communities', *Journal of Medieval Religious Cultures*, 40 (2014), 75–100; Virginia Blanton, Veronica O'Mara, and Patricia Stoop (eds), *Nuns' Literacies in Medieval Europe: The Kansas City Dialogue* (Turnhout: Brepols, 2015); Virginia Blanton (ed.), *Nuns' Literacies in Medieval Europe: The Hull Dialogue* (Turnhout: Brepols, 2013).

[55] Herbert Grundmann, *Religious Movements in the Middle Ages*, trans. Steven Rowan (1935; Notre Dame: Notre Dame University Press, 1995), pp. 14–15.

[56] Johan Van Engen, *Sisters and Brothers of the Common Life: The Devotio Moderna and the World of the Later Middle Ages* (Philadelphia: University of Pennsylvania Press, 2008) pp. 77–9.

[57] McGinn, *The Varieties of Vernacular Mysticism*, pp. 71–6.

[58] M. A. Screech, *Ecstasy and The Praise of Folly* (1980; London, Penguin, 1988).

Cusanus read as closely as he read any ancient.[59] The convergence of the Socratic gadfly and Pauline folly was a learned tradition among Cusanus' favourite authors. Paul described a man 'caught [*raptus*] up to the third heaven' (2 Cor. 12.2). This image of union with Christ was often superimposed upon Plato's idea of 'divine' madness or melancholic ecstasy, as refracted through Dionysius the Areopagite's widely read treatises.[60] Alan of Lille, Thierry of Chartres, William of Conches, and similar twelfth-century voices all engaged the idea of ecstatic insight through a kind of cognitive rapture or *amentis*. Ramon Llull, another of his distinctive influences, similarly recounted his own spiritual ecstasies. The topos itself was not a denial of hierarchy, but rather encapsulated the idea that spiritual exercises could let one rise through intellectual *translatio* into higher forms of knowledge.

If it remains difficult to imagine Cusanus within the same discourse as late medieval *mulieres religiosae*, then consider his reception. Cusanus himself became an example of such hierarchical movement in the generations after his death. The circle of the French humanist Jacques Lefèvre d'Étaples gathered together his works into the Paris *opera omnia* of 1514, introducing him as particularly skilled in mathematics.[61] Throughout their works, though, Lefèvre and his students mentioned Cusanus as the most significant Christian philosopher since Dionysius the Areopagite himself – whom they saw as Paul's student.[62] Although Lefèvre acknowledged Cusanus' deep learning, he did not see this as chiefly the product of an education. Rather, he presented Cusanus as a self-taught wonder to be compared to the ancients like Hermes Trismegistus, Euclid, and Aristotle, and only a few moderns such as Giovanni Pico della Mirandola: 'perhaps they are more truly called (if the word is clear) "disciplined" rather than "taught", these men of good nature and genius who some call αὐτοδιδάκτους ("self taught" as we say)'.[63] For all his learning, therefore, Cusanus seemed a faithful representative of ancient Christian, apostolic knowledge – and this legitimated his philosophy, rather than undermining it.

---

[59] Cusanus' repeated and central re-readings of Thierry of Chartres in particular have been thoroughly explained by Albertson, *Mathematical Theologies*.

[60] E.g. *On the Divine Names* 712A. For a general exploration of the union with Christ theme in Dionysius, see Charles M. Stang, *Apophasis and Pseudonymity in Dionysius the Areopagite: 'No Longer I'* (Oxford: Oxford University Press, 2012).

[61] Richard J. Oosterhoff, 'Cusanus and Boethian Theology in the Early French Reform', in Burton *et al.* (eds), *Nicholas of Cusa and the Making of the Early Modern World*, pp. 339–66.

[62] Oosterhoff, 'Cusanus and Boethian Theology'. On this genealogy, see Kent Emery, 'Mysticism and the Coincidence of Opposites in Sixteenth- and Seventeenth-Century France', *Journal for the History of Ideas*, 45 (1984), 3–23. More generally, see Yelena [Mazour-]Matusevich, 'Jean Gerson, Nicholas of Cusa and Lefèvre d'Étaples: The Continuity of Ideas', in Thomas P. McTiche and Charles Trinkaus (eds), *Nicholas of Cusa and His Age: Intellect and Spirituality: Essays Dedicated to the Memory of F. Edward Cranz* (Leiden: Brill, 2002), pp. 237–63.

[63] Jacques Lefèvre d'Étaples, *Libri logicorum ad archteypos recogniti cum novis ad litteram commentariis ad felices primum Parhisiorum et communiter aliorum studiorum successus in lucem prodeant ferantque litteris opem* (Paris: Wolfgang Hopyl & Henri (1) Estienne, 1503), 178v. 'Mercurium enim, Euclidem, Aristotelem, et ut ad tempora nostra descendam Cusam, Mirandulam et similes plura reperisse par est, quam que a preceptoribus et in libris monstrata perceperint, et tales verius forsan (si verbum pateretur) disciplinati, quam docti dicerentur, quos et melioris nature et genii viros αὐτοδιδάκτους (quod dicimus per se doctos) nonnulli appellavere.'

This sixteenth-century reading of a philosophically ambitious Cusanus should not be separated too sharply from the devotional context I have outlined in this chapter. Although he had been reading Cusanus since at least 1498, Lefèvre had increasingly focused on monastic reform during the period he assembled the *Opera omnia* of 1514.[64] At Paris, he had trained a generation of young scholars from along the Rhineland and he had developed an epistolary network with abbots and monks in the region. This network hunted through the libraries of monasteries from Groenendaal to Basel – yes, looking for manuscripts of Church Fathers and ancient philosophical treatises, but also searching for important classics of devotional literature to print. Lefèvre's acknowledgements to this network for sending along transcriptions, manuscripts, and news take up a full folio page in the 1514 *Opera omnia*. The network helped Lefèvre with devotional literature too. In the years leading up to this edition, Lefèvre published several key works of medieval mysticism, by Ramon Llull, by twelfth-century Victorines, by members of the *Devotio moderna* such as Jean Mombaer and Jan Ruusbroec, and several others.[65] Elsewhere I have begun to trace through these works a fascination with untutored knowledge.[66] Here let me pick out two examples. One is the first printed editions of medieval female mystics: Hildegard of Bingen, Elizabeth of Schonau, and Mechtilde of Magdeburg (1513).[67] Another is a series of works known as the *Contemplationes idiotae* (1519). Lefèvre found the author's anonymity appropriate to a self-effacing simplicity, observing that 'stilus humilis est, sed purus, syncerusque, et plane Christianismum sapiens' ('the style is humble, but pure and sincere; he is plainly a wise Christian').[68]

Indeed, on this reading, the *idiota* did not need to be a man. Lefèvre's edition of the three female mystics was balanced alongside three male mystics. He prefaced the collection with a letter to Adelheid von Ottenstein, the abbess of the Benedictine convent of Rupertsberg (the one founded by Hildegard of Bingen). He reflected on the state of virginity as a reflection of the purity belonging to the whole Church of Christ. He then concluded with a brief defence against those who

---

[64] Jean-Marie Le Gall, 'Les moines au temps de Lefèvre d'Etaples et Guillaume Briçonnet à Saint-Germain-des-Prés', in Jean-François Pernot (ed.), *Jacques Lefèvre d'Etaples (1450?–1536)*, Actes du colloque d'Etaples les 7 et 8 novembre 1992 (Paris: Honoré Champion Éditeur, 1995), pp. 125–40.

[65] Eugene F. Rice, 'Jacques Lefevre d'Etaples and the Medieval Christian Mystics', in J. G. Rowe and W. H. Stockdale (eds), *Florilegium Historiale: Essays Presented to Wallace K. Ferguson* (Toronto: University of Toronto Press, 1971), pp. 90–124; see also entries in Eugene F. Rice (ed.), *The Prefatory Epistles of Jacques Lefèvre d'Étaples and Related Texts* (New York: Columbia University Press, 1972).

[66] Richard J. Oosterhoff, '*Idiotae*, Mathematics, and Artisans: The Untutored Mind and the Discovery of Nature in the Fabrist Circle', *Intellectual History Review*, 24 (2014), 1–19. See also Guy Bedouelle, *Lefèvre d'Étaples et l'intelligence des Écritures* (Geneva: Droz, 1976), pp. 76–7.

[67] Jacques Lefèvre d'Étaples (ed.), *Liber trium virorum et trium spiritualium virginum. Hermae Liber unus. Uguetini Liber unus. F. Roberti Libri duo. Hildegardis Scivias libri tres. Elizabeth virginis libri sex. Mechtildis virgi. libri quinque* (Paris: Henri (I) Estienne, 1513). The author was found to be Raymund Jordanus in the seventeenth century.

[68] Lefèvre, *Contemplationes Idiotae*, fol. 2r.

dismissed women's teaching, 'who would take from women their trustworthiness in having revelations'.[69] One possible target here was Jean Gerson, who may have already begun to acquire a reputation for criticism of visionary women as teachers.[70] Lefèvre's defence was that their example was 'neither impossible nor new'; Jerome himself had presented women as teaching examples of Christian life. In this context, the modern scholarly account of Jerome's use of women being ultimately self-serving – it was *his* vision of Christian life revealed in these women – is quite beside the point.[71] For Lefèvre's view of Jerome included the spurious *Regula monacharum*, from which Lefèvre quoted Jerome's description of himself in precisely the same terms of humility: 'Scio (inquit) quid loquor carissimae, nam ut meam insipientiam loquar, ego homunculus sic abiectus, sic vilis, in domo domini adhuc vivens in corpore, angelorum choris saepe interfui, de corporeis per hebdomadas nichil sentiens divinae visionis intuitu' ('I know, said Jerome, of what I speak, dear ones. For I speak as of my own stupidity, I being a little man so abject, so mean, living then in the Lord's house often bodily present in the choir of angels, yet for weeks sensing from those bodies no intuition of divine vision').[72] For Lefèvre, Jerome's own example legitimised the example of female eremites. Jerome, like Cusanus, exemplified apostolic simplicity as the proper root of understanding.

Conclusion

Here Cusanus has served not as a cause but a symptom of fifteenth-century efforts to hold the order of books, learning, and power to account. George Duby pointed out that medieval social commentators divided their world into three orders (those who work, fight, and pray) for their own purposes. The division was never absolute, of course. Yet it remains central to our account of Renaissance and early modern Europe that these social divisions became ever more complex from the fourteenth century on.[73] In the now-usual story, the protagonists are the Renaissance merchants from which Cusanus came. The burgeoning networks of trade and banking from the

---

[69] Lefèvre, *Liber trium virorum et trium spiritualium virginum*, sig. ai recto.

[70] This viewpoint stems from editors of his works; recent revision finds Gerson balanced in his critique of corrupt priests and female visionaries: Wendy Love Anderson, 'Gerson's Stance on Women', in McGuire (ed.), *A Companion to Jean Gerson*, pp. 293–315.

[71] Jerome's attitude to women has been very closely scrutinised, not least because his translation of Genesis 3 stressed male mastery over females. On his use of female exempla, e.g. Andrew Cain, 'Rethinking Jerome's Portraits of Holy Women', in Andrew Cain and Josef Lössl (eds), *Jerome of Stridon: His Life, Writings and Legacy* (Farnham: Ashgate, 2009), pp. 47–57.

[72] Lefèvre, *Liber trium virorum et trium spiritualium virginum*, sig. ai recto. Quoted from [Pseudo-] Jerome, *Regula monacharum*, cap. 26, in Migne, *Patrologia latina*, vol. 30, col. 414b.

[73] E.g. Hamish Scott, 'Introduction: Early Modern Europe and the Idea of Early Modernity', in Hamish Scott (ed.), *The Oxford Handbook of Early Modern History, 1350–1750. Vol. 1: Peoples and Places* (Oxford: Oxford University Press, 2015), pp. 1–34 at 3.

Hansa to the Medici, combined with the rising value of artisans and farmers after the Black Death, attracted a rising class of bureaucratic intellectuals, as the Medicis and other new families hired pens to justify their money and power.

I find this context hard to explain purely as a matter of socio-economic hierarchy. One example of such an argument comes from R.I. Moore, whose 'persecuting society' of medieval Europe depended on procedures of inquest, canonisation, and thickening legalese. These were the product of a social dichotomy, as 'triumphs of the expert, of the clerks over the illiterate'.[74] Thus 'the hostility of the *clericus* towards the *illiteratus, idiota, rusticus* ... the clerks constructed from the scattered fragments of reality they found to hand'.[75] But this dichotomy does little justice to the evidence I have considered in this chapter. Grundmann, finetuned more recently by Walter Simons, found that the beguines and other lay groups of the Rhineland did not represent a proto-revolutionary poor, reacting to the rich, but that their wealth and class corresponded rather well to the divisions of society as a whole.[76] Likewise, Cusanus *shared* a viewpoint with the nameless women and unlearned men who dedicated themselves to lives of devotion. Rather than seeing the *idiota* as a theological veneer over ambitious ecclesiastical predation, we should see how the text responds to a groundswell of lay concern. I would argue that the theological equality of all before God becomes the mechanism that 'the hotter sort' used to make more social and cultural space for themselves. But this did not fall along simplistic class dualisms. Such theological – and literary – accounts of hierarchy critiqued socio-economic difference without being reducible to such difference.

---

[74] R. I. Moore, *The Formation of a Persecuting Society* (Oxford: Blackwell, 1987), p. 130.

[75] Moore, *Persecuting Society*, p. 131.

[76] In fact, Grundmann, *Religious Movements*, hypothesised that these 'radical' groups were disproportionately wealthy; Walter Simons showed that they actually mirrored wider socio-economic demographics quite closely, in his *Cities of Ladies: Beguine Communities in the Medieval Low Countries, 1200–1565* (University Park: University of Pennsylvania Press, 2001).

9

Making 'Gypsies' in the English Reformation? Laws, Words, and Texts (1530–1621)

SUSAN WISEMAN*

WHAT IS, WHAT was the 'Gypsy'? Working within a narrow time-frame, this chapter investigates the way connotations of the word 'Gypsy' came to be established in the early seventeenth century. It considers primarily English and, briefly, Scottish texts from a broadly defined sphere of the legal and the literary.[1] Thus, while as David Mayall accurately notes, '[a]ll the representations … of the Gypsy are in one way real: Gypsies are who the writer or speaker thinks they are', it may also be the case that in this period the way they were seen set in place both core 'Gypsy' features of an enduring character, and a situation of very one-side control over image.[2] Accordingly, the chapter works on a small canvas to try to more deeply understand the formation of an enduring idea or type – that of the 'Gypsy' – from the early sixteenth century to the 1620s. It investigates factors in the shaping of the signifier 'Gypsy', and its signifieds during the Tudor and early Stuart Reformation, from a period preceding Gypsy legislation to a moment when, it seems, the features of what writers and readers 'think they are' is established.

Scholarship on Gypsies and Roma people is fairly clearly divided into historicist studies focused on the past and those focused on the shaping of the present, and many

---

* I am grateful to Neil Kenny for working to shape the chapter, to Lorna Hutson and attenders of the Oxford Early Modern Seminar and to the anonymous reader for incisive comments, as well as to Anthony Bale and Georgina Trevelyan-Clark for discussions in parallel.

[1] In a complex terminological landscape this broadly historicist chapter uses the noun 'Gypsy' throughout because it is the term used, indeed made, in the period under discussion, whereas Roma is a much later term. Capitalisation, then, is used not to designate a position on origins or nation versus culture, but to acknowledge the cultural shaping of this idea of Gypsy. It is the formation of this idea, rather than the way of life of Roma people, evidently traduced by this type, that is under discussion throughout the chapter. See also Sujata Iyengar, *Shades of Difference: Mythologies of Skin Colour in Early Modern England* (Philadelphia: University of Pennsylvania Press, 2005), p. 173, 263 n.1; David Cressy, *Gypsies: An English History* (Oxford: Oxford University Press, 2018), pp. x–xi.

[2] David Mayall, *Gypsy Identities 1500–2000* (London: Routledge, 2004), p. 3.

of both kinds are longitudinal, such as the respectively historical and sociological studies by David Cressy and David Mayall. A less clear, intermittently articulated faultline in the scholarly field is between emphasis on recovery of experience and representation or image. In this broad division, Romani Studies occupies a socio-logical position which might most sharply contrast with study of ideas, images, and ideologies within literary studies, to which this chapter primarily contributes. Overall, early modern Gypsies as an assigned identity, and Romani people, remain understudied. Within early modern literary studies Gypsies have been studied as they are brought up by individual texts, such as Ben Jonson's *The Gypsies Metamorphosed* (as discussed by Martin Butler) and by topics, such as the question of race (as discussed by Sujata Iyengar).[3] Within historical studies David Cressy's important work has re-opened debate. As he reminds us, Gypsies are largely absent within a strand of scholarship where we might expect to find them: historico-literary scholarship on internal travel and vagabondage and vagrancy. They are not deeply considered, for example, in Paul Slack's historical studies of poverty and policy, nor in Patricia Fumerton's literary-historical discussion of the unsettling of the labouring poor.[4] However, although their inclusion by scholars such as A.L. Beier does allow the presentation of a more coherent picture of migrant poverty, Slack and Fumerton are also following the logic of legal evidence that, particularly in the early Tudor period, 'Eygptians' are legally distinct from the general poor and vagrant. At the same time, however, this distinction is definitely less clear by the late sixteenth century. As the evidence suggests, the shifting of the boundaries between vagrants and Gypsies is definitely a significant factor in a 'Gypsy' identity coming into being.

This chapter investigates the formation of a set of ideas, images, and expectations making the entity of the 'Gypsy', rather than undertaking the more complex task of researching the life of early modern Roma people. In the absence of any freely given words from Romani people themselves in the textual record, legal and literary texts are the period's two dominant textual strands of representation and evidence. There is no doubt that the images and ideas found in these discourses responded to, overlapped with, and certainly influenced Roma lives, but for the largest part they are not focused on revealing or expressing Roma points of view. It is between lit-erary and legal texts that we can see that to be a 'Gypsy' came to be a recognised condition, what in the modern period might be seen as an assigned 'identity', and

---

[3] Cressy, *Gypsies*; Mayall, *Gypsy Identities*. Several studies are discussed here, and scholarship runs from e.g. Dale Randall, *Jonson's Gypsies Unmasked: Background and Theme of* The Gypsies Metamorphos'd (North Carolina: Duke University Press, 1975) to Iyengar, *Shades of Difference*.

[4] Scholarship focusing on vagrancy and the poor is very extensive. Significant studies include A. L. Beier, *Masterless Men: The Vagrancy Problem in England 1560–1640* (London: Methuen, 1985); Patricia Fumerton, *Unsettled: The Culture of Mobility and the Working Poor in Early Modern England* (Chicago and London: University of Chicago Press, 2006); Paul Slack, 'Vagrants and Vagrancy in England 1598–1664' *Economic History Review*, 27 (1974), 360–79; Paul Slack, *Poverty and Policy in Tudor and Stuart England* (London: Longman, 1988); Linda Woodbridge, *Vagrancy, Homelessness, and English Renaissance Literature* (Champaign: University of Illinois Press, 2001) and, for an argument that gypsies should in included in such studies of poverty and vagrancy, see Cressy, *Gypsies*, pp. 271–3.

one that was in a shifting relationship with other categories of people – pedlars, rogues, thieves, canting criminals, magicians, or even regular citizens.

As the Reformation happened, the kind of person an 'Egyptian' might be shifted and changed. In 1505 'Egyptianis' were understood to be indeed, if in a complex way, from Egypt. However, when, in 1621, Ben Jonson began his masque, *The Gypsies Metamorphosed*, with the entry of 'the five princes of Egypt, mounted all upon one horse', everyone knew that they were Gypsies. Taking the Gypsies of Jonson's masque as its end point rather than its main focus, what follows unpacks some of the events, factors, and textual markers that made 'Gypsies'.

'Owtlandissh': Encounters with Strangers

While the Gypsies encountered in Ben Jonson's masques were familiar to the audience from print and myth, early sixteenth-century texts offer fragmentary and ambiguous responses to outlandish 'Gypsions', 'Egyptians', and 'counterfeit Egyptians'. Between 1513 and 1523, 'Gypsions' are recorded as having entertained at the house of the Earl of Surrey at Tendring Hall, Suffolk.[5] The April 1505 payment '[t]o the Egyptianis be the Kingis command' is but one example of records from this period featuring aristocratic payments to 'Egyptians' to be patronised by kings and lords.[6] Early sixteenth-century records seem thin on the ground in part because the rich seam associated with legislation is not yet swelling numbers of mentions. However, there is evidence that entertainment and performance mark many of these encounters; in 1530 in Scotland money was paid to 'the Egyptianis that dansit before the King in Halyrudhous' and in 1504 Sir John Arundell of Lanhere paid 'the Egyptians when they danced afore me'.[7] Finally, a summary of the life of Sir William Sinclair, a late sixteenth-century lord at Roslin, offers a story which draws together connections between Lords and Gypsies, crime and entertainment. In this a lord, returning from Edinburgh to Roslin:

> delivered ane Egyptian from the gibbet in the Burrow Moore, ready to be strangled, ... upon which accompt the whole body of gypsies were, of old, accustomed to gather in the stanks of Roslin every year, where they acted severall playes, during the moneth of May and June. There are two towers which were allowed them for their residence, the one called Robin Hood, the other Little John.[8]

---

[5] Henry Howard, *Works*, ed. G. F. Nott (London: Longman, Hurst, Rees, Orme, and Brown, 1815–16), 2v., v. I, Appendix II, p. v, pp. iii–v (p. v).

[6] See, e.g., Robert Pitcairn, 'Documents Relative to the "Egyptianis" or Gypsies', in *Ancient Criminal Trials in Scotland*, 3 vols (Edinburgh: Nannatyne Club, 1833), iii appendix v, extracts from *Books of the Lord High Treasurer of Scotland*, pp. 590–5 (591–2); see also Henry Crofton, 'II Early Annals of the Gypsies in England', *Journal of the Gypsy Lore Society* I (1888), citing *Letters Foreign and Domestic Henry VIII* iii pt. I p. 499 (4).

[7] Pitcairn, 'Documents Relative to the "Egyptianis" or Gypsies', pp. 591–2; Cornwall Record Office, Truro AR/26/2 Sally L. Joyce and Evelyn S. Newlyn (eds), *REED: Cornwall* (Toronto, 1999), p. 530, cited in Cressy, *Gypsies*, p. 49.

[8] Father Richard Augustine Hay, *Genealogie of the Sainteclaires of Rosslyn* (Edinburgh: Thomas G. Stevenson, 1835), pp. 135–6.

The evidence surviving is limited, and so leaves it unclear what 'Egyptian' was understood to mean in the early sixteenth century, but, as here, it seems neither to have been solely a history of ostracism nor to have been wholly inflected as negative.

Writing just 14 years after the initial legislation against Gypsies in England, the ex-monk, Andre Boorde, teases out a place for them. Describing the world's nations and languages, Boorde thinks ethnographically about what Egyptians are, where they come from and what they do. He writes:

> The people of the country be swarte, and doth go disgisyed in theyr apparel, contrary to other nacyons: they be light fingerd, and vse pyking; they haue little maner, and euyl loggyng, & yet they be pleas[a]unt daunsers. Ther be few or none of the Egipcions that doth dwel in Egipt, for Egipt is repleted now with infydele alyons. There mony is brasse and golde.[9]

In Boorde's account, Gypsies have mixed qualities and are allowed depth. In some ways contact with them is pleasurable; in some ways they are to be treated as a nation and from elsewhere, but they are also a nuisance. Boorde is unusual in seeking to attach those he meets to a coherent explanation of why they are Egyptian. If Boorde experiences these Egyptians as contradictory and problematic, his text resolves that perception by blending Egypt and England and accommodating a land of 'wyderness' to some of the key features noted about Gypsies in the sixteenth-century reports: their clothing (here a form of disguise), dancing and a feature that was to grow in importance throughout the seventeenth century – their thieving. In 1542 Boorde presents the people he met as ambiguously and distinctively 'Egyptian', without the condemnatory 'counterfeit' prefix, and presents a set of people with marked but not immutable or necessarily criminal characteristics. Boorde calibrates the position of Egyptians carefully in his book; they follow Turks, and precede the final nation described, the Jews. This seems to be both a geographical grouping and an ordering of the abjection of non-Christian groups. The potential association between Gypsies and Jews is found elsewhere, in 'Jewes Jeptyons' or 'Egyptians, and some who do call themselves Jews'.[10] Such references both associate and differentiate Jews and Gypsies apparently through a common ground of fakery though also, possibly, because both are diasporic. While the associations Boorde's text suggest may have been present before the Tudor legislation, it is also likely that the force of the legislative expulsion of Gypsies ordered them with other groups perennially excluded from Christian commonwealth – they are ranged with those expelled.

---

[9] Andrew Boorde, *The first boke of the Introduction of knowledge*, ed. F. J. Furnivall in *Early English Text Society*, Extra Series 10 (1870), p. 218.
[10] *Archaeologia*, xlvj cited in Crofton, 'Early Annals', p. 1.

When Boorde was writing, Gypsies were indeed understood as strangers to be expelled. The first piece of legislation specifically against Gypsies was in Henry VIII's reign in 1530/1:

> Forasmuch as before this tyme divers and many owtlandisshe people calling themselfes Egiptsions using no craft nor faict of merchandise, have comen in to thys realme and goon from Shyre to Shyre and place to place in grete companye and used grete subtile and craftye meanys to deceyve the people bearing them in hande that they by palmestrye could tell menne and Womens Fortunes and soo many Tymes by craft and subtiltie hath deceyved the people of theyr Money & alsoo have comitted many haynous Felonyes and Robberyes to the grete hurt and Disceipt of the people that they have comyn among: Be it therfore by the King our Souveraigne Lord the Lords Sp[irit]uall and temporal and by the comons in this present parliament assembled and by the auctorite of the same, ordeigned establisshed and enacted that from henceforth noo suche persons be suffred to come within this the Kinges realme; And if they doo, then they and every of them soo doing shall forfaict to the King our Souveraigne Lorde all theyr goods and catalls, and then to be comaunded to avoide the realme within xv daies next aftre the comaundement upon payn of Imprisonnement.[11]

The Act is quite expansive in defining its object. It gives one clear definition, that these people are travellers, 'owtlandisshe' (though their claim to be from Egypt is doubtful). At the same time, we have information on the border between crime and identity when we learn that instead of a trade they have tricks and deceits; worse, they are thieves and fortune-tellers. Philip and Mary's legislation once again defines them as entering England. It also further builds a character for the Gypsy; these are promulgating 'devilish and naughty practices'. If they remain for a month they are declared felons. They were deprived of benefit of clergy and, as discussed later, specific privileges with regard to juries were revoked.[12] As well as demonstrating a shift to draconian measures, this Act's justifications show us a key assumption about Gypsies; at this point the law viewed them as genuinely from elsewhere and as something close to an unwelcome 'nation'. The assumption that these people are from abroad means that they can be banished.

Elizabeth I's legislation against 'counterfeit Egyptians' marks a significant change in what or who was being legislated against. When the regime legislated against Gypsies in 1562/3 it responded to the law's discovery that they had been born here. Noting that 'a scruple and doubt' had arisen about whether Gypsies could have been born within England, it offers a new designation of them as a 'company or fellowship of vagabonds, commonly called or calling themselves Egyptians, or counterfeiting, transforming or disguising themselves by their apparel, speech or other behaviour into such vagabonds'; anyone doing this for one month is to fall under the statute.[13] The necessary shift away from the Egyptians being understood as from somewhere left a definitional vacuum filled by a re-alignment of their

---

[11] John Raithby, *The Statutes at Large*, 20 vols (London, 1807–), vol. 3, p. 89.
[12] Crofton, 'Early Annals', p. 13; J. Bentham ed. in G. Britain and Danby Pickering, *The Statutes at Large* (Cambridge, 1763) (v.6).
[13] 5 Elizabeth I, c. 20 cited in Cressy, *Gypsies*, p. 74 and see p. 302 n.55.

relationships so that they are now 'vagabonds, calling themselves Egyptians', as a 'transforming or disguising themselves in their apparrel' – appearance and behaviour – and using 'a certain counterfeit speech or behaviour': how they look and how they speak allows identification. The Elizabethan test for belonging to this group is both heuristic and practical in stating that anyone living as one, apparently being known or 'called' as such, or 'counterfeiting' being one for a month should be judged a felon and suffer pains of death, loss of lands and goods.

Where the status of 'Egyptians' as 'outlandish' had been recognised by courts in the arrangement of 'per medietatem linguae', whereby half the jury could be of Romani language, now they are 'to be tried in the county or place' where 'they or he shall be apprehended', as well as losing benefit of clergy and sanctuary.[14] This was a huge change, and degradation, to their status before the law. As an alternative, they were indeed offered the barbed wire safety-net of the Elizabethan employment market. The decisive step away from 'returning' these figures to an actual location made them known, instead, by a mixture of self-confirming perceptions, defining yet unlocated 'language' (with Romani unmoored from Egypt to be no longer 'of' anywhere but located in the user), and practices. Intended to remove a category of person who was partly self-evident, but in being so also 'counterfeit', this legislation had several unforeseen consequences – including in shaping the 'Gypsy'.

As we see, the Tudors perceived Egyptians or counterfeit Egyptians as both specific and part of a wider social problem. From the point when they ceased to come 'from' somewhere – albeit an uncertain somewhere – Gypsies looked, from a legal point of view, more like vagrants than travellers. However, their nomadic status troubles this; if they are not from far away, nor are they fleeing or travelling towards settlement. Thus, while Gypsies were often part of the focus of the mid-Tudor state on social order, movement, and the poor, attention to Gypsies was also specific. Thus, as we see, in the very act of singling them out for specific legislative force the statute also characterises counterfeit Egyptians as ambiguously a kind of vagabond. As George Nicholls' compendious grouping of poverty, vagabondage, and Gypsy legislation suggests, while the Gypsies might at times – and increasingly after 1562/3, it seems – be incorporated into vagabondage legislation, as they are potentially grouped under 'rogues' and 'vagabonds' in James VI and I's statutes of 1603–4 (and in Scotland under 'vagabounds called Egiptians' in 1609), these figures were in neither perception nor law synonymous with vagrants but the two categories were at a varying and conjunctural distance. They were understood by the authorities as a related subdivision but also a particular problem with legal definition.[15] Certainly, the 1562/3 legislation moved Gypsies close to vagabonds in a general way. It may be more significant, however, that after 1562/3 their criminality inheres not in what they do as much as in the way that they do it – styles of being

---

[14] J. Bentham ed. in Britain and Pickering, *The Statutes at Large* (v.6).
[15] 'Act anent the Egiptians' (1609) quoted extensively, David MacRitchie, *Scottish Gypsies under the Stewarts* (Edinburgh: David Douglas, 1894), p. 80.

are criminalised. The Elizabethan statute, a foundation that was in place for many centuries, makes it a crime to live as a Gypsy.[16]

It was the perception, at least, that the act that made 'counterfeit Egyptians' visible also, by the same logic, made them disappear. Writers thought that this group sought to evade the statute by counterfeiting identities; for instance, Sir Thomas Overbury's character of a 'tinker' describes his fellow traveller as a 'sunne-burnt Queane, that since the terrible Statute recanted Gypsisme, and is turned Pedleresse'.[17] Moreover, in 1577, a case of the common practice of passport-faking amongst these groups was uncovered. Passports were given to vagrants and others to pass from place to place unchecked and given the opposite interests of parishes and travellers they were often forged.[18] The 1577 case traces several passports used by Gypsies to Richard Massie, a schoolmaster of Whitchurch who had forged many clearly effective passports, causing issues about where to arrest the Gypsies and his own imprisonment.[19] In an ironic, but logical, counterpoint to the absence of Gypsy-generated texts, those who paid for and used such passports use the very legal discourse that criminalised them. The law, intended to make Gypsies clear, did so but simultaneously almost certainly made actual Romani people more camouflaged.

Although the Elizabethan legislation endured, and some extreme violence was done in its name, it was not often directly applied. As David Cressy argues, although the 1562/3 legislation was at times vigorously and cruelly prosecuted, the evidence suggests that its application is characterised by a perhaps gradual elision into other methods of managing a problem.[20] Certainly, to apply it properly was bloodthirsty and expensive, and evidence gives us a very different picture from the one the law apparently envisaged.[21] Local constables and others adopted other methods to remove Gypsies and the method of paying them to move on seems to emerge in many records in a way that suggests something of a system. However, given the legislation, it is also hard to completely identify them because only later do they come to be more consistently named.[22] The other side of such obscurity is the way the Elizabethan act, supplemented by earlier legislation, supplied a 'how to' kit for the identification of these figures. We can explore some of the key characteristics of these figures that appear in the statute – some clear but others ambiguous. Thus, we can compare the material before and after the Tudor legislation in relation to the attributed qualities and practices of fortune-telling; place;

---

[16] George Nicholls, *A History of the English Poor Law*, 2 vols (London: John Murray, 1854), vol. 1, p. 199. See Edward, p. 146–7; Elizabeth, p. 176; James, p. 214.

[17] Thomas Overbury, *Sir Thomas Overbury his Wife with Additions of New Characters* (London, 1616).

[18] Paul Slack, 'Vagrants', *EHR* (1974), 361–2.

[19] Frederick G. Blair, 'Forged Passports of British Gypsies in the Sixteenth Century', *JGLS*, 3rd ser., 28 (1950), 131–7.

[20] For an outline and cases see Cressy's summary in *Gypsies*, pp. 72–93.

[21] Cressy, *Gypsies*, pp. 73–91, especially pp. 73–4. Cressy notes that the legislation should be understood as enacted in 1563, being dated by the end of parliament on 10 April 1563 – the new year.

[22] T. W. Thompson, 'Gleanings from Constables Accounts and other Sources', *Journal of the Gypsy Lore Society*, 3rd ser., 7 (1928), 30–47 at 35.

language; and a particular social organisation. These features, and others, come to stand in for Gypsies who can, circularly, be identified from these behaviours. We can trace now the material that went into the legislation and its later correlatives on the specific terms of the statute.

Seeing Gypsies: 'Behaviour', 'Speech', 'Place', 'Fortune', 'Company'

Taking the examples of areas explicitly addressed by the statute – fortune-telling (as a form of 'behaviour'), 'speech' and language, 'fellowship' or 'company' (social organisation), and 'place' (as in the 'place where they be apprehended') – we can investigate how these were written about before and after the anti-Gypsy legislative drive. These, then, offer a small sample of the occupations and traits ascribed to Egyptian, jepsions, and Gypsies.

The ambiguous status of fortune-telling before the era of legislation is evident in one of Thomas More's dialogues from 1514. This canvasses the relationship between witness, storytelling, conspiracy, and credulity. A labouring man is brought forward to stand as a witness to a murder having happened but not only does he turn out not to know himself, but his informant is a woman – one he has 'wist' to 'tell manye mervaylous thynges', such as 'if a thynge hadde been stolen, she would have tolde who hadde it'. His informant is a fortune-teller. Asked if she is in league with the devil he answers:

> 'Nay, by my trouth I trowe,' quod he, 'for I could never see her use anye worse waye than lookinge in ones hande.' Therewith the Lordes laughed and asked 'What is she?' 'Forsoothe, my Lordes,' quod he, 'an Egypcian, and she was lodged here at Lambeth, but she is gone over sea now. Howbeit, I trowe, she be not in her own countrey yet: for they saye it is a great way hence, and she went litle more than a moneth agoe.'[23]

So one of the very earliest references to 'Egypcians' associates them with fortune-telling – indeed with the activity of locating stolen goods – and those who foolishly believe they are from Egypt. At this point the disappeared Egyptian stands for the whole panoply of conspiracy and rumour. The text hints that palmistry is a dark art, but stops short of explicitly finding the devil in the self-deceiver.[24] In 1514, then, Gypsy fortune-telling, like legerdemain, sits on a border between entertainment and being a thing of darkness.

The seriousness of fortune-telling as an offence was deepened by the mention of witchcraft in Mary Tudor's legislation and seems to have changed by the time

---

[23] Thomas More, dialogue in W. E. Campbell and A. W. Reed (eds), *The English Works of Sir Tomas More*, 7 vols (London and New York: Eyre and Spottiswode and Lincoln MacVeagh, 1931), vol. 2, 'The thirde boke. The 15 chapiter', pp. 234–40 at 236.
[24] Compare a case of 1619 in Scotland: *Selections from Ecclesiastical Records of Aberdeen* (Aberdeen: Spalding Club, 1846), p. 87 cited in MacRitchie, *Scottish Gypsies*, p. 97.

of Jonson's masque. For example, looking back on the late sixteenth century, the divine Thomas Gataker associates fortune-telling and witchcraft. He uses an example of a woman he was staying with in Essex who kept her children from having their fortunes told by Gypsies who came to the door, lest 'God should cause somewhat spoken by them, to befall' and 'thereby to punish me in my children, for giving so far forth heed to them' and Gataker elaborates this, to conclude that 'our State-Governers' should avoid 'such Wizards as these' lest a similar awful revenge be taken on them.[25] That Gataker sees Gypsy fortune-telling as a kind of witchcraft the sponsorship of which might indeed provoke God suggests another way in which Gypsies are set apart from other kinds of travelling people. As Samuel Rid puts it in a passage working to renaturalise tricks such as juggling and legerdemain, the Gypsies 'purchased to themselues great credit among the cuntry people, and got much by Palmistry, and telling of fortunes: insomuch they pittifully cosoned the poore cuntry girles', and he associates this with the mentions of magic in Marian legislation.[26] Since Philip and Mary's legislation against 'vagabonds, calling themselves Egyptians' identified them as not merely 'false and subtil', as More's figure might have been, but practisers of 'devilish and naughty' doings.[27] Fortune-telling was characteristic of Gypsies and vice versa, but it was kept as a continuing point of reference by how devilish, how criminal and how pleasurable it was.

Language, addressed explicitly by the statute, was a dominant distinguishing feature of Gypsies. Andrew Boorde, whose words we encountered earlier, gives a conversation:

> A talke in Egyptian and English
> Good morrow! *Lach ittur ydyues!*
> How farre is it to the next towne? *Cater myla barforas?*
> You be welcome to the towne: *Maysta ves barfuras*
> Wyl you drynke some wine? *Mole pis lauena?*
> I wyl go wyth you. *A vauuatosa*
> Sit you downe, and dryncke. *Hyste len pee*
> Drynke, drynke! For God sake! *Pe, pe deue lasse!*
> Mayde, come hither, harke a worde!
> *Achae a wordey susse!*
> Geue me aples and peeres! *Da mai paba la ambrell!*
> Much good do it you! *Iche misto!*
> Good nyght! *Lachira tut!*[28]

Published soon after the first waves of legislation, these words can only feasibly have come from an informant. They clearly constitute a language lesson or phrase book but significantly do so in the form of a basic conversation, possibly representing an encounter. Certainly, if Boorde wanted to find a living language

---

[25] Thomas Gataker, *Vindication of the Annotations by him published* (London, 1653), pp. 56–7.
[26] Samuel Rid, *The Art of Jugling* (London, 1612), B1r-B3r.
[27] *An act for the further punishment of vagabonds, calling themselves Egyptians* (1554). See *The Statutes at Large*, p. 211.
[28] Boorde, *The first boke of the Introduction of knowledge*, p. 218.

to put in his book, the fastest route would be to approach some Gypsies and write down the conversation – as seems to be fragmentarily presented here. Boorde is writing just a decade after the initiation of legislation singling out 'Egyptians' and then 'Counterfeit Egyptians'. His sense of them echoes the ambiguities of the way they were registered in the early writings but there is a sense of relative reciprocity in this conversation – perhaps the closest thing we have to uncoerced chat – that emerges by contrast with another, later, engagement with language.

Boorde's text sits alongside a second account of Romani language, given in a legal confession at Winchester. In 1615–16, when Walter Hindes was 'taken in the Company of the Counterfeit Egiptians' with whom he had lived for 'a month since', he fell foul of the Elizabethan ruling whereby to live as a Gypsy for a month qualified one for punishment. He tried hard to confess his way back into stable society by offering information on the life and language of his hosts.[29] The court recorded his interventions, such as that 'Panno marro' meant 'white bread'; 'pecko mas' was 'roast beef' and 'Trickney Ruckelo' and 'Trickney Ruckey' boy and 'mayden' children. Most often considered in terms of the information it might give on Romani language, Hindes' record is, apparently, a mixed Romani-English vocabulary – and as Ignasi-Xavier Adiego suggests, such a mixed language may have been a halfway house between those outside and inside Romani communities. It was possibly a learner's Romani or a grey-zone, not far from what Edouard Glissant implies by a defensive pidgin.[30] What to the authorities speaks as evidence of criminality discovered and of the seductive permeability of Gypsy groups to parish-dwellers and travellers, suggests perhaps to us the ambivalent place that language occupies in their relation to the authorities. On the one hand, it makes a buffer of incomprehensibility between Gypsies and those who so often coerce them, on the other hand its actual formation as a language keeps them marginal and distant from the benefits of mainstream society. At the same time, the very act of transcribing Romani in many ways traduces it, and that is particularly the case in this court-room evidence.[31] Most significant, however, is that the exchanges are labelled as 'A note of some Canting words as the Counterfett Egiptians use amongst themselves as their Language'.[32] As we see, after Dekker and Rid situated Gypsies with the criminal underworld, and used some of their words in canting dictionaries in popular and widely read books, Romani language becomes, as here, criminal 'canting'. Two examples are hardly a survey, but in this case the polarity is clear as is the apparent shift in understanding Romani. If in 1542 Boorde seems to be shaping conversation as a language-learning

[29] *The Winchester Confessions 1615–16*, transcribed by Alan McGowan (Romany and Traveller Family History Society, 1996), pp. 18–19.

[30] Ignasi-Xavier Adiego, 'Historical Sources on the Romani Language', in Yaron Matras and Anton Tenser (eds), *The Palgrave Handbook of Romani Language and Linguistics* (London: Routledge, 2020), pp. 49–84 at 61–2; Glissant's thinking is helpful here in terms of the group-forming function of a language rather than its origins which are a distinct part of his discussion. See Edouard Glissant, *Poetics of Relation*, trans. Betsy Wing (Ann Arbor: University of Michigan Press), p. 118.

[31] I am very grateful to Neil Kenny for this point.

[32] *Winchester Confessions*, p. 20.

resource and any words may have been fairly freely given, in 1616 Romani is 'cant'. By 1616, after both the Elizabethan legislation singled it out for notice and there was an explosion in the multivalent print analysis of crime, Romani language seems to be have become tightly bound to criminality.

Elizabeth's statute obliquely recognised the nomadism of many Romani in designating that, legally, Gypsies belonged to the place where any one of them was 'apprehended'. Moreover, in mentioning gypsies briefly, the scholarship on vagrancy does not engage with their nomadism as a dominant factor in their behaviour and records. These are key factors of overlap with and distinction from vagrants, from the point of view of the Tudor and Jacobean – and English and Scottish – legislative machine. Up to the Elizabethan statute, as we have seen, banishment had been a key punishment for Gypsydom and, given the nomadic nature of their way of life, it is significant that in Scotland legislative intensification existed alongside English but continued to use the punishment of banishment. In 1541 the king and Privy Council, like Henry VIII, sent out letters to sheriffs for the 'expelling' of Egyptians', and in 1586 they are singled out for legislation – as 'ydle vagabond and counterfeit people calland thame selfis Egiptianis'.[33] David MacRitchie notes that in 1609 an act 'anent the Egiptians' banished them and condemned recidivists to death.[34] After the Elizabethan statute the English and Scottish jurisdictions were in theory out of step in the different ways they partly recognised nomadism, though in practice the treks across the border each way probably continued. At the same time, however, substantial differences can be seen in how the Gypsy groups fitted, or didn't, within the hierarchy and power structures of each nation.

We can ask what the statute might have meant by its passing recognition of social structures amongst 'counterfeit Egyptians' in its reference to their 'company' or 'fellowship'. One feature of the approach to 'Egyptians' found in both England and Scotland before the Reformation period legislation is the legal tradition of Gypsies being treated as a group, with the leader, in such cases often called the 'Captain' (the name we find given to the character played by Buckingham in Jonson's masque), having power over the band. Thus, in May 1540 the Scottish records grant a 'precept' to 'the Earl and Lord of Little Egypt; giving power to him to hang and punish all Egyptians within the Kingdom of Scotland'.[35] Similarly, when in 1537 a murder was committed within one of the best-known and best-documented families of Romani, the Faas who were in England, it was Faa himself who was apprehended and then released.[36] As MacRitchie discusses, John Faw who was termed 'our louit' by James V of Scotland was also endowed with authority to

---

[33] *Register of the Privy Council of Scotland* (Edinburgh: H.M. Register House, 1878) v.2 1569–78 quoted in MacRitchie, *Scottish Gypsies*, pp. 64–6. This was followed up in 1587, when they were associated with witchcraft, and again in 1592. MacRitchie, *Scottish Gypsies*, pp. 70–2.

[34] MacRitchie, *Scottish Gypsies*, pp. 80–1. This refers only to Scotland.

[35] Pitcairn, 'Documents Relative to the "Egyptianis" or Gypsies', p. 594.

[36] See David Cressy, 'The Trouble with Gypsies in Early Modern England', *Historical Journal*, 59.1 (2016), 45–70 at 50–1.

punish 'all those that rebel against him' through the 'executioun of justice' on them according to 'his laws'.[37] A confirming counterexample, again from the records of the famous Faa or Faw family, is a case in which the account specifies the hanging of 'each one' of several Faas caught in Scotland as Gypsies after the 1609 act – a case in which in carefully specifying that it was 'each one', the record notes the change from the Captain as a representative suffering the penalty.[38] Thus, in Scotland in the early seventeenth century it remained a question how far a leader had internal jurisdiction over a company and how far he acted as a spokesperson and, potentially, surrogate for the whole 'fellowship'.

The most thorough of the first wave of historians of early modern Gypsies, David MacRitchie strongly suggests that in Scotland the twin factors of association with powerful figures and being a mobile and autonomous commonwealth with a single leader play out in a specific way in relation to the keeping of retainers in Scotland; MacRitchie traces this through prolonged tussles over the punishment and reprieve of those protecting violent bands of Gypsies in 1608–20.[39] For all that it was repeatedly emphasised 'that quhaever ressavit thame within these boundis ... sould not onlie be thocht culpable of their stouthis [thefts], bot farther compatble' for anything found to be missing, royal pardons meant that these associations between settled lords and bands endured.[40] The Gypsies, and legislation against them, were in Scotland bound up with power struggles between lords, systems of justice, and the crown.[41] Thus, Gypsies moved between England and Scotland at the same time as developing distinct relationships within social structures. It seems that in England the association between Gypsies and problematic clientage did register, in a continuing circulation of ideas, that Gypsies had leaders who mediated with the world and had associations with lord and kings – as when Jonson's Cockerel comments, 'A gypsy of quality, believe it, and one of the king's gypsies this' (l. 667–9). The evidence suggests that this was a perceived alliance rather than an actively problematic association between Gypsies and lords.

Overall, if such a small sample can track a shift in meaning, it is, crucially, a shift from an engagement with a complex 'owtlandish' group with its own laws and languages to a reliance on the perceptions, experience, and assumptions of observers shaped by the law. Older legal traditions shape some of the ways in which Gypsies are written about even during and after the Tudor and Stuart legislation. A significant component in the making of the ideas that we see culturally operational

---

[37] Writ of the Privy Council of Scotland (vol. xiv, fol. 59) quoted in MacRitchie, *Scottish Gypsies*, pp. 37–8; see also pp. 39–45, 51–5.

[38] *Privy Council Register*, vol. 9, pp. 171–205. Cited in MacRitchie, *Scottish Gypsies*, p. 83.

[39] What follows in this section closely follows MacRitchie, *Scottish Gypsies*, pp. 78–96 as a single authority and relies heavily on his account.

[40] *Minute Book of Processes*, cited in MacRitchie, *Scottish Gypsies*, p. 78.

[41] See MacRitchie, *Scottish Gypsies*, pp. 91–3. In the English local case reporting in the post-legislation period there is a slightly similar account of people apprehended who might be Gypsies but seem to be retainers of the ubiquitous Earl of Stanley. Thompson, 'Gleanings from Constables', 45.

in mid-legislation thinking about Gypsies is perhaps best understood as partly legal and partly customary. Custom – and evolving everyday practice – sat operationally, but with some ideological unease, alongside the sequence of measures that incrementally calibrated what people and circumstances constituted the punishable offence of being a Gypsy or counterfeit Egyptian. It is made visible at certain points in the textual record, for example when parts of it that have actual legal status are dismantled as when, in the act that made the entry of 'Egyptians' into England a felony, Philip and Mary's law of 1554 also deprived Egyptians of the right to have a jury half made up of men sharing a language (a jury 'medietatis linguae') – and in her recalibration of the act in 1562/3 Elizabeth ensured that this deprivation applied also to any found simply living as 'Egyptian'.[42] We can turn, also, to the shadowy question of the place of Gypsies in relation to ideas of retaining and clientage – an element of the status of Gypsies before the law in Scotland in particular, and referred to in England only in passing.

The Gypsies Metamorphosed: The Gypsies of 1621

In considering what the relationships might be between the clearly delineated, named 'Gypsies' of the post-legislation period and earlier representations, we can turn to two literary texts which offer more than fragmentary explorations of the complex figure we are exploring. John Skelton's ambiguous description of the ale-wife in his 'Tunning of Elenour Rumminge' is a valuable reminder of the ambiguous and many-named figures of the late fifteenth century:

> With clothes upon her hed
> That wey a sowe of led,
> Wrythen in wonder wyse
> After the Sarasyns gyse,
> With a whym-wham
> Knyt with a trym-tam
> Upon her brayne-pan,
> Like an Egypcyan
> Lapped about.[43]

Skelton's poem is a tour de force in satirical ambivalence, and an instructive reminder of the evanescent power of these figures before the legislative drive. The energetic Rumminge's ale works a wicked magic that partakes of her undecided status as alewife, Gypsy, deceiver. Where the turbaned Elenour Rumminge has perilous charisma, in Ben Jonson's 1621 masque *The Gypsies Metamorphosed* ready-made 'Gypsies' still have the headcloths but, it seems, they have become

---

[42] Crofton, 'Early Annals', pp. 13, 16.
[43] John Skelton, 'The Tunnynge of Elynour Rummyng per Skelton Laureat', in John Scattergood (ed.), *John Skelton: The Complete English Poems* (New Haven and London: Yale University Press, 1983).

unbound and are being used as 'a trace of scarves' to keep multiple small children on a horse. The contrasts between Skelton's powerful and exploitative figure and Jonson's 'Gypsies' are immediate and obvious in other ways too: Rumminge has no attributed identity, but Jonson's figures are Gypsies; Rumminge owns the ale, Jonson's Gypsies are criminals; Rumminge is genuinely frightening, like a 'Saracen' but when Jonson's aristocratic audience are invited to 'Gaze upon' the children 'as on the offspring of Ptolemey, begotten upon several Cleopatras', the idea that such characters have any relationship to Egypt is presented as a joke.[44] However, in assessing how far the clarification of these figures to the point where it is relatively clear what a 'Gypsy' is should also be understood as a demystification, it is informative to remember their past, and their associations with trickery, magic, and disguise, which had been confirmed, not minimised, by legislation.

We can start with the emergence of the 'Gypsy' as an understood designation in Ben Jonson's masque, *The Gypsies Metamorphosed*. Designed for out-of-town production, the masque was staged three times in 1621 – twice at stopping points on James I's summer progress and once, apparently by royal command, at Windsor.[45] Martin Butler (reinforced by Peter Lake) notes that both at Burley and later at Windsor, where state officials were involved, the masque emphasises James's support for Buckingham in the backwash of the parliament of 1621 in which the king protected him from a monopoly scandal.[46] As we have seen, the masque opens with an immediately recognisable Gypsy scene, when the Jackman calls the audience to make way for 'the five princes of Egypt, mounted all upon one horse' (l.1), and a second horse 'laden with stolen poultry etc.'. At the same time as the Gypsies appear, the audience is invited to remember that the masque itself takes place because the court is on the move, its summer peregrination displacing other travellers from the road. James' court on progress is doing what the Gypsies do – wander. In wandering the country court and Gypsies mirror each other.

The masque shows the Gypsies played by aristocrats, including at Burley the Captain being played by the Duke of Buckingham. Part of its impact rested on the audacity with which Jonson instantiated scenes of implicit similarity. For example, once the audience knows that the character asking us to make way is a Jackman or Jarkman he is clearly delineated as the thing he does: he is a man who can make 'jarks' or seals for false passports (as we, and possibly they, know the figure from print, as in Thomas Dekker's popular evocation of a criminal underworld, *Lanthorn*

---

[44] Ben Jonson, *The Gypsies Metamorphosed*, ed. James Knowles in David Bevington, Martin Butler, and Ian Donaldson (eds), *The Cambridge Edition of the Works of Ben Jonson* (Cambridge: Cambridge University Press, 2012), 30 vols, vol. 5 pp. 463–584, 526–7 (p. 463), l. 4–8.

[45] Jonson, *The Gypsies Metamorphosed*, p. 465. Knowles gives two versions of this text and this chapter follows the Burley-on-the-Hill version as edited by Knowles (see his discussion pp. 480–1).

[46] Martin Butler, '"We are one mans all": Jonsons's *The Gipsies Metamorphosed*', *The Yearbook of English Studies*, 21 (1991), 253–73 at 258.

and Candlelight).[47] The king and his lawmakers, of course, give true seals but the author – whose words the Jackman speaks – is definitely a maker of false identities that pass current, like that of the Jackman himself. There are even hints of Gypsy–king relationships to come before transformation happens, as when the Patrico (glossed by Dekker as a priest) restores the stolen goods and Cockerel presciently comments, 'A gypsy of quality, believe it, and one of the king's Gypsies this', noting that the 'king has a noise of gypsies as well as bearwards' (l. 667–9). The masque may hold together Jonson and Jackman, but more clearly it holds together king and gypsy, courtier and gypsy; playmaking and forgery; acting and counterfeiting.

The central transformation of *The Gypsies Metamorphosed* is one of moralised colour, changing dark to light. The force, or lack of force, of the changing of Gypsies into performing aristocrats by the removal of face-paint is the subject of much debate. It is both so small an adjustment that Jonson is described as sleeping and also definitively the masque's turning point. Is it the case that we could miss it, because, after all, the actors don't look very different at all, or is it a coup de théâtre? There is a case for each view. Certainly, the text wants us to notice that the Gypsies are dark, possibly walnut, in colour and the darkness of the Gypsies' faces is emphasised at the outset as a visual shortcut to a 'Gypsy' type – ironically like 'Queen Cleopatra' (l. 104).[48] As the masque plays out, the Jackman sings and speaks of 'yellow' and 'tawny faces' (l. 316; see also l. 486; l.67; see also l.483); the text plays on dark night (ll. 323; 327) and bright stars (such as the prince (e.g. l.286)). When the judiciously named 'Clod' fails to recognise Gypsies he sees 'olive-coloured spirits' (418–30; l. 419). If the masque revels in darkening actors, we are also reminded in the Windsor version that this darkness can be 'changed in a trice' (WIN l. 943). The mechanism of change is itself discussed. Lest we have missed the event in the epilogue, Buckingham emphasises 'what died our faces was an ointment'.[49] The facial darkening, made by the king's apothecary, Johann Wolfgang Rumler, may have been able to be removed quickly because the walnut juice pigment was layered over pig fat.[50] While interpretations of the ease and effectiveness of the ease of the change differ, Martin Butler and Barbara

---

[47] Dekker, *Lanthorne* and see Arthur F. Kinney, *Rogues, Vagabonds and Sturdy Beggars* (Amherst: University of Massachusetts Press, 1990), p. 219. So-called 'rogue literature' covers a huge range of material from true crime to the picaresque romance and novel. For clarity of focus the border between rogue literature and this study of Gypsies is restricted to the identification of strains of spoken Romani with canting language. See also e.g. Eric Otto Winstedt, 'Early British Gypsies' *Journal of the Gypsy Lore Society* NS Vol VII (1913), pp. 5–14. For an incisive analysis of the field and of its exclusion of gypsies see Lee Beier, 'On the Boundaries of New and Old Historicisms: Thomas Harman and the Literature of Roguery', *English Literary Renaissance*, 33.2 (2003), 181–200.

[48] On 'Gypsy' in *Anthony and Cleopatra*, beyond the scope of this current chapter, see Iyengar, *Shades of Difference*, pp. 192–9.

[49] For discussions see e.g. Iyengar, *Shades of Difference*, p. 174.

[50] See Virginia Mason Vaughan, *Performing Blackness on English Stages, 1500–1800* (Cambridge: Cambridge University Press, 2005), p. 12; see also the discussion in Iyengar, *Shades of Difference*, pp. 190–1.

Ravelhofer are convincing in suggesting that its aim is probably to meet the challenge of the masque as a genre where each instance must deliver innovation and bravura performance.

Transformation, whether effective or not, in theory banishes the vivid, dancing, Gypsy characterisation (with mixed dances which Barbara Ravelhofer argues combined courtly French ballet with energetic English dances) – and with it much of the visual and exotic pleasure of the masque.[51] We are presented with 'Gypsies' strikingly pleasurable and entertaining – and utterly disposable in a way that leaves estate, place king and clown in place. In manufacturing the effect of vividly real Gypsies, *The Gypsies Metamorphosed* uses stereotypes drawn from other texts. That these were so readily recognisable, visually clear and pleasurable to audiences (as suggested by multiple performances) suggests not so much (as David Cressy suggests) the belatedness of literary representation as that at this point Gypsies were clearly defined. The textual shorthand visual signifiers and cant words of print were readily and vividly remade for stage.[52] *The Gypsies Metamorphosed* is a very full exploration of what games can be played using the category of the Gypsy and it illuminates clearly how by 1621 'Gypsy' has been shaped into a flexible bundle of signs for English protestant culture to think.

Although the manifested 'Gypsy' types are cultural counters that are easy to think with, their chimerically solidly known, mythic presence does not make them anodyne. While the qualities of the Gypsy might have become clear, they were nonetheless disturbing. Several disparate factors shaping a viewer's reaction might be considered. First, the masque seems to imply that a 'real' Gypsy could not be made fair. However, one of the ways in which counterfeit Egyptians were deemed to be counterfeit was, indeed, in blacking up their faces (presumably to look Egyptian).[53] This uncertainty, at the height of the masque's redemption of the courtier, is certainly not stated and would depend on that aspect of counterfeiting being in the mind of the audience. However, there is much in a name; if, as we have seen, the Jackman makes false identities, then the name by which the Gypsies were known was, in part, 'counterfeit'. Arguably, moreover, a significant part of their attractiveness for audiences is that whatever they 'are' they are foundationally both themselves and, crucially, 'counterfeit'. Perhaps then, the piquant possibility of seeing courtier and Gypsy as similar is never utterly washed away, even as it is completely ended at the level of narrative and – even if it is – it is the Gypsies not the aristocrats who have given the audience pleasure.

We can also consider the performance of Gypsy identities. There may be a bit more to the Gypsy disguising. Andrea Stevens notes Jonson's repeated use of racialised colour transformations, having also explored blacking up in the

---

[51] Barbara Ravelhofer, 'Burlesque Ballet, a Ballad and a Banquet in Ben Jonson's *The Gyspies Metamorphos'd* (1621)', *Dance Research: The Journal of the Society for Dance Research*, 25.2 (2007), 144–55.

[52] David Cressy, *Gypsies an English Story* (Oxford: Oxford University Press, 2018), p. 47.

[53] Iyengar, *Shades of Difference*, pp. 174–5.

earlier *Masque of Blackness*. She also suggests that audience and actors may have experienced blackface as a kind of 'deep making'.[54] Building on this, we can note that at each of the three stagings of the masque performers seem to have performed willingly. Certainly, the fact that three sets of elite actors enjoyed the masque seems to suggest that to imagine being a Gypsy was pleasurable, and we can speculate that the pleasure lay in the power of the features that the law sought to prevent; outlawry, fellowship, trickery, and potentially even magic.

If we return to the statute of 1562/3, which clarified the Gypsy as an identity, we see that there the 'counterfeit Egyptians' are accused of 'transforming or disguising themselves'; statute law carried in itself a sense of their power and even charisma – recognised throughout the legislation in their power over others. The emergence of the Gypsy as a type may have made them arrestable but, at the same time, as Jonson's masque suggests, it gives form to them and freshly mints them as newly fascinating. 'Race' is a significant strand in the building of Gypsies as a distinct and fascinating, different, being. As we also see in the shifting priorities of Jonson's texts the racialisation of these figure co-exists with the understanding of them as disguised and faking cultural difference, and is part not so much of a fixedness of identity as of several layered and jostling ways of thinking. In Jonson's masque's metaphors we can see the Gypsy ready as a complex, yet also solid, category to think with but also, to feel and imagine in relation to.

Making 'Gypsies'?

When we return to the question of what factors shape the figure of the 'Gypsy' in the period preceding and spanning anti-Gypsy legislation, the evidence discussed here suggests that in 1621, as Jonson excitedly circulated it, the stereotype of the 'Gypsy' was fully present, exciting, and pleasurable to audiences. In terms of social hierarchy, then, we find that the partly applied, partly evaded, apparently ambiguously understood legislative programme designed to expel Gypsies from the emerging nation in fact shaped them as a very specific and recognisable group within culture and one available, as Jonson's masque suggests, to projection.

By the mid seventeenth century Gypsies were known (and in some cases tolerated) outcasts beyond the law. Thus it seems that perhaps they are only partly visible in local justice's records because if they were recorded as 'counterfeit Egyptians' the huge juggernaut of the statute would be triggered. Some Gypsies may appear as travellers and others in the record, because of a desire to avoid

---

[54] Andrea Stevens, 'Mastering Masques of Blackness: Jonson's "Masque of Blackness", the Windsor Text of "The Gypsies Metamorphsed", and Brome's "The English Moor"', *English Literary Renaissance*, 39.2 (2009), 396–426 at 407–8. Surprisingly, given the Elizabethan legislation, Stevens describes Gypsies as 'Frequently the target of anti-vagrant legislation but also protected by various statutes as a separate culture', 415.

applying the full force of the law. However, if the 1562/3 statute encourages invisibility in both Romani and parish record keepers, that law also gave Romani a very fully realised profile to be recognised and canvassed cultural types as, for instance, Romani is recirculated as criminal cant and they are deeply associated with crime, violence, fortune-telling, disguise. Thus, it seems that what Gypsies seem to be by the moment of Jonson's masque in 1621 was a textual registering of the diffuse but powerful cultural force of legislation combined with earlier factors and a crystallising of them as criminal in post-legislation popular print. Their fates were worked out in a hinterland of writing; at the same time as they reacted to the laws against them, so did the writing about them, setting long-lasting cultural assumptions in place. In the long moment under discussion, then, it is clear that we see Gypsies as made, between law, event and text but never exactly as the law saw them – the evidence discussed here shows the law's cultural, rather than its literal, force. An already fairly specific pre-Reformation group of people are forcefully and caricaturingly recast in a bloody interaction with an intense period of Reformation legislation which, whether Catholic or Protestant, sought to settle social belonging by place and parish.

Practice and law sit together in terms of local interactions. For example, Gypsy transformation was not only a metaphor: at a literal level the authorities were concerned about people moving in and out of Gypsy society and instituted penalties to attempt to keep them separate from the stable parish residents and from those others travelling. Indeed, in 1577 a yeoman from Buckinghamshire was explicitly accused of 'calling themselves Egyptians, and counterfeiting, transforming, and altering themselves in dress, language, and behaviour to such vagabonds called Egyptians contrary to the statute'.[55] Being a Gypsy in the view of the wider culture is a state that is assigned, not chosen – and the privilege to define is defended in this incident. As we have seen, the border between counterfeit Egyptian and vagrant or pedlar was permeable, but also policed. The 1562/3 legislation, however, did itself give mixed messages; on the one hand it is highly specific to Gypsies and, on the other, placed them under the broad grouping of vagrants. Thus, at the same time that the 1562/3 legislation clarified, if not what a counterfeit Egyptian 'was', at least how to identify and apprehend one, it also described them as a sort of vagrant. Thus, while the fact that Gypsies were a specialised focus within legislation, having their own legislative history, shapes also the logic of there being only brief mentions of Gypsies in the vagrancy scholarship, at the same time the relationship between 'Gypsies' and 'vagrants' was undoubtedly itself reshaped in the period after the Elizabethan statute.

In this chapter, then, 'Gypsies' have been understood in terms of legislation and literature specific to them. They have been analysed here as a specific story not as a subset of vagrants' tales, though they are seen in relation to that category

---

[55] 'Trial and conviction of Rowland Gabriel and others' in T. W. Thompson, 'Consorting with and Counterfeiting Egyptians', *JGLS*, 34.2 (1923), 83.

at various moments, most significantly perhaps in the Winchester trial of Hindes who had, it seems, lived with them but not quite been fully of the 'fellowship'. The period in which the 'gypsy' was forged coincides with the most intense anxieties and laws of the English Reformation and with intense legislation on the ordering of the poor, and particularly the vagrant. As we saw, at the start of the period under consideration Gypsies were distinguishable (if not consistently distinguished), and as the laws about and for them were forged and re-forged in the white heat of the English Reformation they became more, not less, specific as legal entities even as they were also – as 'Gypsies' – integrated into a more everyday understanding of those on the road. The Reformation and the ensuing period – the century up to about the 1620s – saw the emergence of their recognisability as vernacular English and Anglo-Scottish figures. By the early Stuart period, Gypsies had become sharply defined within culture to the extent that, for writers and audiences, as we find in *The Gypsies Metamorphosed* they are good, and even pleasurable, to think with, in the sense that they are put to work as vehicles for meaning and fantasy.

Finally, given that the evidence strongly indicates that Gypsies are made entities in this period – and it is perhaps the most intense period of their making – it poses a problem for scholars that there is a large gap in the primary material where any willingly given words from Gypsies fail to find textual form. It may be that to move from the study of types, like that undertaken here, to investigation of early modern Romani in England, scholarship might need to reconsider its exclusive reliance on textual material. Certainly, the absence of words that are in any sense freely given, beyond Boorde's language lesson, poses the question of how scholarship can more fully recognise these figures, and suggests we might also explore non-literate forms of recovery and investigation. As David Cressy reminds us, because of the wide geographical spread of fragmentary records generated by Romani nomadism, and their being recorded as they encountered the structures of settled dwellers in big houses, counties, or parishes, historians and literary scholars alike are heavily reliant on the nineteenth-century scholarship – particularly *The Journal of the Gypsy Lore Society*, the very first issue of which in 1888 initiates an important series of essays collating primary material from Scotland, Essex, Wales, the Midlands, and beyond. Contemporary historians, like this chapter, draw on these essays and associated publications as they engage with the written record. However, as part of the movement of 'last minute' or emergency history at the end of the nineteenth century, the Gypsy Lore Society was trying to capture as much of the past and present of Gypsies as they could without attention to methods. The Gypsilorists acutely experience the likelihood that the people they meet on the road are not likely to be there in the future, and such a perception was accurate as well as at times nostalgic and mythologising. The core articles that are accepted as the foundation of the field sit next to records of 'folk' song; essays on famous people who might have been Gypsies; lists of terrible persecutions throughout Europe and – above all – interviews with English Gypsies, about their past as well as their present. As Yaron Matras has argued, material in the *Journal of Gypsy Lore* has lent its name to poor scholarship – Matras notes that the term '"Gypsylorist" is like a curse or a charm: by articulating the word with reference to others, one seeks to exonerate oneself'.[56] While the material in the journal varies from anecdote to strong scholarship, to investigate the non-literate past it may well be worth reviewing its use of memory, tale, and anecdote as recorded at the end of the nineteenth and start of the twentieth century. This is not to advocate uncritical acceptance of the material in this journal, where any contributors, working with the rich and untheorised methods of folklorists, interviewers, enthusiasts, and tale-tellers make a reading experience mixing ethnography, oral record, documentary, linguistic, and historicist approaches. However, for all that such material is, evidently, unreliable and layered with mediations to consider it in relation to memory, tale, and work on the ethnography of song, it might be part of an approach to early modern Romani life. It is clear that the material used in this chapter would itself give a strikingly imbalanced field of evidence both in terms of the absence of Romani words given freely but also in terms of an excess of legal and literary material, information about men rather than women, assumptions of criminality and difference. Might it be that song and even oral testimony about past custom begin to give us not solid evidence but new approaches to the central gap in primary evidence? In attempting to trace early modern Romani, rather than the type of the Gypsy discussed here, there may be some suggestions to be found in the scholarship on, for example, New England's events, material culture, and non-literate communication.[57]

---

[56] Yaron Matras, 'Letter from the Outgoing Editor', *Romani Studies*, vol. 5, 27.2 (2017), 113–23.
[57] See e.g. the very different approaches of Christine M. DeLucia, *King Philip's War and the Place of Violence in the North East* (New Haven: Yale University Press, 2018); Matt Cohen, *The Networked Wilderness: Communicating in Early New England* (Minneapolis: University of Minnesota Press, 2010), esp. pp. 1–28.

10

'Greatness going off' in Renaissance Antony and Cleopatra Tragedies

JONATHAN PATTERSON

See High order in this great solemnity.[1]

IN THE FINAL scene of Shakespeare's *Anthony and Cleopatra*, Octavian Caesar demands that 'a pair so famous' are laid to rest with all the pomp and circumstance that their greatness demands. And yet, by this point, the spectator is likely to be more than a little perplexed. How can the lives of a manifestly lascivious, self-loathing rebel and his capricious Egyptian queen truly merit the solemn respect of all Rome? Furthermore, one might ask, what do Caesar's laudatory intentions communicate about the perennial early modern preoccupation with living and dying well? And if Caesar is misguided, how exactly *should* Antony and Cleopatra be remembered?[2] In the sixteenth and early seventeenth centuries, these questions aroused considerable interest on both sides of the Channel and across Europe. Numerous plays about Antony and Cleopatra came into existence, each refashioning the tragic story of these ill-fated lovers. Through a comparison of five versions of the tragedy, I shall interrogate its significance as a representation of greatness – that equivocal obsession of the social and political elites across Renaissance Europe.

My interpretation of Shakespeare's *Anthony and Cleopatra* (first published 1623, but probably performed as early as 1606) will be informed by four other tragedies that preceded it.[3] I shall examine two notable French versions: that of Etienne Jodelle (1552–3; published 1574) and that of Robert Garnier (1578; revised 1585). In the sixteenth century, these two plays were appreciable as drama

[1] Shakespeare, *The Tragedy of Anthony and Cleopatra*, V.ii, 363–4. All quotations are taken from Michael Neill's Oxford Shakespeare edition (Oxford: Clarendon, 1994).

[2] 'Antony' and 'Cleopatra' are the default English names used in this chapter; but where particular sources use vernacular and/or Latin variants, these variants will be retained.

[3] These five tragedies enjoyed different and often mixed fortunes – even Shakespeare's was not regularly performed until the mid-nineteenth century. Besides the plays to be discussed in this chapter, one might also mention Nicolas de Montreux's *Cleopatre, tragedie* (1594). Four sixteenth-century

to be read or declaimed; moreover, stage performances of both plays have been attested.[4] I shall set the works of Jodelle, Garnier, and Shakespeare in dialogue with two lesser-known English closet dramas: that of Mary Sidney Herbert, Countess of Pembroke[5] (1592; reprinted 1595) and that of Samuel Daniel (1594; revised 1607).[6] The Antony and Cleopatra tragedies of Jodelle, Garnier, Pembroke, Daniel, and Shakespeare cover a range of dramatic forms and formats. Their emergence is a story of transcultural reception, encompassing public and private performance, domestic recitation, and printed editions. But within that wider story of diversity we discover compelling points of intersection. The play-texts of these five works enable us to constellate a number of perspectives – and staging difficulties – around a particular problem of greatness. Shakespeare succinctly captured it as 'greatness going off' (*Anthony and Cleopatra*, IV.xiv, 6): a notion of debasement harking back to Plutarch's *Lives*.

Across the Renaissance world, greatness could mean many things. My approach will be oriented by what it meant to be great in the context of Anglo-French thinking about social hierarchy. In the sixteenth and early seventeenth centuries, a period that instantiated profound social reorganisation across Europe, both France and England witnessed a surge in attempts to stratify society

---

Italian versions are known: Giulio Landi's *La Vita di Cleopatra* (1551); Giambattista Giraldi Cinthio's *Cleopatra tragedia* (c. 1542, published 1583); Cesare de' Caesari's *Cleopatra* (1552); and Celso Pistorelli's *Marc'Antonio e Cleopatra* (1576). A Spanish version was also in circulation: Diego López de Castro's *Marco Antonio y Cleopatra* (c. 1582). On the plays' development in a wider European context, see Enrica Zanin, *Fins tragiques: poétique et éthique du dénouement dans la tragédie de la première modernité (Italie, France, Espagne, Allemagne)* (Geneva: Droz, 2014), pp. 191–200. For an earlier study which covers medieval sources (Dante, Boccaccio, and Chaucer), see Marilyn Williamson, *Infinite Variety: Antony and Cleopatra in Renaissance Drama and Earlier Tradition* (Connecticut: L. Verry, 1974).

[4] Jodelle's *Cléopâtre captive* was first staged before a royal audience at the Hôtel de Reims (the Paris residence of Charles de Guise, Cardinal de Lorraine), probably in early 1553. Garnier's subsequent *Marc Antoine* may have been staged in the year of its first publication (1578) at Saint-Maixent; it was performed in Touraine (1579), and in Paris (1594 or 1595), according to Raymond Lebègue, *Marc Antoine / Hippolyte* (Paris: Belles Lettres, 1974), p. 217.

[5] Mary Sidney (the sister of Philip Sidney) married Henry Herbert, 2nd Earl of Pembroke, in 1577. Her name is a source of scholarly divisions: Gavin Alexander discusses the problem in *Translation and Literature*, 8.1 (1999), 78–91 at 80–1. I adopt his suggestion of calling her 'Pembroke', the title by which she referred to herself after her husband's death.

[6] The term *closet drama* is ambiguous. It elides various kinds of unperformed English drama including those that were intended for reading rather than performance, and those that were not only read but also performed in a private or semi-private domestic context (sometimes as a staged reading). Recent scholarship has challenged the traditional view that Pembroke and Daniel produced unperformable closet dramas that were destined for reading alone. Daniel's *Tragedie of Cleopatra* was likely to have been staged in Lady Anne Clifford's household: see Yasmin Arshad, Helen Hackett, and Emma Whipday, 'Daniel's *Cleopatra* and Lady Anne Clifford: From a Jacobean Portrait to Modern Performance', *Early Theatre*, 18.2 (2015), 167–86. There are no attested stagings of Pembroke's *Antonius*; yet Pembroke was by no means averse to stage productions, and at the very least her text suggests she may have envisioned some kind of spatialised performance (upon '*The stage supposed Alexandria*'): see Marie-Alice Belle and Line Cottegnies, *Robert Garnier in Elizabethan England: Mary Sidney Herbert's 'Antonius' and Thomas Kyd's 'Cornelia'* (Cambridge: MHRA, 2017), pp. 25–7.

according to fine-grained notions of rank or standing (*état*, *degree*, *order*, *sort*, among other labels commonly used).[7] Within the numerous treatises propounding an overarching vision of the social edifice we find a calibration of degrees of 'dignity' (*dignitas*) among the nobility, 'the better sort' or 'les grands'.[8] Socially speaking, their degree of dignity, the measure of their greatness, was to be judged in accordance with the quality of their bloodline, their lordship over property, and their exercise of public office. Yet these factors alone were not enough: nearly all commentators insisted that the great could only preserve their dignity through honourable conduct commensurate with the demands of their rank and office. Maintaining a firm grip on one's dignity was by no means a foregone conclusion: Christian morality warned of all humanity's penchant for vice, from the lowliest to the greatest. When urging the nobility or royalty not to let moral standards slip, commentators frequently drew upon historical examples illustrating the precariousness of greatness. In this regard, Plutarch's *Lives*,[9] available in Greek, Latin, and the vernacular, provided an irresistible subject from Roman history: the sensuous warrior-statesman Mark Antony whose dalliances with the voluptuous Cleopatra made civil war the price of personal pleasure.[10]

Renaissance Antony and Cleopatra tragedies repeatedly ask: how far can one maintain great status without dignity? And conversely: how can those of humble status act 'nobly'? In response to these questions, a comparative analysis of our five plays reveals numerous incidents where rank and dignity are manifestly misaligned. Such misalignment, I shall argue, was nonetheless productive in a wider cultural sense. It afforded an unusually close focus on historical individuals who could inspire challenging, present-oriented reflection on the evils of luxury, on the dangers of civil war, and, more broadly, on what and who was truly noble.[11] In the tragic

---

[7] Case studies of particular social strata are too numerous to mention. For an overview, see *Dire et vivre l'ordre social en France sous l'Ancien Régime*, ed. Fanny Cosandey (Paris: Editions EHESS, 2005); Keith Wrightson, 'Estates, Degrees, and Sorts: Changing Perceptions of Society in Tudor and Stuart England', in Penelope Corfield (ed.), *Language, History and Class* (Oxford: Blackwell, 1991), pp. 30–52.

[8] In the modern West, dignity is considered universally inherent in all humanity from birth; in the Renaissance, only persons of noble blood were thought to be born with dignity – although others could attain it on merit. On this subject, see especially Lyndan Warner, *The Ideas of Man and Woman in Renaissance France: Print, Rhetoric, and Law* (Farnham: Ashgate, 2011); Carole Levin, Jo Eldridge Carney, and Debra Barrett-Graves (eds), *High and Mighty Queens of Early Modern England: Realities and Representations* (New York: Palgrave Macmillan, 2003).

[9] All other references unless otherwise stated are to the Loeb edition: Plutarch, *Lives: Demetrius and Antony; Pyrrhus and Caius Marcus*, trans. Bernadotte Perrin (Cambridge, MA: Harvard University Press, 1920).

[10] For further studies of ancient sources (Plutarch, Dio Cassius, Appian, not discounting Lucan's *Pharsalia* and Seneca's historical tragedy, *Octavia*), see Geoffrey Bullough, *Narrative and Dramatic Sources of Shakespeare*, 8 vols (London: Routledge & Kegan Paul, 1957–75), *V: The Roman Plays*.

[11] It has become established practice to read individual plays, particularly those of Garnier, Pembroke, and Daniel, as political allegories of a war-torn France and of her unsettled English neighbour. Instead, my comparative approach is modelled on that of Richard Hillman in *French Reflections in the Shakespearean Tragic: Three Case Studies* (Manchester: Manchester University Press, 2012), ch. 3. Hillman's analysis differs from mine in that his is less directly concerned with questions of social representation.

genre, this process of cultural critique came about through echoes of the earlier, vulgar narratives about Antony and Cleopatra found in Plutarch – narratives which were simultaneously finding outlets in more unruly forms of Renaissance popular culture. Even where it aspired to a neoclassical elitism, tragedy could not adequately address the problem of greatness without an active contribution from 'baser sorts'. Commoners and servants, we shall see, play a vital role in Renaissance tragedians' questioning of what made Antony and Cleopatra great – right up to their deaths.

Baseness in the Backstories

Much of what Plutarch said about the lives of Mark Antony and Cleopatra was quietly omitted from Renaissance tragedies based on his work. And yet, large sections of the commonly excluded material tell a colourful story of youthful indiscretion that deserves a second look. Though the tragedian may not have cared for such incidents (or even deliberately sought to avoid them), other early modern readers of Plutarch reacted very differently. One such reader was Simon Goulart (1543–1628) whose knowledge of the *Lives* had few equals. A Calvinist theologian and pastor, as well as a tireless editor of texts ancient and modern, Goulart brought out a French version of the *Lives* in 1583 based on Jacques Amyot's vernacular translation.[12] Goulart wanted to use Ancient philosophers in the service of a Calvinist humanism aimed particularly at statesmen.[13] His augmented version reached a wide readership across Europe, through no less than 17 editions in the period 1583–1620.[14]

An outspoken moralist, Goulart had no hesitation in supplementing Amyot's translation of Plutarch's text with his own laconic and often severe commentary. On Antony, Goulart certainly did not pull his punches. He views Antony's youth as the first instalment of a 'vie immonde' ('filthy life') anticipating a 'deshonneste mort' ('dishonourable death'). Antony came from noble stock, particularly on his mother's side (she was of the house of Caesar). As a young man, we learn, Antony inherited his father's commendable generosity, and showed great military potential (fol. 598r). But a juvenile propensity for seeking out bad company, combined with a flaring temper, meant that his public image

[12] Amyot's *Vies des hommes illustres grecs et romains* first appeared in 1559, with multiple further editions. It is likely that Thomas North may have used the Goulart edition for his augmented English translation of Plutarch's *Lives* (1603). On Goulart in general, see *Simon Goulart: un pasteur aux intérêts vastes comme le monde*, ed. Olivier Pot (Geneva: Droz, 2013).
[13] Amyot, a Catholic humanist scholar, had translated Plutarch for his royal pupil, the future Charles IX.
[14] All French quotations are from Goulart (ed.), *Les Vies des hommes illustres grecs et romains* (Cologne: Jacob Stoer, 1617). See further Jacques Pineaux, 'Un continuateur des *Vies Parallèles*: Simon Goulart de Senlis', in Michael Balard (ed.), *Fortunes de Jacques Amyot: actes du colloque de Melun (18-20 avril 1985)* (Paris: Nizet, 1986), pp. 331–42.

was always questionable. An astringent marginal comment (fol. 598r) makes a didactic overture to socially elite readers:

> Mais c'est chose indigne en tous, et encores plus es hommes de qualité d'estre maquereaux et rufiens, aussi tels vices sont les sources de tous malheurs tesmoin ce qui avint finalement à Antonius.

> Yet it is an indignity for all ranks, and all the more so for men of the better sort, to behave as pimps and ruffians; such vices are the sources of all ills, as we witness in what eventually befell Antonius.

For Goulart, Antony was a quintessential example of a highborn, aspiring leader who from the outset of his career showed a constant weakness in matters of sexual conduct. Read in this way, the seductive Cleopatra was not the start of Antony's debasement but rather the consummation of it – 'le comble de tous ses maux' (fol. 604r). Goulart is in no doubt that the Egyptian queen was nought but a whore (even though his source text allows for a more positive consideration of her supreme self-confidence, charm, and gracefulness). At no point are we given the impression that the Antony–Cleopatra partnership was one of stainless noble affections. Antony, lest we forget, was at this stage on his third wife, the irascible and rebellious Fulvia; after divorcing her he would enter a fourth marriage to the irreproachable, long-suffering Octavia, a union which also ended in divorce on account of his on-off relations with Cleopatra.

When they had returned to Egypt, Antony, we learn, began to invite Cleopatra to join him in his nightly routine of ale-house roistering – an invitation she readily accepted. Thinly disguised as a 'valet' ('domestic servant') and 'chambriere' ('chambermaid'), the amorous pair would visit the haunts of 'petites gens mechaniques' ('the meanest sort'), where the rough merriment often came to blows. The local Alexandrians allegedly took it all in good spirit, amused as they were by Antony's play-acting abilities: they got to enjoy his comic side whereas to his fellow Romans he showed only his austere side. Harmless, even endearing fun and games that allow readers to empathise with Antony and Cleopatra as lovers?[15] Not for Goulart. When the great despise their own dignity, he sententiously averred, there is no tomfoolery, no filthy pastime to which they will not stoop, to make fools laugh and wise men weep (fol. 604v). Such warnings should not be instantly dismissed as heavy-handed moralising. In Goulart's view, those who have the most to lose, socially speaking, are those who are most likely to descend into irreversible patterns of self-humiliation, the moment they start behaving beneath their social status. For Goulart, Antony's early affections for Cleopatra clearly presaged this danger, and are thus vital to the reader's understanding of his deeply ignominious end; one which, in overtly theatrical language (fol. 619r), Goulart will signal as the catastrophe of a 'tragique et malheureuse vie' ('tragic and ill-fortuned life').

---

[15] Williamson, *Infinite Variety*, p. 41.

Of Renaissance Antony and Cleopatra plays, only the Shakespearean version extracts further dramatic potential from this tragicomic backstory. With its hyperbolical language, fluid geographical displacements and ambitious dramatic time-span, *Anthony and Cleopatra* forms a marked counterpoint to the neoclassical restraint of earlier French and English versions of the play. Moreover, as is well known, Shakespeare got plenty of mileage from Thomas North's 1579 English translation of Plutarch's *Lives*. So it is unsurprising that Shakespeare's *Anthony and Cleopatra* interpolates base material from the Plutarchian backstories largely shunned by his contemporaries. From the outset Shakespeare uses socially inflected dichotomies to have his audience observe how the great *triumvir* is being 'transformed / Into a strumpet's fool' (I.i, 12–13). Sure enough, we are soon presented with a reluctant statesman who derives 'the nobleness of life' in whatever mutual (and often carnal) pleasure he can enjoy with Cleopatra. The Shakespearean Antony is one who wears his Roman titles lightly when he is far removed from Rome. He readily exploits opportunities to pass with anonymity, relishing the opportunity to accompany Cleopatra on a new nightly wander through the streets of Alexandria where they can both observe the 'qualities of the people' and mingle with the common crowds (I.i, 55–6).

In Shakespeare's *Anthony and Cleopatra*, the lovers' lowly sport is no mere frivolity; it has become an obsession. Antony seeks ever more extreme ways of testing how every passion makes itself 'fair and admired' in his lover (though interestingly, much of this is reported rather than directly enacted onstage). Enobarbus explains why Antony can never tear himself from the Egyptian queen: she is a woman of 'infinite variety'[16] such that even 'the vilest things / Become themselves in her' (II.ii, 241–6). Enobarbus's judgement will be tested on multiple levels as the play unfolds. In due course, the ever-changing queen, facing political defeats and suicide, will be tasked with dignifying much more demeaning vileness than perfecting Antony's love of cheap pastimes, be they fishing, or drinking with 'knaves that smell of sweat' (I.iv, 1–21), or bedroom cross-dressing (II.v, 20–3). It is no small irony that when all is lost, the prospect of renewed contact with the lowborn – this time the 'Mechanic slaves' of Rome – strikes Cleopatra as a fate more humiliating than death. What, after all, could be baser than ending her days listening to her 'Alexandrian revels' retold in extemporised street songs performed by 'Saucy lictors' and 'quick comedians' (V.ii, 214–18)?

In the course of *Anthony and Cleopatra*, undignified recreation shifts from a mutually satisfying mingling of the highborn with the lowborn, to a form of grotesque play-acting that would gratify only the commoner. Cleopatra's fond reminiscence of counterfeiting gender roles is transformed into a distinct threat – 'I shall see / Some squeaking Cleopatra boy my greatness / I' th' posture of a

---

[16] An epithet possibly suggested by the description of Isis in Plutarch's *Moralia*, according to which the goddess has an infinite number of names, forms, and shapes. See J. H. Walter, 'Four Notes on "Antony and Cleopatra"', *Notes and Queries*, 16.4 (1969), 137-b-139.

whore' (V.ii, 219–21).[17] Distorted souvenirs of Plutarch become part of a forward-projecting ploy – one that, à la Goulart, spies the catastrophe in the early warning signs of indecorous sports. Renewed evocations of baseness are an indispensable irony in Shakespeare's version, where the power mimetically to renew Cleopatra's humiliation would appropriate her infinite variety among the meanest sorts as a paradoxical reflection of Caesar's immortality.[18]

'How? Not dead?' Antony's Botched Assisted Suicide

> O que c'est une chose vile
> Sentant son courage imbécile,
> Qu'au besoin ne pouvoir mourir![19]

> How abject him, how base think I,
> Who wanting courage can not dye
> When need him therto calleth?[20]

So speaks the chorus midway through the Garnier tragedy, and in its English translation by Pembroke.[21] A servile fear of death is deemed an unthinkable prospect for the distraught Antony and his unfortunate queen facing down their defeat at Actium (31 BC); instead the chorus eagerly anticipates how their yearning for death may yet rob a victorious Caesar of his triumph. Thus Garnier and Pembroke challenge their audiences to consider whether death – and specifically *these* deaths – can provide the means for restoring the greatness of Antony and his Egyptian queen; and if not, could the lovers at least prepare to die with honour and thereby avoid a posthumous reputation for vileness and shame? Faced with a double suicide that posed considerable dramatic and staging difficulties,[22] late Renaissance tragedians saw an opportunity to question, and even counteract, a wider neo-Stoic preoccupation with 'noble' deaths that afforded the ultimate liberation from tyranny.

From the ancient records, the scope for transforming Antony's passing into a fully ennobling death was limited. Plutarch's account speaks of the progressive isolation of a once-great general, fast running out of honourable ways to die. Shakespeare's remorseful traitor, Enobarbus, interrupts this demise, recognising

[17] See further Michael Shapiro, 'Boying her Greatness: Shakespeare's Use of Closet Drama in *Antony and Cleopatra*', *Modern Language Review*, 77 (1982), 1–15.

[18] See Hillman, *French Reflections*, p. 112.

[19] Garnier, *Marc Antoine*, III, 1320-2, ed. Charles Mazouer, in *La Tragédie à l'époque d'Henri III. Deuxième série, vol. 1(1574–1579)* (Florence and Paris: Olschki, 1999), ed. Enea Balmas and others, pp. 217–320 at 293. All quotations are from this edition.

[20] Pembroke, *Antonius*, III, 1334-6, in *The Collected Works of Mary Sidney Herbert, Countess of Pembroke*, ed. Margaret Hannay, Noel Kinnamon, and Michael Brennan, 2 vols (Oxford: Clarendon, 1998), I, pp. 139-207, at 189. All quotations are from this edition.

[21] On the social significance of Pembroke's debut in print culture though the publication of *Antonius*, see Belle and Cottegnies, *Robert Garnier in Elizabethan England*, pp. 20–1.

[22] For a further discussion, see Zanin, *Fins tragiques*, pp. 192–3.

in Antony's pardon a friend 'Nobler than my revolt is infamous' (*Anthony and Cleopatra*, IV.x, 19).[23] For Eugene Waith this generosity suggests that Antony *does* recover a degree of his erstwhile greatness: a personal heroism rather than heroic achievement despite – or perhaps because of – circumstantial adversity over which he has no control.[24] However, as Jonathan Dollimore has argued, heroism of a public figure such as Antony can never be entirely personal.[25] Nowhere is Antony able to demonstrate much more in the way of living proofs to Enobarbus's claim.

Arguably the critical missed opportunity was the duel declined by Octavian Caesar: a final chance for Antony to set the military record straight by facing his adversary directly. Caesar, as those who knew their Plutarch would have recalled, briskly rejected the challenge (*Life of Antony*, LXXV) – and in so doing, turned a promising heroic show-down into a deeply insulting put-down. Garnier, Pembroke, and Shakespeare each noted this humiliation. In the Garnier and Pembroke versions, Antony fulminates against fortune and the gods for taunting him thus: that Caesar, 'un homme effeminé de corps et de courage', 'a woman both in might and mind', should have denied a grey-haired warrior one last opportunity to prove his mettle (*Marc Antoine*, III, 1048–69; *Antonius*, III, 1059–80). Richard Hillman foregrounds the wider anxieties about age, manliness, and fate triggered by this incident, to which I would add revilement in a socio-cultural sense. In Garnier, Caesar behaves 'vilainement': an adverb suggesting scorn. As such, Caesar's conduct is tantamount to that of an ignoble *vilain* (peasant) and thus unworthy of martial honour befitting those of noble rank. Turning to Shakespeare, and Caesar responds with a socially inflected taunt to match: 'old ruffian' (IV.i, 4). In the late Renaissance lexicography of John Florio and Randle Cotgrave, *ruffian* (a cognate of *villain*) suggested shades of lowborn bawdiness in either sex.[26] Hence, Antony's indecorous backstory returns to haunt him, with echoes of his youthful exploits among pimps and ruffians (cf. Goulart, *Les Vies des hommes illustres*, fol. 598r, 619v). Now an old ruffian, Antony will never attain personal greatness on the battlefield commensurate with the status of 'emperor' frequently ascribed to him by his followers. Though in the Shakespearean play he may still stumble on, and even hold out valiantly for a time, as in all other versions, there can be no overturning Caesar by the sword.

---

[23] The social connotations are marked. Enobarbus the disloyal vassal dies the death of a 'master-leaver' (IV.x, 22), a phrase deriving from the world of early modern livery and military companies to denote the worst kind of wayward, fugitive apprentice. See John Archer, *Citizen Shakespeare: Freemen and Aliens in the Language of the Plays* (Basingstoke: Palgrave Macmillan, 2005), p. 142.

[24] Eugene Waith, *The Herculean Hero in Marlowe, Chapman, Shakespeare and Dryden* (London: Chatto & Windus, 1962), pp. 118–21.

[25] Jonathan Dollimore, *Radical Tragedy: Religion, Ideology and Power in the Drama of Shakespeare and His Contemporaries* (Durham, NC: Duke University Press, 2004), p. 206.

[26] See Florio's Anglo-Italian *World of Words* (1598), s.v. 'Roffiano' and 'Roffiana': both defined as 'a bawd', 'a pander', 'a ruffian'; Cotgrave, *Dictionarie of the French and English Tongues* (1611), s.v. 'Maquereau' and 'Maquerelle' (a male and female bawd respectively): 'Ruffien' (m.), 'a Bawde, a Pandar'.

In the three main interpretations of Antony's death (Shakespeare, Pembroke, Garnier), suicide emerges as Antony's only remaining option to prevent a servile surrender to Caesar. In the Garnier play, Antony's hopes are lodged high: in quasi-religious tones he endeavours to take his own life as atonement ('expier') for his sins, thus washing away the dishonour of his long-standing infatuation with the Egyptian queen (*Marc Antoine*, III, 1234–41).[27] The theological naivety of Antony's sudden piety would not be lost on the likes of Garnier, whose notion of suicide approximated to the criminal act of *homicide de soy-mesme* (*self-homicide*, or *felo-de-se*), for which, traditionally, the church gave no quarter.[28] Furthermore, the underlying Plutarchian intertext militated against a swift realisation of such high-minded ideals. Plutarch's *Life of Antony* (LXXVI–VII) related in copious detail the protracted manner in which Antony finally expired. After valedictory oaths to the supposedly departed Cleopatra, and following the suicide of his slave Eros, Antony effected an unsuccessful attempt on his own life. Then, we are told, he received news of Cleopatra's non-death, whereupon his wounded body was taken to her place of refuge (a monument) and hauled in through an upper window; having still survived this lacerating entry, he then held death at bay long enough to recognise his queen, stop her wringing laments, and issue her with instructions about preserving herself and his memory with dignity.

Such a prolonged passing would not straightforwardly transfer in its entirety to any form of theatrical representation. We find elements of it enacted onstage in Shakespeare, and sections of it reported to the audience in the Garnier and Pembroke versions, suggesting doubts as to what – and how – the symbolic values of Antony's death should be ascribed. Faced with the prospect of a staging a technically demanding suicide, Garnier and Pembroke opted for a discursive solution: a messenger (Dircet / Dircetus) who appears in Act IV to narrate the disaster in Senecan fashion, thick with gory disfigurement. Thus we are to imagine the

---

[27] Whilst Garnier's religious vocabulary in *Marc Antoine* is far from precise, it tends to be more marked than Pembroke's (see Hillman, *French Reflections*, pp. 132–3). The connotations of atonement in 'expier mon diffame et mes nuisants ébats… que ma fin suprême / Lave mon déshonneur, me punissant moi-même' (*Marc Antoine*, III, 1235, 1240–1) are flattened to 'I must… Conclusion make of all foregoing harmes… that my last daie / By mine own hand my spotts may wash away' (*Antonius*, III, 1247–8, 1253–4).

[28] Garnier, a devout Catholic and distinguished magistrate, held the office of Lieutenant Criminel du Maine (from 1574) and eventually membership of the Grand Conseil du Roi (1586). He would doubtless have understood the long-standing embarrassment of *homicide de soy-mesme* to the community at large. Self-murder warranted forfeiture of a Christian burial, legal confiscation of property, imprisonment, or execution (if the attempted self-killing failed). And yet, the suicides of high-ranking nobles or clerics were often concealed or excused as an act of insanity, a legal loophole that guaranteed that normal burial ceremonies could proceed; influential family connections could also intervene to safeguard property and family reputation. See Georges Minois, *Histoire du suicide: la société occidentale face à la mort volontaire* (Paris: Fayard, 1995); Dennis Hoffman and Vincent Webb, 'Suicide as Murder at Common Law', *Criminology*, 19 (1981), 372–84; Alan Marks, 'Historical Suicide', in Clifton Bryant (ed.), *Handbook of Death and Dying*, 2 vols (Thousand Oaks and London: Sage, 2003), I, pp. 309–18.

direful scene: Eros flatly refusing to fulfil his obligation to kill his master, instead plunging his sword into his own breast, and then collapsing in a blood-spurting, soul-spewing heap. When it comes to Antony, both tragedians are in agreement that gushing fountains of his blood should freely flow – but his life remain – as soon as he has had his turn with the sword (*Marc Antoine*, IV, 1606–9; *Antonius*, IV, 1623–6). Nonetheless, Pembroke makes a much more conscious effort to accentuate the contrasting volumes of gore between master and servant. The net effect of this contrast is to accentuate the irony of Antony's flamboyant but incompetent imitation of Eros's quieter, efficient, and 'most noble acte' of disobedience. Antony's lack of courage and failed self-killing falls well short of these standards. Instead he is reduced to the ignominy of 'extreame wretchednes' brought on by 'lingr'ing death' that none can or will hasten (*Antonius*, IV, 1634–5). Debased to a 'life-dead' corpse encrusted with blood, the Antony of the Pembroke play does not survive its final ordeal, its laborious 'pull'd' entry into the monument to the accompaniment of a weeping populace below. Though all of this comes in the form of an off-stage report, the Senecan combination of blood and bombast still make for an intense theatre of affect, in which onstage characters and their audience beyond become immersed.[29]

Shakespeare's rendering of Antony's end is markedly different in tone and staging. He is far less preoccupied with gushing blood, and much more focused on the enacted exchanges between Antony and Eros. It is only when the last traces of his power are erased that Antony finally reneges on his convictions of heroic omnipotence. Antony realises that he is not a 'man of steel' or a 'firm Roman', but experiences his dishonour in what Dollimore calls extreme dissolution:[30] 'Eros, now thy captain is / Even such a body: here I am Anthony, / Yet cannot hold this visible shape' (IV.xv, 12–14). Amplifying Plutarch's laconic mention of Eros's inability to fulfil his master's death wish, Shakespeare spins out a tense dialogue in which Antony exhibits increasing frustration at his slave's holding back (*Anthony and Cleopatra*, IV.xv, 55–94). We see that no amount of persuasion, nor even the prospect of witnessing his master humiliated before Caesar in triumphal procession, will sway Eros to fulfil his grim duty. This is a far cry from the decisive Eros of the Garnier and Pembroke tragedies, who instantly slays himself; instead, in a manner that could be construed as almost comic,[31] the Shakespearean slave puts off his suicide for as long as he possibly can with flattering farewells, and a slow drawing of his sword which he will not use until given a direct martial order ('Now, Eros').

---

[29] On neo-Senecan tragedy as affective rather than mimetic, see Helen Slaney, *The Senecan Aesthetic: A Performance History* (Oxford: Oxford University Press, 2016), especially ch. 3.

[30] Dollimore, *Radical Tragedy*, p. 211.

[31] See Neill, *The Tragedy of Anthony and Cleopatra*, 'Introduction', p. 76. Modern productions which have injected humour into this scene include Giles Block's 1999 production at the Globe, of which 'Antony's bungled suicide comes across like a scene in the worst sort of minor opera', according to Katherine Duncan-Jones (*Times Literary Supplement*, 6 August 1999), 'except that we are entirely free to laugh at it'. See Bridget Escolme, *Antony and Cleopatra* (Basingstoke: Palgrave Macmillan, 2006), p. 133.

This combination of Eros procrastinating and then suddenly stabbing himself affords Shakespeare a critical opportunity to distance his action from classical models of heroic suicide. Though Antony's subsequent actions result in a drawn-out mutilating of his body, redolent of Cato (it is sometimes argued),[32] the net outcome amounts to a botched assisted suicide. Eros has refused the role of compliant assistant, unlike, say, the doctors who eventually ended Seneca's life.[33] Antony is twice undone, firstly by his failure to anticipate Eros's insubordination, and secondly, by his failure to imitate Eros's death as he falls on his sword. The anti-climax is remarkable. The subject's almost speechless surprise and dismay at his failure to die ('How? Not dead? Not dead?') is then compounded further: three guards and another comrade (Dercetas) arrive, each refusing to heed their master's feeble pleas to finish him off.[34] The dramatic impasse ends only upon the arrival of yet another comrade, Dolabella, bringing news that Cleopatra still lives: and so the irony of unassisted death shifts gear once more, with a still-sentient Antony transported aloft into Cleopatra's monument for the lovers' final parting. Extracting every last ounce of drama from this scene, Shakespeare has Cleopatra shoulder the physical burden of winching Antony into her mausoleum – 'sport indeed!', she tersely comments (IV.xvi, 34). No other Renaissance tragedian would attempt such a spectacle, and many have since have baulked at the sizeable technical challenge it necessitates.[35]

Grinding to a dolorous conclusion, the passing of Antony in late Renaissance tragedies keeps calling into question what status each of its key players has achieved. Recognition of 'noble' dignity is constantly displaced, from Antony to Eros (Pembroke and Garnier), and from Eros back to Antony, when the latter is hailed by Cleopatra as the 'noblest of men' by his 'former fortunes' (Shakespeare).

---

[32] The Younger Cato's allegedly honourable suicide is recorded in Plutarch's *Life of Cato Utican*. In protest against Julius Caesar Cato failed to inflict death upon himself at the first attempt, and expired only after ripping out his innards on the second. For a reading that stresses self-authenticating manliness and dignity in this act, comparable to that of Antony, see Coppélia Kahn, *Roman Shakespeare: Warriors, Wounds, and Women* (London: Routledge, 1997), pp. 125–7.

[33] The Younger Seneca's drawn-out death in protest against Nero is recorded by Tacitus in *Annals* XV.60–4. A combination of bleeding, poison, and hot water eventually brought about his end, during which he retained an extraordinary composure. The incident was well known to Renaissance commentators (see for instance Montaigne, *Essais* II.35).

[34] Wounded, bleeding, and lacking agency, Antony adopts what some critics have taken as a typically feminine position, as his masculinity and heroic valour sink to their lowest ebb. See Cynthia Marshall, 'Man of Steel Done Got the Blues: Melancholic Subversion of Presence in *Antony and Cleopatra*', *Shakespeare Quarterly*, 44 (1993), 385–408.

[35] According to stage historian Richard Hosley, early productions would have used a winch, pulley, and harness to lift Antony 14 feet above the level of the main stage to the gallery. See Hosley, 'The Staging of the Monument Scene in *Antony and Cleopatra*', *Literary Chronicle*, 30 (1964), 62–71. Performance critics have worried about 'a high monument aloft, a missed handhold, a flimsy railing', which could precipitate 'a slapstick catastrophe, as Antony plummets to the stage [floor]'. See William Worthen, 'The Weight of History: Staging "Characters" in *Antony and Cleopatra*', *Studies in English Literature*, 26 (1986), 295–308 at 295.

Mutilation notwithstanding, the Renaissance Antony may still claim, as in Plutarch, that he does not 'basely die' in submission to his chief Roman rival (*Anthony and Cleopatra*, IV.xvi, 55–7). But in return, his immediate legacy is to bequeath an abject corpse quite literally on his lover's shoulders, and a bloody sword to Caesar that speaks ambivalently of 'taints and honours' (V.i, 30).

'O rarely base'! Cleopatra's Parting Shots

What, then, of Cleopatra, all the while holed up inside her Alexandrian monument? Her spirited demise is the focal point of the tragedies of Etienne Jodelle, Samuel Daniel, and Shakespeare. Not that this struggle made her eventual death any less ambivalent. Her celebrated suicide by snake bite had long been enveloped in delicious mystery, since so little forensic proof could be adduced. Daniel and Shakespeare supplied the missing links such as they could be recovered from Plutarch's inconclusive account: an unlikely agent, a poor 'countryman' (Daniel) or garrulous 'clown' (Shakespeare), smuggling a beguiling, aspic-laden basket of figs past the guards;[36] and a pair of loyal maids, one of whom (Charmian) survives to confirm the deed, but almost (in Shakespeare) beats the queen out of 'this vile world' (*Anthony and Cleopatra*, V.ii, 310–12). This instrumentalisation of various subordinates and 'baser sorts' justified a degree of artistic leeway in which Renaissance dramatists could offset rank and dignity in the build-up to the queen's end. Representing Cleopatra's death as a noble act was no straightforward process, not least because the Egyptian queen had to overcome several obstacles just before she died that might rob her of a dignified, reginal departure – and with it, a posthumous reputation for greatness.

The first obstacle was enforced captivity: Caesar's intention for the Egyptian queen. The Cleopatra of Renaissance tragedy has no intention of exploring what, at least in Plutarch, was voiced by the dying Antony as a living possibility: that by remaining alive she had the chance to consult her own safety without disgrace (*Life of Antony*, LXXVII). Ongoing life under Caesar is simply unthinkable for a queen who, as Shakespeare explains, cannot see past the social humiliation of Caesar's gloating triumph, Octavia's chastising sober eye, and the shouting varletry of censuring Rome (*Anthony and Cleopatra*, V.ii, 53–7). Here Shakespeare touched upon what would emerge elsewhere as a deeper philosophical quandary. As Brian Cummings has shown, Renaissance suicidal argument only appears on the surface to be one about self-murder, because the real subject is even more painful

---

[36] From Plutarch onwards, commentators have expressed doubts about the snake-bite theory: see Lucy Hughes-Hallett, *Cleopatra: Queen, Lover, Legend* (London: Pimlico, 2006), pp. 138–9, 191; Colin Burrow, *Shakespeare and Classical Antiquity* (Oxford: Oxford University Press, 2013), pp. 209–10.

and troubling.[37] What it is to die conceals the underlying question: what it is to live, especially when one is prevented from dying.[38]

For Cleopatra, life must end; but the final moments of life are just as important as death itself. She still has to answer legendary accusations of lasciviousness and betrayal.[39] In most versions of the tragedy, the audience has been cued to sympathise, at least partially, with images of a faithless seductress who ostentatiously accepts full responsibility for corrupting, then betraying, and even 'murdering' Antony by deceitful enticements (as per Jodelle's version). Everything thus hinges on the prospect of Cleopatra restoring honour – her own and Antony's – by orchestrating and seeing through to completion a death ceremony that befits them both. This is tantamount to attempting what Mary Ellen Lamb has called a 'heroics of constancy',[40] by which Cleopatra will adopt the posture of faithful, loving 'wife',[41] against the pleas of various confidantes who counsel her to remain alive for the greater good. Pembroke's version neatly splits audience sympathy between Cleopatra, the self-styled 'wife kindhearted', and the 'hardhearted mother' perceived instead by Charmian (*Antonius*, III, 563). Through tense, stichomythic exchanges between the queen and her maidservants, we see that the flipside of Cleopatra's heroic constancy is a stubborn, even chilling refusal to live on in the interests of her children and country.

These quandaries notwithstanding, there is a more immediate obstacle: the queen must face Caesar before making any attempt on her life. Several Renaissance tragedians seized upon this opportunity to switch off Cleopatra's regal composure: facing her overlord, the Egyptian monarch unleashes raw affective responses that can only unsettle the spectator. These sudden outbursts are particularly marked in the Jodelle, Daniel, and Shakespeare plays. In each play, Cleopatra's dignity transmutes into a savage resistance towards her conqueror and to any who would seemingly assist him.

Particularly striking is Jodelle's early rendering of this theme.[42] His 1552 play *Cléopâtre captive* attests to a keenness for images of physical robustness

---

[37] Brian Cummings, *Mortal Thoughts: Religion, Secularity, Identity in Shakespeare and Early Modern Culture* (Oxford: Oxford University Press, 2013), pp. 273–4.

[38] However, failed suicide need not equate to lasting dishonour. In *Essais* II.35, Michel de Montaigne considers the length to which Seneca's devoted wife Paulina went to take her life at the point when he took his. Her efforts were ultimately unsuccessful; she lived on, yet 'tres-honorablement' ('most honorably'), in Montaigne's estimation. See Cummings, *Mortal Thoughts*, pp. 262–4.

[39] See Hughes-Hallett, *Cleopatra*, especially ch. 1.

[40] See Mary Ellen Lamb, *Gender and Authorship in the Sidney Circle* (Madison: University of Wisconsin Press, 1990), especially pp. 129–30.

[41] From the middle ages, Cleopatra was repeatedly put forward as an exemplar of patient, self-denying virtue, alongside the likes of Lucretia, Griselda, Penelope, and Dido.

[42] All quotations are from *Cléopâtre captive*, ed. Enea Balmas, in *La Tragédie à l'époque d'Henri II et de Charles IX. Vol. 1, 1550–1561*, ed. Enea Balmas and others (Florence: Olschki, 1986), pp. 55–117.

and defilement that complement the plaintive and 'rauque' ('hoarse') voice of the queen preparing for suicide. Jodelle is noticeably coy about Cleopatra's suffering that has entailed the loss of her 'blancheur pompeuse' ('haughty whiteness') and 'beau teint' ('beauteous complexion'): hints, therefore, at the loss of racialised European ideals of beauty inflected by neoclassical aesthetics that elsewhere eroticised Cleopatra even to the point of death.[43] Physically, the heroine of *Cléopâtre captive* is a far cry from her later, alabaster-faced counterparts in Garnier's *Marc Antoine* and Pembroke's *Antonius*. Instead, Jodelle stages a half-dead queen confronting Caesar (*Cléopâtre captive*, III, 882–3), with 'deux mammelles ... maigres et déchirées' ('two ... withered and lacerated breasts'). The vile side of Cleopatra's demise comes to the fore, as related in Plutarch:[44] a story of Caesar's struggle to restrain the queen from destroying herself and her enormous treasure, replete with degrading incidents some of which will recur in the Shakespeare and Daniel versions.

Daniel wrote his *Tragedie of Cleopatra* as a companion piece to Pembroke's *Antonius*.[45] Daniel's play picked up the story at the point where Pembroke, his patroness, had left it: the final hours of the Egyptian queen's life. In some respects, Daniel is retracing ground already covered by Jodelle and (perhaps) by Shakespeare.[46] But what follows is far from a straightforward rewriting of either. Instead, Daniel's intersecting plot-lines unfold different forms of debasement, corruption, and villainy, through which the total destruction of Egypt becomes an ever more imminent reality. In Daniel's play, none come off with great glory, whilst the grievous shortcomings of Cleopatra's staff – Philostratus the court philosopher, Rodon the royal tutor, and Seleucus the treasurer – become an integral feature.

Across the Daniel, Shakespeare, and Jodelle tragedies, one of the most salient features is the celebrated 'Seleucus episode' in which treasurer and queen are

---

[43] An artistic trend notably reproduced in curvaceous semi-nudes of the sixteenth-century school of Fontainebleau. See Hughes-Hallett, *Cleopatra*, especially chs. 5 and 6. Jodelle does not deliberately play on shades of white/non-white in Cleopatra's skin colour, as does Shakespeare, whose Cleopatra embodies these racial ambiguities with frank, mature sexuality (thereby stimulating a prurient male fascination, according to modern feminists). See Linda Fitz (later Woodbridge), 'Egyptian Queens and Male Reviewers: Sexist Attitudes in *Antony and Cleopatra* Criticism', *Shakespeare Quarterly*, 28.3 (1977), 297–316; more generally, Yasmin Arshad, *Imagining Cleopatra: Performing Gender and Power in Early Modern England* (London and New York: Bloomsbury, 2019), ch. 5.

[44] 'Le sein tout meurtri ... en plusieurs lieux ulceree avec inflammation' ('her breast beaten black and blue ... ulcerated and inflamed in several places'), as Amyot's equally lurid translation reads (*Les Vies des hommes illustres*, fol. 620r).

[45] The first version of Daniel's *Tragedie of Cleopatra* appeared in 1594; a substantially revised version was published in 1607, from which all quotations are taken. On Daniel's literary career, see Joan Rees, *Samuel Daniel: A Critical and Biographical Study* (Liverpool: Liverpool University Press, 1964).

[46] On Daniel's use of Jodelle, see Howard Norland, *Neoclassical Tragedy in Elizabethan England* (Newark: University of Delaware Press, 2009), pp. 211–18. Hillman (*French Reflections*, pp. 103–15) discusses Daniel in relation to Jodelle and to Shakespeare. He notes that Daniel may have revised his text with knowledge of Shakespeare's play: 'there is no settling the issue of priority, but likewise no questioning the interreferentiality of the two texts' (p. 104).

at odds over the latter's declaration of her wealth to Caesar.[47] Much has been said about this scene (particularly its appearance in Shakespeare's *Anthony and Cleopatra*), where some have seen it as a put-up job designed to distract Caesar from Cleopatra's suicide; or alternatively (in Daniel's version) the latest in a series of queenly impostures.[48] Across the three versions, Cleopatra is not, however, a villain, even if Seleucus is more evenly portrayed that way. Minor differences between the treasurers may be still observed: in Jodelle's *Cléopâtre captive*, Seleucus gives a wordy disavowal of his monarch's good faith (III, 989–1011); Daniel's Seleucus is much more of a minimalist, chipping in briefly that 'some things she hath reservd apart' (*Tragedie of Cleopatra*, III.ii, fol. 22v); somewhere in between is Shakespeare's embarrassed Seleucus, who would rather not affirm that which he knows to be false (*Anthony and Cleopatra*, V.ii, 140–8). All three versions agree on Cleopatra's angry reaction; but the intensity of her anger varies considerably. Daniel's queen is highly affronted:

> What? Vile ungratefull wretch durst thou controwle
> Thy queene, and soveraigne, caytiffe as thou art?
>
> (*Tragedie of Cleopatra*, III.ii, fol. 22v)

Shakespeare's blushing Cleopatra goes much further, flying into an ungovernable rage:

> The ingratitude of this Seleucus does
> Even make me wild …
> Go back, I warrant thee, but I'll catch thine eyes
> Though they had wings! Slave, soulless villain, dog,
> O rarely base!
>
> (*Anthony and Cleopatra*, V.ii, 153–8)

'Slave', 'villain', 'dog' – in Shakespeare, these terms are frequently instruments of heavy hitting verbal abuse;[49] but here they also expose Cleopatra's hyperbolic inflation of her own status, and her desperation to remain in a self-delusional state of control. Hence her violent outburst, with more than a whiff of Jodelle:

> Ah ! Faux meurtrier! Ah! Faux traître! Arraché
> Sera le poil de ta tête cruelle.
> Que plût aux Dieux que ce fût ta cervelle!
> Tiens, traître, tiens.
>
> (*Cléopâtre captive*, III, 1012–15)

---

[47] The historical source for this incident is Dio Cassius's *Roman History*: see Joan Rees, 'Samuel Daniel's *Cleopatra* and Two French Plays', *Modern Language Review*, 47 (1952), 1–10.

[48] For a discussion, see Brents Stirling, 'Cleopatra's Scene with Seleucus: Plutarch, Daniel, and Shakespeare', *Shakespeare Quarterly*, 15 (1964), 299–311.

[49] See further Mary Nyquist, 'Base Slavery and Roman Yoke', in Lorna Hutson (ed.), *The Oxford Handbook of English Law and Literature, 1500–1700* (Oxford: Oxford University Press, 2017), pp. 624–46 at 627.

> Ah! False murderer! False traitor!
> I'll tear your hair from your cruel head.
> I wish to the Gods that I could grab your brains!
> Take that, you traitor, and that!

In *Cléopâtre captive*, we see Cleopatra's most disturbing display of womanly violence in a sustained assault. In both Shakespeare and Daniel, Caesar immediately intervenes to protect Seleucus from the raging Cleopatra. In Jodelle, however, Caesar appears at first taken aback by Cleopatra's unleashed fury (1016), eliciting the terrified plea of Seleucus for him to restrain the queen who starts on him again (1019–29). This unusual three-way exchange does not, however, remain a 'woman-on-top' situation for long. Caesar duly intervenes with a mocking sneer at Cleopatra's 'grinçant courage' ('gnashing courage') and a belittling commonplace about unparalleled female wrath (very much in the Plutarchian idiom, where he openly laughs at her anger). In the Renaissance, queens who attacked a government minister or member of the court laid their dignity on the line; a discreet recovery was virtually impossible.[50] Jodelle insinuates as much, through Caesar's snide remark that the female assailant has abruptly curtailed her assault (1027–8). One might say, with Hillman, that this brief flare-up is not a clumsy lapse of neoclassical decorum but a daring metadramatic effect. By temporarily stepping outside of convention, Jodelle throws Cleopatra's 'performance' into relief precisely as such; tragic decorum is violated in the cause of dramatic irony.[51]

And socio-political irony too. Jodelle and his later English counterparts all accentuate the augmenting and the diminishing that make up the fealty dynamics of the Seleucus episode. Seleucus has manifestly broken rank by questioning his queen's declaration to Caesar. This treasonous betrayal by a 'vassal subject' (Daniel), 'villain' (Shakespeare), and, most notably 'slave'/'serf' (Jodelle) has to be exposed, lest Caesar be misled that Seleucus's word carries a regal authorisation. (Ironically it does in Shakespeare, when Cleopatra enjoins Seleucus to address Caesar (V.ii, 142–4), unaware that her treasurer will immediately betray her.) Jodelle provides the most expansive exploration of these ironies. In *Cléopâtre captive*, the audience already expects the 'serf' to act basely before he speaks. Immediately

---

[50] Catherine of Aragon, reputedly a woman who possessed all the virtuous qualities of 'a noble woman borne', came in for severe criticism in Holinshed's *Chronicles* (1587) when she directly accused Cardinal Wolsey of being her enemy in open court. Earlier chroniclers report that she blamed Wolsey on personal grounds for her divorce proceedings and departed in silent disgrace. See Matthew Hansen, '"And a Queen of England, Too": The "Englishing" of Catherine of Aragon in Sixteenth-Century English Literary and Chronicle History', in Levin *et al.* (eds), *High and Mighty Queens of Early Modern England*, pp. 79–99 at 88–9. The spectacle of a queen resorting to physical violence, moreover, could spark a diplomatic incident. Witness George Chapman's notorious 'slap scene' in *The Tragedy of Byron* (1608): a defamatory representation of the court of Henri IV which drew a formal complaint from the French Ambassador, Antoine Lefèvre de La Boderie, for its portrayal of the king's consort slapping the face of his mistress, Henriette d'Entragues. The ignominious scene was banned forthwith. See J. J. Jusserand, 'Ambassador La Boderie and the "Compositeur" of the Byron Plays', *Modern Language Review*, 6 (1911), 203–5.

[51] Hillman, *French Reflections*, p. 111.

preceding Seleucus's controversial disclosure, the chorus has remarked that tyrants all too easily extract servile confessions from their captives (III, 967–78). Seleucus is almost an exception to this rule in that no tyrannical pressure is required. In Jodelle (and later again in Daniel), he models a kind of *servitude volontaire* – a voluntary acceptance of tyranny with an ulterior pursuit of promotion in the new Octavian regime. Even after Seleucus's ambitions have purchased nothing but his vilification and eternal shame, the ironic social disparities have not run their course. Caesar elects to continue the Egyptian queen's captivity in the utmost prosperity (*Cléopâtre captive*, III, 1050). Given the taunting comments that preceded his decision in Jodelle's version, one cannot but notice the cruel restoration of hierarchy that undermines Caesar's apparent generosity. Cleopatra's reward is to be kept alive, haggard, subjugated – and rich. Now the consummate vassal-monarch, Cleopatra's treasure remains in her own hands – as does, moreover, the means and opportunity for staging her own lavish queenly death-bed scene. And so the ironies of order are again inverted, with Cleopatra suddenly empowered to die on a gilded 'riche lit' ('sumptuous couch').

Shakespeare is fully attentive to the symbolic ambivalence of this moment. At the climax of the drama (*Anthony and Cleopatra*, V.ii), the monument's opulent interior would have probably occupied the entire globe stage, enabling, as Michael Neill observes, an exceptionally powerful connection between the bravura of Cleopatra's performance and the monumentalising power of the dramatist's own art.[52] It is a feast for the spectator's eyes and imagination. With subtle hints of Plutarch, and of the Gospel accounts of the Last Supper and the Crucifixion, Cleopatra dresses for her 'noble act' of death by donning her robe and crown. 'Immortal longings' for Antony make her spurn a final cup of 'Egypt's grape' (V.ii, 277–81).

An otherworldly manifestation of greatness? Or another theologically naïve affectation, paralleling that of Garnier's Antony? Goulart would have said the latter, pointing with disdain to the lavish meal Cleopatra reportedly ate before poisoning herself with a concealed serpent: a metaphor for her 'poisonous' lifestyle and the divine judgement it incurred (*Les Vies des hommes illustres*, fol. 621r). Shakespeare's audience may not have judged her this severely, since the final banquet is all but omitted from *Anthony and Cleopatra*; but at the mention of the Egypt's grape, a savvy Jacobean theatre-goer might have thought back to her filling bowls on a final 'gaudy night' with Antony (III.xiii, 183–4). Indeed, going beyond Shakespeare's direct allusions, other feasts from her past might have sprung to mind, with even less propitious connotations.[53] By the early 1600s, Cleopatra's legendary pearl banquet, first told in Pliny, was becoming a stock motif of travel literature, and of City comedies. These regularly invoked the banquet to portray disgust with and desire for

[52] Michael Neill, *Issues of Death: Mortality and Identity in English Renaissance Tragedy* (Oxford: Clarendon, 1997), pp. 37–8.

[53] Cf. Thomas Nashe, who portrays his hapless traveler, Jack Wilton, caught with his courtesan/lover 'like Antony and Cleopatra when they quaffed standing bowls of wine spiced with pearl together', *The Unfortunate Traveller and Other Works*, ed. J. B. Steane (Harmondsworth: Penguin, 1972), p. 312.

profligate consumption in late Renaissance England.[54] Wherever Cleopatra appears, notes Alison Scott, the Egyptian queen is inherently theatrical – capable of *luxuria*'s illusory and enchanting arts, and dangerous in her attractions right up to her death.[55] Seen in this light, Cleopatra's opulent death preparations are perhaps the ultimate illusion: the *sine qua non* of greatness veering off course, recalling the dubious enticements of those who 'trade in love' (*Anthony and Cleopatra*, II.v, 2) – from Egypt to Venice, where latter-day Cleopatras ply their overpriced trade to hapless Antonies bound for the debtors' prison.[56]

Again and again, we are forced into dilemmas of judgement: between what is *said* about Antony's magnanimity, Cleopatra's alluring charms, or Caesar's tyranny, and what is *shown* of their remorse, clumsiness, even physical debility, as they struggle to embody true greatness commensurate with their elevated rank.[57] This struggle foregrounds an uncomfortable transcultural theme in the Renaissance: vileness is the lurking shadow behind any claims to greatness, dignity, and valour among the highborn. It is a modern critical commonplace to assert that tragedy transcends moralism; but does it always have to? Pre-modern drama affords intriguing interpretative possibilities when we consider it working *with* rather than against the ethical grain. As such, Renaissance Antony and Cleopatra tragedies continually remind us of one of Goulart's lessons: a noble or ruler who shows repeated signs of debasement makes a mockery of the social concept of dignity by degrees. Hence, the prospect of salvaging personal honour, even through an exemplary death, is put to a searing test.

Spectacles of greatness under duress place peculiar demands upon the spectator's tolerance of ceremonial display among the highborn. After so many protracted valedictions, Shakespeare was wise to let his public go with the thought of 'high order', rather than play on, and risk turning the solemn, state burial of Antony and Cleopatra into a painful anti-climax. Lengthy funeral rituals with their litany of ostentatious displays were by no means to every Renaissance spectator's taste. In the words of Florio, translating Montaigne: 'Happie is that death, which takes all leasure from the preparations of such an equipage.'[58]

---

[54] See Alison Scott, *Literature and the Idea of Luxury in Early Modern England* (London: Routledge, 2016), p. 62.

[55] Scott, *Literature and the Idea of Luxury*, p. 66.

[56] Hence Thomas Coryat's titillating portrait of the Venetian courtesan: 'For thou shalt see her decked with many chaines of gold and orient pearle like a second Cleopatra ... yet if thou shalt rightly weigh them in the scales of mature judgement, thou wilt say ... that they are like a golden ring in a swines snowt' (*Coryats crudities* [London: William Stansby, 1611], pp. 266–7).

[57] See Neill (*The Tragedy of Anthony and Cleopatra*, 'Introduction', p. 68), for whom 'overreaching' is the basic rhetorical and structural motif of Shakespeare's *Anthony and Cleopatra*, whereby high hopes are anticlimactically dashed, thus creating the 'perceived gap between expectation and performance'. On these dilemmas more broadly, see Graham Bradshaw, *Shakespeare's Scepticism* (Brighton: Harvester, 1987).

[58] Florio, *The Essayes of Lord Michaell de Montaigne: The First Booke* (London: Valentine Simmes for Edward Blount, 1603), p. 39.

11

Tragedy, or the Fall of Middle-Class Men

RICHARD McCABE

WHEN APPLIED TO sixteenth-century England the term 'middle class' embraces a variety of social possibilities. As contemporary commentators such as Sir Thomas Smith and William Harrison note, merchants, master tradesmen, lawyers, gentry, and even wealthy yeoman might be accounted 'of the middling sort' – as distinct from the nobility at the top of the scale and those who earned their bread by the sweat of their brow at the bottom.[1] Such was the social fluidity of the age, however, that Smith and Harrison struggle to identify a permanent structure in what was, in fact, a dynamic process.[2] Yeomen were a case in point. 'This sort of people', Smith observes,

> confesse themselves to be no gentlemen, and yet they have a certaine preheminence and more estimation than labourers and artificers, and commonly live welthilie, keepe good houses, do their businesse, and travaile to get riches ... by these meanes [they] doe come to such wealth, that they are able and daily doe buy the landes of unthriftie gentlemen, and after setting their sonnes to the schooles, to the Universities, to the lawe of the Realme, or otherwise leaving them sufficient landes whereon they may live without labour, doe make their saide sonnes by those meanes gentlemen.[3]

A class of men who disclaim gentility capitalise on the decay of 'unthriftie gentlemen' to confer gentility on their sons. As this suggests, contemporary social categories were rather permeable than discrete, and that of 'gentleman' especially

---

[1] See Sir Thomas Smith, *De Republica Anglorum*, edited by M. Dewar (Cambridge: Cambridge University Press, 1982), pp. 66–77; William Harrison, *The Description of Britaine*, in Raphael Holinshed, *Chronicles of England, Scotland, and Ireland*, 6 vols (London: J. Johnson, 1808), I, 273–6. See also Hugh Trevor-Roper, *The Gentry, 1540–1640* (Cambridge: Cambridge University Press for the Economic History Society, 1953); Christopher Brooks, 'Apprenticeship, Social Mobility and the Middling Sort, 1500–1800', in J. Barry and C. Brooks (eds), *The Middling Sort of People: Culture, Society and Politics in England, 1550–1800* (Basingstoke: Macmillan, 1994), pp. 52–83; K. Wrightson, 'Estates, Degrees, and Sorts: Changing Perceptions of Society in Tudor and Stuart England', in P. J. Corfield (ed.), *Language, History and Class* (Oxford: Basil Blackwell, 1991), pp. 30–52.
[2] See Ian W. Archer, *The Pursuit of Stability: Social Relations in Elizabethan London* (Cambridge: Cambridge University Press, 1991), pp. 18–27.
[3] Smith, *De Republica Anglorum*, p. 74.

Proceedings of the British Academy, **246**, 219–238, © The British Academy 2022.

so. But, problems of precise taxonomy aside, all members of the middling sort had one thing in common: in the view of contemporary neoclassical critics neither they nor their dependants were fit protagonists for 'tragedy'. It was generally agreed to the contrary that the dramatic metier of the middling was the comic. This perception arose from a predominantly social, as opposed to moral or aesthetic, interpretation of Aristotle's assertion that comedy tends to represent people inferior, tragedy superior to ordinary beings (1448a16–28).[4] The tragic protagonist had to be noble or elevated (*spoudaios*), to match the seriousness of the action and style (1448a2, 1449b24). He or she was someone 'belonging to the class of those who enjoy great renown and prosperity such as Oedipus, Thyestes and eminent men from such lineages' (1453a10).[5] Writing the first full commentary on the *Poetics* in 1548, Francesco Robortello understood this to mean that the characters of tragedy should be 'praestantes' and those of comedy 'viles'; according to this view, those 'worse than ourselves' became 'humiliores' and those better 'praestantiores', all terms denoting social demarcation.[6] According to the even more influential Julius Caesar Scaliger writing in 1561, comedy 'employs rustic or low life characters ... in middling affairs [é pagis ... loco humili ... de medio]' while tragedy is preoccupied with 'kings and princes whose concerns are those of the polis, fortress, and camp [ex urbibus, arcibus, castris]'.[7] Such attitudes lie behind Sir Philip Sidney's condemnation of the practice of 'mingling Kings and Clownes' in what he denigrates as the 'mungrell Tragy-comedie' of his day.[8]

One of the ironies arising from all of this is the striking disparity between the classes presented on the early modern tragic stage and the vast majority of those attending the public playhouses. What, one might ask, was Hamlet to them or they to Hamlet that they should weep for him? The issue was raised in the 'Induction' to *A Warning for Fair Women* (1599), one of the earliest English tragedies to defy the traditional social expectations of the genre. Here personified representations of 'Comedie' and 'Hystorie' dispute Tragedy's relevance to its audience.[9] What had it to offer but hackneyed accounts of blood and gore remote from the experience of the common man?: 'How some damnd tyrant, to obtaine a crowne, / Stabs, hangs, impoysons, smothers, cutteth throats' until 'a filthie whining ghost ... Comes skreaming like a pigge half stickt, / And cries *Vindicta*, revenge, revenge' (ll. 50–7). For her part Tragedy ridicules the 'slight and childish' material of Comedy and damns with faint praise her 'sparkes of wit, / Some odde ends of old jeasts scrap't up togither' (ll. 39–49). In Aristotelian terms, that is to say, she dismisses comedy as

---

[4] Stephen Halliwell, *Aristotle's Poetics* (London: Duckworth, 1986), p. 267.
[5] All quotations are from *Aristotle, 'Poetics'; Longinus, 'On The Sublime'; Demetrius, 'On Style'*, ed. and trans. D. C. Innes (Cambridge, MA: Harvard University Press, 1995).
[6] Robortello, *Aristotelis De Arte Poetica Explicationes* (Florence, 1548), pp. 20, 23.
[7] Scaliger, *Poetices Libri Septem* (Augsburg, 1561), p. 11.
[8] *Elizabethan Critical Essays*, edited by G. Gregory Smith, 2 vols (Oxford: Clarendon Press, 1904), I, 199.
[9] All quotations are from *A Warning for Fair Women*, ed. C. D. Cannon (The Hague: Mouton, 1975).

trivial [*phaulon* or *geloion*] rather than serious [*spoudaion*]. Yet while she demands weightier matter, 'passions that must move the soule ... Extorting teares out of the strictest eyes ' (ll. 44–5), she has a trick up her sleeve to fox both her opponents. 'My Sceane is London, native and your owne', she tells the audience (l. 95). What she offers them is 'true and home-borne Tragedie' based on actual events that occurred within living memory among persons like themselves (ll. 2723–9). Admittedly the play involves remarkable violence, but enacted not by 'some damnd tyrant, to obtaine a crowne' but by a 'gentleman' to obtain a merchant's widow. It therefore harmonises elements from all three of the contending genres: it elevates the client-ele of comedy to tragic status and accords them their proper place in 'history'. Its social implications are easily as radical as its generic innovations. Indeed the two are symbiotic. When in the epilogue Tragedie claims to have wielded 'the launces that have sluic'd forth sinne, / And ript the venom'd ulcer of foule lust' (ll. 2718–19), we hear echoes of Sidney's assertion that the genre 'openeth the greatest wounds, and sheweth forth the Ulcers that are covered with Tissue; that maketh Kinges feare to be Tyrants'.[10] The 'warning' he would deliver to monarchs, the anonymous playwright delivers to the middle class.

While the middle class in its many manifestations may not have been as militantly 'on the rise' in the 1590s as has sometimes been claimed, it exercised immense social and economic influence in both provincial and metropolitan com-munities.[11] And popular literature increasingly reflected its status. In the narrative and dramatic works of authors such as Thomas Deloney, Thomas Dekker, and Thomas Heywood, the middling sort were not merely the subjects of 'comedy', but the heroes. In *Jack of Newbury* (1597) and *The Gentle Craft* (1597–8), for example, Deloney fabricates mythical origins for the guilds of clothiers and shoemakers designed to rival the claims of 'ancient lineage'. His *Thomas of Reading* (c. 1598) is duly praised in Will Kemp's *Nine Daies Wonder* (1600), for celebrating the lives of such 'honest men' as are normally omitted from the official chronicles.[12] The point was enforced by Deloney's practice of dedicating his works not to the nobility but to the guildsmen themselves: *Jack of Newbury* is dedicated to 'all the famous Cloth-Workers in England'; the first part of *The Gentle Craft* to 'all the good Yeomen' of the trade of shoemakers; the second 'to the Master and Wardens of the worshipfull company of the Cordwaynors'; and Thomas of Reading (essentially if not formally) to the clothiers.[13] The very act of dedication promotes the social aspirations of the dedicatees.

In their presentation of the middle classes Deloney, Dekker, and Heywood exploit one of the greatest ambiguities of the Tudor class system, the definition of

---

[10] *Elizabethan Critical Essays*, I, 177.

[11] For a balanced assessment of the influence of the middle class see J. H. Hexter, *Reappraisals in History* (London: Longmans, 1961), pp. 71–116.

[12] William Kemp, *Kemps Nine Daies Wonder* (London, 1600), sig. D3ᵛ.

[13] The earliest extant edition of *Thomas of Reading*, that of 1612, claims to be the fourth. That of 1680 notes that the work was written to '*The honour of the cloathworking trade*'.

'gentleman'. According to Harrison, for example, 'gentlemen be those whome their race and bloud, or at the least their vertues doo make noble and knowne'.[14] The phrasing is deliberately cautious. While the mention of 'race and bloud' genuflects to the traditional components of gentility, 'vertue', an ambiguous term in itself, threatens to render both unnecessary if not redundant. Deloney illustrates the issue perfectly when Katherine of Aragon greets Jack of Newbury by the style of 'gentleman' and he demurs:

> Most gracious Queene (quoth hee) Gentleman I am none, nor the sonne of a Gentleman, but a poore Clothier, whose lands are his Loomes, having no other Rents but what I get from the backes of little sheepe: nor can I claime any cognisance but a wodden shuttle. Neverthelesse, most gratious Queene, these my poore seruants and my selfe, with life and goods, are ready at your Maiesties command, not onely to spend our blouds, but also to lose our lives in defence of our King and Country. Welcome to mee *Iacke* of *Newberie* (said the Queene) though a Clothier by trade, yet a Gentleman by condition, and a faithfull subject in heart.[15]

The term 'condition' seems carefully chosen to combine associations of substance and sensibility while leaving their relationship indeterminate.[16] Several factors are operative here. Deloney fabricates an extraordinary rapport between the guildsmen and the monarchy, and members of the royal family are frequently made to ventriloquise claims for the importance of trade to the nation. Deloney's title-page explains how Jack 'set continually fiue hundred poore people at worke, to the great benefit of the common-wealth'. In fact, 'there is no trade more beneficiall to the Commonwealth, than is the most necessary Art of Clothing'.[17] Trade has become a 'vertue' in itself and the good of the nation is now assessed in commercial terms: the 'commonweale' is now unequivocally the common wealth. But the wealth generated by trade militates against the traditional restrictions of class. It enables Jack, for example, to entertain the royal couple in his own house as lavishly as any aristocrat and stage the equivalent of a courtly masque for their amusement, a masque that prefers the industrious worker ant to the feckless courtly butterfly.[18] The message is that merchants matter: the murder of Thomas of Reading in Deloney's darkest middle-class fiction is presented as a cause for national mourning.[19] The rise of domestic tragedy in the same period is by no means coincidental. We have reached the point at which the status of the middling sort was regarded as sufficiently important for treatment in what was regarded as the highest form of drama. Generic hierarchy reflects and promotes social aspiration. One might even say that the status of the middle class was confirmed by its capacity for tragedy, a confirmation that entailed intense scrutiny of its values.

---

[14] Harrison, *Description*, p. 273.

[15] *The Works of Thomas Deloney*, ed. F. O. Mann (Oxford: Oxford University Press, 1967), p. 24. All quotations are from this edition.

[16] See OED, 'Condition', 10a, 11a,b.

[17] *Works of Thomas Deloney*, p. 1.

[18] *Works of Thomas Deloney*, pp. 30, 37.

[19] *Works of Thomas Deloney*, p. 260.

Corrosive criticism of mercantile values is, of course, a staple of Stuart city comedy, but domestic tragedy elicits even darker energies. Perhaps no better illustration of the link between the two is Philip Massinger's transformation of Thomas Middleton's Pecunius Lucre, from *A Trick to Catch the Old One* (1607), into the proto-tragic Sir Giles Overreach of *A New Way to Pay Old Debts* (1625). What makes the difference is the sheer intensity of Overreach's obsession with using his ill-gotten gains to attain social respectability by having his daughter marry into the aristocracy and become 'right honourable'. As his plans falter, his wits give way and his language descends into a parody of the Marlovian 'overreacher': 'is not the whole world / Included in myself? To what use then / Are friends, and servants?' (V.i.355–7). The title-page classifies the play as 'a comoedie', but not for Sir Giles.[20] To look more closely into the economies of self-interest and class, Massinger implies, is to discover not just hypocrisy but insanity at the core. Peter Holbrook observes that domestic tragedy demonstrates how 'the same motives leading to the falls of princes are at work in the lives of humbler folk' (93), but the effect is even more radical. It entails not just similar 'motives' but equivalent values.[21] In plays such as *Arden of Faversham* (c. 1592), *A Warning for Fair Women* (1599), Robert Yarington's *Two Lamentable Tragedies* (1601), Thomas Heywood's *A Woman Killed with Kindness* (1603), George Wilkins' *The Miseries of Enforced Marriage* (1607), *A Yorkshire Tragedy* (1608), Thomas Dekker, William Rowley, and John Ford's *The Witch of Edmonton* (1621), and Heywood's *The English Traveler* (1633), middle-class conflicts are presented as though they were just as significant as matters of state. In fact they are matters of state, pertaining no less to the maintenance of hierarchy and social order than the business of the court. Accordingly they are mediated through all the conventions of 'high' tragedy: prophetic dreams and premonitions, supernatural agency, rhetorical lamentation, allegorical dumb-shows, and pervasive classical allusion and analogue.[22]

Precisely because the 'middle' is a contested area with permeable boundaries, domestic tragedy is obsessed by class, and class is invariably calibrated by a 'vertue' known as 'credit'.[23] The concept was complex. 'Credit' was largely a matter of one's public reputation – one's 'public fame' – but that assessment depended on the interaction of social, moral, and financial factors. When Shylock muses whether 'Antonio is a good man', Bassanio bridles in his friend's defence: 'Have you heard any imputation to the contrary?' But they are speaking at cross-purposes.

[20] All quotations are from Philip Massinger, *A New Way to Pay Old Debts*, ed. T. W. Craik (London: Ernest Benn, 1964).
[21] Peter Holbrook, *Literature and Degree in Renaissance England: Nashe, Bourgeois Tragedy, Shakespeare* (Newark: University of Delaware Press, 1994), p. 93.
[22] See Malcolm Gaskill, *Crime and Mentalities in Early Modern England* (Cambridge: Cambridge University Press, 2000), p. 214.
[23] See Craig Muldrew, *The Economy of Obligation: The Culture of Credit and Social Relations in Early Modern England* (Basingstoke: Macmillan, 1998); Jennifer Panek, 'Community, Credit, and the Prodigal Husband on the Early Modern Stage', *English Literary History*, 80 (2013), 61–92.

'Ho, no, no, no, no', Shylock explains, 'my meaning in saying he is a good man is to have you understand that he is sufficient' (*Merchant of Venice*, 1.3.11–15).[24] As the exchange makes clear, 'good' is simultaneously a moral and financial category. We still speak of creditors being 'good for the money' in the sense that they are both 'sufficient' and trustworthy, and Shylock hesitates only because Antonio's resources are currently in 'supposition'. The credit of the middle sort depended to a large extent on their ability to maintain their 'estate' by defraying their debts. While prodigality, particularly of the sort portrayed in *A Yorkshire Tragedy*, was condemned for destroying this ability, habits of thrift and hard work were seen to promote it. Domestic tragedy is therefore pervaded by the language of credit and debit – and it is in those terms that the nature and extent of any 'fall' is measured.[25]

At the outset of *Arden of Faversham*, the seminal domestic tragedy, Arden insists upon his station – 'I am by birth a gentleman of blood' (I.36) – and he is addressed as 'Master Arden' throughout the play.[26] While he has more than sufficient means to maintain this estate his public fame is imperilled by his wife's liaison with Mosby whom he regards as a 'villain' and 'base groom' (I.304–5). He is amazed that a woman of Anne's station, 'descended of a noble house' (I.202), seems impervious to the 'common speech of men / Who mangle credit with their wounding words' (IV. 3–4). Anne is equally aware of her 'narrow-prying neighbours' (I.135), but her passion for Mosby is measured precisely by her determination to hazard her reputation. 'Forsooth, for credit sake I must leave thee!', she snorts derisively (X.91). 'All the knights and gentlemen of Kent', Arden tells Mosby, 'Make common table-talk of her and thee' (I.343–4). What the knights and gentlemen are talking about, however, is not just adultery but what they regard as social miscegenation. Mosby is,

> A botcher [jobbing tailor], and no better at the first;
> Who by base brokage getting some small stock,
> Crept into service of a nobleman,
> And by his servile flattery and fawning
> Is now become the steward of his house,
> And bravely jets it in his silken gown. (I.25–30)

The sartorial detail is important. As an impoverished younger brother remarks in *The Miseries of Enforced Marriage*, 'Credit must be maintained which wil not be without money, Good cloaths must be had, which will not be without money' (ll. 1232–3).[27] In this period of strict sumptuary laws, the semiotics of dress matter intensely. Dress

---

[24] All quotations are from *The Merchant of Venice*, ed. J. R. Brown (London: Methuen, 1955). For a discussion of the play's commercial values see David Landreth, *The Face of Mammon: The Matter of Money in English Renaissance Literature* (New York: Oxford University Press, 2012), pp. 150–83.

[25] See Ceri Sullivan, *The Rhetoric of Credit: Merchants in Early Modern Writing* (Madison: Farleigh Dickinson University Press, 2002), pp. 23–43.

[26] All quotations are from *Three Elizabethan Domestic Tragedies*, ed. K. Sturgess (Harmondsworth: Penguin, 1969). This edition conveniently reprints the plays' source materials.

[27] All quotations are from George Wilkins, *The Miseries of Enforced Marriage*, ed. G. H. Blayney (Oxford: Oxford University Press for the Malone Society, 1964).

both denoted and potentially disguised class. During their first altercation Arden humiliates Mosby by publicly stripping him of his sword on the grounds that 'the statute makes against artificers'. The reference is to a statute of 1363 which restricted the wearing of swords to the rank of gentleman and above.[28] Arden claims to be a born gentleman, a 'gentleman of bloud', but that was not the only kind. Having risen in the world, Mosby regards himself as a gentleman, dresses accordingly, and covets the style of 'Master'. His aim, announced in a Machiavellian soliloquy that might come from the lips of Richard III, is to 'sit in Arden's seat' (VIII.31), and Arden's Anne, like Shakespeare's, is only a means to that end. Mosby's ambition, as the source makes clear, is directly equivalent at his level of society to that of the 'damnd tyrant' who murders 'to obtaine a crowne'. The anonymous author found the story in Holinshed where it illustrates the correspondence between public and domestic politics. The murder of a husband by a wife, or a master by a servant, was regarded as 'petty treason', tantamount to regicide because the same principles of hierarchy were seen to obtain in the public family that was the state, and the private state that was the family.[29] The plot is accordingly articulated through the language of usurpation and rebellion. In order to gain her ends Anne enlists the services of the Elizabethan underworld and suborns Arden's servant, Michael, to join the conspiracy. He is all the readier to do so because it furthers his personal ambition to become a land owner by killing his older brother (I.170–5). In this way Anne's activities simultaneously import the forces of public anarchy into the domestic sphere and export them into the wider community. This is a matter of public concern to be treated with appropriate dramatic formality: Michael becomes probably the first servant on the English stage to deliver a deliberative soliloquy – in fact he delivers two.

Whereas on one level Anne realises that Mosby is indeed a 'base peasant' (I.198), an emotional imperative, tellingly couched in classical allusion, overrides that recognition:

> I shall no more be closed in Arden's arms,
> That like the snakes of black Tisiphone
> Sting me with their embracings …
> There is no nectar but in Mosby's lips;
> Had chaste Diana kiss'd him, she like me
> Would grow love-sick, and from her wat'ry bower,
> Fling down Endymion and snatch him up. (XIV.148–56)

The dramatist did not find such language in Holinshed, nor is it what we might expect from a person of Anne's background. But that is the point. The various forms of 'murder literature' on which so many domestic tragedies are based conceive of 'tragedy' in very different terms from the plays. While they externalise the characters to provide 'examples', the plays internalise the examples to generate

---

[28] See the commentary in *A Woman Killed with Kindness and other Domestic Plays*, ed. M. Wiggins (Oxford: Oxford University Press, 2008), p. 293.
[29] See Gaskill, *Crime and Mentalities*, p. 210.

personal drama. Divorce is not an option for Anne under Tudor law. Hers is not
just an act of disobedience but a compulsion, on a par with that of Aeschylus's
Clytemnestra or Euripides's Phaedra. Despite, or perhaps even because of,
their incongruity, the Classical allusions sprinkled so liberally through *Arden
of Faversham* lend the middle the same frame of reference as the high thereby
equating their social significance.

But such elevation entails increased exposure and scrutiny. While the dramatist ignores Holinshed's suggestion that Arden connived at his wife's affair with
Mosby, he exacerbates the suggestions of greed and injustice. The scenes in which
Arden is confronted by Greene and Reede, both of whom he has deprived of what
little land they possessed, present the 'gentleman of bloud' as a predator. Once
Arden rejects Reede's heartfelt petitions for restitution, the luck or providence (and
the protagonists are uncertain which) that had formerly defeated the conspirators
forsakes him. In the epilogue his murder is directly related to Reede's curse and
entails a remarkable *damnatio memoriae*:

> But this above the rest is to be noted:
> Arden lay murder'd in that plot of ground
> Which he by force and violence held from Reede;
> And in the grass his body's print was seen
> Two years and more after the deed was done. (Epilogue, 9–13)

While this by no means exonerates Anne and her allies for the murder of her 'saving
husband' who 'hoards up bags of gold' (I.220), it directly links their acts of petty
treason to his acts of petty tyranny. The clear implication is that the same standards
of political justice are demanded of king and gentleman because the same values
are at stake.

A Warning for Fair Women, the second earliest domestic tragedy extant, revolves
almost entirely upon similar matters of class and credit. The principal source in this
case is Arthur Golding's *A Briefe Discourse of the Murther of G. Saunders* (1573),
a moralising account that ironically uses theatrical metaphors to depersonalise the
action and universalise the example: 'when God bringeth such matters upon the
stage, unto ye open face of the world, it is not to the intent that men should gaze and
wonder at the persons … His purpose is that the execution of his judgements, should
by the terrour of the outward sight of the example, drive us to the inward consideration of ourselves'.[30] Ideally domestic tragedy was supposed to operate in the same
way, and *A Warning* duly rehearses the famous story of how a woman at Lyn in
Norfolk was moved to confess to the murder of her husband by witnessing a similar
event 'written by a feeling pen, / And acted by a good Tragedian' (ll. 2036–48).[31]
While providential overtones of this sort are by no means lacking in *A Warning* –
including such obligatory details as a victim's wounds bleeding in the presence of

---

[30] Quoted from *A Warning*, ed. Cannon, p. 226.
[31] A more elaborate account is provided in Thomas Heywood, *Apology for Actors* (London, 1612), sigs.
G1ᵛ-G2ʳ.

the murderer – the overall effect is quite distinct from that produced by Golding. Here we are made to 'gaze and wonder at the persons' precisely because their social positions are so closely delineated. As the play opens Anne Saunders is happily married to a wealthy 'merchant' who spends much of his days at the Royal Exchange, recently founded by Sir Thomas Gresham.[32] Her would-be seducer, Captain George Browne, finds her sitting at the door with her youngest son awaiting his return. While she rebuffs his first approach, a contemporary audience would note the potential ambivalence of the scene – a woman sitting at the door might betoken wifely concern or provocative display.[33] The episode encapsulates the essence of the social tragedy about to unfold: if a Tudor woman's place was in the home, the doorway was a dangerous liminal area. Ultimately Anne will invite Browne across the threshold into her husband's domain and an ordinary domestic door will become a 'fatall doore' (ll. 796, 1620).

What gains Browne entrance is a matter of 'credit'. When Saunders is obliged to discharge a bond on the exchange he is forced to call in all his outstanding loans: 'take heed unto my credite', he instructs his man, 'I do not use (thou knowest) to breake my worde, / Much lesse my bond' (ll. 568–70). In order to raise the full sum, however, he has the same servant deny Anne the 30 pounds she requires to pay her draper and milliner, 'so that my breach of credite', she observes, 'in the while / Is not regarded' (ll. 629–30). The recognition of her husband's priorities occasions her intense social embarrassment. 'I am a woman', she tells her confidant,

> and in that respect,
> Am well content my husband shal controule me,
> But that my man should over-awe me too,
> And in the sight of strangers, mistris *Drurie*,
> I tell you true, do's grieve me to the heart. (ll. 655–9)

'What signifies it', Drury replies, 'but he doth repose / More trust in a vilde boy, than in his wife?' (ll. 662–3). Now that Saunders' 'trust' is in question, Drury can denigrate his trade. He is a mere merchant (a 'merchant tailor', according to Golding), but Browne has independent means and access to the court. Were she to become Browne's wife Anne would be entitled to wear the clothes Saunders sells to other women:

> Now you are araide
> After a civill manner, but the next
> Shall keepe you in your hood, and gowne of silke,
> And when you stirre abroad, ride in your coach,
> And have your dozen men all in a liverie
> To waite upon you... (ll. 709–14)

---

[32] See John Guy, *Gresham's Law: The Life and World of Queen Elizabeth I's Banker* (London: Profile Books, 2019), pp. 140–50.

[33] Robert Cleaver, *A Godlie Forme of Householde Governement* (London, 1598), pp. 223–4. Quoted in Catherine Richardson, *Domestic Life and Domestic Tragedy in Early Modern England* (Manchester: Manchester University Press, 2006), p. 32.

While Mistress Arden is tempted by a social upstart, a mere 'botcher', Anne is enticed by the prospect of transcending the world of trade. None of this is in the source material. Rather, the dramatist has taken Golding's moral parable and turned it into a social tragedy. To emphasise the point he introduces three elaborate dumb shows more suggestive of the operations of Classical fate than Christian providence. During the course of the first, the Furies lay a courtly banquet at which 'Lust drinckes to Browne, he to Mistris Sanders, she pledgeth him: Lust imbraceth her, she thrusteth Chastity from her … the Furies leape and imbrace one another' (ll. 810–15). The incongruity of this 'masque' to the studied commercial 'realism' of the preceding scenes is both evident and intentional. Imported from Classical tragedy, the Furies represent the destructive forces underlying the civil veneer of middle-class society, forces identical to those that tear apart Aristotle's 'ancient lineages'. In the aftermath of Saunders' murder both Browne and Anne suffer agonies of conscience equivalent to those the Furies provoke in Orestes. While Golding saw this merely as the hand of providence, the dramatist develops it along other lines.

A Warning was staged by Shakespeare's Company, the Lord Chamberlain's Men, in 1599 the same year as *Julius Caesar* and similarities would have been evident to a contemporary audience. Like Brutus, Browne broods upon the murder to come: 'I would be alone, / My thoughts are studious and unsociable, / And so's my body, till the deede be done' (ll. 1339–41). Like Brutus, too, he loses all sense of time and direction: 'what time a day ist now? / It cannot be imagin'd by the sunne, / For why I have not seene it shine to daie' (ll. 1342–4). Similarly, when confronted by the multiple stab wounds on Saunders' servant, he finds them identical to those described by Mark Antony: 'I gave him fifteene wounds, / Which now be fifteene mouthes that doe accuse me, / In ev'ry wound there is a bloudy tongue, / Which will all speake, although he hold his peace' (ll. 1995–8).[34] These 'mouthes' effectively destroy Browne's credit: 'You were a man respected of us all, / And noted fit for many services … Now all your favours cannot do ye good' (ll. 2135–9). Browne's fate is to have his corpse hung in chains as a public spectacle – a *damnatio memoriae* worse than Arden's and the one thing he fears more than death (ll. 2232–5, 2264).

But who is Browne really? Drury's assessment is largely based on his appearance, and throughout the murder enquiry repeated reference is made to his conspicuously costly clothing, his 'white doublet and blew breeches' both made of silk but twice perceived to be flecked with blood. The yeoman of the court Buttery comfortingly suggests that 'a little sope and water' will remove the stain (l. 1520), but the dramatist has a more disturbing interest in 'blood' and its relation to gentility. In one of the most telling changes to the source material, and one that speaks powerfully to the theatrical and political moment, he makes Browne a denizen of the Irish Pale. Golding either knew nothing of this association, or had no interest in it. He needed Browne to be as similar to his readers as possible in order to point his moral: 'Were those whom we saw justly executed in Smithfield

---

[34] Compare *Julius Caesar*, II.1.61–9; II.1.100–10; II.1.259–61.

greater sinners than al other English people?' he asks. 'Were they greater sinners than all Londoners? … No verily: but except their example leade us to repentance, we shall all of us come to as sore punishment in this worlde, or else to sorer in the worlde to come'.[35] The drama plays out very differently. Ireland was in the grip of the Nine Years War and Shakespeare's *Henry V*, also staged in 1599, celebrates Essex's dispatch to reduce it to order while simultaneously calling in question the nature of Captains Macmorris and Browne's 'nation'. Browne begins *A Warning* by assuring Saunders that his people live, 'as civill in the English Pale as here, / And lawes obeide, and orders duly kept' (ll. 117–18), and proceeds to murder the man to whom he gives the assurance.[36] As in the case of the Medeas imagined by Euripides and Seneca, there are suggestions of something atavistic in Browne's recourse to violence. On his way to execution he meets his brother, arraigned for similar crimes in York. Between them, he notes, these two Palesmen have filled 'Englands two greatest townes' with slaughter (l. 2413). Rather than reducing everything to Golding's common denominator, he takes the opposite course:

> It is my other selfe hath done the deede,
> I am a thousand, every murtherer is my owne selfe,
> I am at one time in a thousand places. (ll. 2398–400)

This almost existential internalisation of evil raises the matter of domestic drama to Classical heights. In a particularly brutal form of self-discovery, the very spokesman for civil values finds the opposite endemic to himself. His passage from Whitehall to a gibbet on Shooters Hill describes the trajectory of a personal tragedy that implies a link between civility and race, echoing the prevalent suspicion that English clothing merely disguised Irish 'savagery', that gentility was born not tailored.[37]

But if Irish blood provided an all too convenient explanation for the horrors of the Saunders' case, no such assurance could be provided in that of Walter Calverley. The slaughter of his two young sons and wounding of his wife became a cause célèbre – the subject of two pamphlets, a ballad, two plays, and rampant gossip – principally because of the culprit's social status. He was local gentry, one of the 'Calverleys of Calverley' and a 'gentleman' worth 'seven or eight hundred pound a year', according to the one surviving pamphlet, the anonymous *Two most unnaturall and bloodie murthers* (1605).[38] The event focused public attention on what Ulinka Rublack has termed 'the cultural meaning of murder' and its challenge to social values.[39] The woodcut illustrating the pamphlet shows

---

[35] *A Warning*, ed. Cannon, p. 227.

[36] For the Irish on stage see Stephen O'Neill, *Staging Ireland: Representation in Shakespeare and Renaissance Drama* (Dublin: Four Courts, 2007).

[37] Richard McCabe, *Spenser's Monstrous Regiment: Elizabethan Ireland and the Poetics of Difference* (Oxford: Oxford University Press, 2002), pp. 74–7.

[38] *Two most vnnaturall and bloodie murthers*, p. 1.

[39] Ulinka Rublack, *The Crimes of Women in Early Modern Germany* (Oxford: Oxford University Press, 1999), p. 167. See also Leanore Lieblein, 'The Context of Murder in English Domestic Plays, 1590–1610', *Studies in English Literature*, 23 (1983), 181–96.

a scene of butchery more reminiscent of illustrations of New World 'savagery' than English country life – except, of course, for the gentlemanly style of the perpetrator's costume (Figure 11.1). The pamphlet enforces the incongruity by describing how Calverley held his four-year-old son at arm's length 'that the blood might not sprinkle his cloths which had staind his hart and honor' (p. 13).[40] Why had this happened? To the left of the fashionable figure brandishing an axe over the bodies of the victims we glimpse the devil encouraging the deed. That was one possible solution but, as Peter Lake has demonstrated, the woodcut is adapted from an earlier pamphlet, *Sundrye Strange and Inhumaine Murthers* (1591), describing a different event.[41] Better a demonic explanation, the publisher may have felt, than no explanation at all. Yet the woodcut is misleading in any case. Calverley's murders occurred indoors, in the very sanctum of the family home. They horrified people because of the uncanny intrusion of savagery into gentrified domesticity, and because the perpetrator was the sort of person expected to set a moral standard. The author of *Two most unnaturall and bloodie murthers* blamed prodigality, attributing its onset to divine vengeance for breach of contract.[42] But the matter remained profoundly troubling and the search for alternative explanations continued onstage in Wilkins's *Miseries of Enforced Marriage* and the anonymous *Yorkshire Tragedy*, both staged by the Lord Chamberlain's Men.[43]

In *The Miseries of Enforced Marriage* the 18-year-old Scarborough (the Calverley figure) is forced into a breach of contract by his legal guardian, Lord Faulconbridge, in what amounts to an indictment of the evils of wardship.[44] What follows is not the result of divine vengeance but social injustice. Forced to marry against his wishes, Scarborough adopts prodigality as an act of rebellion, ironically behaving like a spoilt child to prove his maturity.[45] At least in his own view, his is very much a social tragedy:

> O tis too miserable:
> That I a Gentleman should be thus torne
> From my owne right, and forcst to be forsworne. (ll. 469–71)

A gentleman's word should be his bond. Breaking it in this instance entails dishonour – to Scarborough himself, the woman he is forced to abandon but regards as his wife, the woman he marries but won't acknowledge, and the offspring he

---

[40] *Two most unnaturall and bloodie murthers* (1605), p. 13.

[41] Peter Lake, *The Antichrist's Lewd Hat: Protestants, Papists and Players in Post-Reformation England* (New Haven: Yale University Press, 2002), pp. 45–6.

[42] *Two most unnaturall and bloodie murthers* (1605), pp. 3–4.

[43] For a comparison of the two plays and the source see F. Whigham, *Seizures of the Will in Early Modern English Drama* (Cambridge: Cambridge University Press, 1996), pp. 121–87.

[44] See Glenn H. Blayney, 'Wardship in English Drama (1600–1650)', *Studies in Philology*, 53.3 (1956), 470–84.

[45] See Whigham, *Seizures of the Will*, p. 149.

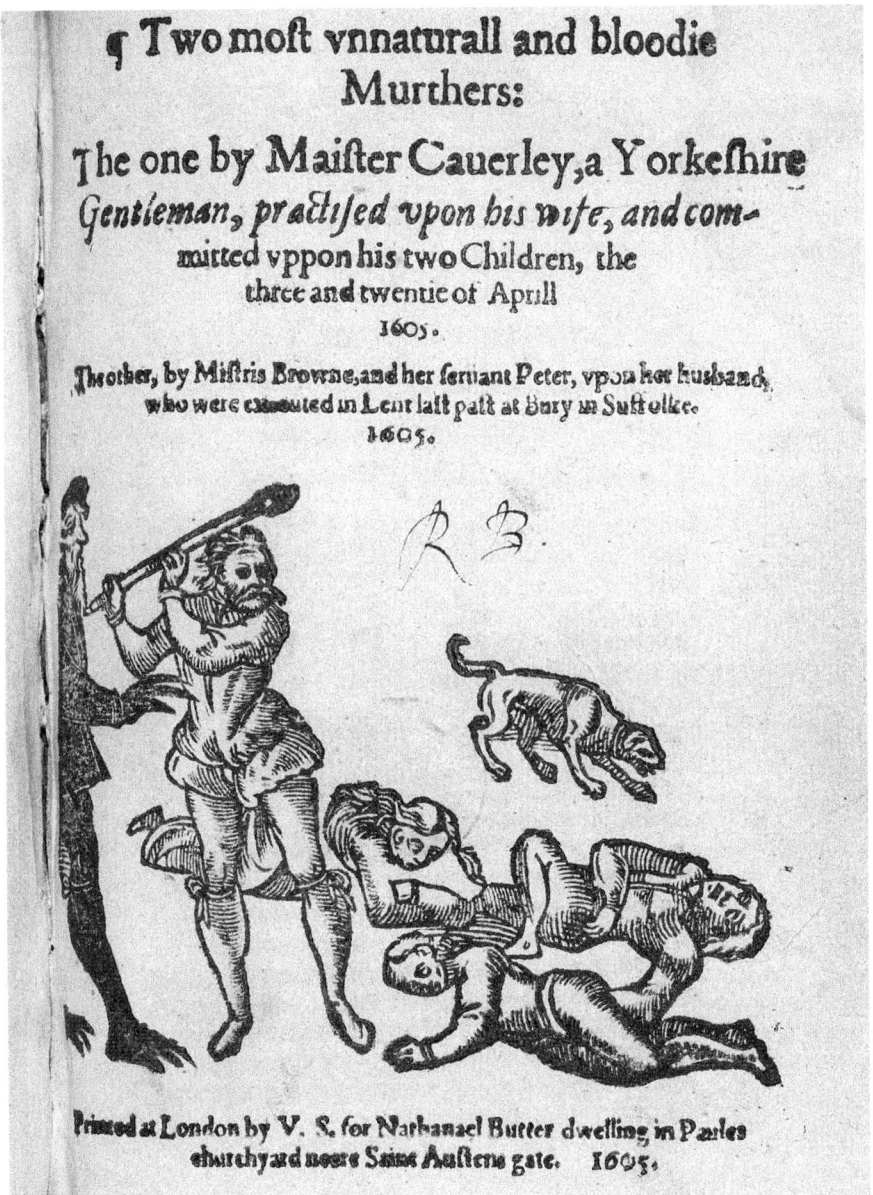

Figure 11.1 Anonymous, *Two Most Vnnaturall and Bloodie Murthers* (1605), title page. The Bodleian Libraries, University of Oxford, 4° C 16 ART BS (27).

regards as illegitimate.[46] His position is comparable to that of Frank Thorney in *The Witch of Edmonton* who marries bigamously to save his father from financial ruin and proceeds to kill his unwanted bride. The *Miseries*, however, is a tragi-comedy and the means through which Wilkins averts disaster is designed to ameliorate the social damage of actual events. Unlike Calverley, Scarborough is prevented from hurting his family by a lowly Butler who validates the social system by lecturing his master in the duties of his class. Having suffered at the hands of his guardian, Scarborough bridles at any form of 'control' or any suggestion of being 'tutored' like 'a school boy' (ll. 1325–8), but the rebuke his Butler administers exploits his own sense of *noblesse oblige*:

> **Butler:** Tis not the aime of gentry to bring forth,
> Such harsh unrellisht fruit unto their wives,
> And to their pretty pretty children by my troth.
> **Scarborrow:** How rascall.
> **Butler:** Sir I must tel you your progenitors
> Two of the which these yeares were servant to,
> Had not such mists before their understanding,
> Thus to behave themselves.
> **Scarborrow:** And youle controule me sir?
> **Butler:** I, I will. (ll. 2491–500)

'Turnes the world upside downe, that men orebeare theyr Maisters?', Scarborrow asks in amazement (ll. 2572–3). Unable to refute the Butler's arguments he orders him to doff his livery – an act equivalent to Arden's stripping Mosby of his sword – but the servant defiantly dons it again in loyalty to the family values his master has betrayed (ll. 2527–64). Matters are ultimately resolved by the convenient death of the guardian leaving his former ward a large legacy, but this was to resolve the plot without addressing the issues it raises. Faced with the horrors of the Calverley murders, Wilkins replaces recorded fact with social fantasy, one in which a Butler first restrains and then redeems his master: 'You are an honest servant, sooth you are', Scarborrow concludes, 'To whom, I these and all must pay amends' (ll. 2853–4). In this way the class system, called in question by actual events, is made to seem self-regulating and therefore 'natural'.

   A Yorkshire Tragedy takes a far more uncompromising look at its dynamics. Here the characters are denominated solely by the familial roles Calverley violated – 'Husband', 'Wife', 'Son' – and most of the action is set within the claustrophobic confines of the ancestral home.[47] There is no suggestion of an enforced marriage and the master's debauchery is presented as a social vice, stemming from what today might be termed a sense of entitlement. Not until confronted by the social

---

[46] For the legal implications of pre-contract see T. G. A. Nelson, 'Doing Things with Words: Another Look at Marriage Rites and Spousals in Renaissance Drama and Fiction', *Studies in Philology*, 95 (1998), 351–73; Diana O'Hara, *Courtship and Constraint: Rethinking the Making of Marriage in Tudor England* (Manchester: Manchester University Press, 2002).
[47] All quotations are from *Three Elizabethan Domestic Tragedies*.

consequences of his prodigality does the Husband realise how inextricable are the
financial and social components of 'credit':

> How well was I left? Very well, very well. My lands showed like a full moon about
> me, but now the moon's I'the last quarter, waning, waning; and I am mad to think that
> moon was mine. Mine and my father's, and my forefathers': generations, generations!
> Down goes the house of us, down, down it sinks. Now is the name a beggar, begs in
> me; that name, which hundreds of years has made this shire famous, in me and my
> posterity runs out. (IV.70–8)

The possible echo, or at least analogue, of Richard II's 'down, down I come ... Come
down? Down, court! Down king!' (*Richard II*, 3.3.178–82) indicates the immensity
of the loss for someone of the speaker's 'name'. But there is no element of morality in the recognition. The Husband's thoughts are worldly: 'I that did ever in
abundance dwell, / For me to want exceeds the throes of hell' (IV.92–3). With a
twisted logicality he determines to prevent the fall of the house by exterminating
it, and the sheer brutality of the following scenes well capture the horror of the
actual event. In this case a Servant's attempts to intervene – like those of Cornwall
and Regan's servants in *King Lear* (III.7.71–81) – prove wholly unsuccessful.[48]
But the real 'tragedy' of the play's title lies in what follows. The Husband is
described as having preternatural strength during the murders of his children
but, like the similarly potent homicidal protagonists of Euripides' *Herakles* and
Seneca's *Hercules Furens*, he suffers a moment of devastating anagnorisis when
the madness passes:

> I did my murders roughly out of hand,
> Desperate and sudden ...
> ... Now glides the devil from me,
> Departs at every joint ... (VIII.15–19)

The woodcut's Devil, the Christian equivalent of the envious pagan gods operative in
Euripides and Seneca, was present all along it seems. Or was he? The play does not
necessarily endorse the Husband's perception. The even more disturbing possibility
arises that it was not the Devil but the over-valuing of status that occasioned the catastrophe. Looking at the bodies of his children the Husband has cause to revise his horror
of material loss:

> Oh, that I might my wishes now attain,
> I should then wish you living were again,
> Though I did beg with you, which thing I feared. (VIII.43–6)

---

[48] For this issue see Richard Strier, 'Faithful Servants: Shakespeare's Praise of Disobedience', in H.
Dubrow and R. Strier (eds), *The Historical Renaissance: New Essays on Tudor and Stuart Literature
and Culture* (Chicago: University of Chicago Press, 1988), pp. 104–33; Mark T. Burnett, *Masters and
Servants in English Renaissance Drama and Culture: Authority and Obedience* (Basingstoke: Macmillan,
1997); Catherine Richardson, *Household Servants in Early Modern England* (Manchester: Manchester
University Press, 2010); H. Shin, 'Fatherly Violence, Motherly Absence, Servant's Resistance in
Shakespeare and his Time', *Renaissance Studies*, 25 (2011), 666–83.

If the Husband has not quite seen through a social order that discriminates between 'vassals' and 'masters' as though they were different orders of creation, he has learned something albeit too late.

The most significant factor in causing the Yorkshire Husband's change of heart is the remarkable 'kindness' shown by his wife in his fall: 'thou has devised / A fine way now to kill me' (VIII.16–17), he tells her. The exact nature of this mark of gentility is subjected to intense scrutiny in what is undoubtedly the most dramatically powerful of all the domestic tragedies, Heywood's *A Woman Killed with Kindness* (1603).[49] The disquieting question at the heart of the drama is what sort of charity, if any, a credit-driven society allows. 'He lost my kindred', says Old Mountford of the fallen Sir Charles, 'when he fell to need' (231). Kindness is supposed to be instinctive to kinship, but there are no free gifts in a world where stronger bonds are formed by commerce than consanguinity. Heywood makes the point explicitly in *The English Traveller* (1632) when Dalavill comments upon the diction of bourgeois 'courtesy':

> **Wincott:** We are bound to you, kind Master Geraldine,
> For this great entertainment. Troth, your cost
> Hath much exceeded common neighbourhood.
> You have feasted us like princes.
> **Old Geraldine:** This, and more
> Many degrees, can never countervail
> The oft and frequent welcomes given my son …
> **Wincott:** And in this,
> By trusting him to me, of whom yourself
> May have both use and pleasure, you're as kind
> As monyed men, that might take benefit
> Of what they are possessed, yet to their friends
> In need will lend it gratis …
> **Dalavill [aside]:** What strange felicity these rich men take
> To talk of borrowing, lending, and of use,
> The usurer's language right. (3.1.1–26)[50]

Though untrustworthy in other respects, Dalavill is right. Old Geraldine 'trusts' his son to Wincott in the hope of a large legacy, effectively loaning him out for interest. In this characteristic exchange, as throughout *A Woman Killed with Kindness*, 'kindness' operates through the language of the market, of credit and debit. It is not just that words from different registers are thrown together but that the registers themselves are made to blend – as in the case of the term 'bound' – creating an emotional economy that operates on the same principles as Gresham's Royal Exchange.

---

[49] All quotations are from *Three Elizabethan Domestic Tragedies*. For the most recent assessment of Heywood see Richard Rowland, *Thomas Heywood's Theatre 1599–1639: Locations, Translations and Conflict* (Farnham: Ashgate, 2010).
[50] Quoted from *A Woman Killed with Kindness and other Domestic Plays*.

When Sir Francs Acton determines to win Susan's love by defraying her brother's debts, he determines to 'fasten such a kindness on her, / As shall o'er come her hate and conquer it' (III.3.66–7). This is not a gift but an obligation and Sir Charles takes the point:

> His kindness like a burden hath surcharged me
> And under his good deeds I stooping go
> Not with an upright soul. (V.1.63–5)

Sir Charles's credit cannot bear such a 'surcharge', and his reaction exposes his true value-system. Though guilty of double homicide, he regrets his fall more than his fault. His conscience, in so far as it operates, is all too easily placated: 'It was not I but rage did this vile murder, / Yet I, and not my rage, must answer it' (I.3.51–2). The courts acquit him, but 'in this suit of pardon, he hath spent / All the revenues that his father left him, / And he is now turn'd a plain countryman' (II.2.6–8). Therein lies the rub. Even in the most straitened circumstances, and reduced to rustic dress, Sir Charles continues to pride himself on his 'gentle style'. It is invested, in very sense of the term, in his remaining land. As he explains to the usurer Shafton,

> My great great grandfather,
> He in whom first our gentle style began,
> Dwelt here, and in this ground increas'd this molehill
> Unto that mountain which my father left me.
> Where he the first of all our house begun,
> I now the last will end and keep this house,
> This virgin title never yet deflower'd
> By any unthrift of the Mountford's line. (III.1.17–24)

Should he and his sister lose this land 'our names should then be quite / Raz'd from the bead-roll of gentility'. But his debt to Sir Francis is a gentleman's debt of honour, and the only way to defray it is to reverse the 'surcharge'. It is just a matter of arithmetic. He owes Sir Francis 500 pounds. 'What do you think', he asks the unwary Susan, 'would Acton give might he enjoy your bed?'

> **Susan**: He would not shrink to spend a thousand pound
> To give the Mountford's name so deep a wound.
> **Sir Charles**: A thousand pound! I but five hundred owe;
> Grant him your bed, he's paid with interest so. (V.1.41–6)

If this were an exchange in contemporary city comedy it would doubtless be taken as an expression of the social cynicism for which the form is notorious. But this is domestic 'tragedy' and we have reached the point at which the value system of the gentry renders principle indistinguishable from parody. The man so anxious to preserve the 'virgin title' of his land will sacrifice his sister's virginity, her 'precious jewel' (V.1.53), to maintain his honour. By determining 'in one rich gift to pay back all my debt' he confounds both of the concepts involved (IV.1.124). What emerges when Sir Francis unexpectedly offers to marry Susan instead is indeed what Dalavill terms a 'strange felicity' in the sense that its elements are fundamentally incongruous. Realising the extent to which Sir Charles has 'engaged' his 'reputation' to 'grow out of my debt', Sir Francis 'recompenses' the act by accepting Susan as a 'gift' in 'satisfaction of all former wrongs' although he had previously 'thought her for her wants / Too base to be my bride' (V.1.135–46). Affection is readily commodified and the audit made up. The plot concludes not so much with a happy ending as an accountant's approval.

The mainplot, involving Sir Francis's own sister, is even more disconcerting. Although recently married to Master John Frankford, 'the most perfect'st man / That ever England bred a gentleman' (II.3.19–20), Anne succumbs to the temptations of his impoverished friend, Wendoll. The play is sometimes criticised for failing to supply adequate motivation for her 'fall', but it is writ large in its language. Frankford is the epitome of the middling sort, revelling in the 'mean':

> How happy am I amongst other men,
> That in my mean estate embrace content.
> I am a gentleman, and by my birth
> Companion with a king; a king's no more.
> I am posses'd of many fair revenues,
> Sufficient to maintain a gentleman.
>   … But, the chief
> Of all the sweet felicities on earth,
> I have a fair, a chaste, and loving wife,
> Perfection all, all truth, all ornament.
> If man on earth may truly happy be,
> Of these at once possess'd, sure I am he. (II.1.1–14)

'Possess'd' is clearly the key term. When he learns of Anne's affair, Frankford reassesses the value of his 'ornament': 'is all this seeming gold plain copper? (III.2.102).

To Frankford's calculating language of possession, sufficiency, and thrift, Wendoll opposes the sensuality of expenditure, debt, and 'hazard':

> Go, tell your husband; he will turn me off,
> And I am then undone. I care not, I;
> 'Twas for your sake. Perchance in rage he'll kill me.
> I care not, 'twas for you. Say I incur
> The general name of villain through the world,
> Of traitor to my friend; I care not, I …
> For you I'll live and in your love I'll die. (II.3.131–9)

Anne's seduction is played out on the level of imagery. Whereas Frankford's golden mean expresses itself in emotional tepidity, Wendoll's attraction is that of the passionate prodigal. The play's dramatic energy depends on violation of the virtues it overtly inculcates.

The intrusion of passion into the domestic court of 'king' Frankford takes imme-diate effect. Even so genteel an activity as a game of cards becomes beset with double meanings – 'you have serv'd me a bad trick, Master Wendoll' (III.2.180) – and the servants are forced to choose between loyalty to the master and betrayal of the mistress. The situation is fraught with danger, but it is not in Frankford's nature to risk credit for passion as Sir Charles had done. Not only does he allow himself to be restrained (and by a maid), but regards the restraint as providential.[51] When he acts it is the product not of passion but calculation – and while he calculates Anne is left to experience the full public consequences of her actions, a fall not so much from divine as social grace: 'See what guilt is; here stand I in this place, / Asham'd to look my servants in the face' (IV.4.148–9). The 'kindness' Frankford affords her is not by way of a gift but a 'usage', and one from which he extorts exorbitant interest:

> I'll not martyr thee,
> Nor mark thee for a strumpet, but with usage
> Of more humility torment thy soul,
> And kill thee, even with kindness. (IV.4.151–4)

For 'humility' read humiliation. Frankford's actions belie his words. By publicly rejecting his wife while at the same returning 'everything that hath thy mark' (V.4.162) – including, as an afterthought, the lute which formerly symbolised the 'harmony' of their union – he leaves her no way to settle the 'surcharge' but suicide. She starves herself to death, taking nothing to repay the crippling gift of everything. The contrast with the subplot is stark. Though guilty of double homicide Sir Charles resumes his position in society whereas Anne can be restored only in death. The 'providence' supposedly operating in the play is an expression of social prejudice and accordingly as arbitrary as Classical fate.

All domestic tragedies end in repentance, an overtly spiritual turn, but examined more closely the spiritual invariably reveals its social priorities. 'My fault so heinous is', Anne tells Frankfurt, 'That if you in this world forgive it not, / Heaven will not clear it in the world to come' (V.4.87–8). Even where the rhetoric seems pervasively religious, as in Yarington's *Two Lamentable Tragedies* (1601), it is generally delivered in the form of a 'gallows speech' as the culprit goes to secular justice.[52] The moral Yarington draws is appropriately civil: murder will never succeed 'where faire *Eliza* Prince of pietie, / Doth weare the peace adorned Diadem' (ll. 2737–8).[53] What I am suggesting here is that English domestic tragedy complicates the traditional distinction, more evident in the murder pamphlets, between 'shame' and 'guilt' societies. Such is the importance it vests in class that the vocabularies of sin and crime, though technically discrete, become inextricably confused:

> Oh what a horror brings this beastlinesse,
> This chiefe of sinnes, this selfe accusing crime
> Of murther: now I shame to know my selfe
> That am estrang'd so much from that I was,
> True, harmlesse, honest, full of curtesie,
> Now false, deceitfull, full of injurie.
>
> (*Two Lamentable Tragedies*, ll. 941–8)

---

[51] For Shakespeare's relationship to this type of drama see Sean Benson, *Shakespeare, 'Othello', and Domestic Tragedy* (London: Continuum, 2012).

[52] Yarington's English plot is based on accounts of a notorious murder of 1594 that was the subject of one sensational pamphlet and numerous ballads. See Lake, *The Antichrist's Lewd Hat*, pp. 24–6.

[53] All quotations are from Robert Yarington, *Two Lamentable Tragedies*, ed. C. Hanabusa (Manchester: Manchester University Press, 2013).

As it is never entirely clear what the penitent repent of – sin, crime, exposure, or loss of status – domestic tragedy hovers uneasily between validation and rejection of the morality it overtly cultivates. The setting is Christian but the ethos owes more to credit than creed. Tragedy is generated less by a conflict between the spiritual and the material than by confronting the material on its own terms. It is as though the 'rise' of the middle class, such as it was, prompted dramatic exploration of its potential for 'fall', disconcertingly linking the two through the value-system perceived to promote both. In the process early modern dramatists expanded the parameters of tragedy and anticipated the theatre of Eugene O'Neill, Tennessee Williams, and Arthur Miller.

Part IV

A Two-Way Relation

12

The Scribes of the Old Pillory:
Hired Hands and their Customers
in Sixteenth-Century Lisbon

SIMON PARK

IF THE SIXTEENTH-CENTURY *lisboeta* needed to write a letter, but lacked the enthu-
siasm, knowhow, or wherewithal to do so, there was one place where they would be
sure to find help: the Old Pillory. Just off the city's busiest shopping street, the Rua
Nova dos Mercadores, the square of the Old Pillory was where a dozen or so scribes
set up their stalls daily. At these one-stop text shops, you could order all manner of
documents, written on demand to match your needs. Their customers came from all
over the city and from all walks of life.

The scribes of the Old Pillory, then, count among those 'hidden helpers' who
have been the object of recent (and not-so-recent) studies by intellectual and cultural
historians seeking to expose the fundamentally social nature of scholarly activity
and the production of texts more broadly in the early modern period. But the scribes
of the Old Pillory do not quite fall into the same category of helper (often salaried
or part of a writer's household) whose part in the Republic of Letters Ann Blair has
been working to recuperate.[1] Nor are they quite those 'others' Armando Petrucci
has studied, namely, a set of literate individuals to whom writing was informally
delegated by others of the same social status.[2] Rather, these scribes were freelance
hands for hire, accessible, it seems, to many.[3] The scribes' commissions illustrate

---

[1] See, for instance, Ann Blair, *Too Much to Know: Managing Scholarly Information Before the Modern
Age* (New Haven: Yale University Press, 2010), pp. 104–14, and 'Erasmus and his Amanuenses', *Erasmus
Studies*, 39 (2019), 22–49. See also: Douglas Biow, *Doctors, Ambassadors, Secretaries: Humanism and
Professions in Renaissance Italy* (Chicago: University of Chicago Press, 2002).

[2] Armando Petrucci, 'Scrivere per gli altri', *Scrittura e Civiltà*, 13 (1989), 475–87.

[3] Fernando Bouza has written briefly, though on several occasions, about the scribes of the Old Pillory,
see, for instance, his 'Cultura escrita e história do livro: A circulação manuscrita nos séculos XVI e
XVII', *Leituras*, 8–9 (2002), 63–95 at 85–9. José Camões also brings together a number of the texts
written about the scribes in his introduction to the play: José Camões (ed.), *Teatro Português do século
XVI*, vol. 1 (Lisbon: Imprensa Nacional—Casa de Moeda, 2007), pp. 18–22. References to the play in
this chapter pertain to this edition and follow in the main text.

Proceedings of the British Academy, **246**, 241–257, © The British Academy 2022.

just to what degree texts were part of the everyday life of those who could not write themselves: the illiterate too, with helping hands like these – and, one might add, helping eyes and mouths, for reading was also a task to be delegated – participated in those paper exchanges of passions, complaints, petitions, and gossip alongside the lettered elite. People did not have to be able to sign their name or to decipher script to participate in the traffic of written material in early modern society.[4] The scribes served the upper strata of society too, though, finding themselves ambiguously in the middle of the social hierarchies of the period, as this chapter will show.

One might not immediately peg a city's scribal services as something to write home about, but Lisbon residents and foreign visitors alike thought them worthy of note when writing about the Portuguese capital. One scribe, sitting at his folding table, appears in the background of a painted cityscape of Lisbon from the sixteenth century found today in Kelmscott House, Oxfordshire.[5] And they even became the subject of a play. Three key sources of information about the scribes are urban registers from the 1550s that survey Lisbon's geography, built environment, and population (including very detailed statistics about the occupations of the city's inhabitants): Cristóvão Rodrigues's *Summario* (*Summary*) of 1551; João Brandão's *Grandeza e abastança de Lisboa* (*Greatness and Abundance of Lisbon*), a manuscript dating from 1552; and, finally, Damião de Góis's *Urbis Olisiponis Descriptio* (*Description of the City of Lisbon*) printed in 1554. These texts praise the city in the tradition of the *laudes civitatum*; Rodrigues and Brandão's books advertise the prosperity and grandeur of Lisbon, using demographic information and lists of churches, institutions, and employment to cast Portugal's capital as a vibrant metropolis.[6] Brandão's survey is particularly striking for its attempt to account for the city's economic activity numerically: he crunches the numbers on the amount of goods sold and the money earned by everyone in the city, converting salary in kind, such as wine, clothes, and food, into cash figures in order to quantify the 'greatness' of Lisbon, which he informs the king will be a 'coisa de admiração nas orelhas de quem o ouve' ('a thing of marvel to the ears of anyone who hears it').[7] By tabulating the salaries of all the city's population and the goods produced and sold, he gives a grand total for the capital's economic productivity, a statistic not so far removed from the modern economic measure, Gross Domestic Product. From

---

[4] For further discussion of the contact the illiterate had with the written word in early modern Iberia, see Fernando Bouza, *Corre manuscrito: Una historia cultural del Siglo de Oro* (Madrid: Marcial Pons, 2002), p. 68, and Manuel de Peña Díaz, *El laberinto de los libros. Historia cultural de la Barcelona del Quinientos* (Madrid: Fundación Germán Sánchez Ruipérez, 1997), pp. 49–53.

[5] Annemarie Jordan Gschwend, 'Reconstructing the Rua Nova: The Life of a Global Street in Renaissance Lisbon', in Annemarie Jordan Gschwend and Kate Lowe (eds), *The Global City: On The Streets of Renaissance Lisbon* (London: Paul Holberton, 2015), pp. 101–19 at 112.

[6] See José da Felicidade Alves, 'Introdução', in João Brandão, *Grandeza e abastança de Lisboa em 1552*, ed. José da Felicidade Alves (Lisbon: Horizonte, 1990), pp. 17–18 and Jeffery S. Ruth, 'Introduction', in Damião de Góis, *Lisbon in the Renaissance: A New Translation of the Urbis Olisiponis descriptio*, ed. and trans. Jeffery S. Ruth (New York: Italica Press, 1996), pp. xxvii–xxxi.

[7] Brandão, *Grandeza e abastança*, p. 69.

my perspective, the benefit of Brandão's study is that he estimates an income for every kind of employment, allowing us to compare to some extent the earnings of very different sectors of society. Góis's text is more conventionally chorographic, narrating the city's history and descriptively mapping its locales, but nonetheless reserves special emphasis for our surprising scribes and their business. He claims, falsely as it turns out, that such public scribes were a novelty in Renaissance Europe.[8] Even if such scribes are believed to have been widespread, though, information about these kinds of hands for hire is often limited, as Fernando Bouza and Miguel Ángel Extremera Extremera both note in the case of Spain.[9] Indeed, notaries and scribes who provided legal assistance have tended to be those most investigated by historians, rather than those who penned love letters or other less formal missives. Christine Métayer, though, has studied extensively the Old Pillory scribes' parallel in Paris, the scribes of the Saints-Innocents cemetery, who also provided a range of services particularly to the lower rungs of the social hierarchy.[10] Finally, Rodrigues's summary focuses principally on the religious institutions of the city, pronouncing that foreigners will be amazed by the 'obras pias' (holy works) that go on in Lisbon, but he nevertheless provides a long list of the different secular institutions and forms of occupation to be found in the city in the second half of his book.[11] It is here that the scribes make their appearance. Our professional scribblers also turn up in the travelogue of a Spaniard, Bartolomé de Villaba y Estañá, and in an anecdote from a sixteenth-century manuscript repertory of courtly stories, which is today held in the Library of Congress.[12] Their most sustained representation comes, however, in the anonymous farce, the *Auto dos escrivães do Pelourinho* (*The Play of the Scribes of the Pillory*).

The play exists as a pamphlet printed in 1625 in Lisbon, although, as José Camões notes in the introduction to his modern edition of the text, it was likely written a century earlier given a series of references in the text that would date it to 1520–4.[13] We know from Nicolau de Oliveira's *Livro das grandezas de Lisboa* from 1620, however, that scribes still had stalls at the Old Pillory in the seventeenth century.[14] The action proceeds in the processional manner of most plays of

---

[8] Góis, *Lisbon in the Renaissance*, p. 27.

[9] See: Bouza, *Corre Manuscrito*, p. 72; and Miguel Ángel Extremera Extremera, 'La pluma y la vida: Escribanos, cultura escrita y socieded en la España Moderna (siglos XVI–XVIII)', *Litterae*, 3–4 (2003–4), 187–206 at 194.

[10] Christine Métayer, *Au tombeau des secrets: Les écrivains publics du Paris populaire; Cimetière des Saints-Innocents, XVIe–XVIIIe siècles* (Paris: Albin Michel, 2000).

[11] Cristóvão Rodrigues, *Summario ẽ que brevemente se contem alguas cousas (assi ecclesiasticas como seculares) que ha na cidade de Lisboa* (Lisbon: Germão Galharde, 1551), sig. [F vii^r].

[12] See: Bartolomé Villaba y Estañá, *El pelegrino curioso y grandezas de España*, 2 vols (Madrid: Miguel Ginestra, 1886–9), vol. II (1889), 57; and *Anedotas Portuguesas e Memórias Biográficas da Corte Quinhentista*, ed. Christopher Lund (Coimbra: Almedina, 1980), pp. 74–5.

[13] Camões, *Teatro do século XVI*, p. 23. The relevant details are that Francisco de Casal is mentioned as the *meirinho das cadeiras* and that the king was in Évora.

[14] Nicolau de Oliveira, *Livro das grandezas de Lisboa* (Lisbon: Jorge Rodrigues, 1620), fol. 95^v.

the early sixteenth century, particularly those of Gil Vicente, where a rolling cast of characters arrive on stage to meet a set of individuals who remain static; here, after an opening scene between two servants, a carousel of customers approach two scribes stationed at the Old Pillory and ask them to prepare letters, just as, for instance, plaintiffs and defendants approach the clownish judge, Pêro Marques, in *Juiz da Beira* (*The Beira Magistrate*, 1525). The customers in the play come from those we would traditionally place among the lower orders: an *atafoneiro* (miller), a *vilão* (village dweller), a *ratinho* (a migrant to the city from the countryside, who usually took up an unskilled job), a black man, an old woman, and a squire's servant. They are also stock characters of sixteenth-century farce, who, more often than not, attempt to cross social boundaries and end up ridiculed for this: for example, in this play, the old woman seeks a husband, transgressing the sexist and ageist expectations of the period, and the servant's master is in love with a woman considerably further down the social hierarchy.

The usual caveats about taking any text at face value must be heeded here – particularly when dealing with texts that are supposed to be funny – but considering that all the texts that mention the scribes offer a more or less coherent view of their activities we can at least infer that there was something of a shared idea of what these scribes did and who their customers were in the middle decades of the sixteenth century. What is particularly clear from accounts of the textual commissions made at the Old Pillory is that the scribes occupied an ambiguous place in the social hierarchy. They are something of an object lesson in how tricky it can be to grapple with professional identity in the early modern period and to draw any straightforward conclusions about how earnings related to social standing or, indeed, to determine what an occupation outside the principal institutions of power in Lisbon meant for social status and financial success. In trying to explore what we might be able to draw from the stories told about the scribes of the Old Pillory, I will deal firstly with the scribes and their own position within the shifting terms of social appraisal in sixteenth-century Portugal, before turning to their interactions with their customers and what this might tell us about the intersection between social status and written culture.

The scribes refuse to fit neatly into taxonomies of social status or occupations of the period, not least because any such taxonomies were far from neat themselves. In response to social mobility, particularly the upward clambering of the increasingly wealthy bourgeoisie, monarchs tried on more than one occasion in the sixteenth century to stabilise the categories of the nobility. Most notably, the *Ordenações Manuelinas* (1512–13) set financial restrictions on nobles, requiring them to maintain a certain degree of wealth to keep their status, and then, later in the century, D. Sebastião rationalised existing categories to establish two sets of more rigidly defined hierarchies within the court and to make the court records the ultimate arbiter of noble status. One order of the nobility was supposed to be restricted to the blood aristocracy while the other (with confusingly similar nomenclature) was intended to be a secondary hierarchy for those who rose through the ranks by the good graces of the king (see Table 12.1)

Table 12.1 Regulations for noblemen in the royal household from 1573

1st Order	2nd Order
Fidalgo Cavaleiro	Cavaleiro-fidalgo
Fidalgo escudeiro	Escudeiro-fidalgo
Moço-fidalgo	Moço de câmara

Source: This table is taken from João Cordeiro Pereira, 'A estrutura social e o seu devir', in *Portugal do Renascimento à crise dinástica*, ed. João José Alves and A. H. de Oliveira Marques (Lisbon: Presença, 1999), pp. 277–336 at 294.

As João Cordeiro Pereira notes, though, there were always individuals who slipped between categories.[15] These laws made more difficult, but did not entirely curb, the entry of the lower orders into the highest official ranks of Portuguese society.

Beyond the nobility, hierarchies were fuzzier still. A central bias of writings from the period that seek to present a global picture of Portuguese society is how top-heavy they are; those at the pinnacle are sifted into several categories, while those below are lumped together into fewer, broader heaps. To write accounts of how social status was perceived among those below the upper crust of the elite, social historians have had to venture beyond the tracts of scholars and officials and mine different forms of evidence, such as court records, for patterns of mutual and self-appraisal. Their findings encourage us to resist broad-brush categorisations – such as the traditional division of society into the three estates – that derive from elite documentation and to consider instead how status was negotiated dynamically in specific texts and circumstances.[16]

A telling example of the sizeable grey areas in Portuguese descriptions of the social hierarchy written 'from above' is the ambiguously named category, found between *escudeiros* (squires) (the lowest category of the nobility) and the 'mechanical occupations', of the 'outra gente limpa' (other clean people) – a label which served as something of a catchall to demarcate the rather heterogeneous group who occupied the middle rungs of society well into the sixteenth century.[17] The idea of *limpeza* (cleanness) here has to do with not working with one's hands (or being descended from someone who did) and being a Christian. Yet, the idea of what counted as a 'clean' occupation was up for debate in the period as artisans sought to establish the dignity of their craft by the value of the end product they created or of the materials that they worked with. For example, architects claimed

[15] Pereira, 'A estrutura social', p. 287.
[16] See the discussion in Alexandra Shepard, *Accounting for Oneself: Worth, Status, and the Social Order in Early Modern England* (Oxford: Oxford University Press, 2015), pp. 2–8.
[17] See Pereira, 'A estrutura social', p. 282. Portugal's official historiographer, João de Barros, also uses this term in the mid century: João de Barros, *Terceira decada da Asia de Ioam de Barros* (Lisbon: João de Barreira, 1563), sig. R iii[r].

the magnificence of buildings lifted them above the lowliness of the materials they worked with and goldsmiths sought to claim a status above others who created things with their hands by the luxury of the raw materials they chased and hammered into glittering shape.[18] Even when more rigid restrictions on 'blood purity' were established in 1570, the services of genealogists could be enlisted to obscure or erase any 'dubious' origins that might prevent access to the upper echelons of society.[19] Our scribes, as we will see, occupied this ill-defined and ever mobile middle ground in the social landscape.

At first glance, the secular section of Rodrigues's *Summario* appears uncon-cerned with the language of social distinction and, instead, focuses on occupations performed by and institutions made up of those from across the social spectrum. However, the final subdivisions of his survey do intersect with those of traditional hierarchies: he splits those working outside government institutions into 'gente d'oficios' (professionals), 'officiães mechanicos' (mechanical occupations), and then 'molheres' (women) – that women constitute an entirely separate category, relegated to the end of his survey, tells us very plainly that gender habitually usurped many other markers of identity.[20] That Rodrigues includes a category for 'gente d'oficios' already marks his demography as different from traditional hierarchies that tended to use vaguer terms for this middle zone. Moreover, on closer inspection, Rodrigues's catalogue of institutions, which comes before the section for 'gente d'oficios', reveals an order of precedence between them: firstly the courts, which he moves through in terms of their relative importance, starting with the Court of Appeal ('Casa da Soplicacam'), the 'principal and supreme justice of the land' ('a principal E suprema da justiça de todo o reyno'),[21] and proceeding down to the lesser tribunals, before he moves on to government institutions that dealt with imports, taxation, etc. This is interesting as it suggests that status might be influenced not only by *what* kind of job an individual had but also *where* they performed it. That the courts and governmental institutions are separated from other kinds of occupa-tion perhaps signals the importance typically accorded to positions in the govern-ment or military because of the fact that these counted as service to the crown. It is a commonplace of the historiography on the period to state that such public offices were the most sought after for the regularity of the benefits that came with them (typically *tenças*, i.e. annual pensions) and the possibilities for rising through the

---

[18] Mafalda Soares da Cunha and Igor Knezevic, 'Iberian Society', in Fernando Bouza, Pedro Cardim, and Antonio Feros (eds), *The Iberian World, 1450–1820* (Abingdon: Routledge, 2019), pp. 142–65, at 155. See also my discussion of poets and their relation to artisans and nascent ideas of professionalisa-tion in *Poets, Patronage and Print in Sixteenth-Century Portugal: From Paper to Gold* (Oxford: Oxford University Press, 2021), pp. 32–4.

[19] Cunha and Knezevic, 'Iberian Society', p. 147.

[20] Cunha and Knezevic suggest that notaries and scribes were placed among the 'mechanical' occupations by those above them in the social hierarchy, but this does not appear to be the case here. See Cunha and Knezevic, 'Iberian Society', p. 154.

[21] Rodrigues, *Summario*, sig. E iiiiᵛ.

ranks that they offered.[22] As Virginia Rau notes in respect of the Casa dos Contos, jobs as scribes drawing up official documents were often used as rewards for service and many saw such a position as a first rung on the professional and social ladder.[23]

Unlike most of the scribes listed in urban registers, though, those at the Old Pillory operated outside the walls of any institution. Damião de Góis notes that those who set up stalls at the Old Pillory were not bound to an official city role ('nullis tamen ciuitatis ministeriis obligatos').[24] Rodrigues includes the 'escrivães do Pelourinho' alongside 'tabeliães das notas' (notaries) in a subsection that lies in his survey between the section detailing the occupational composition of the courts and that dealing with other civil institutions, which, in itself, suggests their liminal place in society.[25] One might call them, then, a species of freelancer. Crucially, by where he situated the scribes within the pages of his survey, Rodrigues differentiates the scribes of the Old Pillory from those in so-called 'mechanical' occupations or indeed from the 'gente d'oficios', such as physicians, surgeons, botanists, musicians, grammar teachers, reading teachers, singing teachers, and dancing teachers, who also provided services.[26] In other words, as neither professionals, nor artisans, nor government functionaries, nor traders, nor labourers, the scribes' exact place in social hierarchy remains challenging to parse: it is much easier to say what they were not rather than what they were. They hovered somewhere in the interstices between the lower nobility and the mechanical occupations, both categories with fluctuating fringes of definition themselves. As with freelancers today, the scribes had no structured career path, they operated outside those institutions of government, household, military, church, or guild that had their own internal pecking order (and, indeed, relative, inter-institutional status).

When we consider their earnings, the scribes begin to seem even more unusual. The court anecdote, the play, and Brandão's *Grandeza e abastança* all indicate that the scribes charged a flat fee of a *vintém* (=20 reais) per letter. This appears to have been an accessible price and suggests that their business model was based on selling missives to the many by charging a low rate. For comparison, in 1520, around when the play was possibly written, an *alquiere* (standard volume measure for cereals = 13.1 litres) of wheat costed 30 reais in Lisbon, rising to 72 reais by 1531 (excluding the years of famine in this decade where prices skyrocketed).[27] A dozen eggs was priced at a *vintém* in 1524.[28] When Brandão was writing, where he

---

[22] For the idea that government or military offices were the most sought after, see Pereira, 'A estrutura social', pp. 286–8, 323; Carroll B. Johnson, *Cervantes and the Material World* (Urbana: University of Illinois Press, 2000), pp. 25–6; and Cunha and Knezevic, 'Iberian Society', p. 143.

[23] Virgínia Rau, *A Casa dos Contos* (Coimbra: Faculdade de Letras da Universidade de Coimbra, 1951), pp. 281–7.

[24] Damião de Góis, *Vrbis Olisiponis Descriptio* (Évora: André de Burgos, 1554), sig. C iii[v].

[25] Rodrigues, *Summario*, sig. [E vii[r]].

[26] Rodrigues, *Summario*, sig. F iii[r].

[27] For prices of wheat, see Mário Viana, 'Alguns preços de cereais em Portugal (séculos XIII-XVI)', *Arquipélago*, 2nd ser., 11–12 (2007–8), 207–79 at 241–4.

[28] This price is taken from the 'Lisbon Prices: Animal Products' file as part of the online datasets: *Prices, Wages and Rents in Portugal 1300–1910*, http://pwr-portugal.ics.ul.pt/, accessed 3 June 2015.

also gives the 20 reais price for the letters, he cites a figure of 67 reais for an *alquiere* of wheat and adds that this price 'não é muito caro nem muito barato' ('is neither very expensive nor very cheap').[29] As for the sorts of figures who appear in the play, the scribes' services were certainly not out of reach of the average miller who earned 105,600 reais/annum – a figure which exceeded many professionals and middle-ranking officials – and were likely within the grasp of domestic servants, like the 'moço' [servant], who earned around 2,000 reais a year, in addition to food, lodging, and clothing, or even in the reach of unskilled day labourers whose rates in Lisbon average between 30 and 35 reais/day in the 1520s rising to 50 reais/day by 1552.[30]

From all accounts, the scribes had no shortage of custom. Helpfully, Brandão estimates the average annual salary of each of the scribes for us: 60,000 reais.[31] This figure is around double the salary of many of the institutional scribes listed in Brandão's survey.[32] It is comparable to the earnings of lower-ranked lawyers and exceeds estimates for skilled day-labourers such as masons, painters, and carpenters, placing the scribes at the salary-level one would expect of someone in the middle of the social order.[33] Yet, Brandão adds to his description that this scribal work proved extremely lucrative for one scribe in particular: he notes that 'entre eles há homem que ganha com que casa filhos e filhas, e compra propriedades' ('there is among them a man who earns enough that he can marry his sons and daughters and buy properties').[34] The ability to afford dowries and to own properties was typically associated with those of high social status, so this points rather intriguingly to how ostensible markers of status were becoming accessible to a broader range of individuals – particularly merchants – troubling the hierarchies of old.[35] The scribes were far from the only 'self-made' entrepreneurs in sixteenth-century Lisbon. Brandão, to take one surprising example, remarks that there were *tripeiras* (women who sold tripe) rich enough to wear gold jewellery and who ended up at dinners in monasteries and great houses. The success of vendors of petty goods certainly points to the muddling of markers of social status, but also suggests, as in the case of the scribes, how hawking a low-value good in bulk – the cooked tripe sold for 5–15 reais, i.e. a little less than the letters – was an effective way of turning a profit in the city. We might thus conclude from the scribes' takings that they benefited from operating outside the regulated institutions that employed most of Lisbon's professional scribes: being self-employed, they had the potential to draw in a better income and one without any of the pre-determined limits of a regular salary.

[29] Viana, 'Alguns preços de cereais', 248.
[30] Brandão, *Grandeza e abastança*, p. 70. For the rates for unskilled labourers, see the 'Daily Wages Lisbon' file as part of the *Prices, Wages and Rents in Portugal 1300–1910* dataset.
[31] Brandão gives a figure of 5 cruzados a day and an estimate of 1500 cruzados a year for their combined salary, which gives 60,000 reais each per annum. See Brandão, *Grandeza e abastança*, p. 109.
[32] See, for example, the figures quoted for the scribes of the treasury and the sheriff in Brandão, *Grandeza e abastança*, pp. 176–8.
[33] For the lawyers, see Brandão, *Grandeza e abastança*, p. 151. For the day-rates for skilled labourers, see the 'Daily Wages Lisbon' file as part of the *Prices, Wages and Rents in Portugal 1300–1910* dataset.
[34] Brandão, *Grandeza e abastança*, pp. 108–9.
[35] Cunha and Knezevic, 'Iberian Society', p. 159.

Brandão's observations about the wealth of the scribes are also borne out by the anonymous *auto*'s more indirect clues to the scribes' financial situation. In the *auto*'s opening scene, a conversation between the two servants, Duarte, a professional pickpocket, says that his friend, Gonçalo, is foolish for ditching the scribe as his master because he was given enviable conditions when working for him (ll. 91–5) – Gonçalo has, before the play begins, stolen his master's folding table and gambled away the money he earned from selling it (ll. 86–90). In Gonçalo's absence later in the play, his master offers a fool ('parvo') a job as his servant ('criado') and promises to offer him food, lodging, and clothing. That he can afford to provide this for his *criado* is further suggestion of relative material comfort. This economic information also has a literary historical dimension: the farce riffs on, and upturns, the dramatic trope of the penniless squire, whose servants grumble about the penury they find themselves in. Several of Gil Vicente's *autos* from the same era as the anonymous play give voice to the gripes of servants stuck in the retinue of an *escudeiro* with not much money.[36] For instance, in the opening dialogue of *Quem tem farelos?* (*Who has bran?*) (1505), Ordoño asks Apariço how things are going with his master. He replies 'S'eu moro c'um escudeiro/ como me pode a mi ir bem?' ('If I live with a squire/ what can be going well?'), before complaining about having nothing to eat and living in poor conditions. The financial precarity of those on the fringes of the nobility in the sixteenth century has been much discussed and is regularly portrayed in Vicente's theatre in contrast to the wealth of the upwardly mobile lower and middling sorts.[37] The reason that Apariço stays is the promise of access to the court through the connections of his master, the cacophonous songster, Aires Rosado. So when Ordoño asks him why he does not leave, he replies plainly: 'Diz que m'há de dar a el rei' ('He says he will present me to the king'). The conversation between Duarte and Gonçalo in the play about the scribes of the Old Pillory mirrors this Vicentine sketch, but offers us the image in reverse: unlike Apariço, Gonçalo was onto a good thing and squandered it. Working for the *escrivão* offered much better conditions than working for an *escudeiro*; where the master is routinely the satirical butt of the roguish knave's jokes in Vicente's plays, here the employers come off as reasonable and likeable. Considered in parallel, the texts seem to offer two options for the low-status characters that each involves a trade-off: the possibility of material comfort in the employ of a scribe, or the (doubtful) hope of social advancement in service to an impoverished *escudeiro*. This parallels the choice the scribes themselves potentially faced between the prospect of profit as a freelancer or the opportunity for rising through the ranks as a civil servant. Within these scenes, we see a calculus of

---

[36] For the character of the *escudeiro* in Vicentine theatre, see José Augusto Cardoso Bernardes, *Gil Vicente* (Lisbon: Edições 70, 2008), p. 214.

[37] For instance, Shankar Raman reads Vicente's *Auto da Índia* as, in part, inflected by the struggles of the nobility to regain their status against the upwardly mobile merchant class: Shankar Raman, *Renaissance Literatures and Postcolonial Studies* (Edinburgh: Edinburgh University Press, 2011), p. 103. One could also see this tension in the *Farsa de Inês Pereira* in the decision the eponymous heroine has to make between the *escudeiro*, Brás de Mata, and the wealthy bumpkin, Pêro Marques.

benefits that weighs long-term social aspiration against immediate material comfort, formalised status against what could (quite literally) be afforded by money.

The scribes offered a variety of services to their customers. Góis lists an impressive gamut of textual products that they could produce: 'letters, amorous messages, eulogies, speeches, epitaphs, verses, encomiums, funeral prayers, petitions, notes and other things of this kind that are asked of them'.[38] Although what they appear to have been especially known for, at least insofar as it offered material for a courtly anecdote or comic scene, are love letters. Even when it came to a particular genre, though, the scribes could serve a range of functions: reading letters aloud, transcribing letters dictated to them, or indeed composing them from scratch once informed of the client's predicament. In the play, the *ratinho*, Gonçalo, for instance, appears on stage clutching a letter of which the contents and the identity of the correspondent remain an enigma. He has to ask one of the scribes to read it for him, but not before lamenting his unfortunate situation:

> Ah, cartinha quem te fez?
> Por que não queres falar?
> Ai, ajuda-me a suspirar
> porqu'é certo que tu vens
> da causa do meu penar.
> Como vai a Catalina?
> Não me queres responder?
> Por quem te mandou escrever?
> Nam quer a minha mofina
> que o tu saibas dizer. (ll. 632–41)

> Oh, little letter, who is your author?
> Why don't you want to speak?
> Ah, help me to yearn,
> for it is certain that you come
> from the cause of my woes.
> How is Catalina?
> Do you not want to reply to me?
> Who ordered you be written?
> My misfortune does not wish
> that you be able to tell me.

His apostrophe to the letter must have raised a chuckle from the audience. But his seemingly silly soliloquy also does something surprising to the idea of literacy itself. Agency shifts from man to missive; Gonçalo recasts his inability to read as the recalcitrance (or, indeed, incompetence) of the letter: it does not *want* to speak ('não queres falar') or respond to his queries ('Não me queres responder?'). At one level, this is a reminder of the frustrations of receiving, but not being able to read, a letter, particularly when one desperately awaits news from a beloved, but it also suggests that for the illiterate, who can speak a language, just not decipher its script, there is something unintuitive, almost wilfully resistant, about the written word.

---

[38] Góis, *Lisbon in the Renaissance*, p. 27.

However, most of the characters in the play are confident in their powers of expression and ask the scribes to write down what they say. Although it must be said that from the initial interactions between several characters and the hands they sought to hire that the scribes themselves did not assume this would be the case: one of the scribes asks the Vilão twice who is to 'notar' (compose) the letter (ll. 450–1, 465) to his beloved. In his response to the second question – the first is answered only with complaints about his situation – the Vilão underlines that it is he who will compose this piece of correspondence and that the scribe's task was one of transcription only: he does this by distinguishing between two verbs, namely, 'notar' (composing) and 'escrever' (writing down). Even so, we can detect in the play's dialogue that a certain amount of anxiety accompanied the delegation of the task of writing. The customers frequently ask for the letter to be re-read aloud before they will let the scribe seal it and write the 'sobrescrito' (address): a check perhaps both of what they have said, but also the accuracy of what the scribe had written.

At times, however, the scribes were more involved in the compositional process. The court anecdote, for instance, describes the client, D. Simão da Silveira, giving only the simplest brief to his servant to pass on to the scribes who then composed the required missive themselves in its entirety. The anecdote is worth quoting in full for the details it gives:

> Dom Simão da Silveira, filho 2° do conde da Sortelha, D. Luís da Silveira, de quem se já falou, foi um dos melhores cortesões do seu tempo, muito discreto e muito estimado por tal. Tanto que estando o príncipe D. João, pai del rei D. Sebastião, concertado a casar com a princesa Joana, filha do emperador Carlos 5°, com quem casou, assentou el rei D. João o 3°, seu pai, em seu Conselho que convinha escrever o dito príncipe à dita princesa ũa carta, cuja matéria havia de ser amores. E mandando el rei a todos os cortesões que fizessem cartas de amores pera que de todas se escolhesse a que no Conselho parecesse melhor para ir em nome do príncipe á princesa, cada um se cansou muito em compor a sua. E julgando D. Simão este trabalho por escusado, mandou um moço com um vintém aos escrivães do Pelourinho que lhe trouxesse uma carta de um galante pera sua dama, e que fosse a primeira que lhe mandasse. Esta carta foi com as mais ao Conselho e por ir em nome de D. Simão foi julgaga por melhor e se mandou à princesa.[39]

> D. Simão da Silveira, son of the second Count of Sortelha, D. Luís da Silvera, who has already been mentioned, was one of the greatest courtiers of his age, very discreet and esteemed for being so. When Prince João, father of the future King D. Sebastião, had agreed to marry Princess Joana, daughter of the Emperor Carlos V, the king, D. João III, agreed with his Council that it would be appropriate for the aforementioned prince to write a love letter to this princess. Because the king ordered all the courtiers to write love letters so that the Council could choose the best one and send it in the prince's name to the princess, they all toiled over their letters. D. Simão, though, thinking that this was a waste of time, sent one of his men with a *vintém* to the scribes of the Old Pillory to get a letter written by a chivalrous (*galante*) man to his lady, and asked that it be written as though it were the first time he was writing to her. This letter was submitted with all the others to the Council and because it was D. Simão's submission it was judged to be the best and was sent to the Princess.

---

[39] *Anedotas Portuguesas*, pp. 74–5.

All the scribes needed to know, then, was that the style needed to be *galante* (just like the letters in the *auto*) and a little about the context: i.e. this was the first time the man was writing to the lady in question. That the letter, penned by a scribe of the middling sort, goes first in the name of the noble, D. Simão, and then in the prince's points to the ease with which authorship (and therefore social status) could be elided in written materials. Just as the king passed on the task of writing to his courtiers, D. Simão does the same by delegating (via his boy) to the scribes of the Old Pillory. The job of composition is passed down the social hierarchy in both cases, but the signature (or, perhaps, even just the name) of the social superior erases the trace of this delegation. The anecdote specifies that the letter was chosen out of all those in the competition because it had D. Simão's name on it and that he was known for being 'discreto' (discreet). His reputation mattered in the reception of this love note and he knew exactly how to trade on his good name to avoid breaking a sweat. This story also foregrounds differing reasons for deputising writing: for the king, delegation involves a search for the best quality epistle, but for D. Simão it was about not wasting his time: while the other courtiers fretted over their submissions, he found a cunningly easy workaround. One assumes too that the scribes were able to produce a letter of credible enough *discrição* (a style coterminous with the court) not to have given the game away.

With this lazy (or ingenious?) courtier, there is something of an assumption made that the scribes will be able to rattle off the sort of letter of amorous initiation required of a courtier. But when a different 'moço' (servant) comes to the scribes, this time in the play, having been tasked with being the amorous go-between for his master, the scribe he commissions provides a more bespoke service still:

ESCRIVÃO SEGUNDO: Ora diga ao que vem
                      servi-lo-ei se mandar.
MOÇO: Quero que seja informado
                      do caso a que venho aqui:
                      eu estou com um pelado
                      de um escudeiro assi
                      muito grande namorado.

                      E tem-m' ele prometido
                      se lhe eu arrecadar
                      isto que quero contar
                      um muito fino vestido
                      diz que mo há logo de dar.
                      E é que anda d'amores
                      c'uma filha da sardinheira
                      que agora é tripeira
                      ela não lhe dá favores
                      do que ele tem canseira.

E mandou-me um recado
agora a sua casa
e eu não sei o que faça.
Sequer por ir aviado
faça-me ũa carta falsa.
Como que vem da sua mão
ganharei eu o vestido
e mostre ter-lhe afeição
dizendo que o coração
só por ele tem perdido.

ESCRIVÃO SEGUNDO: Eu farei isso mui bem
se me for mui bem pagado.
MOÇO: Aqui trago eu diputado
para isso um vintém.
ESCRIVÃO SEGUNDO: Como dizia o recado?
MOÇO: Dizia, senhor, assi:
eu sou mui pouco alembrado
senhora do meu cuidado
mas alembrai-vos de mim
que por vós vivo penado.

Escreve o Escrivão a carta entre si desta maneira:
Senhor,
Cá me mandou um recado
em que dá a entender
que eu que lhe dou cuidado
e que de mi não é lembrado
e que o deixo morrer.
Por certo que tudo isso
se encerra em mim senhor
que sam presa de seu amor.
Por ver-lo em seu serviço
não lhe escrevo mais senhor.

ESCRIVÃO SEGUNDO: A moça como se diz?
MOÇO: À moça chamam Maria
segundo a mãe dizia.
ESCRIVÃO: Sua servidora Maria.
Ora escutai o que fiz
vereis cousa à maravilha.

Lê o Escrivão a carta acima escrita e acabada diz o Moço:
Está, meu senhor, tam bem
que não pode mais estar
há-ma logo de cerrar. (ll. 357–413)

SECOND SCRIBE:	So tell me why you're here And I'll help you out, if you wish.
SERVANT:	Let me tell you about why I've come here: I'm the servant of a Completely penniless squire Who's madly in love.

And he's promised me
That if I can sort out
What I'm about to tell you
He says he'll give me
A very fine garment.
The situation is: he's besotted
With the daughter of a fishmonger
Who's a tripe-seller now
And she won't give him a second look
And he's really fed up with this.

So he sent me with a message
To her house
And I don't know what to do.
Maybe if you write me a fake letter
That looks like it's written by her
I'll be able to resolve this situation
And I'll get my garment:
Make it look like she likes him,
That she's only got eyes for him.

SECOND SCRIBE:	I can certainly do that for you, If I get a good fee.
SERVANT:	I've got a *vintém* here specially put aside For that very purpose.
SECOND SCRIBE:	So, what did the letter say? It said the following: All my cares have been ignored By you, my lady, But think of me now Because I'm living a life of suffering because of you.

The scribe writes the letter:

                    Sir,
             You've sent me a letter
             That says that
             I'm causing you pain
             And that I haven't acknowledged you
             And that I'm letting you die.
             Certainly, all this
             Is my doing
             Because I'm imprisoned by your love.

> So that you get back to your duties
> I won't write to you again.

SECOND SCRIBE: What's the girl called?
SERVANT: They call her, Maria,
According to what her mother said.
SCRIBE: Your servant, Maria
Right, listen to what I've written,
And you'll be blown away.

The Scribe reads the letter written above and when he finishes the servant says:

SERVANT: Sir, I couldn't have put it better myself!
Seal up that letter for me now.

The response that the scribe provides for the Moço's predicament deploys the tropes of courtly love, wittily using the commonplace figure of love as a prison to imply that she is unable to respond to him, but still in love. In this act of composition, the scribe goes from transcriber to problem solver verging on agony uncle. The scene is funny for the scribe's lack of scruples. Indeed, he suggests to the Moço that he is very familiar with this kind of customer and knows just what will work for him: 'Isto para homens vãos/ não é senão marmelada' ('This is pure catnip for ridiculous men'). The scribes' skill is in analysing a social situation and matching a missive to its recipient to have the desired effect; they are social advisors as well as writers. For the servant, the *vintém* spent on the scribe is a small price to pay for the prospect of the 'muito fino vestido' he might get as his reward – clothes in any luxury cloth would have been a significant prize. If D. Simão da Silveira won the kudos of pleasing the king by delegating to the scribes (and the eventual notoriety of the anecdote), the servant could get a much more direct, material return from his outlay with the scribes.

Some of the same issues around the elision of authorship present in the courtly anecdote also recur here in a weave of interactions between characters of differing social status. Communication is again doubly mediated: first by the servant as messenger and then by the scribe. One begins to think that with the scribes of the Old Pillory, written communication slides rather easily into deceitful ventriloquism. To use the distinctions between 'notar' and 'escrever' that operate in the play, a name signed at the bottom of a letter was no guarantee that it had been either physically written ('escrito') or composed ('notado') by that person.

We might take this idea of ventriloquism further by thinking about how the lowly characters in the play themselves replicate a discourse of love usually associated with the court. That the servant and scribe think that such a witty letter would seem believable coming from a tripe-seller's daughter, perhaps makes the *escudeiro* seem all the more delusional. And yet, at the same time, perhaps she really could have sent such a letter: certainly, most of the lowborn characters in the play gush with courtly turns of phrase. To take one example, the miller,

Afonso Gil, dictates a letter containing the quintessential trope of courtly lyric, namely, dying while living:

> Digo que mouro vivendo
> por vos ver minha senhora
> não sejais vós causadora
> de m'eu estar cá morrendo
> vinde vós já dessa Évora. (ll. 600–4)

> I say that I die while living
> when I see you, my lady,
> don't be the cause
> of my being here dying
> come back already from Évora.

This letter sounds like one that would be sent by a courtier, or even, as the courtly anecdote suggested, by a king. This could simply be pure invention for the sake of a gag, but it might just hint that courtly forms of expression leaked out of their traditional social milieu. The poet, Diogo Bernardes, at least, reports in a verse letter of a fish-fryer adopting a form of address that was supposed to be restricted only to the noblest of the noble.[40] The monarchy even legislated against such slippage of social categories, but it never quite tethered the drift of language.[41] Of course, whether real or imagined, words or expressions with courtly associations might sound quite different coming from people like the characters in the play. A proverb of the period encapsulates this tension: 'donde vem Pedro a falar galego?', which literally means, 'how did Pedro come to speak Galician?', but which was flung as a put-down at people who suddenly used rarefied words or elaborate *periphrasis* thought to be beyond their ken and kind.[42] In Gil Vicente's theatre, characters who speak in affected cadences are frequently the object of ridicule because the (attempted) sophistication of their speech is usually at odds with their financial situation, occupation, or the object of their affections. As the pun integral to the name of the squire in *Quem tem farelos?* suggests, people like Aires Rosado put on airs in (often botched) efforts to seem more than they truly were.[43] The *Auto dos escrivães do Pelourinho* encourages the audience to respond similarly to the lovestruck senders of letters. One of the scribes, for instance, gets rather annoyed at the *ratinho* who says he is ill, but whose only ailment, it transpires, after a set of serious suggestions about getting

---

[40] Diogo Bernardes, *O Lima*, ed. J. Cândido Martins (Braga: Caixotim, 2009), p. 349.

[41] See, for instance, the regulations established by Phillip II, as discussed in José Martínez Millán, 'El control de las normas cortesanas y la elaboración de la pragmática de cortesías (1586)', *Edad de oro*, 18 (1999), 165–200.

[42] Fernão Mendes Pinto outlines that he uses plain words in his travelogue so that he would not be mocked with this phrase, see Fernão Mendes Pinto, *Peregrinaçam* (Lisbon: Pedro Craesbeeck, 1614), fol. 122ʳ. The proverb also appears in several sixteenth-century plays, as noted in Camões, *Teatro do século XVI*, p. 80.

[43] For a discussion of the pun, see Gil Vicente, *Gil Vicente: Farces and Festival Plays*, ed. T. R. Hart (Eugene: University of Oregon, 1972), p. 32.

treatment on the part of the scribe, is lovesickness, pushing the audience to find him ridiculous as well. So too are we supposed to laugh at the *escudeiro* who is inappropriately in love with the daughter of a tripe-seller. Hence, while forms of language might migrate beyond their habitual social confines, even if only in the realm of a play, laughter could rob such language of the power it might have had in different circumstances. A dramatist could shape how audiences responded to the language of courtly love in many ways, but one was by playing off the social and financial standing of the characters involved against the aristocratic associations of this way of speaking.[44] This problem of the spread of supposedly 'elite' forms of writing also provides the backdrop to problems that many writers faced in the period when trying to assert the value of their work. Poets, in particular, spent verse after verse spelling out the rules and expectations of poetry in epistles sent to fellow writers, as a means of trying to limit those who could be classified as poets to a small group and not to everyone who turned their hands to verse. They told patrons too that they needed to be discerning about the quality of writing they supported. Rewards should accrue, poets said, only to the very best.[45] They were perhaps trying to avoid exactly the situation described in the court anecdote, where the courtiers' work is rejected in favour of a text produced by the Old Pillory scribes.

The scribes-cum-writers-cum-problem-solvers of the Old Pillory were, then, mediators extraordinaires. Hidden helpers, who deployed their literacy skills not to advance in the court or civil service, but as profitably self-employed businessmen offering their services to all and sundry. They were entrepreneurial intermediaries in exchanges between monarchs, labourers, and everyone in between. The evidence for their lives lived, in multiple senses, in the middle, thus shows us the blurry edges between social categories and how letters, as forms of social connection, might be particularly susceptible to such blurriness: the illiterate might have composed missives like courtiers; the middling sort could write for kings without them realising; correspondence might be intercepted, and a fake response sent back to the sender. While we may not often think twice about the addressee named at the top and the sender's name signed at the bottom of a letter, the tales told about the scribes of the Old Pillory suggest that the invisible work of others might lie behind these names. Although archives containing letters tend to have preserved those written by, or on behalf of, the most powerful, the evidence explored here shows that those sending missives were far from always among the literate or the elite.

---

[44] On courtly love in Gil Vicente and the various ways it is treated, see T. R. Hart, 'Courtly Love in Gil Vicente's *Don Duardos*', *Romance Notes*, 2.2 (1961), 103–6.

[45] For more on the topic of poets and their struggle for professional and social status, see my *Poets, Patronage, and Print in Sixteenth-Century Portugal*, pp. 15–56.

13

Authorship and Social Status in Early Modern England

COLIN BURROW

THERE ARE NO simple truths about the relationships between literature and social hierarchy in early modern England. This is partly because social status is inherently multifaceted and elusive, and partly because literature is too. Social status depends on facts such as birth and wealth. But it can also depend on an agent's behaviour, their aspirations, the institutions and conventions within which they express and hold that status, and on other people's perceptions of the agent. Literary status in the early modern period could derive in part from social status, but it could also be established or expressed by a broad set of behaviours and conventions which could be transferred between agents. By alluding to a writer of 'high' literary or social status, or by choice of genre, or by printing works in a particular form, individual authors could lay claim to a fictive social status far above their socio-economic bracket. Publishers, always keen to elevate their wares, could by adroit use of paratextual materials – by ornamental title-pages, by dedications, by the add-ition of honorifics to an author's name – enhance or even sometimes strategically diminish the status of the authors and of the works that they published. For these reasons, as this chapter will argue, the social status of authors needs to be thought about in conjunction with book history. The chapter begins with an overview of the rapidly changing and complex interplay between markers of literary status and of social status in late Elizabethan England. It ends by considering how these changes influenced the ways in which sonnets were written and presented to their readers.

Types of Status

Sir Thomas Smith in *De Republica Anglorum* (written in the 1560s but published in 1583) divided 'the Parts and Persons of the Common Wealth' into four groups: 'gentlemen, citizens or burgesses, yeoman artificers, and laborers'.[1] Smith

---

[1] Sir Thomas Smith, *De Republica Anglorum*, ed. M. Dewar (Cambridge: Cambridge University Press, 1982), pp. 64–77.

Proceedings of the British Academy, **246**, 258–285, © The British Academy 2022.

discussed 'gentlemen' – the group of which he was himself a member – in detail. This category is remarkably wide: it runs from dukes and marquesses down to those who had acquired the status of gentleman by obtaining a university degree, or by paying a Herald to 'give him for mony, armes newly made and invented'.[2] An entire chapter is devoted to the question of 'Whether the Maner of England in Making Gentlemen so Easily is to be Allowed'. Although Smith answers that question in the affirmative, he allows that it needs to be asked.

By contrast to this finely shaded analysis of the category of gentlemen, Smith's treatment of the 'fourth sort' 'which do not rule' is strikingly brief, although it includes a wide range of different groups of people: 'Taylers, Shoomakers, Carpenters, Brickemakers, Bricklayers, Masons, &c ... have no voice nor authoritie in our commonwealth'.[3] As social and economic historians have long recognised, early modern taxonomies of social status are highly dependent on the perspective of the observer: close to, distinctions are fine-grained and clear; from afar they become blurry. They also seek to imposed dichotomised schemes on systems of status which on the ground were dependent on a number of factors (wealth, birth, education, occupation, power, location), not all of which might be present in any given member of a group, and some of which could change rapidly.[4]

Late twentieth-century taxonomies of literary activity displayed a similar, and similarly limiting, tendency towards the synchronic and the binary. In two very influential books from the 1970s and 80s Richard Helgerson set out a 'literary system' within which later Elizabethan writers operated.[5] He divided writers into three main groups, all of whom Smith would have included in his broad class of 'gentleman', who were distinguished by the kinds of things they wanted to do with their writing. There were 'amateurs' (including Sir Walter Ralegh, Edward Dyer, and Ralegh's cousin Sir Arthur Gorges), who eschewed printing their poems;[6] there were professional writers (Robert Greene would be an exemplary instance) who scraped a living from their pens; and then there was a group Helgerson called 'self-crowned laureates' (Spenser and Jonson in particular), who sought to create

---

[2] Smith, *De Republica Anglorum*, p. 72.

[3] Smith, *De Republica Anglorum*, p. 76.

[4] See Alexandra Shepard, *Accounting for Oneself: Worth, Status, and the Social Order in Early Modern England* (Oxford: Oxford University Press, 2015), pp. 2–9 for an overview; Keith Wrightson, *English Society 1580–1680* (London: Hutchinson, 1982), pp. 18–23; Keith Wrightson, '"Sorts of People" in Tudor and Stuart England', in J. Barry and C. Brooks (eds), *The Middling Sort of People: Culture, Society and Politics in England, 1550–1800* (Basingstoke: Macmillan, 1994), pp. 28–51; Keith Wrightson, 'The Social Order of Early Modern England: Three Approaches', in L. Bonfield, R. Smith, and K. Wrightson (eds), *The World We Have Gained: Histories of Population and Social Structure* (Oxford: Basil Blackwell, 1986), pp. 177–202; David Cressy, 'Describing the Social Order of Elizabethan and Stuart England', *Literature and History* 3 (1976), 29–44.

[5] Richard Helgerson, *The Elizabethan Prodigals* (Berkeley: University of California Press, 1976) and Richard Helgerson, *Self-Crowned Laureates: Spenser, Jonson, Milton and the Literary System* (Berkeley: University of California Press, 1983).

[6] See Steven W. May, *The Elizabethan Courtier Poets: The Poems and their Contexts* (Columbia: University of Missouri Press, 1991).

elevated literary personae which transcended their social origins, and who believed that 'poetry was itself a means of making a contribution to the order and improvement of the state'.[7] These groups Helgerson saw as mutually defining and relatively closed.

This taxonomy was not intended to be complete or to reflect the material realities of social status, but its shortcomings are not hard to see. Literary status depends not only on the wealth or rank of an author but also on 'softer' markers of status such as genre, the form in which a work is published, its dedication or prefatory matter. The latter were to a large extent independent of the former. So in the 1560s and 1570s a group of poets with connections to the Inns of Court – George Gascoigne, George Turbervile, and Barnabe Googe – published volumes of verse. These clearly indicated the social status of their authors: Googe's volume was even emblazoned with his coat of arms.[8] Their paratexts sought to establish a fiction that they had only been published as a result of the interference of over-eager friends or of avaricious publishers. That meant these volumes were designed to emulate the preference among poets with direct links to the royal court for circulating their works in manuscript within relatively narrow groups.[9] Aspirational mimicry of this kind was a central feature of the late Elizabethan literary landscape.

Further complexities emerge if we examine the group of 'professional' writers. Robert Greene (1558–92) was probably the most successful such writer in the Elizabethan period, and his literary career, in the course of which he tirelessly poured out pamphlets, plays, and romances, served as an example to a wide group of younger men who sought to earn a living chiefly by writing. Greene was one of several writers in the 'professional' group who had acquired the right to be called 'gentleman' or 'Master' by virtue of his university degree. From his first publication (*Mamillia* of 1583) onwards he was often described as 'graduate in Cambridge' on title-pages. From these cues literary histories since George Saintsbury's of 1887 have traditionally distinguished a group of 'University Wits' – Marlowe, Peele, Greene, Lodge, Lyly – from other 'professional writers', be they playwrights such as Shakespeare and Ben Jonson, or pamphleteers such as Thomas Dekker, who did not have university degrees.[10] In practice this distinction was only contextually activated. So university educated playwrights could collaborate happily with grammar school educated playwrights, as George Peele did with Shakespeare over

[7] Helgerson, *Self-Crowned Laureates*, p. 29.

[8] For the coat of arms, see Barnabe Googe, *Eglogs Epytaphes, and Sonettes* (London: Thomas Colwell, for Raffe Newbery, 1563), sig. A4v. For markers of status on title-pages, see George Gascoigne, *The Poesies of George Gascoigne Esquire* (London: H. Bynneman for Richard Smith, 1575); George Turbervile, *Epitaphes, epigrams, songs and sonets. Newly Corrected with additions, and set out by George Turbervile Gentleman* (London: H. Denham, 1567).

[9] Colin Burrow, 'Fictions of Collaboration: Authors and Editors in the Sixteenth Century', in L. Erne and G. Bolens (eds), *Medieval and Early Modern Authorship* (Tübingen: Narr, 2011), pp. 175–95.

[10] George Saintsbury, *A History of Elizabethan Literature* (London: Macmillan, 1887).

Titus Andronicus, for instance.[11] But professional rivalry could activate vigorous attempts at social differentiation. The most notorious instance is Robert Greene's attack in his posthumous *Groatsworth of Wit* (possibly ghost-written by another very active professional writer, Henry Chettle) on the 'upstart Crow, beautified with our feathers' grammar school boy William Shakespeare.[12] Scholars have debated whether this was an attack on Shakespeare as a social upstart or as a plagiarist.[13] It was probably a mixture of the two: literary mimicry – writing plays which used the conventions established by Christopher Marlowe – could be attacked as akin to social mimicry. Describing someone as an 'upstart' could be a means by which an established author sought to slap down a successful newcomer who had learnt to adopt the style of a successful group.

Because 'actual' lowly social status tended to be invoked chiefly in polemical contexts, more is known about the social origins of those writers who happened to have irritated their contemporaries than about those who did not. A good instance is the Cambridge don and pamphleteer Gabriel Harvey. We know that his father was a rope-maker because his behaviour prompted Robert Greene, in the first edition of *A Quip for an Upstart Courtier*, to introduce a rope-maker from Saffron Walden into his satire on social upstarts. The rope-maker delivers a speech saying how his three sons, who are unmistakeably Gabriel Harvey and his brothers, are variously fools and vainglorious asses.[14] Thomas Nashe in his series of pamphlet attacks on Harvey relentlessly drew attention to his adversary's low birth (Nashe's own father was probably a minor cleric) as a means of demolishing Harvey's claims to be a literary innovator. A similar process is clearly visible on the late Elizabethan stage. When the playwright and prose writer Thomas Dekker (about whose parents' status nothing is known) described Ben Jonson as a bricklayer in *Satiromastix* (1602) he did it as part of a (literally) staged argument with Jonson. Jonson had sought to elevate his own literary status by identifying himself with Horace in *Poetaster* (1601). He also remained a member of the Bricklayer's Company in order to secure citizenship and social advancement.[15] His literary aspirations were so nakedly expressed that they provoked his rivals to draw attention to his actual social origins and his notional profession. The figure of the 'upstart' – a person who affects greater status than his actual position warranted – was so widespread in the literature of the period not just because late sixteenth-century England was a period of significant

[11] Brian Vickers, *Shakespeare, Co-author: A Historical Study of Five Collaborative Plays* (Oxford: Oxford University Press, 2002), pp. 148–243.

[12] Robert Greene and Henry Chettle, *Greenes Groats-worth of Witte, Bought with a Million of Repentance* (London: [J. Wolfe and J. Danter] for William Wright, 1592), sig. F1v.

[13] See Brian Vickers, '"Upstart Crow"? The Myth of Shakespeare's Plagiarism', *The Review of English Studies*, 68 (2016), 244–67. On the authorship of the pamphlet, see John Jowett, 'Johannes factotum: Henry Chettle and Greene's Groatsworth of Wit', *Papers of the Bibliographical Society of America*, 87 (1993), 453–86.

[14] Robert Greene, *A Quip for an Vpstart Courtier* (London: John Wolfe, 1592), sig. C4r (STC 12300).

[15] Ian Donaldson, *Ben Jonson: A Life* (Oxford: Oxford University Press, 2011), pp. 88–9.

social mobility, but because representing a rival as an 'upstart' could strip off the 'borrowed feathers' of status-markers and leave behind the bald socio-economic facts about that author's social origins.

But feathers – in the sense both of markers of social status and of literary excellence – *could* be borrowed. Socio-literary status – as Jonson's self-identification with Horace in the late 1590s and early 1600s might remind us – is in part a performance. The genres in which an author wrote or the texts to which they alluded were potentially props and costumes for the performance of literary rank. This is true of Edmund Spenser, the archetypical instance of Helgerson's 'self-crowned laureate', who was probably the son of a clothier (the reason we do not know this for sure is that Spenser never annoyed his fellow writers sufficiently for them to make a point of it), and who graduated at Cambridge as a sizar or poor scholar. Spenser's *The Shepheardes Calender* was anonymously published in 1579, and adopted from the Inns of Court poets of the 1570s a staged reluctance to be identified in print.[16] The elaborate setting forth of the volume, however, adorned with woodcuts and notes which made it appear to be an early work by a future Virgil, made it plain that the anonymous author was somebody to be reckoned with.[17] The social status of writers, viewed as a species of performance, was radically entangled with the status of literary genres and with bibliographical markers of status. A writer could seek to 'rise' – as Spenser clearly did – by writing in a genre of high status or by adopting a career structure which had social and poetic progression built into it. Doing so anonymously avoided the risk of a satirical attack which drew attention to the author's actual low social status. This is one reason why pastoral poetry was so popular among writers of the later sixteenth century: an obscure shepherd might glance at high politics and hint at associations with courtier poets, at the same time as indicating that in time the author would become a new Virgil.

The example of Spenser raises a further general point. The majority of his works after the *Calender* were printed by William Ponsonby, who had been entrusted by the family of Sir Philip Sidney with publishing his works after his death. Literary status in this period could be expressed through what Jerome McGann has called bibliographic codes, which include choice of publisher.[18] Dedications, typefaces, engraved title-pages, the ways in which an author's name was presented, could all implicitly situate a book within a hierarchy of authors as well as within social hierarchies in the wider world.[19] These codes were heterogeneous, and in the final

---

[16] See Marcy L. North, *The Anonymous Renaissance: Cultures of Discretion in Tudor-Stuart England* (Chicago: University of Chicago Press, 2003), pp. 99–104.

[17] See Ruth Luborsky, 'The Allusive Presentation of *The Shepheardes Calender*', *Spenser Studies*, 1 (1980), 29–67. On career criticism, see Patrick Cheney, *Spenser's Famous Flight: A Renaissance Idea of a Literary Career* (Toronto: University of Toronto Press, 1993) and Philip R. Hardie and Helen Moore (eds), *Classical Literary Careers and their Reception* (Cambridge: Cambridge University Press, 2010).

[18] Jerome J. McGann, *The Textual Condition* (Princeton: Princeton University Press, 1991), pp. 13–14.

[19] For the transmissions of fashion in typeface and format, see Mark Bland, 'The Appearance of Text in Early Modern England', *Text: An Interdisciplinary Annual of Textual Studies*, 11 (1998), 91–154.

decades of the sixteenth century they changed rapidly. They were highly dependent on the material resources of printers (their stock of ornaments and typefaces, the availability of engravers to create bespoke title-pages) as well as immaterial factors such as a printer's level of experience in producing analogous volumes, or the skill of their compositors. They were also connected with the output of particular publishers, who might specialise in a particular kind of work.[20] But despite their range and variability, bibliographical markers of status were in many respects more significant than the 'actual' social status of writers. They, rather than a family tree or evidence about an author's income or capital worth, were what readers of books actually saw; and they could be used both to express and generate cultural credit. There was potential for feedback, too, between 'actual' social status and biblio-graphical markers of status: a poet from relatively low material origins (a son of a clothier like Spenser, say) who could produce a book which looked like a work by Sir Philip Sidney might enjoy an enhanced future status in the eyes of his peers, while a pamphleteer working with a printer at the lower end of the market (such as John Danter, who published Nashe's attacks on Gabriel Harvey) might attract negative comment about the status of his works and of his social origins.

One exceptional but influential example will illustrate this point. In 1591 John Harington (1560–1612) published his folio translation of Ariosto's *Orlando Furioso*. It was the most lavishly printed work of vernacular literature to have appeared by that date, and was carefully modelled on Francesco Franceschi's edition of Ariosto from 1584.[21] Harington was the queen's godson, although he was eventually knighted not by the queen herself but (to the queen's fury) by the Earl of Essex during his campaign in Ireland in 1599. On the engraved title-page of Harington's Ariosto (Figure 13.1) the translator's own portrait, fashionably clad in ruff and slashed doublet, appears in a roundel which is rather larger than that which surrounds the laurelled portrait of Ariosto at the top of the page.[22] Harington's spaniel Bungy lies at the foot of the page. This detail quietly tells Harington's readers that he enjoys aristocratic sporting pursuits and can even afford to have a picture made of his dog. The volume was dedicated to Queen Elizabeth, and Harington presented customised copies to many prominent figures, including Lord Burghley.[23] Harington was unusually aware that the printed book was an act of social communication, and so micro-managed the presentation of the volume. He chose as his publisher Richard

[20] See Zachary Lesser, *Renaissance Drama and the Politics of Publication: Readings in the English Book Trade* (Cambridge: Cambridge University Press, 2004), pp. 26–51.

[21] Cf. Lodovico Ariosto, *Orlando furioso in English Heroical Verse*, trans. J. Harington (London: Richard Field, 1591) and Lodovico Ariosto, *Orlando furioso di M. Lodouico Ariosto nuouamente adornato di Figure di Rame da Girolamo Porro* (Venice: Francesco de Franceschi, 1584).

[22] On the history of author portraits, see Sarah Howe, 'The Authority of Presence: The Development of the English Author Portrait, 1500–1640', *The Papers of the Bibliographical Society of America*, 102 (2008), 465–99.

[23] Richard A. McCabe, *'Ungainefull Arte': Poetry, Patronage, and Print in the Early Modern Era* (Oxford: Oxford University Press, 2016), pp. 98–9; Jason Scott-Warren, *Sir John Harington and the Book as Gift* (Oxford: Oxford University Press, 2001), pp. 49–55.

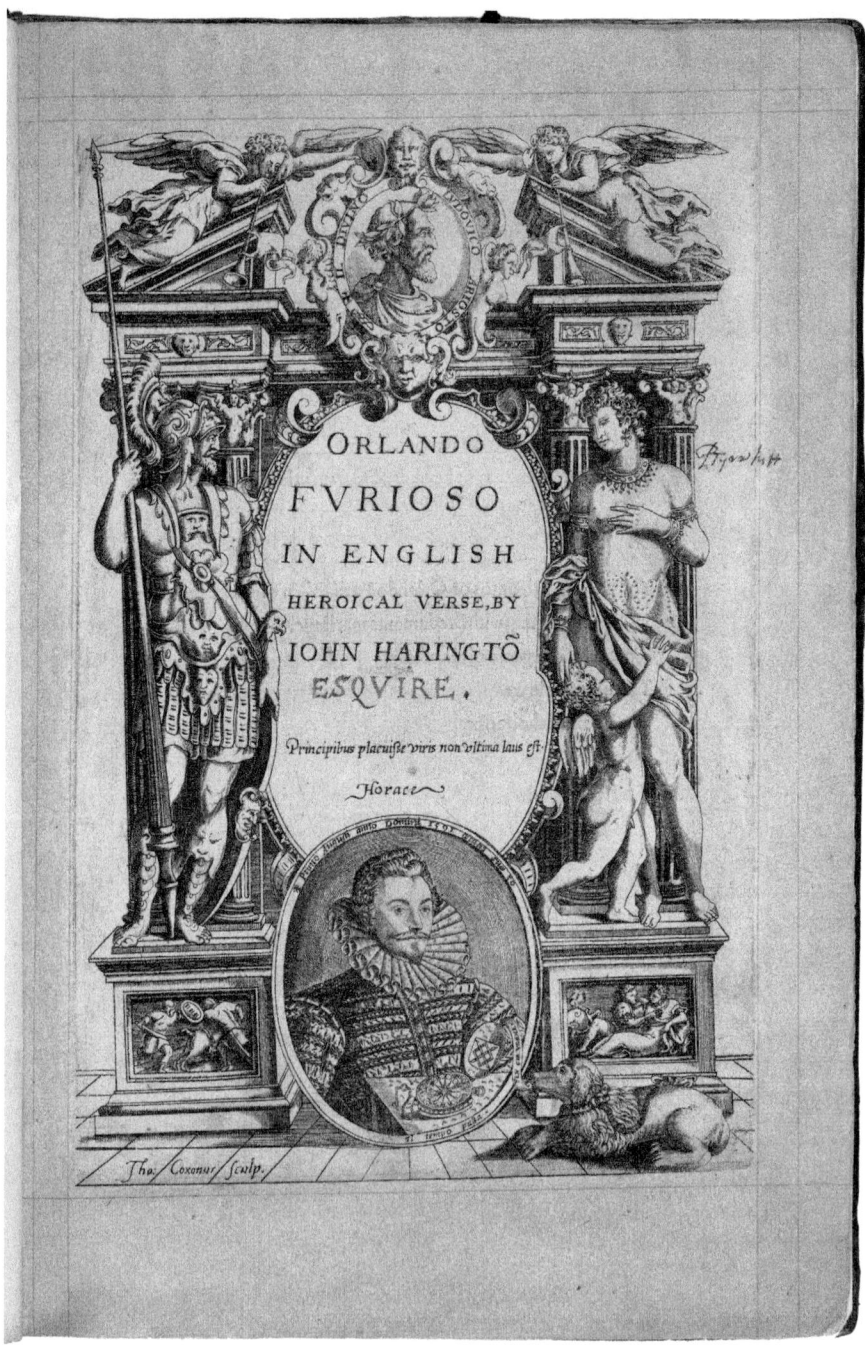

Figure 13.1 Title-page of Sir John Harington's translation of *Orlando Furioso* (1591), reproduced under CC-BY-SA 4.0 license from Folger Shakespeare Library STC 746 copy 1.

Field, who enjoyed a monopoly over the printing of a number of Latin literary texts, and whose press-work was notably high quality. Moreover he gave Field precise instructions that all prose in the volume be set 'in the same printe that Putnams book ys', which is to say in the typeface Field had used in 1589 for George Puttenham's *Arte of English Poesie*.[24] Puttenham's volume was dedicated to Lord Burghley, but was written in the form of an address to the queen herself. Not only a particular publisher but even a particular typeface could create a network of associations – position a book, as it were, within a virtual family – and so make a claim to status. And Harington, who according to legend was out of favour with the Queen in 1591 for having circulated a bawdy tale from Ariosto among her maids of honour, needed to combine together as many markers of social status as he could. Later authors who published vernacular poems with Field – including William Shakespeare with *Venus and Adonis* (1593) and *Lucrece* (1594) – were implicitly associating themselves with these markers of high literary status.

Social Dynamics of Genre: The Case of Drama

Harington's Ariosto enjoyed what might be called the social advantage of kind: an epic intrinsically invited high status presentation, and might naturally suit a high status dedicatee. Other literary kinds did not have such prestige, but might gradually borrow the markers of status from works which enjoyed higher status. Printed texts of plays originally performed on the public stage were the clearest instance. Before 1594 these rarely carried the name of their author on their title-page, even if it was someone as famous as John Lyly, whose massively popular prose narrative *Euphues* (1578) declared on its title-page not only the name of the author but that he was 'Master of Arte. Oxon.'. Lyly's play *Campaspe* was presented to its readers in 1584 as though its status derived solely from its place of performance: 'Played before the Queenes Majestie on new yeares day at night, by her Majesties Children, and the Children of Pawles.' But the fashion changed very rapidly after 1594. Between that date and 1610 about half of printed plays carried an author's name on the title-page and during the same period about 12 per cent included a mark of status such as 'master of arts'.[25] By 1597 John Lyly was duly described as 'Master of Arts' on the title-page of his play *The Woman in the Moone As it was Presented before Her Highness*. Bibliographical

---

[24] British Library MS Add. 18920, fol. 336r. See Simon Cauchi, 'The "Setting Foorth" of Harington's Ariosto', *Studies in Bibliography*, 36 (1983), 137–68.

[25] These statistics are derived from the Database of Early English Playbooks, http://deep.sas.upenn.edu/adv ancedsearch.php, accessed July 2019. They include plays for boy and adult companies. There are inevitable variations in the figures depending on exactly which classes of drama are included and the terminal dates used: Douglas A. Brooks, 'Dramatic Authorship and Publication in Early Modern England', *Medieval and Renaissance Drama in England*, 15 (2003), 77–97 at 86 states that roughly 50 per cent of plays are ascribed 1580–99, with a sharp rise to 75 per cent in 1600. Markers of status were significantly more frequent on the title-pages of plays for indoor theatres: see Alan B. Farmer and Zachary Lesser, 'Vile Arts: The Marketing of English Printed Drama, 1512–1660', *Research Opportunities in Renaissance Drama*, 39 (2000), 77–165.

codes and conventions for marking social status clearly evolved in ways which were partially autonomous from the 'actual' social status of writers: Lyly in 1597 enjoyed exactly the same social status as he did in 1584. What had changed were genre-specific conventions for indicating that status.

There were many reasons for these changes. The so-called University Wits were among the earliest to have their names associated with markers of social status on the title-pages of plays: so *A Looking-glass for London* of 1594 was described on its title page as 'Made by Thomas Lodge Gentleman, and Robert Greene. In Artibus Magister'. Lodge and Greene were here borrowing if not the feathers, then the bibliographic codes associated with slightly more elevated kinds of writing. In the mid-1590s there was a small rash of printed closet dramas, and particularly of closet dramas translated from the French of Robert Garnier.[26] Closet dramas routinely included dedications, and their title-pages routinely included authors' names, some of which were of very high status: *The Tragedie of Antonie Done into English by the Countesse of Pembroke* (Mary Sidney Herbert, who was Sir Philip Sidney's sister) appeared in a separate edition in 1595, having previously been published in 1592 along with the Countess's translation of Philippe de Mornay's *Discourse of Life and Death*.[27] It was rapidly followed by a reissue of *Pompey the Great, his faire Corneliaes Tragedie ... Written in French, by that excellent Poet Ro: Garnier; and translated into English by Thomas Kid*, which was dedicated to the Countess of Sussex. Kyd's translation had appeared in the previous year with a notably spare title page ('CORNELIA'), but either poor sales or the example of the Countess of Pembroke's volume prompted a reissue with a new title-page that gave the translator's name – and made it the only dramatic work ascribed to Kyd in print.[28]

The authorship of plays for the public stage grew in visibility and status by borrowing conventions from closet drama. It also took an upward nudge from a sad accident. Christopher Marlowe was stabbed in the eye with a dagger of value 12d in a tavern in Deptford in May 1593.[29] This event belonged to a different social world from the Countess of Pembroke's experiments in closet drama at Wilton House, but nonetheless it aided the rise to prominence of the theatrical author. In 1594 two plays with titles which sounded very similar to closet dramas (*The Massacre at Paris* and *The Tragedie of Dido Queene of Carthage*) were published with Marlowe's name attached – and the title-page of *Dido* declared it had been co-written by Marlowe and 'Thomas Nashe Gent.'. Status-markers on title-pages

---

[26] For the complex and reciprocal relationships between closet dramas and the public stage, see Marta Straznicky, *Privacy, Play Reading, and Women's Closet Drama, 1550–1700* (Cambridge: Cambridge University Press, 2004), esp. pp. 48–56.

[27] See May, *Courtier Poets*, pp. 166–70 and, on Mary Sidney Herbert's *Antonie*, Jonathan Patterson's discussion in Chapter 10 of this volume.

[28] For the commercial failure of the first issue, see Lukas Erne, *Shakespeare and the Book Trade* (Cambridge: Cambridge University Press, 2013), pp. 94–5.

[29] See Charles Nicholl, *The Reckoning: The Murder of Christopher Marlowe* (London: Jonathan Cape, 1992), p. 18.

are easy to quantify. They are rather less easy to interpret. In the course of one of his arguments with Gabriel Harvey, Thomas Nashe self-defensively claimed that 'it hath pleased M. Printer, both in this booke and Pierce Pennilesse, to intaile a vaine title to my name, which I care not for, without my consent or priuitie I here auouch'.[30] By making this claim he was of course attempting to avoid a revenge attack by the 'upstart' Harvey by denying that he was a pot who vociferously drew attention to the soot on the kettle; but it should serve as a reminder that it could be publishers or printers as much as authors who recognised that status-markers on title-pages could be an aid to marketing works such as play-texts. Markers of status – be they explicit indicators of social standing or implicit markers of high literary value – sold books.

Nonetheless, it is helpful to regard 1594 as a watershed in the ways of marking the social status of playwrights. Playwrights after this date might *appear* to be more status-aware, even though they or their publishers were more or less following convention by including marks of status in their printed texts. George Chapman was described as 'George Chapman Gentleman' on the title-page of his first printed play, *The Blind Beggar of Alexandria* (1598). This probably was not an indicator that Chapman – the grandson of the keeper of Henry VIII's dogs – was unusually keen to emphasise his social standing. It is more likely to have been just a consequence of the relatively late date at which Chapman began to publish plays. Chapman was, however, one of the first playwrights to dedicate a printed play to a member of the nobility.[31] In 1608 he dedicated *The conspiracie, and tragedie of Charles Duke of Byron* to Sir Thomas Walsingham. Again the scent of closet drama might be detected in that title, and that is presumably why Chapman took the risk of aiming so high with his dedication. When writing in non-dramatic genres Chapman was very skilled at deploying and developing bibliographic codes for marking authorial status. He went on to emulate Harington's Ariosto by publishing in folio his *Whole Works of Homer* (1616), posthumously dedicated to Henry, Prince of Wales, and printed by Harington's printer, Richard Field. This volume appeared complete with an authorial portrait (Figure 13.2) which blurs the distinction between Homer and his translator, since the balding and bearded Chapman (the clouds behind him hinting at a laurel wreath) has more than a passing resemblance to the figures of Hector and Homer as they are illustrated on the title-page.[32] In the text surrounding

---

[30] Thomas Nashe, *Works*, ed. R. B. McKerrow and F. P. Wilson, 4 vols (Oxford: Blackwell, 1958), 1.311–12.

[31] On dedications to plays, see David M. Bergeron, *Textual Patronage in English Drama, 1570–1640* (Aldershot: Ashgate, 2006), pp. 77–8. Jonson inserted custom dedications into copies of *Cynthia's Revels* (1601) to William Camden and Lucy, Countess of Bedford, and dedicated *Volpone* (1607) to 'The Two Most Noble and Most Equall Sisters, The Two Famous Universities'. Marston dedicated *Antonio and Mellida* (1602) to 'Nobody' and *The Malcontent* (1604) to Jonson. See Franklin B. Williams, *Index of Dedications and Commendatory Verses in English Books before 1641* (London: Bibliographical Society, 1962), p. x.

[32] See John A. Buchtel, 'Book Dedications and the Death of a Patron: The Memorial Engraving in Chapman's Homer', *Book History*, 7 (2004), 1–29. For the 'explosion' of author portraits after 1610, see Howe, 'Author Portrait', 467.

Figure 13.2 Portrait of George Chapman from *The Whole Works of Homer* (1616), reproduced under CC-BY-SA 4.0 license from Folger Shakespeare Library, STC 13624.

his portrait he is given the virtual honorific 'Homeri Metaphrastes', the translator of Homer. Authorial status is not separable from the physical forms of books or from the status of genres; and indeed in the case of Chapman's Homer the author seems finally to draw his status from his literary activity. He is no longer a (mere?) gentleman, but the translator of Homer.

It is often said that Shakespeare, the glover's son from Stratford-upon-Avon, was unusually careless about publishing his plays. Shakespeare began his career before 1593. His name began to appear on title-pages in 1598 and came to be 'a crucial feature in the authorization of his drama in print'.[33] Although he obtained a coat of arms by purchase in 1596 he is not described as 'gent.' or gentleman on any of the works that were printed during his lifetime. There may have been personal reasons for this: it is often thought that Ben Jonson satirised Shakespeare's motto of 'Non sans Droict' (not without right) in *Every Man Out of His Humour* when Sogliardo buys a coat of arms and Puntarvolo suggests the motto 'Not Without Mustard' for him.[34] Even if that was not a direct or a palpable hit, the general tendency of policing social aspirations by satirical mockery, combined with the convention that gentry status acquired by a university degree seems to have been valued more highly (or at least marked more frequently in printed books) than the acquisition of a coat of arms by purchase may explain why Shakespeare did not become a gentleman in print until after his death. *King Lear* was ascribed to 'M. William Shak-speare' in 1608, and the posthumous 1623 folio of *Mr. William Shakespeares Comedies, Histories, & Tragedies* did include, in its first, inconspicuous two-letter word, an indicator that Shakespeare should be called 'Master'. The authorial portrait in the first folio, its dedication to William Herbert, Earl of Pembroke, and Philip, Earl of Montgomery, were all declarations of social prestige.

The Shakespeare folio built on the precedent of the first folio of Ben Jonson's *Workes* (which contained both plays and poems) printed by William Stansby in 1616. Jonson's folio is generally regarded as 'monumental, path-breaking, trend-setting'.[35] It is probably better regarded as the most influential example of the way bibliographic status markers could migrate between different kinds of publication. William Stansby's engraved frontispiece for Jonson's *Works* was by William Hole (Figure 13.3). It was similar to the engraved title-page which Hole had provided for Hooker's *Laws of Ecclesiastical Polity* in 1611, and its design followed that for Thomas Lodge's translation of Seneca's prose works in 1614.[36]

[33] Erne, *Shakespeare and the Book Trade*, p. 96.

[34] Ben Jonson, *The Cambridge Edition of the Works of Ben Jonson*, ed. D. M. Bevington, M. Butler and I. Donaldson, 7 vols (Cambridge: Cambridge University Press, 2012), 1.336 (3.1.193). S. Schoenbaum, *William Shakespeare: A Documentary Life* (Oxford: Clarendon Press, 1975), pp. 166–73.

[35] Bergeron, *Textual Patronage*, p. 129.

[36] Lucius Annaeus Seneca, *The Workes of Lucius Annaeus Seneca, both Morrall and Naturall*, trans. T. Lodge (London: William Stansby, 1614); Richard Hooker, *Of the Lawes of Ecclesiastical Politie* (London: William Stansby, 1611). On the technical development of engraved frontispieces, see Margery Corbett and R. W. Lightbown, *The Comely Frontispiece: The Emblematic Title-page in England, 1550–1660* (London and Boston: Routledge and Kegan Paul, 1979).

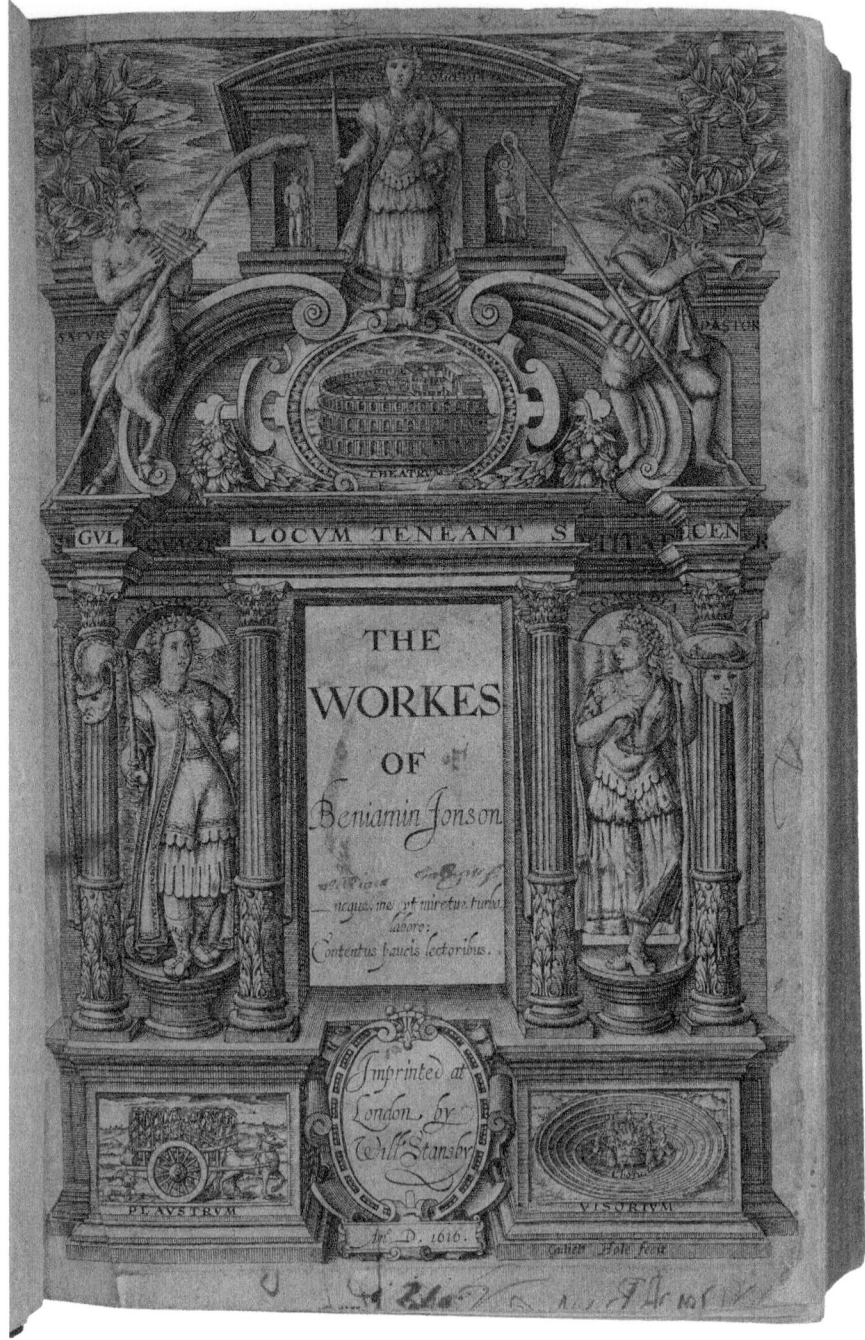

Figure 13.3 Title-page of *The Workes of Beniamin Jonson* (1616), reproduced under CC-BY-SA 4.0 license from Folger Shakespeare Library, STC 14751 copy 2.

The layout of these title-pages was familiar from continental folios, and indeed from Harington's Ariosto. The title and the author's name appear within a neo-classical edifice flanked by monumental figures backed by columns. The relation between Jonson's *Works* and Lodge's Seneca, however, is worth pausing over because the name of Thomas Lodge was so persistently associated with indicators of status. He is usually 'Thomas Lodge' or 'T.L' 'of Lincolnes Inne, Gentleman' on the title-pages of his Elizabethan publications, and in the pivotal year of 1594 his play *The Wounds of Civil War* was described as 'Written by Thomas Lodge Gent.'. By 1601 he was generally termed 'doctor of physic', and this was the style used by Stansby on the title page to Lodge's translation of Seneca. This might draw the eye towards a striking feature of the engraved title-page of Jonson's *Works*. It borrows codes of status from Lodge's Seneca but – pointedly, it seems – omits the verbal markers of status. Indeed William Hole left a slight gap below Ben Jonson's name and in exactly the space in which a marker of social status might be expected to appear, into which a former owner of the Folger Shakespeare Library's copy has inserted his own signature. Jonson at this point did not have a degree (his honorary degree from Oxford came three years later in 1619) or any inherited entitlement to call himself a gentleman. Hence the blank is at once explicable and eloquent: Jonson's name appears sufficient to stand on its own. If Chapman had turned 'Homeri Metaphrastes' into an honorific, Jonson in the folio *Works* implicitly makes an overt *lack* of social status a marker of literary authority.

The elevation in the status given to authors of play-texts is frequently treated by theatre historians as a more or less autonomous narrative. In fact it was intimately linked with a much more general rise in the visible status of printed literary texts during the 1590s. As early as 1601 Samuel Daniel (who had a remarkably strong and consistent relationship with the publisher Simon Waterson) had published a volume of *Works* in folio, dedicated to the Queen. A number of large paper copies survive, which were presumably intended as customisable gifts to members of the nobility or to elite institutions such as the University of Oxford.[37] By 1609 Daniel followed his *Works* with an edition of his epic *The Civil Wars* which bore his portrait on its title-page. This was engraved by Thomas Cockson, who had been responsible for engraved portrait on the title-page of Harington's Ariosto,[38] and it declared Daniel's relatively new status as groom of her majesty's privy chamber. This position (first mentioned on the title-page of *Certaine Small Workes* from 1607), with a stipend of £60 per year, appears chiefly to have been a reward for having written masques for Queen Anne. But Daniel was generally reluc-tant to grant value to the theatrical writing from which he derived both material

[37] For example, Bodleian Library Arch. G d.47 (1).
[38] Arthur M. Hind, Margery Corbett, and Michael Charles Norton, *Engraving in England in the Sixteenth & Seventeenth Centuries: A Descriptive Catalogue with Introductions*, 3 vols (Cambridge: Cambridge University Press, 1952), 1.240–1.

advancement and (during a difficult period in which he was Master of the Queen's Revels) a great deal of trouble.[39] Indeed it was not until 1635, 16 years after his death, that a collected volume of his theatrical writings appeared. Even then they were presented as his *Dramaticke Poems*.[40]

Jonson's folio therefore used the bibliographical codes in part developed by Daniel. But it did so implicitly to claim high status for theatrical works, to which Daniel had himself been reluctant to accord high value. And after the 1616 folio there continued to be a self-elevating cycle of feedback between Jonson and other poets. Michael Drayton produced around six collected editions of his *Poems* in the early seventeenth century, but it was not until 1619 – three years after the Jonson folio – that they were published in folio, accompanied by a portrait of Drayton wearing a laurel wreath within a roundel which described him as 'armigeri' (Figure 13.4). It is no coincidence that the publisher of the 1619 edition of Drayton's *Poems* was the same William Stansby who had three years before published the folio of Ben Jonson's *Works*. Not to be outdone, Ben Jonson was later depicted wearing a laurel wreath in an engraving probably produced in around 1627 by Robert Vaughan.[41] This was presented as a portrait of 'doctissimi poetarum Anglorum', 'the most learned of the English poets'. Drayton's social honorific was replaced by a direct claim to literary eminence. That portrait of Jonson is often found bound with copies of the first Folio, despite being a later emulation of Drayton's image. Jonson, as was his wont, was rude about both Daniel and Drayton: he declared that Daniel was 'no poet' and that 'Drayton feared him, and he esteemed not of him'.[42] One reason for his aggression was that these two poets helped to establish the bibliographical codes and markers of literary status which Jonson was able to exploit. They were also revealingly different from Jonson in the kinds of work to which they implicitly attached value. They not only wrote sonnets – a form to which Ben Jonson was notably averse – but included them in collected volumes of their works. Both wrote plays, but neither presented them as a major part of their authorial *oeuvre*. These were indicators that they operated in a slightly different socio-literary sphere from Jonson, as the next section will show.

Household Laureates: Daniel, Drayton, and the Sonnet

The subject-position of the Petrarchan sonneteer, abjectly loving a tyrannical mistress and seeking to persuade her to love, has often been seen as analogous to that of a courtly petitioner seeking within a competitive environment to influence a royal

---

[39] See Joan Rees, *Samuel Daniel: A Critical and Biographical Study* (Liverpool: Liverpool University Press, 1964), pp. 96–9.

[40] *Drammaticke poems. VVritten by Samvell Daniell Esquire, one of the groomes of the most honorable prive chamber to Queene Anne* (London: John Waterson, 1635).

[41] Donaldson, *Ben Jonson*, p. 399.

[42] Jonson, *Cambridge Edition*, 5.360, 5.367. Quotations from and parodies of Daniel are in *Every Man in his Humour*, 1.3.114–19; 5.3.235–8.

Figure 13.4 Portrait of Michael Drayton from *Poems: by Michael Drayton Esqvire* (1619), reproduced under CC-BY-SA 4.0 license from Folger Shakespeare Library STC 7222 copy 1.

mistress or patron. The rise of the sonnet sequence is usually associated with the social dynamics of the Elizabethan court, and its decline with the different social and gender dynamics of the reign of James.[43] There are other equally plausible reasons for its decline which follow from the general history outlined in the previous section. The secret emotions of a sonneteer, loving, aspiring, but not daring to reveal his love in public, made the sonnet sequence a perfect form for an age in which reluctant or anonymous publication could be a marker of social status. But what happened to this form in a period when authors proclaimed both their identity and their social status in collected volumes of works?

From 1592 onwards Samuel Daniel's published works carried a motto on their title-page: 'aetas prima canat veneres postrema tumultus', 'let the first age sing of loves, and the last of battles'. This not only encoded purpose into his literary career from its very start, but suggested that sonnet sequences might be a natural prelude to epic ambitions. His sonnet sequence *Delia* was duly included in his *Works* (1601) along with his epic *Civil Wars*. The material realities beneath the purposive appearance of Daniel's works in print were, however, precarious. He often struggled for money. His social origins are not known, though Wood says that he came from 'a wealthy family in Somersetshire'.[44] He attended Oxford but left (as Wood put it) 'without the honour of a degree'. This is gently intimated by the title-page of his first publication, which was a translation of a book of *imprese* by Paulus Jovius in 1585, where he is described not as a master of arts but as 'late Student in Oxenford'. At Oxford he became friends with the translator of Montaigne, John Florio.[45] Daniel's skill in French and Italian probably helped him to win employment with the English ambassador to Paris in 1586. He then travelled to Italy with Sir Edward Dymoke. This gave him a wide knowledge not only of European languages but also of continental conventions for presenting literature to its readers. From an insular perspective it is remarkable that Daniel published his *Works* as early as 1601, but in doing so he emulated the collected *Oeuvres* of Francois Villon (1533) and particularly those of Ronsard (1572). This volume opened with Ronsard's sonnets, the 'Amours', and was adorned with a portrait of the author. Bibliographical markers of status could migrate across seas as well as generic boundaries.

Daniel was what might be called a household laureate. His imaginary if not his actual status was that of a learned though lower-born companion to a noble man or woman – a subject-position which he best captured in his philosophical epistles to female aristocratic patrons, in which the 'we' of generalised philosophical reflection unites him with his addressee.[46] His knowledge of modern languages fitted him for a position as tutor or secretary to a noble household – a position of

---

[43] See the classic article, Arthur F. Marotti, '"Love is Not Love": Elizabethan Sonnet Sequences and the Social Order', *ELH*, 49 (1982), 396–428.

[44] Antony à Wood, *Athenae Oxonienses*, 4 vols (London, 1813–20), 2.267.

[45] Wood states that Florio married Daniel's sister, *Athenae*, 2.269.

[46] E.g. 'To the Lady Lucie, Countess of Bedford', ll. 63–4 'vnlesse we finde vs all within, | We neuer can without vs be our owne', Samuel Daniel, *Poems and A Defence of Rhyme*, ed. A. C. Sprague (Chicago and London: Chicago University Press, 1965), p. 117.

cultured above-stairs service analogous to that held by his brother, who served as a music master in several aristocratic households. By around 1598 he became tutor to Anne Clifford, daughter of the Countess of Cumberland. During the early 1590s he seems to have acquired a role as secretary or tutor at Wilton House, although the chronology is by no means clear. By 1592 he was addressing the Countess of Pembroke as his patron.[47] Later Elizabethan literature frequently explores the status of gentlemen servants akin to the Daniel brothers. Shakespeare's unfortunate steward Malvolio (literate, trusted, but absurd) belongs to the lower end of this group – although in reality the steward of a vast noble household such as that of the Earl of Leicester might be knighted and become a member of parliament, and even in smaller households might expect a decent wage of £10 a year.[48] The secretary in George Gascoigne's *Adventures of Master F.J.* (who becomes the erotic servant of his mistress), as well as the music master Thomas Whythorne (whose autobiography relates a series of amorous misadventures in an aristocratic household), indicate that in smaller households roles of this kind provided close contact with elite groups, but also an invitation to social over-reach and consequent humiliation.[49] Both Gascoigne's F. J. and Whythorne become entangled in erotic confusions as a result of exchanging lyrics within a noble household. This class of learned servant was represented so frequently in the period after 1560 because its status was a potentially admonitory double to that of many authors. They were at once gentlemen and servants. They knew that the intimacy they enjoyed with their social superiors could dissolve instantly into ridicule or dismissal if they over-reached themselves. Daniel seems generally to have benefited from that kind of position even if at times he fretted against it: he described Wilton as his 'best Schoole', where he learnt rather than taught.[50] From that association he acquired a set of connections with Sidney's family which gave him a literary status well above his social standing. And it may be significant that he instinctively associated the revision of poems and the building of an authorial *oeuvre* with the construction and reconstruction of houses: he regarded his 'works' as itself a kind of noble house.[51]

---

[47] Rees, *Samuel Daniel*, pp. 76, 11–12.

[48] Kate Mertes, *The English Noble Household, 1250–1600: Good Governance and Politic Rule* (Oxford: Basil Blackwell, 1988), p. 68. Simon Adams (ed.), *Household Accounts and Disbursement Books of Robert Dudley, Earl of Leicester, 1558–1561, 1584–1586* (Cambridge: Cambridge University Press, 1995), pp. 464–5.

[49] For the secretary who could 'prick such faire large notes' on his mistress that F. J. falls out of favour, see George Gascoigne, *A Hundreth Sundrie Flowres*, ed. G. W. Pigman (Oxford: Clarendon Press, 2000), pp. 199; Thomas Whythorne, *The Autobiography of Thomas Whythorne*, ed. J. M. Osborne (Oxford: Oxford University Press, 1961).

[50] Samuel Daniel, *A Panegyrike Congratulatorie ... Also Certaine Epistles, with a Defence of Ryme* (London: Edward Blount, 1603), sig. E8v.

[51] In 'To the Reader' prefixed to *Certaine Small Workes* (1607) he compares himself to 'the curious builder who this yeare | Puls down, and alters what he did the last'. The epistle to the Countess of Cumberland praises her for having built a 'glorious dwelling for your honoured name', Daniel, ed. Sprague, *Poems and A Defence of Rhyme*, p. 115.

Christopher Warley has argued that Elizabethan sonnets 'are a site for the creation of class as a new means of producing social distinction'.[52] The example of Daniel suggests something more specific. The sonnet sequence was the ideal vehicle through which to represent the experience of the lettered servant, socially aspirant but constricted in upward mobility by the ornamented plaster ceilings of those whom he served. Daniel was from the very start of his poetic career implicated in the public circulation of sonnets as akin to the secrets of the nobility. In 1591 an unauthorised edition of Sir Philip Sidney's *Astrophil and Stella* appeared, which was billed on its title-page as containing 'sundry other rare sonnets of divers Noble men and Gentlemen'. These included 28 sonnets ascribed to 'Daniel'. Daniel's role in the publication will never be known for sure, but given his association with the Countess of Pembroke at around this date he was, and remains, one of the key suspects for having leaked Sidney's sonnets to the press, and for having piggy-backed on the social and literary standing of his patroness's brother as one of the 'divers Noble men and Gentlemen' to appear in that volume.[53]

A year later Daniel dedicated the authorised 1592 edition of *Delia* to the Countess of Pembroke, and insisted to his patroness that 'I rather desired to keep in the private passions of my youth' and that he was 'betraide by the indiscretion of a greedie Printer' (sig. A2r) in having his sonnets published with those of Sidney. The first poem in the 1592 sequence (which had not appeared among the 28 sonnets printed with *Astrophil and Stella*) is in effect a continuation of the volume's self-defensive paratexts. The sonnet deliberately diminishes the role of the poet to that of a humble secretary or book-keeper:

> Heere I unclaspe the booke of my charg'd soule,
> Where I haue summ'd my sighes, heere I enroule
> Howe they were spent for thee; Looke what they are.
>   Looke on the deere expences of my youth,
> And see how iust I reckon with thyne eyes:
> Examine well thy beautie with my trueth,
> And crosse my cares ere greater summes arise.[54]

The sonneteer here becomes a quasi-scribal figure, or a moral accountant who sums up the charges and expenses of his soul and submits them to a social superior for verification. His mistress has the power to cancel ('crosse') them all. This directly imitates the language of Sidney's Sonnet 18: 'With what sharpe checkes I in my selfe am shent, | When into Reason's audite I do go: | And by just counts my selfe a banckrout know | Of all those goods, which heav'n to me hath lent: | Unable quite to

[52] Christopher Warley, *Sonnet Sequences and Social Distinction in Renaissance England* (Cambridge: Cambridge University Press, 2005), p. 152.

[53] See Henry Woudhuysen, *Sir Philip Sidney and the Circulation of Manuscripts, 1558–1640* (Oxford: Clarendon Press, 1996), pp. 376–83.

[54] Samuel Daniel, *Delia, contayning certayne sonnets: with the complaint of Rosamond* (London: I.C. for S. Waterson, 1592), sig. B1r. For the relationship between this sonnet and *Astrophil and Stella* 18, see Warley, *Sonnet Sequences*, pp. 98–9.

pay even Nature's rent, | Which unto it by birthright I do ow'.[55] But Daniel imitated those lines by the brother of his patroness with a distinctive difference, which Mary Sidney Herbert might be expected to notice. Sidney assesses his own bankruptcy, and his own reason is the authority that oversees the accounts. Daniel, by contrast, presents the ledger of his debts to his mistress, who can cross and check them as she sees fit. Daniel was prone to represent himself as mere accountant or a secretary on occasions when he had reason to fear he might have overstepped a social boundary. In around 1598 he wrote a fictional complaint from Octavia to her husband Antony, which he dedicated to the Countess of Cumberland. The poem (which may have been written at the request of the Countess) risked appearing to ventriloquise his patroness's unhappy marriage,[56] and to offset that risk it was accompanied by a dedication which insisted that Daniel was simply 'B'ing Secretary now, but to the dead' (1602, sig. Diir). The opening poem in the 1592 edition of *Delia* reflects a similarly awkward situation: someone of low status was associated with the indiscreet publication of Sidney's sonnets and so takes cover under the persona of a humble household clerk. Daniel imitated French and Italian sonnets liberally, but he imparted a distinctive clerkly flavour to the English sequence. A writer who operated within a noble household was, from the perspective of a Sir Thomas Smith, of the same status as any other literate gentleman; but being a secretary carried with a range of social skills and risks which could generate a whole range of distinctive subject-positions.[57] This suggests that social status – accepted marks of rank or social credit – may be less significant for the understanding of literary activity than subtle shadings and variations in social *experience*.

Samuel Daniel's *Delia* appeared in 1592 with no name on the title-page. It was reissued a year later in a volume containing a closet-drama called *Cleopatra*, which is a companion-piece to the Countess of Pembroke's translation of Robert Garnier's *Antonie*.[58] This volume duly carried Daniel's name as well as his motto, as it extended the bibliographic conventions for printed closet dramas to include sonnets. Sonnet sequences in the 1590s generally did not bear their author's name or any mark of their status on the title-page: so it was with *Phyllis* (1592) by the Thomas Lodge who is elsewhere 'Thomas Lodge of Lincoln's Inn, Gentleman', or Doctor of Physic. But after the 1593 edition of *Delia* they might do so: Edmund Spenser's name appeared on the title-page of his sonnet sequence *Amoretti and Epithalamion* in 1595. When Daniel incorporated his sonnet sequence into the 1601 *Works*, being a scrupulous secretary attuned to observe the finer points of feminine rhyme and the evolving literary landscape around him, he revised his poems carefully for inclusion in that high status volume.

[55] Philip Sidney, *The Poems*, ed. W. A. Ringler (Oxford: Clarendon Press, 1962), pp. 173–4.

[56] 'Daniel, Samuel', Oxford Dictionary of National Biography online, accessed July 2019. For the date, see Rees, *Samuel Daniel*, pp. 76–9.

[57] See further Richard Rambuss, *Spenser's Secret Career* (Cambridge: Cambridge University Press, 1993).

[58] Daniel's *Cleopatra* is discussed by Jonathan Patterson in Chapter 10, this volume.

Michael Drayton came from much lower social origins than Daniel (Aubrey states that 'he was a Butchers son'),[59] but he too was highly skilled at manipulating bibliographical codes to enhance his status – though he did so with such care that none of his contemporaries drew attention to his lowly origins. Drayton published volumes of verse from 1593. In his earlier printed works his name usually appeared, in the plain form 'Michael Drayton', as a signature at the foot of dedicatory epistles prefixed to his poems. This was standard practice at this date: the name 'William Shakespeare' appeared in a similarly sparse form at the end of the dedications to *Venus and Adonis* (1593) and *Lucrece* (1594). From early in his career Drayton dedicated poems to a range of aristocrats, chief among whom was Lucy Harrington, Countess of Bedford. In 1596 he made an extraordinarily daring dedication of *Mortimeriados* (1596) to his patroness, in which he declared his verse would 'ad more vigor' to her fame 'Then earthly honors, or a Countesse name'.[60] Presenting himself in this way as the source of the status of his patroness, rather than the other way around, seems to have been a serious blunder: his relationship with the Countess seems to have collapsed after 1596.[61] But Drayton's name continued to grow: in 1604 its usual form on title-pages became 'Michael Drayton, Esquire'. This was because his regular patron in these years, Sir Walter Aston, had been made Knight of the Bath at the coronation of James I, and Drayton acted as one of his esquires. For that occasion he acquired the right to bear arms. The arms he adopted were a naked expression of aspiration, both poetic and social: they depicted Pegasus salient (leaping) on an azure ground *guttée d'eau*, or flecked with raindrops.[62] This visibly united poetic status (it was from a blow of Pegasus's hoof from which the waters of Helicon flowed), with social status, since it was very similar to the coat of arms of what was, to someone of Drayton's generation, an inner sanctum of poetic status, the Inner Temple. Drayton was not mocked for his social aspirations as Shakespeare had been by Jonson. This may be because he rose with his patron rather than simply by purchasing a coat of arms.

The following year (four years after Daniel's *Works*) 'Michael Drayton Esquire' published a volume of *Poems* (1605), the title-page of which sets out in reverse chronological order a quasi-Virgilian career path, with Drayton's epic *The Barons' Wars* at the top and his *Pastorals* near the bottom in a veritable pyramid of generic aspiration. This went through five editions before 1619, when the aspirant Drayton published the revised version of his *Poems* with an authorial portrait. Unlike Daniel, Drayton did not enjoy a stable relationship with one publisher, although

[59] John Aubrey, *Brief Lives*, ed. K. Bennett, 2 vols (Oxford: Oxford University Press, 2015), 1.516. Aubrey also says that Shakespeare's father (a tanner) was a butcher, 1.365. Bernard Newdigate, *Michael Drayton and his Circle* (Oxford: Shakespeare Head Press, 1961), pp. 4–7 suggests Drayton's father was also a tanner.

[60] Michael Drayton, *Mortimeriados. The Lamentable Ciuell Warres of Edward the Second and the Barrons* (London: I.R. for H. Lownes, 1596), sig. A3r.

[61] McCabe, *Patronage*, pp. 76–7.

[62] Newdigate, *Michael Drayton and his Circle*, pp. 150–1.

William Stansby published collected editions of his works from 1610 onwards. As he gathered his works together Drayton was strikingly reluctant to follow Jonson's example and associate his name with published dramatic works. During the period 1597–9 Henslowe's diary records payments to him for about 20 named plays for the Admiral's Men.[63] None of these was ever ascribed in public to Drayton and only one (*The Life of John Oldcastle* (1600)) was printed. This may be because his dramas were speedy hack work (he seems to have worked on more than a dozen titles in 1598 alone), but generational factors may also play a part: Drayton was born in 1563, nearly a decade before Jonson. Like Shakespeare (born in 1564) he was in his thirties by the time the publication and ascription of plays to authors became the norm rather than the exception. But it is also significant that during the late 1590s Drayton was seeking to raise his status by an intensive – one might almost say frenzied – series of dedications to members of the nobility. *Englands Heroical Epistles* (1597) dedicated each epistle to a different patron, and in the extended 1599 edition of that work he was explicit about the social function that such dedications could serve: 'It is seated by custome ... to beare the names of our friends upon the fronts of our bookes, as Gentlemen use to set theyr Armes over theyr gates' (sig. H3r). That kind of pressure for social status through dedications was for Drayton in 1597 not compatible with being named as the author of plays. Jonson, born just a crucial few years later in 1572, could pursue a different path.

Again the quirks of personal history probably also played a part in determining exactly how Drayton sought to bring prestige to his works. Despite having being born into what Smith would have described as 'fourth sort' 'which do not rule', Drayton had early experience of service as what he termed 'a goodly page' within a household of the higher gentry.[64] He was by the mid-1580s in the household of Thomas Goodere, uncle of Donne's friend and patron Sir Henry Goodere, in Collingham, Nottinghamshire. He was trusted as a witness to discussions about the lease of his master's manor, and, in 1595, acted as a witness to the will of Sir Henry Goodere the elder, whom he described as 'the first cherisher of my Muse'.[65] Jean Brink has suggested that Drayton exaggerated these connections, but the documentary evidence clearly indicates that he became a close and trusted servant to the Gooderes.[66] That background of service in an upper-gentry household is the most likely reason why he, like Daniel, had the social instincts of a household laureate, who tended to identify authorial and patronal status.

[63] Philip Henslowe, *Henslowe's Diary*, ed. R. A. Foakes (Cambridge: Cambridge University Press, 2002), pp. 64, 65, 74, 85, 88, 90, 91, 92, 93, 96, 97, 100, 103, 125, 129, 135, 183, 201, 202. The phrase 'm[r] drayton hath geuen his worde for yt the boocke to be done wth in on fortnyght' (96) suggests that Drayton worked at a frantic pace.

[64] 'Of Poets and Poesie', 25–40, Michael Drayton, *The Works*, ed. J. W. Hebel, K. Tillotson, and B. Newdigate, 5 vols (Oxford: Basil Blackwell, 1961), 3.226–7.

[65] Michael Drayton, *Englands Heroicall epistles. By Michaell Drayton* (London: For N. Ling, 1597), sig. E1v.

[66] J. R. Brink, *Michael Drayton Revisited* (Boston: Twayne, 1990), pp. 5–7. Kathleen Tillotson, 'Drayton and the Gooderes', *The Modern Language Review*, 35 (1940), 341–9 sets out the evidence for a strong connection with the households of the Gooderes.

And as with Daniel, there is a distinct secretarial flavour to his much-revised sonnet sequence. The French-sounding title of the first edition, *Ideas Mirrour Amours in Quatorzains* (1594), marked an aspiration to be considered alongside both Ronsard's *Amours* of 1552, the sparse presentation of which Drayton's volume emulated, and *L'Idée* of Claude Pontoux – whose collection of *oeuvres* appeared in 1579.[67] Drayton repeatedly revised both the sequence and the wording of his sonnets, which he included in his increasingly capacious collected editions of his works.[68] The version which appeared in the 1605 *Poems* begins in the world of the schoolroom, with 'Thine eyes taught me the Alphabet of love, | To kon my crosse-row ere I learnd to spell ... My loves Schoole-mistris now hath taught me so, | That I can read a storie of my woe' – a version of a sonnet which had appeared as number 11 in the 1594 edition. Sonnet 3 in the 1605 sequence continues very much in the idiom of Daniel:

> Taking my penne, with words to cast my woes,
> Duely to count the summe of all my cares,
> I finde, my griefe innumerable growes,
> The reck'nings rise to millions of despaires,
> And thus dividing of my fatall houres,
> The paiments of my love, I reade, and crosse
> …
> My heart hath paid such grieuous usurie,
> That all this wealth lies in thy beauties bookes,
>   And all is thine which hath been due to mee,
>   And I a Bankrupt, quite undone by thee.[69]

The sonneteer becomes a household accountant who is hopelessly in debt to his mistress. An expression of an overwhelming debt might not seem a natural pathway to love, but it could be in this period, when 'every businessman was at the same time a debtor and a creditor, indebtedness, far from creating subordinate relationships reinforced connections and confidence'.[70] Debt implies credit (in the sense of epistemic trust) and hence (potentially at least) a relation of affect between creditor and debtor. As Drayton revised his sequence he gradually moved this sonnet towards its start.[71] In the revisions to the sequence he also emphasised his elite connections and his singular artistry, as if to create the impression that the increasing grandeur of the volumes in which his sonnets appeared seeped through into their contents.

[67] On Drayton and Pontoux, see Sidney Lee, *Elizabethan Sonnets*, 2 vols (Westminster: A. Constable and Co., Ltd, 1904), 1.lxxxviii–xc.
[68] On the revisions, see Drayton, *The Works*, 5.137–9; Louise Hutchings Westling, *The Evolution of Michael Drayton's 'Idea'* (Salzburg: Institut für Englische Sprache und Literatur, Universität Salzburg, 1974); Warley, *Sonnet Sequences*, pp. 152–74.
[69] Michael Drayton, *Poems* (London: Printed for N. Ling., 1605), sig. Bb1v.
[70] Richard Grassby, *The Business Community of Seventeenth-Century England* (Cambridge: Cambridge University Press, 1995), p. 177.
[71] A version had appeared as Sonnet 10 in the edition of 1594. In the revised version of 1599 appended to *Englands Heroicall Epistles* it was Sonnet 6.

The 1605 *Poems* included a group of 'Certaine other Sonnets to Great and Worthy Personages', which directly address patrons from James VI and I down to Lucy, Countess of Bedford. These appeared along with a sonnet first published in 1599 which emphasised Drayton's singularity:

> Thinkst thou my wit shall keepe the packe-horse way,
> That eu'rie dudgen low invention goes?
> Since Sonnets thus in bundles are imprest,
> And eu'rie drudge doth dull our satiate eare?
> Thinkst thou my Loue shall in those ragges be drest,
> That eu'rie dowdie, eu'rie trull doth weare?
>> Vnto my pitch no common iudgement flyes,
>> I scorne all earthly dung-bred scarabies. (1605, sig. Bb8v, Sonnet 31)

In another poem added in 1605 Drayton confesses that once 'With those the thronged Theaters that presse, | I in the circuit for the Lawrell strove', but that now 'No publique glory vainely I pursue, | All that I seeke is to eternize you' (Sonnet 47). That opposition between pursuit of the laurel in the theatre and the private language of praise is highly significant as well as completely disingenuous: it was by praising a patron in terms of singular excellence that Drayton sought to elevate his own status as a poet.

Taken as a whole, Drayton's revisions to his sonnets suggest that as the ephemeral and courtly form of the sonnet moved into the collected works of a professional writer, so the persona of the sonneteer was pulled in two distinct directions. One impulse was to elevate the status of the form in order to make it a worthy companion to the weighty (and indeed epic) poems dedicated to noble recipients with which it shared a volume. The other was to insist that the author was no more than a mere secretary or accountant, a humble recorder of the mistress's virtues, who sought eternity of fame only through praising those virtues.

This was the form taken by printed sonnet sequences in the Jacobean period. And that fact casts some light on that famous and mysterious volume entitled *SHAKE-SPEARES SONNETS. Neuer Before Imprinted* which appeared in 1609. The debates about Shakespeare's sonnets are endless and will remain so. Was publication authorised? Who is the mysterious dedicatee Mr W.H.?[72] Situating the volume within the evolving bibliographical codes which surrounded the publication of sonnet sequences in the early seventeenth century will not answer these questions, but it does enable some of the most striking features of the volume to snap into focus. Shakespeare's surname is very prominent on the title-page. There is no authorial dedication or epistle, apart from the publisher's dedication to Mr W.H., the 'onelie begetter'. The gap of 18 years between the publication

---

[72] On the title and the debate about authorization, see Katherine Duncan-Jones, 'What Are Shakespeare's Sonnets Called?', *Essays in Criticism*, 47 (1997), 1–12; Katherine Duncan-Jones, 'Was the 1609 Shakespeares Sonnets Really Unauthorized?', *Review of English Studies*, 34 (1983), 151–71; Colin Burrow, 'Life and Work in Shakespeare's Poems', *Proceedings of the British Academy*, 97 (1997), 15–50; William Shakespeare, *The Complete Sonnets and Poems*, ed. C. Burrow (Oxford: Oxford University Press, 2002), pp. 91–103.

of Shakespeare's Sonnets in 1609 and the publication of Sidney's *Astrophil and Stella* in 1591 was a very long time in the history of printing conventions. Thomas Thorpe and George Eld had never printed a volume of Sonnets before, and are unlikely to have had examples to hand of printed volumes of sonnets from the 1590s which they could use as a template, though *Sir P.S. His Astrophil and Stella*, which presents its author's name with similar prominence, and which, like the 1609 volume, breaks individual sonnets over page-endings was the closest precedent for the physical form of *Shake-speares Sonnets*. The volume, that is, does not simply look like a collection which has spilled out into print against its author's wishes, but it resembles the ultimate example of such a high status publication. But Shakespeare's publishers also knew that earlier sonnet sequences were coming back from the dead in collected editions of authorial works such as those of Drayton and Daniel. Within the context of Jacobean reprints of sonnet sequences the prominence given to Shakespeare's name in *Shakes-speares Sonnets* is not surprising. Certainly it might indicate the status that the name of Shakespeare had acquired by 1609 and its power to sell books: that, after all, is part of the force of 'Never before imprinted'. But it is also an example of lateral drift in printing conventions, from collected works which included sonnet sequences, to sonnet sequences themselves. That drift continued: the much-maligned reprint of the sonnets in *Poems: by Wil. Shake-speare. Gent* published in 1640 by John Benson carried both an authorial portrait and a clear marker of Shakespeare's status as a gentleman on its title-page.

The ways in which the language of social status is used within *Shake-speares Sonnets* is a topic in itself.[73] But viewed against the context of the seventeenth-century reprints of Daniel and Drayton's sonnet sequences and their emphasis on the sonneteer as secretary or accountant Sonnet 58 stands out:

> That God forbid, that made me first your slaue,
> I should in thought controule your times of pleasure,
> Or at your hand th' account of houres to craue,
> Being your vassail bound to staie your leisure.
> Oh let me suffer (being at your beck)
> Th' imprison'd absence of your libertie,
> And patience tame, to sufferance bide each check,
> Without accusing you of iniury.
> Be where you list, your charter is so strong,
> That you your selfe may priuiledge your time
> To what you will: to you it doth belong,
> Your selfe to pardon of selfe-doing crime.
> > I am to waite, though waiting so be hell,
> > Not blame your pleasure be it ill or well.[74]

[73] See e.g. David Schalkwyk, *Speech and Performance in Shakespeare's Sonnets and Plays* (Cambridge: Cambridge University Press, 2002); Warley, *Sonnet Sequences*. Lynne Magnusson, *Shakespeare and Social Dialogue: Dramatic Language and Elizabethan Letters* (Cambridge: Cambridge University Press, 1999), pp. 35–57 focuses particular attention on Sonnet 58.
[74] William Shakespeare, *Shake-speares Sonnets. Neuer before imprinted* (London: By G. Eld for T[homas]. T[horpe], 1609), sig. E1r.

The speaker of Shakespeare's sequence sounds at its beginning like a schoolmaster or advisor to a nobleman, and even adopts the voice of Erasmus as he advises a young man to marry. He also presents himself as someone who is concerned for the continuation of his addressee's household.[75] The position of steward, household manager, or the secretary who oversaw correspondence to and from a noble household or who transcribed and cross-checked the expenditure recorded in a nobleman's daybooks into a version of the accounts prepared for auditing, was, as far as we know, not one Shakespeare had ever in fact experienced at close quarters – though what he did or did not do during the 'lost years' is, of course, lost.[76] But the language and strategies of address appropriate to those roles were part of a wider cultural habitus, which was in turn part of the status-language of the sonnet form. Daniel and Drayton gave to *Shake-speares Sonnets* not a social position which could directly be mimicked or to which their author might literally aspire; rather they provided a language of clerkly status which could be used and complicated. Sonnet 58 assumes the modest role of clerk, and then inflates or transforms that role into that of a moral judge. And then it abjures that authority. Its social position, that is, is deliberately dizzying.

This is particularly apparent in the use of the verb 'controule' in line 2, which is deployed in a way that recalls its origins in compiling household records, or what was in French called a *contrerolle*, a register or account book which validated the contents of another register (*OED* vb. 1a), and from which the 'controller' of a household took his name.[77] The usage implies that a mere clerical assistant might actually be able to judge his master, to 'control' him in the sense of 'judge and condemn' him, by checking off his daily deeds against a more authoritative ledger of actions.[78] That lexical register is reinforced by the reference to an 'account'. This could again evoke numbers in a day-book or ledger (*OED* 2a), but that term also blurs over into the language of moral reckoning – indeed anticipates Nature's '*Audite*' in Sonnet 126, of which the 'quietus' is to render up the young man to death. The young man may have his noble charters and his privileges that let him go where he likes, while his 'vassail' poet says he can do nothing to stop him. But a curiously corrosive effect spreads outwards from the scribal/accounting/legal/moral terms used at the start of

---

[75] Thomas M. Greene, '"Pitiful Thrivers": Failed Husbandry in the Sonnets', in P. A. Parker and G. H. Hartman (eds), *Shakespeare and the Question of Theory* (New York: Methuen, 1985), pp. 230–44.

[76] On day-books, see Adams, *Household Accounts*, p. 8 and Mertes, *Noble Household*, pp. 85–6. Aubrey famously said Shakespeare was a 'Schoolmaster in the Countrey' during the lost years, Aubrey, *Brief Lives*, 1.366. The identification of him with the Will Shakeshaft at Houghton generated excitement (e.g. in Richard Dutton, Alison Findlay, and Richard Wilson (eds), *Theatre and Religion: Lancastrian Shakespeare* (Manchester: Manchester University Press, 2003)), but is now generally resisted.

[77] Warren Boutcher, *The School of Montaigne in Early Modern Europe* (Oxford: Oxford University Press, 2017), 1.106.

[78] On the moral component within the language of accountancy in this period, see Adam Smyth, *Autobiography in Early Modern England* (Cambridge: Cambridge University Press, 2010), pp. 57–72, and Ceri Sullivan, *The Rhetoric of Credit: Merchants in Early Modern Writing* (Madison and London: Associated University Presses, 2002), pp. 28–9.

the sonnet. They might prompt a reader of the poem to remember that a 'charter' and 'privilege' are legal documents that convey specific and limited rights over particular commodities, and that charters and privileges are written down by scribes. People who make a living by writing and recording deeds play a role in regulating the behaviour of even their extreme social superiors. They might even claim – or here pointedly *dis*claim – to circumscribe the liberties of their masters. Angel Day in his treatise on letter writing said we should write 'To our betters, always with submission ... to our friends lovinglie: To our enemies sharplie and nippinglie'.[79] Where the social relationship between speaker and addressee is uncertain, as it can be in a sonnet, writing 'with submission' and 'lovinglie' and 'nippinglie' can all be combined into a single address. And where such an unsituated address occurs in a volume of works presented to its readers as enjoying high status – as one of *Shake-speares Sonnets* – the balance of power can shift from the addressee to the addressor. The clerk can become controller.

The overt meaning of Sonnet 58 ('you can do what you like, darling while I just sit humbly with my ledgers at home') is therefore very remote from its illocutionary force. It is written by a master of the figure of thought called 'Ironia, which we call the drye mock: as he that said to a bragging Ruffian, that threatened he would kill and slay, no doubt you are a good man of your hands', which George Puttenham associated exclusively with anecdotes in which social superiors address their social inferiors.[80] Here irony becomes a means of floating through and cutting across social boundaries. The main illocutionary force of the sonnet comes through its secondary senses: you are hurting *yourself*, your interests, your material well-being. Meanwhile the poet-controller, the humble scribe, is watching and writing it all down, recording the growing deficit in his master's cultural credit, and judging. Who enjoys the higher status? The free master with his privileges and licenses, or the poet-scribe, who holds him to account, who reduces his addressee to the unnamed recipient of his epistle? Those questions the poem raises but does not answer.

What more general observations about the representation of social hierarchy arise from this discussion? The main point I wish to establish is that the languages of social and literary status are complex codes. They are connected with social origin and actual material status, but they are partially autonomous from their socio-economic base. They can be articulated through typographical and generic conventions which agents cannot always control, and which can migrate from one form or genre to another. I have also suggested that the ways in which authors articulate their social status is highly dependent on the social experience and perspective of individual agents. That means it is necessary not only to read texts very carefully in order to decode how they are using the language of social status, but

---

[79] Angel Day, *The English Secretary, or Methode of Writing of Epistles and Letters* (London: P. S[hort] for C. Burbie, 1599), sig. B2v.
[80] George Puttenham, *The Arte of English Poesie* (London: Richard Field, 1589), p. 157.

also to read the bibliographical codes through which those texts are presented, and to consider very carefully the minute differences between the social experiences of different authors – both that of literal authors and those implied by authorial personae. Experience of household service can create fine shades of distinction between the voice of one poet and another. But experience both generates and is generated by a language of status, and that language could be used by those who did not directly have the experience. An author can learn how to perform a particular social position from another author's writing. Someone like Shakespeare, who probably had never recorded the debts or actions of a social superior as a member of his household, could nonetheless use the language of those who had done so, and by imitating that language he might generate new and potentially unsettling perspectives on the social status of an author of sonnets. That is the main implication of what I have said about Shakespeare's Sonnet 58.

But one much more general conclusion about the status of writers in the period from about 1580 to 1623 in England can be deduced from the material analysed here. Across that period it became markedly easier to claim quasi-social status by virtue of literary activity: Shakespeare, the writer of Sonnets; Chapman, the translator of Homer; Jonson, the most learned of the English poets and author of *Works*. This status was a form of cultural credit, and might be typographically presented as an honorific broadly equivalent to, though independent of, 'actual' social status. That tendency had many origins: the aspirations of relatively low-born authors not simply to sell books but to become canonical figures; a leaking of status from aristocratic families such as the Sidney/Herbert clan to their servants, to those they patronised, and to those who imitated those whom they patronised; and a gradually enriched language for presenting and establishing the status of printed books and their authors, which was in part a product of the increasing volume of the English book trade. The relationship between literature and social hierarchy, that is, should be thought of as at least a three-way relationship, between 'actual' social status, the status implicitly described or claimed within a text, and the evolving bibliographical codes which determine how those claims are presented.

Index